SECOND EDITION

FAMILY THERAPY: FROM THEORY TO PRACTICE

BY **Jon Winek**

Bassim Hamadeh, CEO and Publisher
Kassie Graves, Director of Acquisitions
Jamie Giganti, Senior Managing Editor
Jess Estrella, Senior Graphic Designer
Elizabeth Rowe, Licensing Coordinator
Claire Benson, Associate Editor
Rachel Singer, Associate Editor

Cover image copyright © Depositphotos/agsandrew.

Printed in the United States of America

ISBN: 978-1-5165-0602-6 (pbk) / 978-1-5165-0603-3 (br) / 978-1-5165-1021-4 (hc)

Contents

SECTION 1

History and Development

This section discusses the historical development of theories of therapy that have been crucial to the development of family therapy. Since family therapy is an approach that developed into a profession, it is important to become familiar with the background of its development. This developmental history provides the context for understanding the theories of family therapy.

Prior to the family therapy movement, family therapy theories were marked for the most part by a linear epistemology. Since epistemology refers to the worldview of the theorist, we see that epistemology is the context in which theory develops.

Chapter 1 describes the shift from a linear to a systemic epistemology, tracing the development of the field. Family therapy shifted as a result of broader shifts in thinking in philosophy and science. These shifts are described to provide the context for understanding theories of family therapy. This chapter also defines key terms and discusses how these terms are useful to describe styles of relating.

Chapter 2 discusses the shift that occurred as family therapy moved from a first-order to a second-order epistemology. This is also referred to as a shift from a modern to a postmodern perspective. This chapter starts with a critique of the structural functional view of families and discusses how this gave rise to a theoretical revolution. This revolution is described in detail as we focus on how it impacted the development of family therapy.

Chapter 3 looks at some issues that have recently challenged how we view family therapy theories. These issues have brought up social justice critiques of the field and challenged our current thinking about systems theory. First we look at issues of the ethnocentric view of families that have been implied by our theories. Then we critique issues of gender and equality in families. Finally, we look at how diverse sexual orientation can be conceptualized in our theories of practice.

CHAPTER

THE SHIFT FROM LINEAR TO SYSTEMIC EPISTEMOLOGY

Introduction

This book represents a departure in how theories of family therapy are taught. I emphasize the relationship of a selected set of theories to each other as well as the relationship of theory to practice rather than just focusing on a theory in isolation. This method provides the student with a meta or higher-level overview of the field of family therapy. Family therapy is a contextual science, so it is appropriate that the various theories are presented in their context. In the same way that it is impossible to understand much about a family unless one knows about its context, it is difficult to know much about a theory of family therapy unless you know about its theoretical context. Two issues are central to understanding a theory's context: First, it is important to know about a theory's development. Second, it is helpful to know the relationship of one theory to other theories.

Prior to Thomas Kuhn's (1962) pivotal work *The Structure of Scientific Revolutions*, it was assumed that the truth of a theory was sufficient to ensure its acceptance. By truth we mean that the correspondence for the theory to the observed data. Kuhn took a higher-order perspective, looked at social forces within the intellectual community, and articulated how these forces influence what we call scientific truth. He was able to show how political, social, and economic forces influence the acceptance of a scientific theory. In some instances, scientific theories that are known to be false are still held for social reasons. Kuhn also demonstrated how an intellectual revolution was required for a new theory to be accepted. Its "truth" was not enough to ensure its acceptance by the scientific community. A theory needs a group of proponents who publicly support the theory as it gains acceptance.

The shift from a linear to a systemic paradigm in psychotherapy is the result of such an intellectual revolution. The basis for systemic thinking in family therapy was inspired by a book by von Bertalanffy (1968) titled *General Systems Theory.* He argued that all systems share similar properties that regulate the relationship among parts of the system. He further suggested that systems seek to maintain stability through a homeostatic mechanism. This homeostasis is maintained by feedback and mechanisms that return the system to this state when it deviates from it.

After the publication of this book, a cybernetics or control model replaced the linear disease model. The emphasis in this new field shifted from how a mental disease has developed to how a family's homeostatic mechanism maintains the problem. A homeostatic mechanism is a set of rules that maintains a steady state in a system by controlling minute changes. Likewise, the shift from the homeostatic, cybernetics, or first-order epistemology to a cybernetics of cybernetics or second-order epistemology represents another intellectual revolution.

The purpose of this chapter is to describe the first revolution. The second revolution will be described in the second chapter. As we see in politics, it is hard to identify exactly where revolutions begin. It is equally difficult to describe all of the individuals that have influenced a given revolution. Therefore, I have selected a few theories that I consider key in the intellectual revolution and that have resulted in the current state of the field.

More recently, some have viewed the family therapy movement as being at a juncture in how we conceptualize our clients and practice our trade. Shields, Wynne, McDaniel, and Gawinski (1994) have argued that family therapy has been, and continues to be, marginalized or not seen as mainstream. Others, such as Hardy (1994) and Anderson (1994), take a less pessimistic view of the profession. The US Bureau of Labor Statistics in reviewing mental health counseling and Family Therapy concluded "Employment of mental health counselors and marriage and family therapists is projected to grow 29 percent from 2012 to 2022, much faster than the average for all occupations. Growth is expected in both occupations as more people have mental health counseling services covered by their insurance policies." At any rate, family therapy was primarily developed by psychiatrists who ignored professional doctrine against seeing members of a family in session (Broderick & Schrader, 1991). Since then, it has come into its own but has not given up the "counterculture attitude" that developed out of its revolutionary history. As a result, systemic theory is most often presented as an alternative to traditional ideas, provoking shifts in students' thinking. Systems thinking was introduced as a more truthful theory of how families function. Given the insights of Kuhn (1962), we see that this may not be the best criterion. It is not our goal to make claims of truthfulness. The criteria for evaluating a theory of family therapy should be its utility in terms of client outcomes and fit with a particular practitioner. Utility refers to the difference therapy makes to the client. While fit refers to the therapist understanding of and ability to execute the theoretical model.

Epistemological Assumptions

In order to best understand a theory it is best to consider some basic philosophical issues first. Epistemology is the branch of philosophy that address issues with the meaning of knowledge. As Dickerson (2010) states "Epistemology is often defined as the theory of knowledge, also stated "knowing what we know" or "thinking about how we think"…"p349. As we explore the theories and issues in family therapy I invite you to pay attention to how the developers of theory thought. I often invite my students to imagine they share the mind set with the developer of the theory as they explore each theory.

Theories of psychotherapy, and specifically theories of family therapy, have two essential components: theoretical assumptions and techniques of change. The assumptions and the techniques of change are so closely tied to each other that it is often difficult for a novice theorist to separate them. However, separating them is necessary for evaluating each theory of family therapy. The assumptions are based on philosophy and merit philosophical evaluation, while the techniques are appropriately evaluated empirically.

The first component is the theoretical explanation or description of functioning. For example, we learned that gravity functions to attract bodies of matter to each other through the story of an apple hitting Newton on the head. Like all scientific theories, the fundamental elements are assumptions about the natural order of the universe, or in our case the natural order of the family.

These assumptions are often referred to as epistemology. Epistemology is a branch of philosophy that concerns itself with the nature of reality. It seeks to answer the philosophic question, "What sort of world is this?" These assumptions are often taken for granted, seen as truths, and not clearly stated. Throughout this text, I hope to spell out the epistemological assumptions made within each theory. Historically, theories of family therapy have focused on exploring the origins of problems or "pathology." More recently, the emphasis has been on the curative factors of treatment. That is, there has been a real shift from explaining the creation of problems to explaining the curative process.

The second component in a theory of family therapy is a methodology of change. Newmark and Beels (1994) define methodology as "what I know how to do and how I go about doing it" (p. 4). Methodologies of change are often in the form of therapeutic techniques. Many of the innovations in family therapy are a result of shifts in practice. Once changes were made in practices and results were produced, theories were developed to explain these successes.

Methodology

In family therapy, advances in the methodology of assisting people with change frequently precede the theoretical explanations of the changes. Such theories are referred to as post hoc: that is to say, the observation of change precedes the explanation of change. However, this process is not linear. How you perceive the world is based on your epistemology or worldview. In other words, something has to be conceptualized before it can be discovered. Constantine (1986) makes this point quite eloquently:

> We cannot get away from the fact that all perception is based on categories and conclusions, on mental maps of reality around us. This should not be seen solely in a negative light, however, because *theory is understanding*; without theory, we have only data, facts, knowledge without meaning. The trick, then, is not to try to eliminate theory (which cannot be done in any event), but to make it explicit, to use it rather than be used by it, and to broaden it to embrace the range of paradigms by which real people in real families organize their life together. (p. 6)

Methodology has always played a role in the development of theories of psychotherapy. Since Freud's time, the most important methodology of the psychotherapist has been to listen to stories people tell about their lives. In psychoanalysis, particular attention is paid to clients' free associations and dreams. Freud reported clients' stories to other therapists through the simple use of case reports, which he published as case studies.

In addition to being influenced by changes in therapeutic methodology, family therapy has been influenced by changes in technology. Family therapy was quick to adapt technology in the therapeutic setting. The use of one-way mirrors and audio and video recordings was pivotal in the development of the field of family therapy. This technology lessened the supervisor's dependence on case reports when training future therapists and allowed researchers to view and review the therapeutic process. Thus, the therapeutic process became observable in real time.

A final important factor in the development of a theory of family therapy is the social context under which it occurs. Just as the social environment plays an important role in the way a family functions, the social situation in which theorists and practitioners work plays a role in how they view the world. Factors such as whether the therapist works in an agency or in private practice affect the development of a theory. Perhaps most influential in shaping a theory is the client population with whom the therapist is working.

To understand the shift to systemic family therapy, we must first understand the presystemic worldview.

The Presystemic Worldview

It is a difficult task to trace the specific origins of family therapy as a profession. In Broderick and Schrader's (1991) comprehensive history of the profession, we see that some of the early pre-pioneers of family therapy started to conduct conjoint therapy sessions prior to the turn of the prior century. While these practitioners were working with a family as a whole, they had not articulated a theory that would adequately explain the process. In addition, these practitioners were rare and in isolated practice. Most did not present their works in public forms out of fear of being sanctioned by their professions, which viewed work with whole families as unethical. Thus, it was not until well after World War II that family therapy clearly identified itself as a profession.

A linear worldview, concerned with causation and effect, dominated thinking about Western psychotherapy from Freud's time to the revolution that brought us family therapy. For example, we can say that mental illness (effect) is the result of childhood trauma (cause). Such a view is a one-way view and does not allow for the study of interaction. Furthermore, such a view carries the implicit assumption that the locus of a person's psychological difficulties is intrapsychic: that is, the problem resulted from difficulty in the individual's mental functioning.

A linear view of the world predominates the physical sciences and, to a large degree, everyday life in Western culture. In this domain of science, the emphasis is on explanation of observations. When faced with a problem, our first response is to question "why" something happened. Also, when we are faced with a person who is different (such as mentally ill), we often seek an explanation of that difference by questioning why he or she is in that state. This can imply that there is a single cause and further implies that there is a single solution.

The systemic concepts of equifinality and equipotentiality fly in the face of this conventional view. The notion of equifinality states that when we view an end state, there are an infinite number of ways one could have arrived at this position. For example, when considering a person with depression, we see that factors such as genetics, family of origin, drug usage, age, socioeconomic status, nutrition, exercise, self-concept, history, head trauma, and lack of social support can all contribute to its development. In fact, the best explanation is one that considers all factors. Equipotentiality speaks of the idea that from any situation or state there are an infinite number of possible future outcomes. This implies that, in the above example, by making changes in any number or all of the factors, the individual can move past his or her present state into an infinite variety of alternative states.

Associated with this linear point of view is a notion about the nature of reality. Reality is seen as having an independent existence from our perception. This is related to the idea that there exists a single universe with knowable, unchanging laws of "nature." Reality exists independently of our minds and perceptions. Implicit in this orientation is the reductionist view that one can observe reality by observing its key elements. If we (the scientist) can reduce the sequences of phenomena we are studying to minute components, we can discover their "true nature" and ultimately, reality. Thus, the goal of the science of psychology became the discovery of the laws of the minds of humans.

Along with this orientation of reality comes a view of the proper methodology for scientific discovery. Research from this perspective is most often quantitative. In its ideal form, a theory is tested by deducing a hypothesis. The hypothesis is then "objectively tested" against data collected. Tests of significance are then used to rule out the influence of chance. From here, it is believed that one will get an objective view of reality.

A related difficulty with a psychodynamic perspective is that its emphasis on childhood socialization leaves us with an emphasis on the past. Thus, we are able to explain the generation of psychopathology in one's childhood, but we are at a loss to change our childhood. To the adult with an emotional problem, understanding that a problem's origin is in an unresolved Oedipus complex does little to direct the person to solve the problem. All too often, the psychoanalytical belief that understanding a problem, or even making an unconscious problem conscious, has little to do with empowering a client to resolve the problem.

Prior to the generation of systemic thinking, the family was seen as a cause of psychopathology. As feminist thinkers have pointed out (see Chapter 3 for the feminist critique), psychology was quick to blame parents, particularly the mother, for pathology. However, the role family members play in the maintenance of a problem was ignored. Thus, the family was seen as central in the development of the problem but not as having an impact on its maintenance. Furthermore, consideration of the family was not included in the cure. Psychiatric practice in the 1940s and 1950s considered it unethical for a therapist to see a client with family members present because of the difficulty with multiple transference issues. Speaking of the early family therapy movement, Broderick and Schrader (1991) state, "The pioneers were mostly psychiatrists who dared to break the rules requiring a therapist to see no more than one member of a family at a time" (p. 4). Seeing multiple family members challenged the current thinking about psychotherapy as a whole.

As they rebelled in practice, clinicians, researchers, and theoreticians started to see differences that led to the challenge of the linear paradigm. This shift occurred as a result of the work of the first generation of family therapists. The second section of this book covers the specific contributions of the main schools of therapy that produced the shift.

Shift to a Systems Paradigm

The central ideas of the systemic view are not new; they existed in philosophy for a long time prior to the family therapy movement. In the 1940s and 1950s, mathematicians, physicists, and engineers brought these ideas together into the form that is known as general systems theory. These researchers built mechanical models approximating certain properties of the human brain. As Guttman points out (1991),

> at that time it was recognized that many different phenomena (both biological and nonbiological) share the attributes of a system—that is, a unified whole that consists of interrelated parts, such that the whole can be identified as being different from the sum of its parts and any change in one part affects the rest of the system. General systems theory concerns itself with elucidating the functional and structural rules. (p. 41)

The pioneers of family therapy, practicing during the 1940s and 1950s, adopted this systemic perspective and began challenging the prohibition against seeing multiple family members. The ability to describe whole families as something more than the sum of their members was very attractive to the pioneers, who were in search of a theory to ground their changes in practice. In contrast to the linear worldview of conventional psychology of that time, the systemic view of family therapy sees causation as circular. For example, rather than looking for the one-way relationship where A causes B, we are now looking at the relationship between A and B. The relationship between A and B is seen as occurring in two directions. That is, not only does A have influence over B, but B also has influence over A.

This perspective does not reject the notion of a linear causal sequence of events. It does incorporate a linear pattern into a circular worldview with the concept of an arc. Borrowed from geometry, this term refers to how a part of a circle will look like a line when the circle is large and the segment is short. Thus, in systemic thinking, the causal sequence A causes B is seen as part of a wider circular loop. For example, in this example, A causes B, which causes C, which causes D, which in turn causes A. Any segment between two letters is an example of an arc.

FIGURE 1.1   **Circular Causation**

In this case, A causes B is part of a whole where B has an influence on A by its relationship to C and D.

For example, consider a wife and husband who have developed a circular style of arguing over the years. The husband nags his wife about spending more time together. This prompts his wife to withdraw into the den and channel surf with the remote control. The constant changing of the channel annoys the husband and he further nags his wife.

In this example, we see that one could say the husband's nagging causes the wife to withdraw. However, it would be equally accurate to say the wife's withdrawing causes the husband to nag. Once the pattern has been developed, there is little to be gained in trying to discover which occurred first. Such knowledge would be of little use to the couple as they struggle to break this pattern. Furthermore, it may be impossible to know, for the pattern may have originated in a prior generation. The husband may have come from a long line of nagging men and his wife from a long line of withdrawing women.

The systemic perspective changes the style of questions a therapist asks. In systemic thinking, key questions take the form of "how?" questions. For example, a family therapist might ask the couple above how each of them contributes to the argument and how they could contribute to a nonargumentative lifestyle. This shifts the role of the therapist. No longer is the therapist seen as a powerful figure who has the answers for the clients. Rather, the therapist is seen as a facilitator who has questions for the family.

This change in the type of questions asked is often referred to as a family therapist's emphasis on *process*. Process is best understood in contrast to *content*. In communication, content refers to the words that are said, while process refers to the way in which the words are said. For example, a loved one saying, "I love you" with a sincere tone will have an entirely different impact on you than the same words spoken with a sarcastic tone. Process is often described as, who says what to whom, in what way, with what outcome? Outcome is viewed in both behavioral (what happens?) and emotional (how does it feel?) terms. Thus, the family therapist is interested in how a family or individual functions, not why a problem exists.

From the systems view, the emphasis shifts from the discovery of objective reality to the understanding of subjective experience or subjective reality. Family therapy focuses on the patterns of the processes that impact the family's physical and emotional well-being. This subjective reality is seen as a product of the organism observing it. Truth is a result of one's experience and not existent outside the realm of experience. The notion of universe is replaced with the idea of a *multiverse* in which each person's unique experience is a universe in itself. The interest shifts from the discovery of universal laws to the discovery of localized rules. Thus, from the systems perspective, the goal of science is the accurate description of clinical phenomena. This stands in contrast to the linear goal of reducing data for analysis. The goal from a systemic perspective is to look at wholes and to expand the phenomenon under observation by considering its context. This holistic view gives the therapist a more complete (more useful) perspective.

From a systemic perspective, a person exists in the context of relationships. These relationships exist as individuals are part of families, families live in communities, and communities exist in the context of culture (see Figure 1.2).

FIGURE 1.2 Possible loci of Problems in Systems

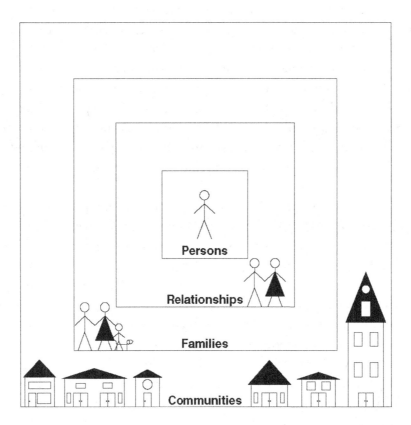

In the figure we see that, like Russian nesting dolls, wholes are in themselves parts of larger systems. In systems theory an individual exists in relationships with others. Families are made up of relationships. Families in relationship to each other make up communities. The systemically oriented therapist sees how problems can exist on a variety of these levels. Understanding allows the therapist to target intervention to a level where he or she expects it to be most effective.

The systemic perspective with its emphasis on wholes creates a science of relationship and interconnectedness. In contrast with a linear view, which is interested in reducing data to cause and effect, a systems theory approach is less interested in "why" problems developed and more interested in relationships and "how" relationships maintain a problem. This scientific methodology shifts the emphasis in systems theory from quantitative to qualitative. Rather than borrowing its methodology from the physical sciences, systemic methodology borrows from anthropology, sociology, and history.

The systemic perspective uses a more inductive rather than a deductive methodology. In an inductive argument, observation, or a premise, leads to a conclusion, or generalization. Thus, observation drives theory, rather than theory driving observation. Systems theory allows for a recursive interaction to occur between the data and the theory via the theoretician.

The emphasis in systemic family therapy has shifted from the past orientation of the linear view to an emphasis on the present. This shift has occurred in two ways. First, a historical view of problems is not emphasized in most theories of family therapy. The emphasis is not on "why" the problem developed but on "how" it is maintained. Second, theories of family therapy focus on change during the therapy session. The goal in treatment is often to change the way family members communicate and interact in the session. Here we see a progression in terms of the time frame that is the focus of therapy. Presystemic theories placed emphasis on change in the past. Systemic family therapists shift this emphasis and target the present as the locus of change. The postmodern or second-order cybernetics family therapy discussed in Chapter 2 goes to the next step and places the emphasis on change in the future.

Key Terms

In order to understand a theory, we need to understand the terminology of that approach. Let us explore the key terms in systems theory.

Cybernetics

Cybernetics is at the core of systemic thinking in family therapy. A diverse group of researchers and theorists came together in the 1940s and 1950s to look at how systems control themselves. According to Becvar and Becvar (1988), this group included mathematicians Norbert Wiener, John Neumann, and Walter Pitts; physician Julian Bigelow; psychologist Kurt Lewin; physiologist Warren McCulloch; and anthropologists Gregory Bateson and Margaret Mead. Rather than looking at the movement of objects, which was the more traditional approach to discovery, the early cyberneticists concerned themselves with organization, patterns, and process.

Wiener defines the term and its origin in his 1948 account:

> The word cybernetics is taken from the Greek kybernetes, meaning steersman. From the same Greek word, through the Latin corruption gubernator, came the term governor, which has been used for a long time to designate a certain type of control mechanism and was the title of a brilliant study written by the Scottish physicist James Clark Maxwell eighty years ago. The basic concept which both Maxwell and the investigators of cybernetics mean to describe the choice of this term is that of a feedback mechanism, which is especially well represented by the steering engine of a ship. (p. 14)

This new science focused on the similarities between control of inanimate machines and control of living systems. This was achieved by looking at how communication and feedback combine to control a system. Consider the following example: Mr. and Mrs. Markus seek marital therapy to address some intimacy issues. The therapist observes how the couple engages in a pattern of mutual influence on each other. In this case, Mr. Markus angrily accuses his wife of not being responsive to his requests for intimacy. She agrees that she is not responsive but sees her nonresponsiveness as a result of his coldness. He admits to being cold to her but responds that he will warm up after she is more responsive to him.

The cybernetics approach involves looking not at what is said but the mutual pattern that exists in the Markus couple. The therapist is concerned with the sum total of patterns of process within the relationship. In this example, each person's attempt to change the other without changing himself or herself is paradoxically keeping the relationship locked in a negative pattern.

Structure

Structure is an important and related concept in systems theory. According to Constantine (1986), "structure is the sum total of the interrelationships among elements of a system, including membership in the system and boundary between the system and its environment" (p. 52). Structure is the relatively enduring framework of a family or system. In fact, we are able to recognize structure by observing its stability. Since we are making observations for stability, observations of structure must accrue over a length of time or through multiple observations. For example, the relationship between mother and daughter is usually lifelong and enduring. However, in some families, the structure is not absolutely permanent. In such a family, a parent may disown a daughter for having premarital sex. While the structure in most instances between mother and daughter is stable, it can be destroyed.

Structure varies based on the point of view of the observer. For example, a family is very different to the youngest child, who feels that her siblings pick on her, than it is to her older brother, who feels that his younger sister gets all of his parents' attention. This perspective is different still from that of a teacher who sees the brother and sister at school. Given the different perceptions of structure, there is no "true" structure because it is dependent on the interest of the observer. In observing structure, it is important to consider the position of the person making the observation. Furthermore, when making observations of structure, one will tend to see examples of what one wants to see. This explains how students who are taking a course in psychopathology see pathology on every street corner and medical students get "med students' disease", or the conviction that they have the disease they are studying. In the Markus couple from the example above, the structure is formalized by the marital contract. Since the couple has agreed to be sexually exclusive, they both have the expectation that they will seek intimacy only from each other.

Boundaries

A boundary is what separates a system's structure from its environment. For example, a boundary of a family may be blood relationships, but even this boundary varies for different families. While most consider brother and sister blood relatives, they may not consider their second cousin a relative. What about third, fourth, and fifth cousins? Regardless of how it is defined, once a boundary has been defined, it serves to separate a system from its environment.

Not all boundaries are clear, and in some instances there is a transitional space between systems. For example, consider a forest and a meadow. It is easy to differentiate between the middle of the forest and the middle of the meadow. However, it may be hard to tell the forest from the meadow in the scrub brush between the two. Or, consider an example from a family. The children refer to their mother's best friend as Aunt Kami, but the father's best friend is called Mr. Jones. Thus, boundaries are not always consistent. This is especially true at the edge of a system. In fact, sometimes boundaries can be identified only when they are crossed.

While all boundaries serve to differentiate two or more systems, they also serve as an interface between systems. We use the terms *open* and *closed* to refer to opposite ends of a system continuum. A closed system has limited interface between itself and other systems in the environment. An open system has extensive interfaces with other systems in the environment. It is apparent that at either end of this continuum, a system cannot exist for long. An entirely open system dissipates into its environment, and an entirely closed system breaks down for lack of resources. However, it is still useful to consider toward which end of this continuum each system falls.

Suppose that boundaries are part of the issues that impact the Markus couple's relationship. Perhaps there is a pattern in which Mr. Markus is connected with his coworker. On one occasion, Mr. Markus brings his coworker to his home to eat after a night at a bar. Mrs. Markus feels that he has violated a boundary by bringing the coworker home without talking to her first. Mr. Markus responds to being confronted by his wife with the statement, "It's my house too"—to which she responds by withdrawing further.

The boundary is the container for a system. This should be contrasted with a systems process, which describes what happens within the boundaries.

Process

Process in a system is the observable, dynamic, relatively transient interaction of the parts: it is movement, action, behavior, and emotional expression. Process is the transient and emergent qualities of a system. We recognize process by its action, reaction, and movement. Consider this example: A husband and wife are talking and she gives him a seductive look. He responds by kissing her. She then takes him by the hand and leads him toward the bedroom. We see that the time scale for observing process is a fraction of that of structure. If, in the above example, the wife is always the one to initiate intimacy and this pattern occurs for years, we could call this a structural pattern. Thus, we can conclude that *process over time becomes structure.*

We can now see that structure and process are at opposite ends of a continuum. Structure is a macro concept while process is a micro concept. Simply stated, everything that happens within relationships is process, but if we observe the same process over time, structural patterns can emerge. If, in the example above, the wife usually instigates intimacy with "that look," we can say that she is the instigator of intimacy. Thus, structure is patterns of process. At this point, we can develop some rules about changing structure and process.

First, *a change in structure results in a change in process.* Since structure is a higher-order phenomenon, any change in structure will be translated to a change in process. In most instances this change happens immediately. For example, bringing an entire family in for therapy changes the structure of the system. The new structure, family plus therapist, results in a different process for the family. As a result, the family will act and speak in the therapy room in ways they would not at home. Unfortunately, the resultant change in process is stable only for as long as the new structure is intact. Frequently, as soon as the family walks out of the therapist's office, old structures and old processes reappear.

Consider the following example: A family has a three-year-old boy who has a problem with night terrors. The boy screams out in fear and anger almost every night. It takes the parents about an hour to calm him down and get him back to sleep. At the second interview, it comes out that he is sharing his bed with his four-year-old brother, who frequently wets his bed. The parents are asked simply to provide a change in structure by getting the three-year-old his own bed. The night terrors stop and, shortly thereafter, the four-year-old stops wetting the bed. Here, a change in the structure of sleeping arrangements changes the process of night terrors and bed-wetting.

Second, *a change in process can result in a change in structure*. Since process occurs on a micro level, its influence on structure is not as direct. In most instances, a new process needs to be established for some time before it will be translated into a change in structure. For example, a family is structured around a rigid traditional gender basis for the division of labor. On one occasion, the mother is sick and can't get the children ready for school. Dad substitutes for Mom during this time and finds it rather enjoyable. This leads him to become more interested in caring for his children. Over time, this leads the family to change the division of labor in the family.

These rules are important to keep in mind when thinking about the numerous theories of family therapy. Some therapists focus on changing structure; others focus on changing process. Still others seek to change both structure and process with their respective interventions.

Communication

Communication in systemic thinking is the exchange of information among components of a system. It is comprised of the message sent and the message received by the system's components. In human systems, we first think of the verbal communication that occurs among members of the system. However, spoken language is not the only medium by which messages are sent and received. We also communicate by our actions. How we act says something about us. The people who observe us are free to interpret our actions, leading to the old saying, "Actions speak louder than words."

Some of the earliest work in family therapy focused on the study of communication. Gregory Bateson and his team (Bateson, Jackson, Haley, & Weakland, 1956), among the first to bring systemic theory to family therapy, started studying communication in families of people with schizophrenia. Their research on schizophrenia led to the development of what some call the communications model of family therapy (the main offspring of which is the Mental Research Institute discussed in Chapter 7). In fact, Nichols (1984) asserted that the communications school died of success. In this statement, he was describing how the ideas of the original communication school have been so instilled in family therapy and psychotherapy as a whole that now few can recognize their origins.

PHOTO 1.1　　**Gregory Bateson**

Communication is a central issue when considering cybernetics. The parts of a system must be in communication in order for the system to function. When we speak of communication in systems theory, we speak of it as broadly defined. Verbal, nonverbal, and emotional communication are important in systems. Four basic principles should be considered when looking at communication in families:

Principle 1: "One cannot not behave" (Watzlawick, Bavelas, & Jackson, 1967, p. 48). We are always behaving. Behavior is any action of our bodies, and it is impossible to do nothing. We are always doing something. Even when we are at rest, we are behaving.

Principle 2: "All behavior is communication" (Watzlawick et al., 1967). Everything we do says something to our audiences. Walking down the street and making eye contact with a stranger communicates something. Ignoring your spouse is a form of communication. Being late for class also says something about you.

Principle 3: "One cannot not communicate" (Watzlawick et al, 1967, p. 51). Principle 3 follows principle 2. Everything we do communicates something about us to others. For example, one can abstain from talking for a period of time. While there is no verbal communication, there is still communication. Most couples' refusal to talk to each other is a sign of a profound disagreement.

Principle 4: "The meaning of a given behavior is not the true meaning of the behavior; it is, however, the personal truth for the person who has given it a particular meaning" (Becvar & Becvar, 1993, p. 76). Principles 1 and 2 focus on the message sent; principle 3, however, focuses on the message received, and principle 4 is about the interpretation of the message or communication. While the message received may not be the message sent, the message received is the truth for the recipient. How one takes a message, independent of the message itself, is important. Here we again enter the realm of subjective meaning. We have also reached a point similar to the one reached in our discussion of process. We can now conclude that everything is communication.

Furthermore, we can distinguish between the *report* and *command* aspects of communication. The report aspect of communication is the message or content. The command aspect is a statement about the relationship between the people in communication. All communication contains both aspects in the message. For example, I tell my students to do their reading so they can understand the course material. The report aspect is that assigned reading has important information. The command aspect of the communication is that I can tell them what to do, namely, read.

It is also important to differentiate further between different modes of communication. The most obvious is the verbal mode, which is often referred to as digital communication. Next, we have the nonverbal mode, which, when combined with observation of the context of the behavior, is referred to as the analog mode of communication.

The digital mode of communication gets the most attention for obvious and important reasons. First, this mode of communication involves the manipulation of symbols. Thus, our verbal conversation is entirely symbolic. By using words that are symbolic expressions of thoughts, we can sometimes successfully express our thoughts, feelings, and desires.

Our culture places a great deal of emphasis on the verbal mode of communication. For example, if a wife comes home and tells her husband about asking her boss for a raise, the first thing he asks her is, "What did your boss say?" Later he may get around to asking how the boss acted. However, in therapy we often find that "how it is said" carries more information about internal emotional states.

Our verbal communication is also linked to our conscious mind. Most people spend a good deal of mental energy thinking about what they are going to say. That is, most conversation is screened. It is also true that when one perceives the conversation to be important, the degree to which one screens increases. Freud's use of free association was one technique to get past the screening to the unconscious mind. It is also with verbal communication that we are more likely to communicate a nontruth. When telling a lie, most people lie only with their verbal communication. Their nonverbal behavior often tells the truth.

The analog mode of communication is important for several reasons. Since it is nonverbal, it is a more basic mode of communication. It is governed primarily by our unconscious mind, and a person is less likely to screen his or her analog communication. Since nonverbal behavior tends to be unconscious, only the most accomplished liar can lie nonverbally. This mode of communication is nonsymbolic. Therefore, the "language" of analog communication may be more idiosyncratic, and it is often necessary to verify any interpretations that are made. For example, I was interviewing a woman who kept turning her head when I was saying something I thought was important. I became concerned that this woman was avoiding listening by turning her head. When I asked her about this behavior, she disclosed that she was unable to hear out of one ear and turned her head to hear me better. Had I not verified my interpretation, I would have continued to make an incorrect assumption about this client.

Congruent Communication

Congruent communication refers to the relationship between digital and analog communication. When someone is transmitting the same message in both digital and analog modes, the message is said to be congruent. When a person is transmitting different messages in the digital and analog modes, the messages are said to be incongruent. When receiving an incongruent message, you do not know which of the two messages to respond to. This situation is frustrating and is sometimes referred to as "crazy making." For example, a 24-year-old man was given a pass from a residential program where he was being treated for substance abuse. During his pass, his parents threw a party for him to celebrate his birthday, as well as his being sober for 30 days. During the party, everyone but the young man drank alcohol. When he confronted his parents about the drinking, they stated, "Honey, we are so glad you're addressing your substance abuse issue. Drinking is just not good for you."

Metacommunication

Metacommunication refers to communication about communication. It involves a discussion about the process of communication. This serves to control a system. By engaging in a conversation about how one is communicating, one is able to control the system. For example, after noticing that the children were fighting more after their move, the parents called a family meeting. In the meeting, they discussed how the children were not being supportive of each other. The parents encouraged the children to talk about how they felt they were getting along with other family members and how they could improve how they were getting along. By discussing how they were talking to each other, the family members were able to resolve some feelings and move toward getting along better.

Thinking about the Markus couple, we see that the process of therapy is an example of metacommunication. By engaging in productive communication about how they communicate with each other, Mr. and Mrs. Markus attempt to control their relationship. Such communication makes the system more deliberate in its purpose and direction.

Feedback

Feedback is the aspect of a system that is recursive or self-correcting. It is the part of communication whereby a system regulates how it is functioning. Feedback provides information about past behavior to the system in a circular manner. When discussing feedback, we can differentiate between positive and negative feedback. It is important to note that the terms positive and negative do not refer to any value judgment. Negative feedback results in the maintenance of the status quo, while positive feedback results in a change in the system.

A negative feedback, or an attenuating feedback loop, functions to maintain the current state within the system. It provides information so the system can operate within specific parameters. An example of this kind of feedback loop can be found in the thermostat of your house. The thermostat is set at a specific temperature. When the temperature drops below that level, the furnace is switched on. As the temperature climbs, the thermostat responds to the increased temperature by switching off the furnace when the preset temperature is reached. This negative feedback loop controls the heating system in most homes.

The steady state caused by a negative feedback loop is referred to as homeostasis. Inherent in this process, however, is a paradox. The steady state is produced by slight variations. In the example from above, the temperature may drop 2 degrees below the set temperature before the furnace is turned on. Once the furnace comes on, the temperature may rise 2 degrees above the set temperature before the furnace is shut off. This gives us a 4-degree variation in temperature. However, the variation in homeostasis is often not part of our conscious experience. This variation is referred to as hunting, such as when a hound following a scent will turn to the left and right as it follows. As the hunt progresses, the hound becomes more efficient at following the scent. However, while hunting can become more efficient, it cannot be eliminated from any true system.

A positive feedback or amplifying feedback loop functions to amplify some aspect of a system. In this type of feedback, a small input is amplified until the system itself either corrects for the amplification or the system is altered. For example, if a speaker gets too close to a microphone, electronic feedback occurs. If the speaker continues, the volume of the feedback increases over time until the speakers are blown. In human systems, we see that positive feedback loops are functioning during times of change. For example, a teenager may start advocating more freedom from parental control as she becomes more involved with peer groups. If the parents respond by treating the teen like a child, she might respond by demanding and possibly taking more freedom. At this point, the parents may continue to treat the teen more like a child and further restrict freedom. Eventually, the conflict may escalate until the teen acts out by running away. However, if the teen is given more freedom at the same time she is given more responsibility, she may experience growth in the form of increased maturity.

Wholes and Parts

A useful way to understand systemic cybernetics is to think of wholes and parts (Hanson 1995). This analogy is helpful in visualizing the interconnected nature of systemic organization. If we start with considering how a system is organized in a hierarchy. This most simply stated is that some systems in nature and social organization are of a larger order than others. Consider how we typically organize our understating of the human body in medical sciences. We can bring medical understating to a variety of levels. Starting with the cell which is organized into organs, organs are organized into systems; system make up an individual, an individual's health is influenced by their living environment and their lifestyle, lifestyle is influenced by culture.

If we look at a level we see that it makes a coherent whole. Take the human heart on the organ level in the example from above. There is a whole specialty of medicine organized around treating diseases and condition of the heart, cardiology. The heart can be seen a whole into itself. However, the heart is made up of cells which have to function for the whole of the heart to function. Likewise, the heart is part of the circulatory system and it needs to function well for that system to focus. This phenomenon is often described with the statement in systems theory that "the sum of the whole is greater than that of the parts".

This hierarchical organization is seen in both natural and human systems. In fact the nature/man distinction is not often made by systemic theorists. Here human environment is seen as a part of the whole of the natural environment. In family therapy we see how families are made up on individual in who are influenced by their biology, as well as their social experiences. The social takes place in the context of relationships. These relationships give rise to families, who live in communities that are parts of cultures and nations. Here again each whole we consider is made up of parts while itself is part of a larger whole.

Styles

Now let us describe some basic styles of relationships that are of interest in family and human systems. Family therapists often concern themselves with pairs of people. These pairs are referred to as dyads. For example, parents are referred to as parental dyads. After dyads, family therapists concern themselves with groups of three, called triads or triangles. Larger groups are often seen as combinations of dyads and triads.

Complementary

The first style of dyad I will describe is referred to as complementary (Bateson, 1972). The form of a complementary relationship is two that fit together in a pair that, when considered together, form a whole (such as a relationship based on dominance and submissiveness or an outgoing nature and reservation). For example, in the child's nursery rhyme, Jack Sprat could eat no fat and his wife could eat no lean, so together they licked the platter clean. Over time, the divisions that occur as a result of the organization become even more pronounced.

Symmetrical

A second style of dyad is called symmetrical (Bateson, 1972). This style of relating is in the form of competition. Here, one is trying to outdo the other. A boxing match and a nuclear arms race can be the result of a symmetrical relationship. A family's effort to "keep up with the Joneses" is likely the result of a symmetrical style of relating. This relationship tends to escalate over time as the competition becomes more intense.

Parallel

The third style of dyad is described as parallel. A parallel relationship has a mixture of both complementary elements and symmetrical elements. This style allows for the greatest variation of behavior and range of role assignment. It is important to note that these styles of relating are mere descriptions and in no way imply that one has an advantage over another. They simply describe the natural variation in the way people relate to each other.

Triad

The next form of relationship to consider is a triad. A triad, made up of three people, is more complex than a dyad. In addition to being more complex, it tends to be more stable. This is why couples who are struggling can be stabilized, at least in the short term, by the birth of their first child. Triads are sometimes referred to as triangles in family therapy. A triad can be either pathological or healthy, given the context. Consider the example of a couple who is having difficulty. The husband enters into individual therapy, thus forming a triangle. In individual therapy, despite intentions to remain neutral, the therapist is drawn into seeing the man's wife as an uncaring villain. Given that the man's therapist seems to understand him so well, and his wife understands him so poorly, the conflict continues and even escalates. Yet, when the same couple goes to the same therapist together, the therapist is able to help the couple talk to each other during the sessions in more productive ways. With their new communication skills, they are able to resolve other conflicts.

Summary

The worldview resulting from the shift from linear to systemic thinking would later be referred to as a first-order cybernetics model. In this approach, we see three central interrelated concepts: First, cybernetics as a mechanism of control entered the discussion on mental health. No longer were mental problems seen as exclusively the product of unconscious pathology. Second, structure was paramount in the discussion of family problems. The discovery that change in structure resulted in a change in process drove family therapy research and interventions for several decades. Finally, communication between family members, as well as between the family and its environment, entered into the analysis. Behavior became synonymous with communication and therapists became interested in interpreting the implicit messages in problematic behaviors.

Learning Exercises

1. Go to a public place such as a restaurant and observe some couples. As you observe them, pay particular attention to their nonverbal communication. Can you recognize couples who are in an early part of their relationship, couples who are mad at each other, couples who are bored with each other, or couples with sexual tension? How do you recognize these couples? What kind of nonverbal communication do they have with each other?

2. Interview a nonclinical couple about the history of their family. As they tell their family story, pay attention to details about structure and process in the family. What metaphors do they use in telling the story?

Discussion Questions

1. Why is it important to understand a context of a theory to understand its application to a clinical situation? What are some of your basic beliefs about the nature of humans and their relationships? Are people inherently good or evil, altruistic or self-serving in nature? How do these beliefs impact the types of relationships you have with your clients?

2. How does "free will" impact our ability to generate objective theories of families that are both predictive of behavior and universal?

3. How does family therapy's emphasis on wholes impact its ability to explain individuals and families in their contexts rather than reducing individuals to impulses or genetic codes?

4. In systemic theory, where observation drives theory rather than theory driving observation, what happens to clinical terminology like *denial resistance* and *avoidance*?

5. Think about a conflict you have had with someone. How did you use a triad in that situation? Did you complain to a third party? Did this help or hinder your ability to resolve this conflict?

6. Think back on your family's response to your going to college. How did the family structure change to accommodate this? What happened to your personal space in your family home?

Suggest Readings

Bateson, G., Jackson, D., Haley, J., & Weakland, J. (1956). Toward a theory of schizophrenia. *Behavioral Science, 1*(4), 251–264.

Broderick, C. B., & Schrader, S. S. (1991). The history of professional marriage and family therapy. In A. S. Gurman & D. P. Kniskern (Eds.), *Handbook of family therapy* (Vol. 2, pp. 3–40). New York: Brunner/Mazel.

Constantine, L. (1986). Family paradigms: The practice of theory in family therapy. New York: Guilford Press.

Kuhn, T. (1962). *The structure of scientific revolutions.* Chicago: University of Chicago Press.

von Bertalanffy, L. (1968). *General systems theory.* New York: George Braziler.

Web Resources

Cybernetics

American Society for Cybernetics: Defining 'Cybernetics':

http://www.asc-cybernetics.org/foundations/definitions.htm

Wikipedia page on Cybernetics:

https://en.wikipedia.org/wiki/Cybernetics

American Society for Cybernetics:

http://www.gwu.edu/~asc/

Cybernetics of cybernetics

Wikipedia page on Cybernetics of Cybernetics:

https://en.wikipedia.org/wiki/Second-order_cybernetics

Echosystemic Psychology

http://ecosystemic-psychology.org.za/home/ethical-psychology/first-and-second-order-cybernetics

Thomas Kuhn/Structure of Scientific Revolutions:

Wikipedia on Thomas Kuhn:

https://en.wikipedia.org/wiki/Thomas_Kuhn

Wikipedia on *The Structure of Scientific Revolutions*—written by Kuhn:

https://en.wikipedia.org/wiki/The_Structure_of_Scientific_Revolutions

Ludwigvon von Bertalanffy:

Wikipedia on Ludwig von Bertalanffy:

https://en.wikipedia.org/wiki/Ludwig_von_Bertalanffy

General Systems Theory

General Systems Theory Quizlet Flashcards

https://quizlet.com/2873390/mft-national-exam-general-systems-theory-flash-cards/

CHAPTER

THE SHIFT FROM MODERN TO POSTMODERN EPISTEMOLOGY

Introduction

This chapter describes a revolution that occurred in the field of family therapy. The field developed rather quickly during the 1960s and 1970s, but after it was established, it took only a few years before a second paradigm shift occurred in the 1980s and into the 1990s. This shift was a move from a modern or first-order epistemological perspective to a postmodern or second-order epistemological perspective. Next we consider the psychosociobiological perspective and discuss how it has led to the development of what has been called medical family therapy. In addition, we discuss how issues of spirituality impact marriage and family therapy. Finally, this chapter addresses recent trends in the field toward theoretical integration and empirical validation.

As we saw in Chapter 1, the field developed as a result of the revolution of systems thinking. In a little over a decade, a second shift in theoretical thinking was starting to occur. At approximately the same time, a similar shift was occurring in the social sciences, which make up the context in which family therapy is practiced. To understand this second shift in the field, we must consider some issues in the philosophy of science.

In part, the shift occurred in response to challenges within the social sciences' "modern" view of the world. Thus, this new era saw the field of family therapy, like the social sciences in general, move from what was called the modern scientific era to what has been called a postmodern scientific era.

Family therapists first used the term *first-order epistemology* to describe what is essentially called the modern paradigm in the social sciences. According to Simon (1992), in first-order epistemology, social systems such as families are seen as having a stable existence independent of the process of observation. Therapy is required when a system deviates from some norm or standard, which indicates a form of pathology. The task of therapy is then to reduce the system's deviance from the norm and return it to a nonpathological functioning.

The Structural Functional View

Central to the modern era in science was its emphasis on structure. Modern science is concerned with analysis of the structure of the phenomenon under study. This view of science is sometimes referred to as the structural functional view. The structural functional scientist studies how structure function in relationship to other structures. Most of the structural functional social scientists took a view developed in Anthropology that define functioning as the ability to adapt to their environment. A structural analysis takes the form of looking at how a structure functions. This structural functional perspective focuses on differentiating dysfunctional, pathological, or disordered structures from functional, healthy, or ordered structures. This set the stage for the attempts of the early family therapy movement to describe the "normal" family. In fact, most of the first and second generations of family therapy theories contain explicit descriptions of "normal" family functioning (see chapter 5).

For example, in psychodynamic theory, the id, ego, and superego are the structures that make up the unconscious mind. The description of how these hypothetical structures function together is the basis for the entire psychodynamic theory of personality development. Consequently, in psychodynamic family therapy, the emphasis is on a family ego mass. This concept describes the collective unconscious of the family (see Chapter 5). In this approach, the goal is differentiation of the ego of individual family members. Such a change is in the structure of the family's unconscious.

Another example is the Mental Research Institute, or communications model, which concerns itself with the structure of communication (see Chapter 8). In this approach, changes are made in the structure of the family's communication, causing changes in the emotional structure.

The most obvious example in family therapy is structural family therapy. This approach concerns itself with how the family's structural organization influences functioning and how a change in the structure can result in a change in functioning. Structural family therapy (see Chapter 9) made direct use of the idea that a change in structure results in a change in process and devised several interventions to take advantage of this phenomenon.

Over time, this modern or first-order perspective came to be challenged for several reasons. Defining what is normal is a difficult enough task when considering an individual. When trying to define a normal family, the task becomes more complex and over time approaches being impossible. Even if we indirectly define a normal family as one without problems, there still is the impossible task of finding a family that is completely free of problems. This is because it is typical for the family to struggle during certain points in its development. For example, couples struggle with issues of intimacy when they first bring home their new baby.

Second, it is hard to describe functioning based on structure. In the structure of a family, there is a great deal of naturally occurring variation. For example, as the divorce rate increases, so does the number of single-parent families. At around the turn of the 20th century, a great deal of change occurred in typical family structures; there was a shift from a predominance of extended rural families to a predominance of urban nuclear families. Other historical examples include the increase in families with same-sex partners who are raising children and families who are remaining childless by choice. The "alternative" forms of families do not fit well with the structural functional models of family therapy articulated in the early movement. Likewise, the field did not initially recognize differences in family structure and functioning as a result of culture, class, or socioeconomic status.

The multiverse view of reality allows for an acceptance of people who have varying beliefs. It took the political stance of the feminist family therapist to bring discussions of power and privilege to the field (see Chapter 3). This shift helped make way for the acceptance of the multicultural view. Since the dominant culture was no longer seen as possessing the correct reality or "truth," other cultures became more valued. Emphasis was now placed on harmony and coexistence rather than assimilation. This increased interested in hearing marginalized voices developed into a social justice emphasis in family therapy (see chapter 3).

A New View of Reality

At about the same time, the very nature of our view of reality was challenged. Reality itself was no longer seen as absolute and existing independent of observation. Instead, it increasingly became seen as a result of the process of observing. Thus, a process becomes constructed by our observation of and discussions about a phenomenon. This new view of reality first called second order epistemology has come to be referred to as postmodernism. In 1999 Kenneth Gergen brought us into the millennium with his *An invitation to Social Construction*. Summarizing this perspective Gergen (2009)states "In a broader sense, we may say that as we communicate with each other we construct the world in which we live."p.4. In addition to being concerned about how reality is constructed, postmodern theorists are also concerned with the narratives in which our constructions are embedded. A narrative is a story that is told to represent and communicate our construction of the world (see Chapter 14).

Thus, the philosophy of science went from the idea of discovering true reality to that of creating reality through observation. The reality that is created is based on the stories that are told. Further, the philosophy of science went from the notion that we consider our universe to creating a multiverse. That is, people can come to understand a variety of perspectives, not just a single perspective, as having truth and validity.

Given this, when new theories are developed, we no longer need to fully discard the old theory. As Simon (1992) points out in his article "Having a Second Order Mind While Doing First Order Therapy," we can use different orders of theories simultaneously. If we take a second-order theoretical position, we are able to hold both first-order and second-order perspectives at the same time. We can describe situations where linear or first-order theories can provide a description of successful therapy, and at the same time we can use a second-order perspective to describe how the therapeutic relationship influenced the same case. Thus, the second-order perspective can incorporate the first-order perspectives. Wilber (2000) explains in his book *The Theory of Everything* would call this process evolution. In this case, Family Therapy evolved from a modern to post-modern perspective incorporating the discoveries and wisdom of the former into the latter.

One of the advantages of the second-order perspective is its ability to allow both/and thinking rather than either/or thinking. This simple shift in perspective increases the number of possibilities available for our clients.

The first-order perspective focused on pathology that was seen as occurring in problems in the structure of the family. This view was criticized because, like the linear perspective, it emphasized pathology rather than health. Furthermore, the emphasis was not on the therapist's actions, but on the actions of the family. What was needed was a theory that could describe not only the interaction among members of the family, but also the family therapist's interaction with them.

In addition, some of the pressure to change came out of the way the field had developed. Clinicians with diverse professional identities were drawn to the excitement of exploring new theoretical territory. In fact, the unifying force in the field may have been dissatisfaction with existing theories and professional identities. This was evident at conferences and in the journals that drew a diverse set of presenters and authors.

Given that the field was loosely organized around its lack of satisfaction with the theories of individual psychology, the field overemphasized the family. The individual became lost in the drive to understand "family" homeostasis. It became standard practice to locate all problems in relationships between family members. This became difficult for two reasons. First, an individual can carry a psychological problem. Research has discovered evidence of a genetic component of several disorders, such as schizophrenia, alcoholism, depression, and bipolar disorder. Second, terms like *abusive family*, *alcoholic family*, and *schizophrenic family* entered widely into the literature during the first-order period. However, to speak of entire families as such is an error in logic. These are individual descriptors that have been used to describe a group of people. It is correct to say the family contains a member who is alcoholic, but it is incorrect to say the family is alcoholic. While the family dynamic can play into the process, it is still an individual that carries the symptom. For example, sometimes family therapists would treat the parents for a problem in a child. The shift of the locus of a problem would lead to a "flight into health" where the clients would terminate treatment prematurely because the parents felt blamed for their child's problem.

As part of the field became interested in a theoretical understanding of change, the first-order theoretical understanding of family therapy became inadequate. The core concept of homeostasis does a good job of describing stability, but it is not effective in describing change. The early family therapy movement developed techniques of change but little or no theoretical understanding of how these changes were initiated. The emphasis on homeostasis was detrimental to the understanding of change. Family therapy was clear in its criticism of the traditional study of pathology. Surprisingly, though, the early movement was unable to recognize that it had fallen into a theoretical pit of similar form in its attempt to describe homeostasis but not change. That is to say, it saw problems as resulting from problems in family structure.

Postmodernism

These pressures and others resulted in the questioning of not only specific theories of science, but also how science itself was conducted. Gergen (2009) provides a thought provoking introduction to post modern theory. The 1980s were a time of challenging the foundations of science.

This occurred as the sciences were "deconstructed." The idea of deconstruction comes from the work of French philosopher Michel Foucault and German philosopher Jürgen Habermas. They argued that mainstream knowledge presented as objective truths is a story that serves to maintain the power distribution or status quo and push out alternative stories. Thus, to deconstruct an idea is to expose the story and analyze what the story is maintaining.

This led to a shift away from the study of structure and function. Constructionism became increasingly important understanding how people develop theories to understand the world. In a postmodern view, reality was seen as a result of a subjective experience that is shared. Since language is the medium that we most frequently use to share experience, family therapy shifted its analysis to that of the interaction of language and experience. Therefore, family therapists started to study how we create or construct reality through the use of conversation. In the constructivist approach (see Chapter 13), the therapist is involved in conversations with the client that result in the client's developing a new reality that is free of her or his problem. In narrative family therapy (see Chapter 14), the therapist is concerned with how the stories clients tell about their history impact how they experience problems. In solution focused family therapy the therapist co-describes a problem and works towards creating solutions for the clients problem.

Scientists using the second-order paradigm also became interested in narratives told by locals or people close to the experiences. Stories are important factors that shape how reality is experienced. In this way, therapists again became interested in content, specifically the content of the stories told. Of particular interest to the postmodernist are alternative stories told by people who have traditionally had their voices marginalized or even suppressed. These included the mentally ill, minorities, women, and people of alternative sexual orientation. Since this approach takes a stance against oppression, these voices are given attention. Again this helped shape the current movement towards social justice in family therapy (see chapter 3).

Due to the increased attention on narratives and the emphasis on the constructive nature of the therapeutic process, therapy came to be seen as a collaborative undertaking. Golann (1988) includes this in his description of second-order or postmodern therapy:

> If family therapists remain aware of the indivisible and recursive nature of their interactions with families, and if they use this awareness to form collaborative rather than a hierarchical therapeutic system, and at the same time minimize their attempts to change individual or family structures in strategic or predetermined ways, then they may be said to be practicing a second order family therapy. (p. 51)

Given the postmodern perspective, the goal of therapy shifts from being curative to co-constructing a new reality or to re-authoring a person's or family's story.

This view of therapy as a process of collaborative conversation takes away some of the expertise in the role of the therapist. The appropriate goal of therapy is no longer seen as the cure of pathology. The new goal of therapy is to direct a conversation from which a new "pathology"-free reality can be co-constructed. This perspective does not completely remove the therapist from an expert role. The therapist is the expert in guiding the conversation in ways that will increase the likelihood of such realities emerging, thus allowing the clients to be experts in their own families and lives.

The postmodern perspective developed in part as a response to the problems in developing a description of normalcy. In the postmodern perspective, normalcy is deconstructed; it is seen as a construction designed to exclude a certain percentage of the population from mainstream society. As Berger and Luckman (1966) pointed out in their pivotal treatise on the social construction of reality, all psychotherapy is a form of social control. Thus, psychotherapy is an attempt to have all clients act in a socially acceptable manner. For example, therapists are mandated to intervene directly with law enforcement when clients disclose plans to harm themselves or others. Family therapists noted the social control elements and brought this into their analysis of therapy.

Related to the insight on the social control aspects of therapy came other insights into the nature of reality. Postmodern theoreticians came to view reality as the result of a shared social construction. From this perspective, our beliefs regarding the nature of our world are a result of our shared relationships. Although this paradigm shift was also occurring in other social sciences, family therapy was in a unique position to study this phenomenon. It is in the intimate relationships of families that our first construction of reality develops and that later constructions are modified. Psychopathology was no longer seen as simply an emotional illness. The second-order view sees emotional problems as the result of a view of reality that does not allow one to live efficiently in one's set of social circumstances.

As the second-order perspective started to discover the self of the therapist, it also strived to rediscover the individual in the family. Since problems were seen as located in conversations, a reemergence of interest in individuals occurred. We can make a distinction between an external conversation between two or more people and an internal conversation, or internal dialogue. With this distinction, we can reintroduce the individual as a topic of inquiry. Therefore, where we locate pathology has shifted. Recall that from a linear perspective, pathology is located in the individual, and from a modern or first-order perspective, pathology is located in relationships. In the second-order perspective, the conversation that leads to pathology is located both in relationships and in individuals. This transcends an either/or perspective and allows for a both/and view of pathology.

At about the same time, there was also a critique of the cybernetics metaphor that was at the core of the family therapy movement. This critique occurred on two levels. First, there was concern that the therapist was underemphasized in early models of family therapy. Families were viewed as "black boxes" that therapists would observe in their offices. This metaphor is based on the idea that you can discover the nature of a family by simply studying the inputs and outputs. That is, through the study of what information the family receives and what information its members transmit, we can understand a family. However, one can question the assumption that the family would be the same in the therapist's office as they would be in their homes. Second, the homeostatic metaphor was challenged as being too mechanical: appropriate to predict and control the behavior of machines, but not able to account for the unpredictability and free will of humans. For example, the homeostatic metaphor could not explain the occasional situation where families report that they spontaneously resolve their issues.

The first point of the critique was addressed by adapting the cybernetics metaphor to incorporate the observer or therapist in the analysis of a family. By raising the abstraction one level, one can describe cybernetics of cybernetics. This is to simply include a system that is engaged in control of a lower-order system. This is sometimes referred to as second-order cybernetics. In family therapy, the therapist and client are viewed as a cybernetics of cybernetics system.

The second point of the critique has not been adequately addressed. Alternative metaphors, such as the constructionist metaphor, have been suggested as a replacement for the systemic metaphor. However, no alternative has been fully developed, and systems theory remains central to the field. Table 2.1 spells out the differences in the first-order and second-order perspective as they relate to some key issues in family therapy.

TABLE 2.1	Differences Between Modern and Postmodern Epistemology	
Issue	Modern Epistemology	Postmodern Epistemology
What is the prominent theoretical style?	Structural Functional	Social Construction of Reality
How is reality viewed?	Single reality or truth (single universe)	Personal reality and truth (multiverse)
How are clients problem conceptualized?	Problems are the result of significant deviation from normal behavior	Problems exist when two or more people agree a problem exists
What is the goal of therapy?	To cure illness by returning functioning to normal	To construct (create) a problem free reality
Who is responsible for creating change?	The therapist provides the client with insight or tools to create the change	Change emerges from client therapist interaction

The Psychosociobiological View

An additional challenge to the modern, linear epistemology that dominated scientific thinking, and specifically the medical field, occurred in 1977 when George L. Engel disputed the traditional reductionist medical approach with an inclusive systematic model he called a "psychosociobiological view." He was concerned that medicine's reduction of disease processes exclusively to biochemistry unnecessarily split the mind from body. The biomedical view has led to cures and effective treatments to many diseases that have plagued us for centuries. However, while this view of health is able to explain cellular function with some degree of success, it is at a loss to explain the emotional component of most illness. In addition, we are at an almost complete loss to explain how emotions affect our physical health.

Engel looked to general systems theory as a possible solution for the crisis he saw in biomedicine. By considering different levels of the processes above the cellular level, one is able to develop a more holistic approach to medicine and ultimately psychiatry. Engel (1977) clearly states,

> To provide a basis for understanding the determinants of disease and arriving at rational treatments and patterns of health care, a medical model must also take into account the patient, the social context in which he lives, and the complementary system devised by society to deal with the disruptive effects of illness, that is, the physician role and the health care system. (p. 132)

In an essay addressed to psychiatry, Engel (1980) more fully develops his model. At its core, the hierarchical model has each level represent a dynamic whole in itself as well as part of a larger whole (see Figure 2.1). Each of these wholes in itself is the subject of considerable scientific inquiry. However, rather than reducing each level to be studied in isolation, Engel placed emphasis on the interconnected relationships (see Figure 2.2).

FIGURE 2.1 **Hierarchy of Natural Systems**

George L. Engel, "Hierach of Natural Systems," The chemical application of the biopsychosocial model. American Journal of Psychiatry, vol. 137, no. 5, pp. 535–544. Copyright © 1980 by American Psychological Association.

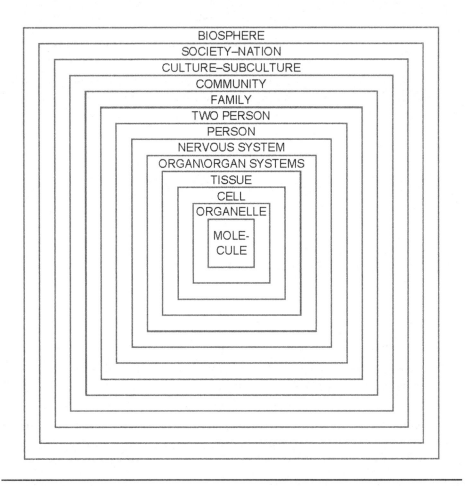

Source: From Engel, 1980.

As one goes higher in level of abstraction, each becomes larger and more complex, made up of organized collections of lower-level processes. For example, a person's experience and behavior are influenced by her or his nervous system, organ systems, tissues, cell, organelles, and so forth, down to subatomic particles. Likewise, each person is a member of two-person (dyad) relationships; a member of a family, community, and culture or subculture; and ultimately part of the biosphere. Engel (1980) also points out that a "person (or individual) represents at the same time the highest level of organism hierarchy and the lowest level of social hierarchy" (p. 536).

As we see, central to this view and to systems theory in general is the concept of *isomorphism*. According to Constantine (1986), this term, borrowed from mathematics, simply means "same structure." It is common that similar structures occur at different levels of analysis. For example, the impact of addiction in a person may result in cognitive disorganization and loose boundaries. As a result of isomorphism, we find families with alcoholic parents are often disorganized themselves. Likewise, a co-therapy team who is treating a conflicted couple is likely to experience a conflict over the best way to help the couple.

FIGURE 2.2	Continuum of Natural Systems

George L. Engel, "Hierach of Natural Systems," The chemical application of the biopsychosocial model. American Journal of Psychiatry, vol. 137, no. 5, pp. 535–544. Copyright © 1980 by American Psychological Association.

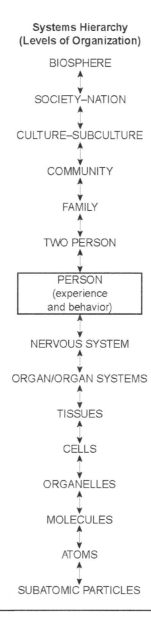

Source: From Engel, 1980.

Medical Family Therapy

From a family therapy perspective, the intersection of mind and body makes family therapy a natural fit for medicine. This idea led McDaniel, Hepworth, and Doherty (1992) to call for the development of a new field of medical family therapy. To these authors, medical family therapy's development was inevitable. They state, "Like it or not, therapists are dealing with biological problems, and physicians are dealing with psychosocial problems. The only choice is whether to do integrated treatment well or do it poorly" (p. 2). Hodgson, Lamson, Mendenhall, & Crane (2012) point out that "...approximately 70% of patients seen in primary care have a psychosocial issue. p. 143. This leads to their optimistic assertion "Family Therapist, grounded in a systemic and relational lens, are well positioned to be leaders in this evolution across integrated and collaborative care services in primary, secondary, and tertiary care settings." p. 144. Thus we see that medical family therapy is a collaborative approach of which family therapists are a part. Through this collaboration are opportunities to bridge the mind–body split.

McDaniel and colleagues originally (1992) identify two universal goals for medical family therapy: agency and community. "Agency refers to a sense of making personal choices in dealing with illness and the health care system, both of which offer contributions to a patient's feeling of passivity and lack of control" (p. 9). This goal involves allowing the client to be in charge of her or his care, including deciding which situations to receive care for. In 2014 Doherty, McDaniel & Hepworth discussed how Medical Family Therapy target the "Triple Aim" in healthcare reform of , improving quality and satisfaction of care, improving health of populations, and reducing per capita costs of health care. "We see medical family Therapy not just as a form of treatment, but as a contributor to the transformation of health care."p. 541. Concludes Doherty, McDaniel & Hempworth (2014).

Community is an emotional goal that involves patients' degree of connection to others in their environment. According to McDaniel and colleagues (1992), " it is the sense of being cared for, loved, and supported by a community of family members, friends, and professionals" (p. 10). This involves bringing the family together to support each other during illness. The crisis of the acute phase of illness can provide an opportunity for change in long-standing family patterns.

Video Call Out 2.1: Strategic/Medical Family Therapy

In the video Pamela Richey R.N., M.S. addresses issues of both agency and community when they discuss issues of infertility in a couple. Agency is explored as they discuss their struggle with making the choice to use a donor eggs. Pam points out that they can decide not to utilize the donor eggs and accept their situation. In this case there are also significant issues of community as the couple struggles with their extended family. They also discuss how the extended family responds to the couple's infertility. In this case the wife's sister in law got pregnant in a short time and her mother in law asked her to plan a baby shower. Pam helped the couple process their feelings of hurt and grief over their infertility.

In 2014 Hobson, Lamson, Mendenhall & Crane edited a comprehensive text of advanced applications in Medical Family Therapy. They organize their view of Medical Family Therapy into 4 sections; Training, Research, Policy, Finance. By including chapters on Policy and Finance the authors are recognizing issues in the context where it is practiced. In reviewing research from 30 years Crane & Christenson (2014) "… demonstrates that family therapy is an effective and relatively inexpensive modality of psychotherapy treatment." P. 419. Regardless of your position on healthcare reform cost effectiveness will become an increasingly important in the focus of development of Family Therapy and Medical Family Therapy.

Another significant contribution made by medical family therapy was the modification of the biopsychosocial model developed by Engel (1977 1980) to include issues of spirituality which is referred to as the biopsychosocial-spiritual model (BPS-P) Watson, Bell & Wright (1992) and Wright Watson and Bell (1996). Spirituality is increasingly being recognized as an important component to whole person and family healing. When family member experience illness and other life changing events spiritual and religious belief and practice are often a source of reflection and comfort family can turn to. Hospital chaplains and other staff that are trained and able to work with clients within their spiritual belief(s) are able to support their client family during the stress times of dealing with illness. Family Therapy sister fields of psychology and counseling have recognized this to a greater degree teaching classes in spirituality in Counseling. Miller 2003 published the first edition of her influential and insightful text on "Incorporating Spirituality in Counseling and Psychotherapy." Some theorists have come to see shifts in spiritual and religious beliefs and practices as a third order change. This builds on the work or Watzlawick, Weakland, and Fisch (1974) of the Mental Research Institute who describe first and second order change (see chapter 8)

In addition to having a collaborative relationship with traditional medicine, the field has recently been developing a relationship with complementary and alternative medicine (CAM) approaches. We find that systematic family therapists are increasingly bridging the theoretical gap between mind and body by developing working relationships with a variety of health care providers. CAM practices are those systems of health care that are currently not considered part of conventional medicine. They include traditional Chinese medicine, meditation, herbal therapy, massage, and therapeutic touch (to name a few examples).

In a national survey of clinical members of the American Association for Marriage and Family Therapy, 88% of respondents reported recommending CAM practices to their clients and 45% reported having a relationship with a CAM provider to whom they make referrals (Caldwell, Winek, & Becvar, 2006). Further study revealed that most respondents found CAM to be "an imparted expansion of their therapeutic repertoire, or theoretically, … a fit with the systematic/holistic paradigm according to which they work" (Becvar, Caldwell, & Winek, 2006, p. 120).

Spirituality

Despite Freud's early dismissal of religion, there has been a long history of attention to issues of spirituality in professional marriage and family therapy (MFT). As Broderick and Schrader (1991) point out, much of the early interest in marriage and family therapy was in the clergy. In churches and in pastoral care, the notion of seeing families as the unit of treatment or care is a natural fit.

Also, it is often the clergy who are called on to help newly married couples deal with the transition into married life, and it is the clergy to whom families look for assistance in times of stress, such as loss of a loved one.

Despite the fact that many MFT professionals have a background in religion, only recently have issues of spirituality and religion been discussed in major journals. In 1994, Stander, Piercy, MacKinnon, and Helmeke found that only 13 articles addressed spiritual issues in the major MFT journals. However, in more recent years, some books have been published on spirituality and MFT (e.g., Becvar, 1997; Walsh, 1999). A notable example is Blanton's (2013) exploration of how centering prayer can change neurobiology which in turn can change a couple's relationship. In a 2002 random sample of clinical members of the American Association for Marriage and Family Therapy (n = 153), 72% saw spirituality as relevant to their practice (Carlson, Kirkpatrick, Hecker, & Killmer, 2002).

Belief in God has been a consistent belief in American Culture. According to Gallup (2011) 9-10 American have believed in God since they started asking about it in the 1940. In the same Poll when the question was changed to do you believe in a universal spirit or higher power a full 98% agreed. Not only do people believe in God, but they also believe that spiritual beliefs are good for you. Spirituality has been linked to both physical health (Rippentrop, Altmaier, Chen, Found, & Keffala, 2005) and emotional well-being (Cotton, Larkin, Hoopes, Cromer, & Rosenthal, 2005; Rippentrop et al., 2005). In a 2008 gallop pole 80% of people in the U.S. find religion fairly important and 54% describe religion as very important.

The systemic paradigm positions MFTs to assist clients who are struggling with issues of spirituality and religion. Systems theory's emphasis on connection can be used to assist clients in reconnecting or connecting with their spirituality, as well as to help them reconnect with their connection to the greater good—or what the Alcoholics Anonymous community would call their "higher power."

Like Multicultural Counseling that requires a basic competency of different cultural practices and believes MFT are called to have competency and understanding of basic spiritual practices of a variety of faith traditions. Carson, McGeorge & Anderson (2011) explore training in spiritual issues and find a disparity between what is taught and practiced. Their conclusions echo that of Helmeke and Bischof (2002) when they state "..educators need to help therapists move beyond the idea that talking about spirituality represents an imposition of the therapist's personal beliefs and begin to see spirituality as a potentially rich cultural resource to be explored in therapy with the clients". p.10.

Not only family therapy, but also psychiatry, has started to pay more attention to issues of spirituality. In 1994, the *Diagnostic and Statistical Manual of Mental Disorders (DSM)*, published by the American Psychiatric Association, first listed spiritual problems as an area on which to focus treatment. The *DSM* is the primary classification system for mental health professionals, and its inclusion of issues of spirituality legitimizes a focus on faith in psychotherapy. This is carried through to the revised DSM V (American Psychiatric Association 2013) which sought to be more even sensitive to religious and spiritual beliefs by including language calling for diagnoses to be made in the context of belief.

Empirical Validation

Since the inception of family therapy, it has been strongly linked to research. Gregory Bateson, by profession an anthropologist and philosopher, was one of the first contributors to early systems thinking as well as one of the early researchers in family dynamics. Bateson's interest and charisma inspired Don Jackson to found Mental Research Institute in 1958 (W. A. Ray, personal communication, Feburary 6, 2009). Prior to this, Bateson led a group of researchers in studying the origins and process of schizophrenia. This project identified six conditions in a family's communication that they saw to be associated with the development and maintenance of schizophrenia (Bateson, et al., 1956). This linked the study of family patterns and process to the study of mental illness.

Evidence Based Practices

As family therapy has matured as a profession, it has moved even farther toward embracing a scientific paradigm. Initially, family therapy was based on broad anecdotal claims of effectiveness. However, as the MFT field has developed, there has increasingly been a call to focus on empirically based claims of effectiveness. Evidence Based Practices (EBP) refers to the practice of utilizing empirically based treatment procedures. For some the definition is narrow calling for the exclusive use of only approaches that have been shown effective in experiments and clinical trial. Williams, Paterson Edwards (2014) take a much broader view. As they link research to practice that have identified 5 types of research:

1. Research that provides better understanding of a client's experience.
2. Research that guides our assessments.
3. Research instrument that have merit in clinical assessment.
4. Research which shows which treatment is effective with what problem.
5. Identify which elements of treatment are important for success. (Williams Patterson Edwards 2014)

For now, let us briefly consider some of these EBP approaches specifically 4 which is commonly referred to as outcome research and 5 which is commonly referred to as process research. Both of these approaches will be covered in greater detail in Chapters 15 and 16.

Outcome Research

The first area of research that is important to consider has been described as *therapeutic outcome research* (see Chapter 16). This approach seeks to empirically establish how therapy progresses successfully. This is carried out using two different research traditions. I refer to the first as research on effectiveness, which seeks to establish what approaches are empirically shown to be most effective. This can be done by either comparing different approaches to each other or by testing an approach's ability to treat a specific population. I call the second tradition common factor research, which looks to empirically identify factors associated with success independent of the theoretical orientation of the therapist.

Process Research

The second area of research is referred to as *process research* (see Chapter 13) by Broderick (1993). As you recall, process is a description of the interactions that occur in the family. Process research seeks to describe "normal" processes that occur in families. Through an understanding of what normal processes are, therapists can assess family functioning and design interventions to help restore normal functioning.

Integration

There has also been a shift away from a homogenous (single) theoretical approach. The early 1980s marked a period where eclectic approaches were increasingly popular. In eclectic practice, a therapist borrows interventions and theoretical constructs from a variety of theories. These are placed in a metaphorical therapeutic tool bag that therapists draw on to meet the needs of their clients. Thus, the boundaries between some of the schools decreased.

In 1997, Jay Lebow declared, "We have entered the era of integration in couple and family therapy" (p. 1). Eclecticism came under criticism for borrowing techniques from different schools without regard for the fit of the underlying assumption of the schools. Thus, the various tools, when assembled, might not make a coherent whole or might be incompatible with the personality of the therapist (see Chapter 15). The integration movement called for the therapist to develop a collection of therapeutic tools that fit together to make a coherent whole. Not only was it expected that the tools would fit together and work as a whole, but it came to be expected that the therapist would have a theory to describe how they would work. This theory would be based on the therapist's own worldview, including a degree of self-awareness. This is one of the ways the idea of self of the therapist entered the field.

The idea of self of the therapist also flows from our postmodern paradigm, where the therapist is no longer seen as a passive observer but as an active participant. This theoretical position implies that we can no longer assume that the therapist, as a person, is not a variable that impacts the outcome of a therapy session. So, with a postmodern paradigm, we must assume that a therapist's feelings affect the therapeutic process and ultimately the outcome. Of the family therapy models discussed in this book, the experiential model pays the most attention to issues of self of the therapist (see Chapter 7).

Summary

This chapter has covered major trends in family therapy that occurred after its initial development and led to a shift in the epistemology associated with theories of marriage and family therapy. This shift arose out of a general trend in the social sciences as well as some concerns within the family therapy movement. Family therapists increasingly became dissatisfied with the structural function view that predominated in the social sciences during the modern period. In particular, the degree of diversity in the American family frustrated attempts to describe "normal" family functioning and prompted theorists to abandon the first-order epistemological view, or modern paradigm.

This led to a shift in epistemology in family therapy, and we entered the postmodern theoretical period. The postmodern paradigm is unique in that it is a meta theory. That is, it is a higher-order theory that explains modernism without replacing it; it incorporates it as part of the description of a wider reality. Thus, we can move past an either/or perspective and adopt a both/and perspective.

At about the same time, there was a theoretical shift in psychiatry that influenced the social sciences in general. This became known as the psychosociobiological model. This model deals with the issues of hierarchy inherent in systems. Rather than leaving the gap between levels of analysis unexplained, this new theory sought to explain the relationship between levels of hierarchy. We see the individual as the highest-level biological system while also the lowest-level social system.

Finally, we have explored issues of spirituality, empiricism, and integration as recent influences in our current level of understanding of systems. Spirituality is a factor that binds many families together, but it is often not considered in secular approaches to family therapy. Family therapy has recently moved into an era of empirical validation of its theoretical concepts. A trend toward integrating theoretical perspectives through careful consideration of the self of the therapist has also been discussed.

Learning Exercises

1. Bring an organizational chart from an organization that you are familiar with to class. In small groups, discuss how the structure of the organization influences its ability to function.

2. Divide the class into two groups. Have one group take a modern view and the other take a postmodern view. Have each group discuss their view of how problems in families develop.

3. Describe your family you grew up in and what were the stories that were told about it. Does the stories seem more modern or postmodern in their themes. Pay particular attention to how the family view of reality pay part in their viewing of parenting.

4. Research the mission statement from the university that you received your undergraduate degree from. What elements of their mission statements come from a modern perspective and what elements of the mission statement come from a modern perspective?

1. Discuss how psychotherapists engage in social control of their clients in situations where clients are considering harming themselves or others.

2. Discuss how changes in the context in which marriage and family therapy is practiced influenced the shift from a modern to a postmodern paradigm.

3. How does brining oppressed voices to the discussion allow family therapist to take a position on issues of social justice.

4. In what ways have you observed your body to influence your mind and in what ways does your mind influence your body?

Suggested Readings

American Psychiatric Association. (2013). *Diagnostic and Statistical Manual of Mental Disorders* (5th ed.). Washington, DC: Author.

Carson, T. S., McGeorge, C. R., & Anderson, A. (2011). The importance of spirituality in couple and family therapy: A comparative study of therapists' and educators' beliefs. *Contemporary Family Therapy, 33*, 3–16.

Gergen, K. J. (2009). *An invitation to social construction* (2nd ed.). Thousand Oaks, CA: Sage.

Helmeke, K. B., & Bischof G. H. (2002). Recognizing and raising spiritual and religious issues in therapy: Guidelines for the Timid. *Journal of Family Psychotherapy,* 13(1-2), 195–214.

Hodgson, J., Lamson, A., Mendenhall, T., & Crane, R. (2014). *Medical family therapy: Advanced applications.* New York, NY: Springer.

Miller, G. (2003). *Incorporating spirituality in counseling and psychotherapy: Theory and technique.* Hoboken, NJ: John Wiley and Sons.

Williams, P. E. (2014). Clinician's guide to research methods in family therapy: Foundations of evidence-based practice. New York, NY: Guildford Press.

Web Based Resources

Chapter 2

Postmodern Wiki page

https://en.wikipedia.org/wiki/Postmodern_psychology

Rational Wiki

http://rationalwiki.org/wiki/Postmodernism

Structural Functional Theory Wiki Page

https://en.wikipedia.org/wiki/Structural_functionalism

Structural Functional Theory Wiki Books Page

https://en.wikibooks.org/wiki/Sociological_Theory/Structural_Functionalism

A review of Structural Functional Theory

http://www3.uakron.edu/witt/fc/fcnote5.htm

Internet Encyopedia of Philosophy page on Michel Foucault

http://www.iep.utm.edu/foucault/

Encyclopedia Britannica Biography on Michel Foucault

http://www.britannica.chttp://www.britannica.com/om/biography/
Michel-Foucault

Stanford Encyclopedia of Philosophy on Michel Foucault

http://plato.stanford.edu/entries/foucault/

Stanford Encyclopedia of Philosophy Biography on Jurgan Habermas

http://plato.stanford.edu/entries/habermas/

Encyclopedia Britannica Biography on Jurgan Habermas

http://www.britannica.com/biography/Jurgen-Habermas

George Engel Wikipedia Page

https://en.wikipedia.org/wiki/George_L._Engel

Biopsychosocial model Wikipedia Page

https://en.wikipedia.org/wiki/Biopsychosocial_model

Boundless.com explanation of Biopsychosocial model

https://www.boundless.com/psychology/textbooks/boundless-psychology-text-book/stress-and-health-psychology-17/introduction-to-health-psychology-85/the-biopsychosocial-model-of-health-and-illness-326-12861/

Family Therapy Magazine article on Medical Family Therapy

http://www.aamft.org/imis15/documents/jasinglepagefinal.pdf

CHAPTER

SOCIAL JUSTICE: RACE, CLASS, ETHNICITY, GENDER, AND SEXUAL ORIENTATION IN FAMILIES

With Nickolas A. Jordan, Ph.D.

Introduction

In the late 1970s and early 1980s, marriage and family therapy was well established and had become a legitimate profession. Once this occurred, it turned its critical lens on itself and became self-reflective. As a profession, marriage and family therapy has had a long history of being critical of established theories of psychotherapy. It was family therapy's criticism of the linear perspective that helped establish family therapy as a legitimate endeavor. When the profession did turn its critical lens inward, the focus was on issues of inclusion, specifically gender and ethnicity. In the late 1980s and 1990s, the profession looked at issues of race, sexual orientation and domestic violence. These critiques led several theorists to question some of the core ideas of general systems theory. While these questions are being discussed in literature and at professional meetings, systems theory remains the foundation for specific schools of family therapy. The field still concerns itself with the study of homeostasis as maintained through feedback. The critiques have sent many theorists back to the drawing board, but they have not produced a paradigm shift.

In addition to the homeostatic mechanism systems theory view social system as arraigned in a hieratical manner. If you recognize that systems arrange themselves in this hierarchical manner is a separate issues that is the particular arrangement fair and just. Asking questions about the fairness of the hierarchy that occurs in society is what lead us to the "social justice perspective" in Family Therapy.

This chapter examines issues of diversity, gender, and sexual orientation.

It is healthy for a profession to continually look at its context, and yet family therapy largely ignored its own context for several decades. This seems to have occurred for three reasons. First, the context of the profession was missed by most theorists as they tried to describe the context of their clients. Second, during the early period, the profession was struggling with legitimacy. Focusing a self-critical lens on a fledgling discipline might have been seen as dangerous when the profession was receiving criticism from the outside. Finally, family therapy has a lacked a clear, theoretical framework in which to place model and intervention. Only with the profession's increased status and legitimacy as a mental health discipline, and an influx of diverse persons and perspectives was the field mature enough to take a long, hard look at itself.

These views include minority issues. As members of the dominant culture, the founders of the profession were mostly white, middle-class, heterosexual, christian males who developed theories with their culture in mind. As the field developed and women and minorities became involved in the profession, theories and techniques were taken to the margins of our society. It was in these margins of society that the theories broke down. It was also at the margins that the critiques of family therapy took hold.

A Critique of Ethnocentricity in Marriage and Family Therapy

Until the 1990s, this country was seen as a "melting pot" of cultures. The dominant story was of settlers moving from their native lands to the United States, the land of freedom and opportunity. Driven from their homelands by oppression, the new settlers in the US were eager to adapt to "American" values. This mythology prevailed for a significant portion of the past century.

Part of this mythology is that the United States was a democratic society that, by shedding the tyranny of a monarchy, was able to create a meritocracy. A meritocracy is a society where social position is based on the contribution of the holder of that position. The belief that if an individual works hard enough, plays by an established set of rules, pulls themselves up by the "bootstraps", they will attain financial and social success. This is a Darwinist view of the wider social hierarchy that tends to miss the role of class in US society. Issues of race, class, sexual orientation, and gender have a large impact on one's opportunities, but racism, sexism, and ethnocentrism, though dominant forces in US history, were largely ignored. Slowly, and not without the occasional steps backward, the melting pot ideal has been replaced by a pluralistic, multicultural view. One significant factor in this evolution has been the civil rights movements that started in the 1920s and have been raising our consciousness since. Another factor was the election of the United States' first black president

Barack Obama. For the dominant group, his election signaled the beginning of a post-racial society where the problems of oppression were solved (Wingfield & Harvey, 2013). Also, the proliferation of the mass media has made this a smaller world by bringing many cultures and experiences into our homes.

Family therapy seemed to be off to a good start in recognizing the role of class in a family's experience with the 1967 publication of *Families of the Slums* (Minuchin, Montalvo, Guerney, Rosman, & Schumer). Minuchin brought his ideas and experiences of working with urban New York families to Philadelphia when he became the director of the Philadelphia Child Guidance Center. There, he started to train members of the local black and Latino populations to be paraprofessional therapists. These therapists had an easier time establishing credibility with their clients because the perceived differences between them were not as great.

In 1982, McGoldrick, Pearce, and Giordano brought ethnicity to the forefront of family therapy with the edited volume *Ethnicity and Family Therapy*. In her opening essay, McGoldrick (1982) eloquently sums up the state of family therapy:

> It seems so natural that an interest in families should lead to an interest in ethnicity. It is surprising this area has been so widely ignored. Ethnicity is deeply tied to the family, through which it is transmitted. The two concepts are so intertwined that it is hard to study one without the other, and yet we have done just that. (p. 3)

She argues that a culturally sensitive therapist must have an understanding of the shades of meaning a culture presents in order to understand a family's situation. From this perspective, the therapist's role "will be that of a cultural broker, helping family members recognize their own ethnic values and to resolve the conflicts that evolve out of different perceptions and experiences" (p. 23). The therapist works from within the family system.

To facilitate the understanding of different cultures, the first edition of *Ethnicity and Family Therapy* (McGoldrick et al., 1982) presented essays on some 20 different cultural groups. These essays were designed to provide therapists with an overview of the significant issues one might face when working with a family from a particular cultural group. In recognizing the potential limits of one's ability to understand different cultural groups, McGoldrick (1982) states that one cannot understand all family types. She also states, "What is essential for clinicians to develop is an attitude of openness to cultural variables and to the relativity of their own values" (p. 27). The Third edition of *Ethnicity and Family Therapy* (McGoldrick, Giordano, & Garcia-Preto, 2005) expanded on the already significant contribution of the first edition and provides 47 essays on different ethnic groups. This resource belongs in every family therapist's library.

Before addressing specific cultures and families, let us first provide a structure for discussion by defining some key terms to be heard throughout the chapter. We are intentional in our use of language. We use the words "Social Justice" in addition to using terminology like "inclusion" or "diversity". Diversity and Inclusion in their basic form is the presence of multiple voices in a conversation or interaction. We see Social Justice as the negotiation and rules of engagement for the voices present in a conversation or interaction. First, as family therapist and human beings, we acknowledge the reality of Oppression and Privilege in our work as family therapist. We see oppression as systematic discrimination and exclusion of a specific group of people based on attributes such as skin color, gender, and/or sexual orientation. Privilege is an unearned access to social and economic resources (McGoldrick & Hardy, 2008). As family therapists, we understand the need of the feminist informed idea of equity in relationships. Where equality assumes similar treatment will bring about similar results, equity is the understanding that some individuals and families need different treatment to gain similar results.

Differences in culture create tension and conflict in familial relationship; even in the therapeutic relationship itself (Hardy, 1989). To further your willingness to examine your own culture openly, let us start to develop a cultural awareness by looking at African American families, Latino families, and Asian American families. These are the three largest racial groups in the United States and represent the individuals, couples, and families beginning family therapy trainees are likely to encounter. As you will see below, these groups are collections of different nationalities. If one thinks about differences further, it is possible to see the national view of ethnicity as inadequate. Regions of nations have rather different cultures. In fact, people of different socioeconomic means have different experiences, even when they are from the same ethnic background. In no way is this list exhaustive, but it will serve as a beginning of cultural knowledge for family therapists.

African American Families

African American families are unique in that, by and large, their immigration to this continent was not by choice. They were brought out of the African continent through the Transatlantic Slave Trade and forced into unpaid labor. In addition to being torn from native lands and forced to work in brutal conditions, enslaved families were subjected to rape, repeated physical, sexual, and psychological violence. Families were often torn apart as slave men, women, and children were sold to distant plantations. Systems of laws and constitutional amendments legitimized the terrorizing of these families by imposing harsh penalties for attempting escape and determining a slave's life as worth only sixty percent of their White masters. Black & Jackson (2005) point out that in the 1860's "In the South slave ownership was practiced by just 25% of Whites, but the majority of Whites defended Slavery because they believed that their prosperity depended upon it. p.78. While slavery has been outlawed for over a hundred years, oppression and exploitation still prevail. The generational trauma of Slavery, Jim Crow, and the YouTubeification of police violence against Black people have led to serious, negative consequences in the African American families. Consistently, African Americans have less average income, nearly double the unemployment rate, an increased number of deaths due to homicide, a lower rate of college and university enrollment, and a decreased life expectancy when compared to their white counterparts (Hines & Boyd-Franklin, 1996). In addition African American's are significantly more likely to be profiled, arrested, charged, convicted and given a longer sentence. The most recent 2010 Census showed that 38.9 Million people identified as black alone and an additional 3.1million indented as black in combination with another race, making 14% of the population of the United States (Rastogi, Johnson Hoefeel, & Drewery. (2011).

Given the long history of oppression and systematic exclusion, early researchers viewed the African American family pejoratively as disorganized and pathological (Deutsch & Brown, 1964; Frazier, 1966; Moynihan, 1950). Starting in 1970 with Carol Stack's ethnography *All Our Kin,* researchers studying African American families have focused on the families' initiative in the face of adversity. More recently, Boyd-Franklin (1989), Hines and Boyd-Franklin (1982), McAdoo (1981), and Staples (1994) have continued to question the deficit view of African American family life. Clearly, when viewed in the context of their history and current oppression, the accomplishments of African American families are exemplary. The sense of kinship and pride in "Blackness" is a testimony to the strength of families.

African American families are also noted for strong kinship ties. According to Nobles (1980), a tribal mentality prevails in African philosophy where the phrase "We are; therefore, I am" contrasts with more European notions of family. Relatives often live close to one another and share child rearing responsibilities. Kinship ties often go beyond blood ties to include family friends, who are referred to as cousins, aunts and uncles; boyfriends; girlfriends; deacons; pastors; and others. The systematic attack on the Black family has taught African Americans to create attachment bonds where they live. To the majority of African Americans, kinship means that one can expect support from others and is expected to give support in times of adversity. There is a great sense of obligation to one's kin. Children can be transferred to relatives when situations become problematic. For example, when a teenager gets in trouble with gangs, the family may send the child to live on an aunt's farm in a rural area, thus effectively cutting off the gang influence.

It will often take a degree of detective work on the part of a non–African American therapist to find all significant nonblood kin ties. Too much curiosity on the part of the therapist can make the family suspicious. (Suspiciousness is understandable when one considers the significance of the "Tuskegee study." Over a period of four decades, the government studied syphilis in black males by withholding treatment from the subjects without their knowledge or consent.) While a genogram (McGoldrick & Gerson, 1985) is a useful tool for collecting data on a client's kin network, Hines and Boyd-Franklin (1996) caution that "genogram information should be gathered only after the therapist feels that he or she has a bond of trust with the family" (p. 71). Any genogram conducted with an African American family should be considered an on-going process because of the many apparent and hidden kinship ties that transcend blood relationships.

In African American families, the identity of a man is often a function of his ability to provide for the family. Thus, many black men work several jobs. While it is important for therapists to include the family's significant males in the therapy process, the therapist must be flexible in scheduling appointments so the male clients can attend. Hines and Boyd-Franklin (1996) suggest using phone contact and letters to keep the father apprised of progress in therapy, thereby reducing the likelihood of sabotage.

Eye contact is another issue one should be aware of when working with African American men. In this ethnic group it can be a sign of deference or non-aggression not to make eye contact, especially with other men. Sometimes, they will choose to wear sunglasses during a session. A therapist who confronts them about their lack of eye contact or insists that they remove their glasses will be viewed with suspicion. Likewise, an African American man is likely to be very quiet during a session. This may be due to deference, but can be easily misinterpreted. A home visit where a seemingly mute client has a home turf advantage may go a long way toward opening up dialogue between client and therapist (Jones & Seagull, 1977). Franklin (1993) talks of an "invisibility syndrome," where, out of fear, whites treat African Americans as if they are invisible, further marginalizing them. This speaks to the need for white therapists to be aware of and overcome this tendency.

In contrast to their male counterparts, African American women are often seen as central to the family and often have identities tied to the roles of mother and grandmother. Work outside of the home is no stranger to Black women. Cowdery, Scarborough, Kudson-Martin, Seshadri, Lewis, Mahoney (2009) found the African Amereican families enaged in the willful suspension of gender roles when they perceive it is for the good of their family. Frequently, they have been the sole breadwinners for a period of time. Willie (1981) and Willie and Greenblatt (1978) credit this to the fact that African American families tend to have more egalitarian relationships than Caucasians. Hooks (2000b) contends that lack of opportunities due to fear and racism toward Black men inhibit their ability to find steady, meaningful employment or education. Furthermore, African American women tend to identify to a great degree with their spiritual life, and church can be a central influence in their lives. Building upon the importance of church Allen, Davey and Davey (2009) describe an integrative model for delivering mental health services to African American Churches.

African American families often seek therapy out of concern for their children (Hines & Boyd-Franklin, 1996). Problems with children are often identified at school, on which African American families put a great deal of emphasis. Unfortunately, black children are often marginalized by teachers and administrators who automatically identify them as underachievers. This limits their academic potential and lowers the success ceiling. Recognizing the decreased opportunities for their children, African Americans are often very strict and commonly use corporal punishment to control them. "Sparing the rod" and rearing a child that is ill prepared for the challenges of the world are often central concerns. A therapist who responds negatively to the parenting style can drive a family from therapy. Hines and Boyd-Franklin (1996) suggest that, "rather than argue for the elimination of physical punishment, the therapist can expand upon parents' understanding that this practice is a residual of slavery, as well as teach and emphasize the benefits of positive, alternative approaches" (p. 80). Kelcher-Oliver & Smith (2015) describe issues and perspectives in calling for evidenced-based interventions to help African American families parent more efficiently.

Latino Families

The Latino population has grown at an incredible rate over the past few decades. At the time of the 2000 census, there were over 35 million people of Hispanic origin in the United States (Guzmán, 2001). In the most recient 2010 census that number had grown to 50.5 million or 16% of the population of the United States (Ennis, Rios-Vargas & Albert 2011). This number is much higher if one considers that there are many more Latinos who have entered the United States illegally and are undocumented and uncounted. According to Garcia-Preto (1996), Latinos are the fastest-growing ethnic group in America. However, as Garcia-Preto points out, this increase in number does not result in an increase in status. In fact, oppression is increasing as public assistance is discontinued for people without legal standing, healthcare services are severed, and as bilingual education is being threatened. More reciently Garcia-Predo (2005) argues "For many Latinos, the United States has represented a place in the sun, a place to be free, yet upon their arrival they are dismayed by the attitude of non-Hispanics towards them." p.156.

Mexicans, Puerto Ricans, and Cubans are the three largest Latino groups in the United States. Latinos from nations in Central and South America have immigrated for economic opportunity or, more recently, as war and civil unrest refugees. We will review some of the therapeutic issues facing Mexican, Puerto Rican, and Cuban clients. In no way will this be an exhaustive review, and there is a need to recognize differences in these groups. I encourage family therapy students to read further on the specific Latino groups. The Third edition of *Ethnicity and Family Therapy* (McGoldrick et al., 1996) contains a comprehensive review of 8 Latino ethnicities.

Mexico's borders originally contained what is today New Mexico, Texas, California, Nevada, and Utah and part of what are now Arizona, Colorado, Kansas, Oklahoma, and Wyoming (Calvert & Calvert, 1993). Many of the early missions have become major Southwestern cities. As Mexico lost land to the United States, the inhabitants found themselves foreigners in their own land, and lost civil rights and private property (Falicov, 1982). Most Mexican Americans are a mix of the early Caucasian settlers and Native American tribes, including Mayan, Aztec, and Hopi (Novas, 1994). The first major wave of immigrants came around 1900 as an attempt to escape the Mexican Revolution of 1910 (Shorris, 1992). According to the 2010 census, there are 50 million Mexican Americans living in the United States (Ennis, Rios-Vargas & Albert 2011). While some Mexican Americans have become financially successful, the majority live below the poverty line (Garcia-Preto, 1996).

Puerto Ricans are the second-largest Latino group in the United States. At the time of the 200 census, there were 44.6 million Puerto Ricans living in the United States (Ennis, Rios-Vargas & Albert 2011). . The largest concentration resides around New York City. Puerto Rico is an island possession of the United States, and as a result, Puerto Ricans have been U.S. citizens since 1917. Despite citizenship, the majority of Puerto Ricans in the United States live in poverty. According to Garcia-Preto (1996), "Drug addiction, alcoholism, and AIDS have plagued the Puerto Rican population at home and on the mainland" (p. 147). Although Puerto Rico exists as a protectorate of the United States, it has no representation in congress and lacks the ability to vote in the Electoral College for Vice President and President of the United States.

Cubans are the third-largest Latino group in the United States and the most recent immigrants. At the time of the 2010 census, there were 1.2 million Cubans in the United States (Ennis, Rios-Vargas & Albert 2011). Concentrations are in Florida, New Jersey, California, and New York. They started to emigrate to the United States in the early 1960s after Castro came to power. The first immigrants were mainly of European ancestry and came from upper-class backgrounds. Later immigrants were of mixed race and economically disadvantaged. While Cubans are some of the most economically successful of the Latino groups, their average family income still falls short of the national average (Novas, 1994). It will be interesting to observe how the 2015 changes in United States policy toward Cuba—including the reopening of embassies—will impact emigration and presenting problems for Cuban families.

For the most part, Latinos are members of the Roman Catholic Church. According to Garcia-Preto (1996), "there is an emphasis on spiritual values and expressed willingness to sacrifice material satisfaction for spiritual goals" (p. 151). This is related to a deep sense of family and commitment to the honor of the family. This family connection can be confusing to a non-Latino therapist, who might view this strong connectedness as a pathology by labeling it enmeshment. Related to Latinos' loyalty to the Catholic Church is a general respect for authority. This can lead to difficulty in asserting their rights, which is more pronounced for those who are here illegally, as there is political backlash against those without legal status (Garcia-Preto, 1996). Careneiro (2012) analyzed the history of Christianity in Latin America and it's impact on Latin families. Out of repression and punishment of priests and nuns for their social activism in the 1970s she finds that "… many Latino families do not trust the government, and are hesitant to question the Church for fear of retaliation." p.146.

Latino families have a strong extended structure where several generations may live together. They have a more pronounced division of labor based on gender and, as a result, have stronger gender roles than white, middle-class Americans. It is this extended family that first comes to the aid of a Latino family. Formal therapy is often not sought before the situation becomes desperate, and, even when presented to the therapist, the problem is minimized out of respect for authority. Korin (1994) suggests that eliciting, listening to, and validating stories about the family's life in this country helps contextualize their struggles. Garcia-Preto (1996) suggests that families' sense of culture shock and lack of context be addressed as a therapeutic issue.

Asian American and Pacific Islanders Families

White, middle-class people tend to identify Asian Americans as one cultural group. However, Lee & Mock (2005) take the lead from recient census classifications and identifies Asian American and Pacific Islanders as being divided into 51 distinct ethnic groups. Including 21 groups listed as Asian American and 30 Pacific Islander to make up Asian American and Pacific Islander group. Each of these 43 ethnic groups has a unique immigration history. Some came to the United States seeking economic opportunity, while others came as war refugees seeking to escape persecution. There are at least 32 languages spoken by Asian Americans, with even more dialects, making this an even more diverse group (Lee, 1996, Lee & Mock 2005). The Asian American population has been growing faster that any other racial group in the United States, from 1 million in 1960 (Lee, 1996) to over 10 million in 2000 (Barnes & Bennett, 2002) to 14.7 million in 2010 (Hoeffel, Rastogi, Kim & Shahid 2012). In the 2010 census there were 14.7 million people who identified with being Asian and another 2.6 million people who reported being Asian in combination with another race combined together to make 17.3 million people or 5.6% of all citizens in the United States (Hoeffel, Rastogi, Kim & Shahid 2012. Asian Americans practice many religions of Eastern and Western origin. Despite the great degree of diversity within this group, common characteristics can be identified that lead to some suggestions for treatment.

According to Lee (1996), "in traditional Asian families, the family unit—rather than the individual—is highly valued" (p. 230). This belief is highly ritualized in cultural and family customs. Given this, a person's acts reflect not only on himself or herself, but also on the family and all ancestors (Shon & Ja, 1982). Thus, shame and obligation are a social control mechanism to keep family members in their prescribed social role. These roles are based on age, gender, birth order, and social class. Role reversal is a common stressor in Asian American families. It is often the children who first learn English, making the parents dependent on their children for assistance in dealing with issues of acculturation. In addition, role reversal can occur when women are more able to find employment than their husbands.

In many traditional Asian families, marriages are arranged. The Western notion of marriage for love is not an issue in Asian families. Despite this, divorce is not common in Asian American families. Parent–child relationships are more dominant than the husband–wife relationship (Lee, 1996).

Traditional Asian American families have role structures similar to stereotypical American families of the post–World War II era. Males assume roles as authoritarian, provider, protector, and disciplinarian. Females assume roles of homemaker, child bearer, and nurturer. According to Lee (1996), "most parents demand filial piety, respect, and obedience from their children" (p. 231). Most families are extended in structure, including members from three or more generations.

Uba (1994) has shown that Asian Americans have occurrences of mental illness at rates equal to or higher than those of Americans of European descent. According to Lee (1996), Asian American families commonly present with parent–child problems, marital discord, in-law problems, and other domestic problems. Asian American individuals are likely to present with somatic complaints, depression and anxiety, adjustment disorder, schizophrenia, alcoholism, drug addiction, gambling, and suicidal ideation (Lee, 1996). Uba (1994) has identified six factors that predict mental health problems in Asian Americans: (1) financial status, (2) being a woman, (3) old age, (4) social isolation, (5) recent immigration, and (6) postmigration adjustment. Sue and McKinney (1975) have found that Asian Americans who use mental health services are more disturbed than their European counterparts. This is an indication that Asian Americans are likely to delay getting help until problems have become quite intense. Asian Americans and Pacific Islanders continue to have the lowest utilization of mental health services among ethnic groups (Lee & Mock 2005) Lee (1996) identifies five types of data that should be collected when assessing an Asian American family: (1) demographics, (2) data on the family system, (3) data on the community system, (4) pre-immigration history, and (5) immigration history. Lim and Nakamoto (2008) find that the use of genograms is culturally resonant with Asian Cu,lture value and provides an opportunity to understand the importance of family relations,

There are several ideas to keep in mind when working with Asian American families. First, many Asian Americans do not accept a Western biopsychological explanation of mental illness (Lee, 1996). Thus, it is important to discuss with the family what they see as the cause of difficulty. Second, it is essential to keep in mind the role of shame in Asian American families. Questions asked about men may be seen as an attempt by the therapist to shame the family. Third, it is best not to use children as interpreters in families where the children speak English (Lee, 1996). Using the children as interpreters would further invert the system. Finally, it is necessary to keep in mind that the Western notions of self-disclosure and verbal expression may counter Asian American values (Lee, 1996).

Several authors have recommended specific approaches when working with Asian American families in therapy. Kim (1985) has developed an approach based on an integration of strategic and structural therapy. Ho (1987), in an approach based on the theories of Satir and Bowen, teaches families to recognize unspoken rules. Paniagua (1994) and Sue and Zane (1987) do an outstanding job laying out the fundamentals of working with Asian Americans.

TABLE 3.1	Summary of Key Differences in Working With Three Ethnic Groups		
Issue	**African American**	**Latino**	**Asian**
Immigration pattern	History of slavery, Jim Crow laws	Fastest-growing ethnic group, both legally and illegally	Diverse immigration pattern
Gender roles	Egalitarian roles, masculinity connected to ability to take care of family	Traditional gender roles; pronounced division of labor by gender	Traditional gender roles
Spirituality	Strong spiritual orientation	Predominantly Catholic	Diverse Western and Eastern religious practices
Child rearing practices	Strict parenting style	Often the responsibility of females	Practices focus on obedience to family and ancestors
Clinical issues	Therapist needs to be flexible to get men to attend Men may not make eye contact Therapy often focuses on children Suspicion of medical fields Therapist must be aware of how Privilege operates in relationship to the client	Addiction HIV/AIDS Strong family connection can be confused for enmeshment Therapy may not be sought until family is in crisis Therapist must be aware of how Privilege operates in relationship to the client	Extreme pressure not to shame family Western view of mental illness may not be accepted Using children as interpreters inverts family structure Model Minority (citation) expectation Therapist must be aware of how Privilege operates in relationship to the client
Strengths	Strong kinship ties	Deep sense of family	Low divorce rates

Learning Exercises

1. Talk to a member of an ethnic group that is different from yours. Pretend you are an anthropologist trying to understand the person's culture. Ask her to tell the story of how her family came to live in this country. As she is telling the story, pay attention to themes that emerge. Ask the person how she maintains her culture in this country. How does she try to fit in with mainstream

American culture? As you ask the person questions, be sure to probe for as much detail as possible. Pay attention to the types of questions that open up the flow of information.

2. Trace the ethnic ancestry of your family of origin. Talk to the most senior members of your family that live in this country. How did the ancestors who immigrated reach the decision to come to this country? How did they get here? If your family is of mixed ancestry, ask how the family mixes the cultures. Ask what works for the family and what is difficult.

3. Attend a religious service at a church, synagogue, mosque, or temple that is not familiar to you. Observe the rituals and try to infer their meaning. After the service, talk to a member of that religious group. Ask him to interpret the meaning of the symbols in the rituals. How similar or dissimilar are they from the symbols and rituals in your own religion? After you have an understanding of the key beliefs of that religion, reflect on how your life would be different if you had these fundamental beliefs. Spend a day reflecting on this at different times.

A Critique of Gender Bias in Marriage and Family Therapy

When speaking about Gender and the biases connected to it within the field of family therapy, it is important to understand it as a range of physical, biological, mental, and behavioral characteristics pertaining to, and differentiating between, masculinity and femininity. Gender can also refer to sex based social structures and gender identity. Gender identity speaks to psychological and emotional self-identification (Stone Fish & Harvey, 2005). There are more than two genders, gender is not binary, instead, exist on a spectrum. While biology does play a role in determining physical difference, 'gender' is a social construct. Mistakenly so, gender and sexuality are confused or used interchangeably. Sexuality and gender do overlap and exist in relation to understandings of gender, however, they are not the same.

Unlike the ethnic critique of family therapy that came about over time, the gender critique of family therapy struck like a whirlwind. A single article published in *Family Process* 30 years ago triggered this critique of family therapy. Until then, feminist thinking and theory was largely ignored or marginalized as simply "male bashing" (hooks, 2000a). Rachel Hare-Mustin (1978), an associate professor and director of a community counseling training program at Villanova University, published an article titled "A Feminist Approach to Family Therapy" that set off a rethinking of the role of gender in family therapy.

Feminism is an evolving construct. The meaning of that word to others and for others has changed over the decades. Feminism is often mischaracterized as a hatred of men or minimized to the fight to gain equal pay for women. In the early twentieth century, feminism was centered on white women's desire to leave the home and earn a living similar to men. Later, the movement became more inclusive and took on the women's suffrage. More recently, feminism speaks to a collection of ideologies that seek to establish equal economic, social, and political rights for women. Today, feminism is attracting all genders. Instead of a focus on equal rights and equity in society for women, theorists like bell hooks are shifting the feminist focus to bringing about an end to oppressive hierarchy and the destruction of Privilege held by white men or as hooks suggests: a movement to end all racist, sexist, oppression, (hooks, 2000b).

Two features differentiate feminist family therapy from other forms of therapy, such as the gestalt and humanistic therapies, which seek to enhance the self-esteem of the client by exploring his or her social roles. Although "these approaches may encourage individual development free of gender-prescribed behaviors, ... they do not (a) examine nor (b) seek to change the conditions in society that contribute to the maintenance of such behaviors" (Hare-Mustin, 1978, p. 182).

Family therapy initially moved the focus off of the individual and onto the society. With the feminist critique, society has become the patient in family therapy. This view calls on experts educated in the behavior of societies, such as sociologists and anthropologists, to provide information relevant to therapy. Not only has the profession of family therapy come under critique, but American society has also undergone scrutiny. This change of focus has not been accepted by all theorists. Some in the family therapy field have critiqued the new direction offered by theorist such as Hare-Mustin. Scott Johnson (2001) suggests that family therapist thinking of their work as healing society is beyond a family therapist's expertise saying, "... rarely, if ever, in our course of work or credentialing processes are we knowingly offered the tools with which to attack human discord on a national or global scale as we might be, for example, if we were trained as international mediators or foreign service workers." (p. 3)

Historically, changes in the family that occurred during the industrialization of America set the stage for the current structure of the family. Families became dependent on work outside of the home for their economic means. This increased the family's need to divide labor. As Hare-Mustin (1978) points out, "where productivity was rewarded by money, those who did not earn money, such as women, children, and old people who were left at home, had an ambiguous position in the occupational world" (p. 182). Given this, the roles of women shifted to being almost exclusively responsible for child rearing and household labor. Not only was there an increase in the division of labor, but the gender roles became more rigid.

This gender-based division of labor was described as early as 1955 by Parsons and Bales. Taking a structural functional stance, Parsons and Bales (1955) described the division of labor in a family where women engaged in expressive roles and men engaged in instrumental roles. Expressive roles allowed for the expression of emotion in the family environment. Parsons and Bales saw this role as necessary to provide for the maintenance of family cohesion and for nurturance of the children. This left men to provide labor outside of the home in exchange for money. Men provided for the instrumental needs of the family, such as food, clothing, and shelter. This labeling set up two conditions that are of concern to feminists. First, it put women in charge of emotional expression in the family, making them increasingly susceptible to emotional distress. Second, it set up a situation where it became very easy to blame mothers for the emotional distress of their children.

Gender and Mental Illness

Women are much more likely to suffer from a mental illness than men. If we look at the most recient revision of the *Diagnostic and Statistical Manual of Mental Disorders* (DSM-V; American Psychiatric Association, 20013, we see that, except for sexual disorders that are specific to men, there is an increased frequency in mental disease among women relative to men. This is also the case for the class of diagnostic criteria called personality disorders. Unlike mental disorders, personality disorders are seen as long-standing flaws in character that are dysfunctional. Save for antisocial disorder, the personality disorders all have an increased rate of prevalence in females. From this, one can conclude that being a woman in our society is bad for mental health. To a feminist, this is seen as the cost of gender roles where the woman is responsible for the emotional expression and functioning in her family.

Feminists noticed that since women were assigned the role of child socialization and denied the ability to contribute directly to the financial well-being of a household they were often blamed for emotional difficulties in children. This phenomenon is referred to by feminists as "mother blaming." A classic example of this is Fromm-Reichmann's (1948) theoretical construct, "schizophrenogenic mother." In this, the mother was seen as the cause of her child's schizophrenia. In a study by Caplan and Hall-McCorquodale (1985), clinical journal articles were researched from 1970, 1979, and 1982 to discover the rate of mother blaming for children's problems. They found very little difference in the rate of mother blaming across the years or according to the gender of the author presenting the theory. It is as if mental health theory reasons that the mother's natural instinct of nurturance is the cause of any problems developed in her children.

Gender-Sensitive Treatment

The systemic functional model of the family leads family therapy to ignore issues of gender and equality in our society. By correcting for individual biases of traditional psychology, family therapy developed what could be called a systemic bias. As Braveman (1988) points out, family therapists considered themselves far ahead of traditional linear psychology. As a result, she asserts, family therapists "had [their] heads buried in the sand" while others addressed issues of gender.

The machine-like view of simple cybernetics gave way to a machine-like view of family and family functioning. Included in this was the Batesonian view that opposed the use of a power metaphor. In this view, all parties contribute to problems by participation in the system. Not only was the family a machine, but it was a political machine, where all members had equal participation and blame was a linear and irrelevant term.

Goldner (1985) points out that, to a feminist, the idea of equal responsibility seems "suspiciously like a hypersophisticated version of blaming the victim and rationalizing the status quo" (p. 33). James and MacKinnon (1990) point out that blaming the victim is particularly marked in crimes and violence against women. Explanations by psychologists of battery, rape, incest, and the like have included women's provoking or consenting to the crime. For this reason, feminist family therapists are suspicious of the neutrality implied in the systems metaphor.

Feminist family therapy, like the constructionist approach and the ethnicity critique, is more a set of values than a collection of therapeutic interventions of family functioning. Osmond and Thorne (1993) state, "It is not our impression that feminist family therapists call for abandoning general systems theories; rather they are critical, specifically, of non-contextual cybernetic approaches" (p. 604). Feminist family therapy is a set of values used to influence the course of treatment.

Central to feminist family therapy is the idea that gender should be a central organizing component of family theory. Goldner (1988, 1993) and Luepnitz (1988) argue that gender should be given at least the same consideration that generations are given in family theory. Furthermore, by looking at gender as an important factor, therapists can stop blaming mothers for problems in the family. Feminists recognize that, given the role of women and mothers in our society, women are most often interested in change. Many therapists call on the most motivated members of families to do the largest share of the work in therapy. To the feminist, having the woman do the majority of the work in the therapy room is another form of oppression.

Learning Exercises

1. List all of the rites of passage that occurred in your socialization into your gender. How were these marked by members of your family? Describe in detail how you became a man or woman in the form of a developmental history. Be sure to pay attention to transitions from various stages of your gender development. Which stages were more difficult than the others?

2. Pair up with a classmate of opposite gender. Share your developmental history with this person. Try to develop an understanding of the rites of passage of members of the opposite gender. Ask questions that will help you develop an understanding.

3. Spend time in a public place observing the interaction of men and women. Try to observe how intimacy is expressed in these situations. How do men show intimacy with other men? How do women show intimacy with other women? How is intimacy displayed between men and women?

Gay and Lesbian Families

Just as family therapy has been slow to look at the other issues discussed in this chapter, it has a long history of ignoring the issues faced by gay and lesbian families.. The awareness of issues of sexual orientation started in the late 1980s, but it was not until 1991 that the *Family Therapy Networker* published a special article on gay and lesbian issues. It was clear that this topic had arrived when a chapter on gay and lesbian issues was included in the second edition of Froma Walsh's classic text *Normal Family Processes* (1993). Later, Bigner and Gottlieb (2006) coedited a

PHOTO 3.1   Jon Winek & Nickolas Jordan

book titled *Intervention With Families of Gay, Lesbian. Bisexual, and Transgender People: From the Inside Out*, also published as a special edition of the *Journal of GLBT Family Studies*. More recently, Linda Stone Fish and Rebecca Harvey (2005)wrote an in-depth discussion of systemic work with LGBTQIA families called *Nurturing Queer Youth*.

Issues of sexual identity in the development of healthy families are too complex to be addressed by a simple conceptualization of heterosexuality versus homosexuality. We need to consider sexual identity a broad spectrum that includes, but not limit to, persons who have a bisexual, pansexual, asexual, and/or queer, orientation. We also have to consider these issues in their historical context. There is a long history of oppression of people who deviate from the heterosexual assumption. As late as 1973, homosexuality was categorized as a mental illness in the American Psychiatric Association's *Diagnostic and Statistical Manual of Mental Disorders*. This occurred one year after Weinberg (1972) first introduced the term *homophobia*. Homophobia is actions or attitudes based on a fear of homosexuality.

It was not until 2015 that the United States Supreme Court togrant the LGBTQUIA community the right to get married. From a social justice perspective the Supreme Court ruling on the right to marry was a long road to be granted equal access. When chief Roberts wrote a clear statement on the social justice view of this issue: "No union is more profound than marriage, for it embodies the highest ideals of love, fidelity, devotion, sacrifice, and family. In forming a marital union, two people become something greater than once they were. As some of the petitioners in these cases demonstrate, marriage embodies a love that may endure even past death. It would misunderstand these men and women to say they disrespect the idea of marriage. Their plea is that they do respect it, respect it so deeply that they seek to find its fulfillment for themselves. Their hope is not to be condemned to live in loneliness, excluded from one of civilization's oldest institutions. They ask for equal dignity in the eyes of the law. The Constitution grants them that right. The judgment of the Court of Appeals for the Sixth Circuit is reversed. It is so ordered." P.28

Photo 3.3: "Linda Stone Fish." Copyright © by Linda Stone Fish. Reprinted with permission.

As the right to marry was grated also came marital conflict and shortly there after divorce. In all states courts do not have case law to set legal president as couples divorce and will need to develop ways to assist family. In the same vain Marriage and Family therapist therapist will need to develop techniques to help these families through divorce.

Like the melting pot mythologies of race and the ethnocentricity of American culture that led to oppression of people who were different from the Caucasian norm, the normative sexual orientation is heterosexual. Given that segments of our society still see people with alternative lifestyles as deviant, mentally ill, or sinners, it is hard to articulate how families can accept and support their members who are not heterosexual. Likewise it can be difficult for people of gay, lesbian and/or bisexual, (LGBTQIA) orientation to accept themselves. Similar to persons of color and persons with low socio-economic status, LGBTQI individuals suffer from internalized oppression (King, 1991). This is where persons with an oppressed status discriminate against others with the same status. In this case, LGBTQIA persons often act in homophobic ways toward those with the same or similarly oppressed orientations. Internalized oppression exist because marginalized groups receive the same messages as the dominant group (Palma & Stanley,2002)

Given that sexual orientation can be invisible to others, throughout history LGBTQIA persons have chosen to remain hidden and as a result suffered discrimination. The ability to hide a marginalized status is both a blessing and curse. In one way, being able to feign heterosexuality in a dangerous space has immediate, positive results. In a different way, the stress of being closeted inhibits personality development. There is also double and triple discrimination for people who hold marginalized status sexually, racially, and economically. This intersectionality of oppression can place place additional stress on that person and family.

Families with LGBTQIA members are in many ways like other families, and like all families they face issues from time to time that need to be addressed in therapy. As Long, Bonomo, Andrews, and Brown (2006) point out, these families are not inherently unhealthy. "In fact, the problems faced by these families are mainly reflective of the heterosexist, homophobic world in which we live" (p. 9). The question for us is how family therapists can support families with LGBTQIA members.

One way family therapists can help families with these issues is in the area of coming out. Sexual minorities are now self-identifying at a younger age and while living with their parents (Long et al., 2006). This is despite the fact that the process of coming out is emotionally complex (Waldner & Magruder, 1999). The person coming out can fear consequences ranging from being abused or being forced into therapy to simply disappointing his or her family (Coenen, 1998). In fact, some adolescents have chosen to run away after being emotionally, verbally, or physically abused following their disclosures (Savin-Williams, 1994; Savin-Williams & Cohen, 1996). Despite the possible negative consequences, Bepko and Johnson (2000) and LaSala (2002) argue that LGBTQIA people suffer when they keep part of their life hidden from their family and therefore should come out to their family. It can be useful for family therapists to help people these individuals weigh the costs and benefits of coming out. Once a decision is made, the family therapist can help the client with that process to maximize the benefits and reduce trauma.

Families need support in dealing with feelings and issues associated with their teen's coming out (Long et al., 2006). They need to reconcile their assumption that their child is heterosexual with the child's orientation while continuing to love and support him or her. They have to deal with the social stigma associated with having a LGBTQIA family member. According to Long and colleagues (2006), "many parents are extremely fearful that their children will be seriously injured or killed because of their identity" (p. 14). Likewise, there are a variety of stressors for siblings of LGBTQIA children. They suffer from a stigma and on some occasions become jealous of the extra attention their sibling receives to support him or her through the coming-out process.

An additional area where family therapists can assist families is in parents' coming out after they have children. When and how LGBTQIA parents talk to their children can have an impact on the relationship (Long et al, 2006). Long and colleagues conclude, "Researchers have demonstrated that younger children have a smoother adjustment than older ones when learning about their parent(s) being gay or lesbian" (p. 15).

In addition to support through the coming out process, families must be assisted in having difficult dialogues. Difficult dialogues create disequilibrium of thought. This is where long held and sometimes secret beliefs and assumptions are challenged. The therapist creates a space where families can begin to "tolerate" a new understanding of themselves and of others. Ideally, tolerance is the first step toward acceptance of the LGBTQIA members. For the person identifies as LGBTQIA, the therapist creates a space where they can examine their own views of self, independent of the family's tolerance or acceptance (Stone Fish & Harvey 2005).

Helping LGBTQUIA families is a complex process that the field is just starting to address. Aside from the Stone Fish and Harvey work, there is very little written on how each theory can be modified to assist these families. Long and colleagues (2006) provide a brief theoretical analysis of several theories. Since this area is on the cutting edge of development, there is need for well-trained clinicians to apply models of family therapy to sexual minority families and publish on their findings (Long et al., 2006).

Learning Exercises

1. Most openly gay or lesbian people engage in a process of acceptance and "coming out." This process involves disclosing their sexual orientation to significant people in their lives. Think about what a coming-out process would look like in your life. Who would be supportive of you? Who would reject you?

2. Research resources available on your campus to support GLBT students. As you review these services, think about additional services that you think could or should be offered.

Summary

This chapter traces some more recent challenges that the field of family therapy has been wrestling with in recent years. Unlike the challenges discussed in the first two chapters, these challenges did not lead to a shift in epistemology. However, they were great enough to raise the consciousness of the profession.

First we looked at the ethnocentric position of the early family therapy movement. By recognizing the cultural context of our clients, we are able to move to a therapy that considers the cultural context of each client's family. Through an awareness of the impact of culture on family, we can hopefully avoid a family therapy that is culturally inappropriate and ultimately damaging. Cultural Competence allows therapists to assist families in adapting to the broad and diverse American culture without sacrificing their own cultural identity.

Like ethnicity, gender is a contextual factor that was largely overlooked by the early family therapy movement. By examining the often invisible influence of gender, we are able to embrace a more equitable division of labor between the genders. We also see that historically women have taken more of the responsibility and ultimately more of the blame for child rearing. Gender awareness and sensitivity in family therapy allows us to look more closely at issues of power and control in families.

Most recently family therapy has addressed issues of sexual orientation. As family structure has evolved to include families not based on a heterosexual marital bond, our views of families have had to be modified. New views of families need to be developed so we can understand and support these alternative forms of family.

Discussion Questions

1. Describe the social change processes that allow society as a whole to address its biases toward groups of people.

2. Do you feel it is important to make self-disclosures about your ethnicity, race, or sexual orientation when working with clients who are different from you in terms of their ethnicity, race, or sexual orientation? If so, when and how best are the self-disclosures made?

3. To what degree do you think family therapy should take a leadership role in social change? Should family therapy follow the lead of broader society?

4. You are an intake worker for a large community mental health clinic. You are presented with an interracial couple each with three children, who have some concerns about the impact of their engagement and eventual marriage on their children. In your clinic you are thinking of assigning this case to one of two therapists. You think highly of each and their work, one has expertise in working with interracial couples and one has expertise in working with blended families. How do you reach a decision as to who to assign the case to?

Suggest Readings

Johnson, S. (2001). Family therapy saves the planet: Messianic tendencies in the family systems literature. *Journal of Marital and Family Therapy, 27, 1,* 3–11.

Hardy, K. V. (1989). The theoretical myth of sameness: A critical issue in family therapy training and treatment. *Journal of Psychotherapy & the Family*, Vol 6(1-2), 1989, 17–33.

Hooks, B. (2001). Feminism is for Everybody: Passionate Politics. Pluto Press.

Johnson, S. (2001). Family therapy saves the planet: Messianic tendencies in the family systems literature. *Journal of Marital and Family Therapy, 27, 1,* 3–11.

McGoldrick, M. & Hardy, K. (2008). *Re-visioning family therapy: Race, culture, and gender in clinical practice.* New York: Guilford.

McGoldrick, M., Giordano, J., & Garcia-Preto, N. . (Eds.). (2005). *Ethnicity and family therapy* (3nd ed.). New York: Guilford Press.

Stone Fish, L., & Harvey, R. G. (2005). *Nurturing queer youth*. New York: W. W. Norton.

Web Resources

NAACP

http://www.naacp.org/

UNCF

http://www.uncf.org/?gclid=COmt5LKNlskCFQumaQod9MUD8w

NAMI

https://www.nami.org/#

Domestic Violence:

NCADV (National Coalition Against Domestic Violence)

http://www.ncadv.org/index.php

The National Domestic Violence Hotline

http://www.thehotline.org/

RAINN (Rape, Abuse, & Incest National Network)

https://rainn.org/

Gay-Rights Organizations:

HRC (Human Rights Campaign)

http://www.hrc.org/the-hrc-story/about-us

GLAD (Gay & Lesbian Advocates & Defenders)

http://www.glad.org/

GLAAD (Gay & Lesbian Alliance Against Defamation)

http://www.glaad.org/

Wikipedia List of LGBT rights organizations in the U.S.

https://en.wikipedia.org/wiki/List_of_LGBT_rights_organizations_in_the_United_States

Latino support organizations:

National Council of La Raza

http://www.nclr.org/about-us/

National Hispanic Institute

http://nhi-net.org/Pages/Mission.aspx

The Committee for Hispanic Children and Families, Inc.

https://www.chcfinc.org/

Asian support organizations:

National CAPACD (Coalition for Asian Pacific American Community Development)

http://www.nationalcapacd.org/

NCAPA (National Council of Asian Pacific Americans)

http://www.ncapaonline.org/about

JACL (Japanese American Citizens League)

https://jacl.org/about/

KAC (Korean American Coalition)

http://www.kacla.org/about.html

SECTION 2

First-Generation Models of Marriage and Family Therapy

This section introduces the student to three first-generation theories of marriage and family therapy. All of the theories included here were based on linear and individual-oriented theories that were modified by some first-generation family therapist to fit the newly developed systemic paradigm. It makes sense that as systems theory developed as the unifying theory of family therapy, it was first applied to existing theories.

Behavioral family therapy, considered in Chapter 4, is the first of such theories. Behaviorism itself was a challenge to psychodynamic theories. It challenged the idea that intrapsychic issues are responsible for a client's problems. Behaviorism family therapy evolved to incorporate cognations and cognitive behavioral therapy, and is sometimes just referred to as Cognitive Behavioral Family Therapy. This paradigm became systemic as theorists applied it to couples therapy and work with parents in addressing behavioral problems in their children.

Psychodynamic Family Therapy as presented in Chapter 5, is one of the foundational models of family therapy. The influence of several theorist including; Sigmund Freud, Alfred Ackerman, John Bowlby and Nathan Ackerman is explored. We then discuss the impact of contextual family therapy, object relations, as well as attachment based family therapy.

The theory developed by Murray Bowen, discussed in Chapter 6, is a classic example of a first-generation theory. Bowen integrated psychodynamic theory and systems theory to develop a grand and popular approach to thinking about working with families. The genograms provide a graphic representation of families that makes intergenerational patterns appear obvious.

The fourth and fifth first-generation model discussed in this section are satir transformational systemic and symbolic-experiential family therapy. Chapter 7 explores the work of Virginia Satir & Carl Whitaker. These theories builds on experiential gestalt theory and incorporates systems theory into their view of family functioning and change.

CHAPTER

BEHAVIORAL & COGNITIVE
BEHAVIORAL FAMILY THERAPY

Thinking About This Approach

Behavioral family therapy BFT grew out of the application of scientific observations that occurred in behavioral psychology laboratories. Its roots can be traced back to the work of J. B. Watson, Ivan Pavlov, and others working in the early part of the 20th century. Given this tradition, it is closely linked to the logical positivistic view of science. Unlike the other approaches, which have clearly identifiable founders, behavioral family therapy was developed by applying facts learned in the psychology laboratory to the clinical setting. In fact, some would not call this approach a school of family therapy. Falloon (1991) argues, "Behavioral family therapy is a generic term for a number of therapeutic interventions that focus on the family unit and are derived from empirical studies" (p. 65).

Behavioral family therapy focuses on evaluation and assessment of behavior sequences during all stages of treatment. While this theory was developed in academic settings to describe the behavior of individual subjects, current behavioral family therapists are well equipped to deal with the complexity of relational behaviors. Behavioral family therapy has been applied to parent training, marital therapy, anxiety disorders, and sexual dysfunction. It is common for families to present with specific concerns about the behavior of their children. Clinical approaches that quickly and precisely target these concerns are very attractive to consumers.

This theory rests in the first generation of theories of family therapy. The concern for what is observable and quantifiable makes this a more linear theory. Also, the ability to evoke change by using behavioral techniques makes this a particularly appealing approach. Behavioral family therapy is attractive for its utility rather than its theoretical eloquence. Its high degree of usefulness has impacted most, if not all, schools of family therapy. This is especially true of the Mental Research Institute (MRI; Chapter 7) and the strategic (Chapter 9) and solution-focused brief (Chapter 10) approaches.

Ivan Pavlov, a Russian researcher working at the turn of the century, developed classical conditioning in his experimentation with dogs. In his original experiments (Pavlov, 1934), a dog was given food—an unconditioned stimulus that leads to an automatic response in the parasympathetic nervous system, such as salivation, creating an unconditioned response. In the experiment, food was paired with a conditioned stimulus—a bell. After a period of applying the experimental condition, the dog salivated when it heard the bell (see Table 4.1). It was hypothesized that this process could produce phobic responses in humans. This hypothesis was tested in an experiment that would have questionable ethics today. Watson (Watson & Raynor, 1920) induced a phobic response in a small child named "Little Albert" by pairing a bunny with a loud noise. After the application of the experimental condition, Albert displayed a phobic response toward the bunny.

The theorist/researcher who had the greatest impact on behavioral family therapy was the late Harvard psychologist B. F. Skinner. Skinner's term "operant conditioning" refers to the conditioning of voluntary behaviors. Here, the subject is aware of the behaviors she or he is performing in response to the conditioning. The basic idea of this approach is that the likelihood of a person's performing a conditioned act is clearly a function of others' responses to the act. Operant responses that are positively reinforced or rewarded will increase in frequency. Operant responses that are negatively reinforced or not acknowledged will decrease in frequency until ultimately extinguished.

In behavioral family therapy, the treatment of anxiety disorders involves the use of systematic desensitization, a technique developed by Wolpe in 1948. According to Wolpe (1948), an anxiety disorder is acquired through classical conditioning where a fear response is paired with a stimulus. After this conditioning has occurred, the client may or may not have conscious memory of the original event. In the use of systematic desensitization, a response that is incompatible with anxiety is paired with the anxiety-provoking stimulus. Over time, the subject is reconditioned to have no anxiety response to the stimulus. In practice, this involves having clients first relax and then imagine approaching the source of their fear. As they become anxious, they are instructed to stop and relax before imagining being closer to the stimulus.

TABLE 4.1	Classical Conditioning
Pre-Condition Dog + Food → Salvation Dog + Bell → No response	Food = Unconditioned Stimulus Salvation = Unconditioned Response Bell = Neutral Stimulus
Conditioning Dog + Food + Bell → Salvation	Bell = Conditioning Stimulus
Conditioned Dog + Bell → Salvation	Bell = Conditioned Stimulus Salvation = Conditioned Response

Systematic desensitization has proven to be a very effective technique for reducing anxiety. In vivo desensitization is a more intense form of desensitization that involves building the client's ability to relax until she or he is ready to practice approaching the feared stimulus. For example, to overcome her fear of flying, Erica Jong might first be asked to practice relaxation techniques while imagining taking a trip on an airplane. After successfully carrying out the relaxation techniques, she might be taken to the airport to practice them. The next step might involve boarding a plane while practicing the relaxation exercises. Finally, she would be ready to take a brief flight to resolve her fear of flying.

The treatment of sexual dysfunction often involves the treatment of anxiety associated with poor functioning. While good sexual functioning can be one of the most enjoyable parts of one's life, poor functioning can produce a great deal of anxiety.

Cognitive Behavioral Therapy (Ellis, 1962), or Rational Emotive Therapy (Beck, 1976) developed as the behavioral ideas of reinforcement was applied to thinking about the role of thought (Cognition) in the maintained of problematic behavior. Both Ellis and Beck focused their work on uncovering beliefs, attributes and expectancies that underlie symptomatic behavior. Simply put they seek to uncover the assumptions in life that lead to poor behavioral choices. Ellis (1978) describes how "While trying to help family members change their basic irrationalities and thereby make profound emotional or personality changes, the RET therapist would also tend to employ various other cogitative methods-such as information giving, problem-solving techniques, advice and interpretation, many of which overlap with some of the main techniques used by psychodynamic and family systems therapists" (p.46).

Rational Emotive Therapists (RET) help family members understand how irrational beliefs underlie their psychopathology. Ellis developed his ABC model where families place blame for their problem on an event or person (A). They then are encouraged and instructed to look for an irrational belief (B). The therapist then challenges this belief (C). For example a client might decide that their unhappiness is the result of his wife not trusting him after he had an affair (A). This is supported by the irrational belief that he would be happy if she was able to be closer to him (B). The therapist might utilize insight into the belief that his wife being closer would result in his happiness by pointing out the difficulty in basing your happiness in someone else's actions (C). Ellis and Harper (1963) saw problems in relationships as resulting from an unrealistic belief or expectation of the other and extreme negative evaluation of the ultimate failure to meet expectations. This insight has powerful implications for family therapists who incorporate this model into their cognitive behavioral family therapy CBFT.

The profession of marriage and family therapy was shocked by Neil Jacobson's sudden and untimely death in the summer of 1999. Since the 1970s, Jacobson had been one of the profession's most prolific theorists and researchers. He is most noted for his research and contributions to the theory and practice of marital therapy. He developed the concept of couple acceptance (Cordova & Jacobson, 1993: Jacobson, 1991, 1992). Simply put, this concept recognizes that not all problems can be solved and that some things must be accepted as part of a partner's imperfection. This idea is consistent with the MRI approach, which argues that sometimes a solution to a problem can itself become a problem (Watzlawick, Weakland, & Fisch, 1974).

Huber and Baruth (1989) combined systems theory and Rational Emotive Therapy to develop Rational Emotive Family Therapy REFT. This has been a influential integration to the two theoretical approaches. This approach starts with an assessment of the family based on the family's cognitive behavioral and emotional frames. From the assessment the REFT therapist utilizes a variety of strategies to effect change in the family's functioning. According to Huber & Baruth (1989) "... the REFT Therapist can best be seen as a teacher and family member's students in a common new learning experience." P.98. The work inside and homework outside of the therapy session are all designed to teach the family how to live without distortions and more efficiently.

Parent training is based on a specific application of operant conditioning. In this approach, parents are taught how to reinforce their child's appropriate behavior through the use of rewards, such as positive attention. Shaping occurs as parents reward a child's attempts to engage in desirable behavior. As the child gets closer to performing the target task, parents reward her or his efforts. Parents are also taught how to extinguish, or get rid of, negative behavior. By recognizing what form of reinforcement a child is receiving for negative behavior and removing it, the negative behavior can be extinguished. In practice, the frequency of the undesirable behavior increases slightly at first. However, if the parents are consistent in their nonreinforcement, the undesirable behavior is eventually extinguished. It is important to warn clients that, at first, things will get a little worse before getting better.

Behavioral marital therapy is based on social exchange theory (Thibaut & Kelley, 1959). Social exchange theory is an economic theory of interpersonal relationships. It views relationships as the result of participants' efforts to maximize rewards from the relationship while reducing costs. According to this theory, people will be satisfied in a relationship as long as they are getting more than what they put into the relationship. However, a person will not terminate a relationship simply because it is not rewarding. This is because there are costs involved in ending a relationship. A person will remain in a relationship until the cost of ending the relationship is less than that of remaining in it. In behavioral marital therapy, the couple is taught to negotiate mutually rewarding exchanges. For example, if Mrs. Jones agrees to play golf with her husband, Mr. Jones will agree to go with his wife to see a movie.

In the late 1970s a similar emphasis on utilizing behavioral techniques to alter behavior was applied to altering a client's cognitions. Ellis published an article in the *Journal of Marriage and Family Counseling* introducing Rationally Emotive Therapy family therapy. He describe that the RET family therapist "... would place the responsibility for all family members' emotional disturbances squarely on themselves, and not on their childhood upbringing or their present life conditions; and s/he would try to help all of the them to accept this responsibility and to change their basic disturbance-creating outlooks so that no matter what happened to them inside or outside of the family they would tend to feel appropriately sorry, regretful, and irritated at each other and their own poor behavior but not inappropriately angry, self-damning, or undisciplined." (Ellis, 1978, p.46.).

Over the decades CBT has become a heavily researched approach to family therapy in practice; and as Dattilio (2001) points, CBFT has been underutilized. Because of its demonstrated utility and effectiveness it has become the standard of care in the medical community and the mental health system. It also will continue to be a pragmatic set of interventions that therapists will incorporate into treatment plans and manuals. Because of its proven effectiveness, understanding behavioral theory will be important in training future family therapists.

Innovations in Practice

By far, the greatest innovation of behavioral family therapy and cognitive behavioral family therapy has been the challenge to psychoanalysis. Behavioral therapy was probably the first widely accepted approach to be successful at challenging the idea that psychotherapy has to address deep-seated unconscious issues to be effective. The advent of the behavioral approach greatly shortened the time required to treat clients, making behavioral therapy perhaps the first brief therapy approach.

A second innovation of behavioral family therapy has been the impact of behavioral techniques on the practice of sex therapy. Pioneers such as Masters and Johnson (1966, 1970) brought behavioral techniques into play when addressing disorders of sexual functioning. By bringing the couple into the interview room and discussing sexual techniques in behavioral terms, the success rate of these therapies increased dramatically. Likewise, a significant component of most difficulties in sexual functioning is anxiety. Since behavioral therapy is so useful in reducing anxiety, using behavioral techniques with sexual issues addresses both the problem of technique and the underlying anxiety.

A more subtle but equally important contribution of behavioral therapy is the use of technological advances. Behavioral therapy was one of the first approaches to use audiotaping and videotaping in research and training, allowing researchers and supervisors access to real-time data.

Despite the lack of a highly developed understanding of change, behavioral therapy is a powerful tool. In this section, we discuss some additional definitions necessary for using a behavioral approach to family therapy.

Reinforcement

Reinforcement is any reward that is paired with a behavioral response. The act of pairing a reward or reinforcer with a behavior response increases the frequency with which that behavior will be performed. It is important to note that the strength of a reinforcer is a function of its desirability to the person receiving it. Thus, there is no universal reinforcer. What one subject values highly may mean little to the next. Reinforcement may not even be material. Verbal reinforcement in the form of praise, or nonverbal reinforcement in the form of a smile, may be powerful.

In addition to being idiosyncratic to the person receiving it, reinforcement is subject to saturation. Saturation refers to the decrease in the value of a reinforcer that occurs as a result of the frequency with which it is received. For example, the first million Bill Gates made was much more reinforcing than the most recent million he made.

Negative Reinforcement

Negative reinforcement is any stimulus that, when removed, increases the frequency of the behavior. Going home early to avoid too much stress at work would be an example of negative reinforcement. It is important to note that, just as the strength of a reinforcer is a function of its desirability, the strength of a negative reinforcer is a function of its undesirability to the person avoiding it.

Video Call Out 4.1: Behavioral Family Therapy

During this video the clients discuss giving their child a "pop", as euphuism for spanking. Since punishment is not a part of behavioral therapy and proven to be ineffective, she seeks to extinguish this behavior in the parents. During this interview the therapist Bonnie Perkins, M.A. asks about the outcome of the "pop" to assess what the client think and feel about this form of punishment. Here she is accessing the client's perspective on this issue, in essence asking how is that working for you? Since the client reports that it was not particularly effective and did not seem dependent or committed to it use, she simply focused on alternatives. By finding another approach that is more likely to produce behavioral change she expects that the spanking with stop rather quickly, as behaviors that are negatively reinforced are easily extinguished.

Shaping

Shaping is a technique for modifying behavior. It involves reinforcing behaviors that are progressively closer to a desirable behavior. In this systematic manner, new learning takes place. For example, when teaching your son to eat with utensils, you might praise him the first time he picks up a fork. Then you could praise him for spearing a pea with his fork. Finally, you would praise him when the fork finds its way into his mouth.

Schema

Schema is a concept utilized to describe a pattern of thinking. According to Dattilio (2005) "In essence, schemas are used as a template for an individual's life experiences and how he or she processes information" (p.15). In essence they are the assumptions we make. Our assumptions of how the world work has a lot to do with how we organize and live our life. If a person has a negative schema based on a history of trauma or abuse they are likely to distort their thinking. This is referred to as cognitive distortions and could be a thought like, I have no value, I always lose, life has no meaning. Cognitive distortions are usually global and absolute.

When beliefs are held on a collective level among family members and shared they are referred to as family schema. When couples start their own families and develop their own set of beliefs there can be difficulty in how schemas are accepted, modified or combined. For example, when one partner grew up with a family schema around "we don't talk about our problems" marries a person with a "let's all talk this out" schema. There are questions on which approach should prevail or can the couple develop a hybrid family schema. Azar, Nix, & Makin-Byrd (2005) extend the concept of schema to include "adaptive and problematic functioning in the caregiver role." p.45. Understanding a parents schema is essential to helping them engage in effective parenting practices.

Time-Out

Time-out is a behavioral technique that is an effective alternative to corporal punishment of children. It involves having the child take a time-out for inappropriate behavior. When a child is acting out, she or he is instructed to go off to the side and sit quietly for a few minutes. Typically a time-out lasts one minute for every year of age. After the time has expired, the child is allowed to rejoin the activity in a more productive manner. It is often useful to talk to the child at the end of the time-out period so she or he can learn from the experience. However, it is important to view time-out as an opportunity to redirect the child to a positive behavior rather than as a punishment. It is also important that the parent not use anger when placing a child in time-out. If that occurs, the child is likely to seek negative attention in the future. Furthermore, the time-out will be spent reinforcing the child's negative self-concept.

Time-out is also used in couples work to de-escalate an argument that is on the verge of becoming out of control. When a couple find themselves in an argument that is increasing in intensity and becoming a negative experience, they can call a time-out. This involves one of them simply calling time-out. When this occurs, they withdraw to a safe place for a predetermined period. After this time has expired, the couple might try to resolve the argument, or they might even be instructed to suspend the argument until the next therapy session.

Video Call Out 4.2: Behavioral Family Therapy

The therapist Bonnie spends a good deal of time exploring how the family makes use of time out. Throughout this she focuses on what they are doing well. She is generous with complements when she agrees with their technique. When she is less than satisfied she is not critical of their approach; she simply makes suggestions in areas where they are utilizing less than optimal techniques. This approach of the therapist helps shape the parent's behavior, specifically how they put their child in time out without being critical. This positive approach by the therapist is isomorphic with the way she wants the parents to approach shaping their children's behavior. By experiencing this approach themselves it is likely to transfer into the parent's approach to shaping their children's behavior.

The Premack Principle

The Premack principle refers to the notion that an undesirable behavior or task is more likely to be completed if it is followed by a highly desirable one. For example, parents apply this principle by telling their children they can't play video games until they've completed their homework. This is very important in parenting because many parents enjoy making their children happy, thus it is easy to overlook training them to do what is necessary. They think that if they just provide for their child's needs, that the child will learn to be responsible without training. Frequently, children need the motivation provided by the Premack principle for them to learn responsibility.

Modeling

Modeling is learning that occurs by watching another person perform a behavior. We see that people often learn best by example. It is important for parents to model the type of behavior they would like their children to perform. For example, it is unlikely that your children will always be on time for school when you are often late picking them up. Watching seems to be more powerful than being told, and the old saying "Do as I say, not as I do" almost always fails to produce the desired behavior.

Communication Skill Training

Communication skill training involves training the family members to avoid common errors in communication. This is emphasized particularly in behavioral couple therapy. Communication skills can address both the process level of interaction and the content level of interaction. The process level focuses on such issues as speaking with a calm voice tone, making eye contact, taking turns speaking, and not interrupting. The content level focuses on what is being said with such skills as stating feeling, paraphrasing each other, and speaking for yourself. These skills are developed in therapy through a combination of modeling and critiquing the client's performance.

More recently, as the incidence of developmental disorders in children and rates of autism increase, we find that Behavioral Communication Skill training has become more and more common. Miller, Vernon, Wu & Russo (2014) reviewed 45 studies and concluded that there is significant and growing evidence of that usefulness of social skills groups. These approaches utilize behavioral techniques to shape how people with autism interact socially. Michelle Garcia Winner's book "Thinking about you thinking about me" invites young people on the Autism spectrum to look at how they think about social interactions and provides this with some more useful social schema. By combining this learning with behavioral techniques and opportunities to refine their skills in groups, we are entering a rich new area of practice for MFT's. Working with families helping them train their own members how to communicate socially has a lot of possible opportunities for family therapists.

Metaphors

The behavioral approach to family therapy is based on two metaphors for the therapeutic process. The first metaphor equates therapy with learning. In this metaphor, interpersonal problems are the result of clients' lack of knowledge of how to have and maintain good interpersonal relationships. Thus, the goal of treatment is to aid the client in learning new behaviors and ways of relating. This accounts for the close connection between behavioral family therapy and psychoeducational therapy.

The second metaphor used to describe behavioral family therapy is that of social exchange (Thibaut & Kelley, 1959). This metaphor sees relationships as governed by the same law of supply and demand as economics. People are seen as motivated in social relationships by interpersonal rewards or profit. That is, people strive to get as much as possible out of a relationship with minimal investment. It is interesting to note that when a relationship is going well, both parties report that rewards are much more than the costs. However, when the relationship turns poor, both parties typically report that they are getting back far less than they "invest" in the relationship.

This metaphor is extended to underlie the technique of contracting. By assisting clients to learn skills in negotiation, behaviorists help the clients engage in mutually satisfying relationships. This technique is especially useful in cases where the presenting problem is marital discord. Most couples marry prior to negotiating the marital relationship. There is a cultural myth that "love" will make a marriage work. Some couples believe being in love is all that is needed to function in a relationship. However, after the honeymoon is over, they find there is much to negotiate. From simple issues such as what to eat for dinner to complex ones like child rearing, marriage is a series of negotiations and compromises. Having the ability to develop behavioral contracts with your spouse facilitates marital satisfaction.

Questioning

In behavioral family therapy, much of the questioning involves getting an accurate picture of the behavioral sequences that surround the client's problematic behavior. Questions also seek to quantify the frequency of the problem. The behavioral family therapist is interested in both the frequency of the problem and the behavioral sequences that surround the problem. This includes interest in what happens to each family member immediately preceding and following the identified patient's problematic behavior.

From this approach questions tend to be precise as the therapist tries to develop an accurate contextual description of the client's difficulty. The goal of a behavioral interview is to establish the behavioral context in which the problematic behavior occurs. It seeks to establish a precise definition of the problem. It also seeks to develop a description of what behavior by others is providing reinforcement of the problem behavior. The concern here is both positive and negative reinforcement.

In cases where a child is the identified patient, a good deal of attention is paid to improving the skill level of the parents. Therapists are concerned that the parents have age-appropriate expectations for their children. They are also concerned about the parents' ability to be consistent and follow through with appropriate rewards and consequences for their child's behaviors.

While a good deal of evaluation is focused on the parents of a child who presents for treatment, behavioral therapists are cautious about shifting their focus to issues of parenting too quickly. This is because parents often experience this shift as being blamed for their child's issues, and they may have a "flight into health" where they decide not to continue therapy. Clients making a flight into health often cancel their following appointment by message stating that they have decided the problem has either resolved or no longer needs addressing. A gradual shift in emphasis that continues to focus on the child in context may prevent a flight into health. The frame of addressing issues in parenting to support the child's unique needs often allows parents to become active in improving their parenting.

Structuring

The interview in cognitive behavioral family therapy is highly structured. Initially, the therapist may meet with the family for more than an hour to formulate a clear idea of the context of the problem. Behavioral sequences could be observed in the therapy office. On occasion, behavioral therapists will go to the family's home to make observations in the family's natural setting. Also, to get a clear idea of the behavioral sequence, the family might be sent home between sessions with specific instructions to observe and record the behavior sequences that relate to the problem.

Families are often given instructions on how to address the problem. Homework assignments that allow families to work on their issues between sessions are a mainstay of behavioral family therapy. The homework involves being deliberate about extinguishing undesirable behaviors. As these are extinguished, positive behaviors are shaped and intimately reinforced. Follow-up sessions, where the homework is discussed and modified, usually occur on a weekly schedule. Issues are addressed in order of importance until they are resolved. Once issues are resolved, a follow-up is scheduled several weeks later to prevent and address any issues of relapse.

Behavioral family therapists further provide calmness in the chaos that a dysfunctional family experiences. As they selectively focus on the most pressing of the behavioral problems and provide some changes, the family tends to buy into the therapy. This calmness and focus are often a hook to engage the family.

Responding

The behavioral and cognitive behavioral family therapist tries to be responsive to the needs of clients by specifically addressing the problematic behavior. In behavioral family therapy, the clinical focus is on the emotional climate of the family. Emotions are addressed in terms of how they relate to a person's behavior. The skilled behavioral family therapist is able to function in the emotional turmoil that can occur in a distressed family. The therapist seeks to change the emotional climate

Video Call Out 4.3: Behavioral Family Therapy

In the video we see an example of how a behavioral therapist responds. The parents report that they are exhausted by their role as parents of young children. The therapist supports their efforts while normalizing their feelings of exhaustion. By calling attention to how important parenting is to them, she utilizes their own motivation to address the issues in the children. Over time, as the children become more independent and need less direction from their parents, there will be more room for the parents to rest and engage in self-care behaviors. As this occurs, the therapist would bring up the issue of their exhaustion and perhaps help the couple reconnect and spend some time and effort on their relationship and themselves.

of the family by changing the behaviors of family members. Behavioral theory postulates that a change in behavior will change the emotional climate of the family.

Applications

A revolution was started when William Masters and Virginia Johnson applied professional techniques to the practice of sexual therapy. Their publication of *Human Sexual Response* in 1966 and *Human Sexual Inadequacy* in 1970 brought the treatment of sexual dysfunction to the couple counselor. Rather than undergoing analysis, or medical treatment for one of the partners, the couple was counseled in a conjoint session. It was found that a significant number of sexual problems could be addressed by teaching the couple new techniques. While the techniques of this approach produced striking results, such therapy was primarily an inpatient procedure, which for some was a barrier to receiving treatment.

Helen Singer Kaplan (1974) developed an outpatient-based approach to the treatment of sexual dysfunction. By coupling behavioral techniques with psychodynamic techniques, therapy for sexual dysfunction became more effective. This was accomplished by addressing psychodynamic issues of shame, fear, and conflict in the relationship while assisting the couple to use more effective sexual techniques.

A second area of application for behavioral family therapy is using behavioral techniques in clinical work with couples. The application of behavioral techniques to marital problems dates back 45 years to the work of Richard Stuart (1969) and Robert Liberman (1970). Stuart's approach draws from exchange theory and assumes that, at one time in their relationship, couples were rewarding to each other. To draw on this initial positive history, Stuart would have couples make explicit reinforcement contracts. Stuart (1980) expanded his theory to an eight-step model that seeks to accentuate the positive. Liberman's later approaches included elements of behavior theory, including operant conditioning, positive reinforcement, shaping, modeling, and social learning theory (Liberman, Wheeler, de Visser, Kuehnel, & Kuehnel, 1980). When these approaches were linked with general communication skills and the use of contingency contracts, couples were often able to negotiate the resolution of persistent conflict.

Stuart (1980) provided a very creative and useful technique he referred to as "caring day." On this day, one or both partners agreed to act as if they cared for their partner. The clients were to be explicit in their caring and were asked to bring their contracts to the therapy sessions. This technique is useful for helping a couple quickly develop a more positive way of relating and connecting to the therapeutic process.

Behavioral theory has a long history of being applied to improving parenting. Not only is it frequently used in the family setting, but behavioral techniques are the standard of care in the residential treatment facility. Most residential programs are run on a level system where clients earn privileges (reinforcements) as rewards for performing specific targeted behaviors. Commonly, these programs are run as a token economy where clients can earn chips that can be exchanged for privileges. For example, in a group home, a child with issues of hostility might be allowed to watch a move on Friday night if she was supportive to her sibling 10 times during the prior week.

Finally—and perhaps most important, as discussed above—behavioral therapy and the use of behavioral shaping have an impact on parenting. In fact, it would be fair to say that parents have always sought to shape their children's behavior. As behavior techniques were developed in the psychology lab, parents quickly applied lessons learned to the art of child rearing.

Acting as a Behavioral Family Therapist

Like most forms of treatment, behavioral family therapy starts with the therapist's establishing a productive relationship with the family. This is accomplished during the early phases of therapy. The behavioral therapist avoids being critical of the client's prior attempts to solve the problem and quickly takes an expert role, offering the client knowledge in behavioral therapy as a means of addressing the problem.

In behavioral family therapy, the shift to diagnostic assessment is quick. Several factors are hallmarks of behavioral assessment. First, the assessment is nonhistorical. In the thinking of behavioral therapy, how a problem developed is of little consequence in terms of its elimination. The behavioral family therapist is concerned with what maintains the problem. Here, behaviorism fits well with the systemic idea of homeostasis. If you look at feedback as reinforcement of desirable behaviors, we can see the similarities of this approach.

The first step in the assessment is to define the behavior to be addressed. There are three possible outcomes from targeting a specific behavior. First, an undesirable behavior can be extinguished. Second, a new desirable behavior can be established. Third, both an undesirable behavior can be extinguished and a desirable behavior can be established.

Once a behavior is targeted, the next step is to establish a baseline. In behavioral terminology, the baseline is the frequency with which a behavior occurs. It is important to establish an accurate baseline so that the therapist can measure the effectiveness of any interventions. This involves observing the problematic behavior for a period of time. Observations can be made through client record keeping. The record keeping may include observing events prior to and after the problematic incident. Due to the tendency to overreport negative behavior and underreport positive behavior, it is best to use a specific time period for observation. Frequently, clients are asked to collect baseline data between the first and second sessions.

In behavioral family therapy, the intervention phase is rather distinct and precise. The data collected in the assessment phase are used to design a treatment plan. In the case where undesirable behavior is targeted, new reinforcement responses are designed and implemented. For example, parents may be asked to stop reinforcing Mary's failure to pick up her things by picking up after her. Furthermore, they may be instructed to place in a box the items they find left lying around. This box is kept locked away until Saturday, when they allow her to retrieve her belongings. The Saturday Box quickly conditions children to pick up after themselves.

In this phase, the behavioral family therapist acts as a coach for the family. In the interview, the therapist gives direct instructions on how the family members are to respond to each other. Like a coach in a sporting event, the therapist calls the action in the room. Initially, the therapist uses verbal reinforcement to get instructions followed. Over time, however, the change in function itself reinforces the behavioral change. The therapist often relies on specific homework assignments the client is given to work on between sessions.

In instances where new behaviors are desirable, clients may be asked to engage in a discussion of reinforcements for desirable behaviors. Family members may rehearse how to praise and reinforce when progress is made toward the desirable behavior. The process of reinforcing behaviors increasingly closer to a desired behavior is called shaping. The reinforcement of approximations of the targeted behavior occurs until the target behavior is performed. Once this occurs, the target behavior is reinforced. For example, a teenager may be given a later curfew on the weekend if he completes all of his homework during the previous week.

In many instances, families seek to extinguish certain behaviors and establish other new behaviors. In these instances, each behavior is treated separately from the others. Techniques are then applied that are appropriate to each behavior. In behavioral therapy, there is no assumption of an unconscious link between behaviors. Rather, it is assumed that the undesirable behavior is simply the result of reinforcement. Each behavior is treated as a unique issue in the family's life.

Treatment ends when the behavioral problem is extinguished or a new desirable behavior is established. Treatment is terminated as clients are encouraged to discuss the differences in their lives that have resulted from their newfound functioning. In some instances, a follow-up meeting is scheduled for several weeks after the termination of treatment. In other cases, the therapist simply contacts the clients post termination to determine if the family has maintained adequate functioning.

Case Example: The Case of Billy's Temper Tantrums*

Ms. Susan McArthur calls regarding her six-year-old son, Billy. She has become overwhelmed by his temper tantrums and is concerned that he will not be able to go to kindergarten in two months unless he gets over his problem. Over the phone, she states that there are no other problems with her son. In fact, there are no other problems in their family. Billy's older brother, Max, is doing well in second grade, and Ms. McArthur is at a loss to explain the differences in her two children. The only explanation she can come up with is that Billy may not feel he belongs because he was adopted. She reports that he was adopted as an infant and has always been different from Max.

The therapist asks the entire family to attend the first session. When Ms. McArthur is hesitant to bring the whole family in, the therapist asks if they are all affected by the problem. When she replies that they are, the therapist suggests that they should also be interested in its solution.

The setting for this therapy is a counseling center for faculty and staff at a small university. The therapist is a Caucasian woman in her mid 40s with over 15 years' experience. The family is also Caucasian except for Billy, who was adopted from China as an infant. The family has always been open to Billy about his adoption. The community the family lives in is rather diverse, and two of Billy's peers from his day care have also been adopted from China. Ms. McArthur and her husband, Mr. Ron Smith, work at the university in student services positions.

Session One

The family arrives 30 minutes late for their session. Ms. McArthur is very angry at her son, Billy. She reports that he had a "grade A temper tantrum" prior to the session. While Mr. Smith is concerned, he is not as upset as his wife. Max is embarrassed that they are late and seems irritated that his mother is upset. Billy is sullen. He looks a little embarrassed and is very reserved when the therapist tries to talk to him. In fact, when the therapist shakes Billy's hand, Billy tells her that she cannot take him away from his family.

The therapist smiles and inquires how Billy got the idea that she was going to take him away. Billy responds that he heard from his friends that psychologists do those things. The therapist tells Billy that what he heard is not true and explains that she is a family therapist and that her job is to help families live together in better ways. The therapist asks Billy if he likes living in his family, and Billy responds that he does.

At this point, the therapist notices that there are only a few minutes left in the session. She explains to the family that she has to end on time because she has a prior commitment after the session. She thanks the parents for bringing the children to the session and asks to see the parents alone for a few minutes. As Billy and Max go, the therapist shakes their hands and thanks each of them for coming.

The therapist then sets the next appointment and stresses to the parents the importance of coming to the session on time. She suggests that, before attending the next session, they promise that the family will go for ice cream after the session. She further suggests that the parents allow themselves plenty of time so that Billy will not be inclined to respond to their stress.

Ms. McArthur is uneasy about the suggestion of taking the children for ice cream. She states that she does not think it is right to bribe the children to do what is expected of them. The therapist frames the ice cream as a reward for a job well done. The therapist jokes that she works much harder when she knows that she is going to get paid for her work.

Session Two

The family arrives on time for the session and everyone seems to be in a good mood. The purpose of this session is to establish a baseline of temper tantrums. The therapist takes out a calendar and goes through each day, discussing any incidence of tantrums. After the family discusses the frequency of tantrums for the past week, the therapist continues to take a baseline of the problem for the prior week.

The therapist has paper and colored pencils available for the children to play with during the session. As the children are engaged in drawing a series of pictures, the therapist invites the parents to the other side of the room to talk. Several times during the session the children seek attention from the adults by interrupting their conversation.

The third time Billy interrupts the conversation, the therapist redirects him. She informs him that if he needs something, he is to say "Excuse me" before speaking. A few minutes later he does this, and he is given verbal praise by the adults. The therapist and parents takes time to admire each of the children's artwork. At the same time, the therapist asks questions about each of the works and commissions another work based on the last, giving plenty of praise and encouragement. After each work is produced, it is hung in a place of honor in the office.

Based on the conversation that occurs while the children are drawing, the therapist sees a pronounced pattern. In the past three weeks, Billy's tantrums have averaged four times a week. All of these instances were a result of Billy's hesitation to follow a direction from his mother. In response, she would push him toward compliance, and Billy's hesitation would quickly deteriorate into a tantrum. In response to the tantrum, Mr. Smith would enter the room and try to calm Billy.

Until last week, Mr. Smith was successful in calming his son by getting down on the floor and reasoning with him. Last week, there was an incident where Mr. Smith was unable to calm his son. After a period of reasoning, Mr. Smith "lost his temper" and spanked Billy with his belt. Since Ms. McArthur and Mr. Smith do not believe in corporal punishment, this prompted a fight between the parents. As a result of the fight, Max became fearful and withdrew to his room in tears. This incident prompted Ms. McArthur to call for therapy.

As the therapist talks with Mr. Smith about the incident, Mr. Smith reports feeling out of control and concerned that this problem could cross into other parts of his life. When the therapist asks Mr. Smith about his fear, Mr. Smith lists a variety of concerns with parenting. In addition, he is concerned that his neighbors may hear Billy's temper tantrums and call the police.

The therapist then explores with Mr. Smith his fear that neighbors will call the police. Mr. Smith describes an incident where his neighbor had the police called on him for getting into a shouting match with his wife. While no one was arrested, Mr. Smith is still concerned about the incident. Mr. Smith quietly shares that he has a record from college for selling LSD at a rock concert.

At the end of the session, the therapist asks the parents to simply keep track of the frequency of Billy's temper tantrums over the next week and emphasizes that they should pay particular attention to what happens just before and after the tantrums. The therapist asks Billy to try not to have any tantrums over the next week. She also sympathizes with Billy and tells him that if he needs to have a tantrum, it will be okay, and that he will not be taken away from his parents. The therapist then asks the parents if they can come to the next session without the children. When the children object, the therapist simply tells them that she wants to talk to their parents about some adult stuff. After the therapist reassures the boys that they would not be interested in the grown-up stuff, they stop their objections.

Session Three

During this session, the therapist explores with the parents their history of substance abuse. While both used "recreational" drugs in college, both deny any use for the past 10 years. Both report drinking about once a week in social situations and report that they never drink more than two or three drinks. The therapist accepts their reports and clarifies that she was exploring the possibility that substance abuse may have been playing a part in Billy's tantrums.

The therapist also explores with the family how they explained the adoption to Billy. Ms. McArthur reports that she told her son a year ago that his mother gave him up for adoption because she could not take care of him anymore. She states that he did not ask any questions, nor did she offer any more details.

The therapist shares with the parents that she thinks Billy might have some anxiety about being adopted. Mr. Smith defensively asks why the therapist thinks that. The therapist calmly states that she is concerned that Billy's comments about a psychologist breaking up a family in the first session might reflect Billy's anxiety. The therapist is careful to explain that she is not saying the parents made Billy anxious. She explains that children are often anxious about what they do not understand. While Billy might act as if he knows what being adopted means, he may still be very confused. He does know that he came to be a member of the family differently than his brother, and that is enough to produce anxiety.

The therapist also explores with the parents their beliefs about their parenting. By simply asking what they think in general about their parenting skills the therapist was able to access their parenting schema. Mom thinks she will eventually be a failure. She shares that this idea came out of a dissatisfaction of how she was parented. Her husband's response to her disclosure was of disbelief. He saw her parenting style as very different from her mother's. She agreed that his perspective was probably more true and that she could talk with him when she was having anxiety around parenting. Dad discloses that he mostly thinks parenting is about meeting his child's needs. This leads the parents to a discussion about setting self-reliance as a goal of parenting rather than meeting their needs. Simply dad is excited by the idea that good parenting is about teaching children to meet their own needs. This new schema for parenting has potential to helping him be less anxious around tantrums.

When the parents ask how to address adoption issues, the therapist suggests that they have a family meeting and explain to both Billy and Max what adoption means. The therapist suggests that they emphasize that adoption means Billy is as much a member of the family as everyone else, even though he came to the family by a different path.

At this point in the interview, the therapist asks the parents to share their observation of Billy's tantrums. They report six tantrums during the past week. Ms. McArthur then speaks of her discouragement at the increase in frequency. The therapist reassures her by explaining that the frequency of a problem often increases slightly when it is first addressed. She states that this should be taken as a kind of "put up or shut up" message from their son and explains to the parents that they will need to have a lot of patience and give each other a lot of support to help their son get past this problem. The therapist shares that she is confident that the family can eliminate this behavior and that it should take no more than two weeks with consistency. The therapist ends the session by asking the parents to think about whether it is worth addressing the problem and schedules a follow-up in a week. As the family leaves, the therapist reminds the parents to talk with their children about the adoption. They agree to do so, and the therapist asks that everyone attend the next session.

Session Four

At this session, the family brings in a piece of art they created after they talked with Billy about being adopted. In the picture is Billy's mother giving him up because she could not care for him. Across the page is his current family, each drawn with half a heart in her or his chest. On the other side of the picture is the whole family holding hands with whole hearts in their chests.

The therapist raves about how beautiful the picture is. She correctly guesses that the Smith-McArthur family had only partially full hearts until Billy came to live with them. The therapist suggests that the picture be framed and hung in the family home. When Ms. McArthur asks what side of the picture they should hang, Billy says the second side. The therapist agrees, and the whole family takes pride in their community art project.

During the session, the therapist asks the parents to explain to Billy that the time has come for him to stop having temper tantrums. They are asked to tell him that since he is now older, he no longer needs to have temper tantrums.

Billy is asked to pick a reward from each of his parents to be given each night that he does not have a temper tantrum. After careful thought, Billy requests a story from his father each night before he goes to sleep. From his mother, he requests cookies as a late night snack. Both parents agree, and Ms. McArthur adds the condition that the cookie be eaten before Billy brushes his teeth. The therapist encourages everyone to shake hands on the arrangements. The therapist further suggests that Max should also get a cookie and be allowed to listen to the story that Billy picks out for his father to read.

At this point, the therapist asks the boys to leave the room so she can talk with the parents about adult things. Once alone with the parents, the therapist instructs them on extinguishing behavior. The parents have considered the warning from the previous session that things could get worse before getting better, and they are willing to address the issue.

The therapist instructs the parents to ignore any tantrums. She even encourages them to leave the room when Billy has a tantrum. She further instructs the parents to leave the next room if Billy follows them. The therapist lets the parents know that she understands the difficulty of this and shares with them a similar problem she had with her own son. She goes on to share that, while it was hard, she and her husband were able to ignore the behavior and break the cycle.

When Mr. Smith expresses concern about his neighbors calling the police, the therapist laughs and states that she was expecting Mr. Smith to bring up the issue. The therapist then gives Mr. Smith a letter that reads:

Dear Neighbor of the Smith-McArthur Family:

I am a family therapist who has been working with the Smith-McArthur family to help Billy get over his temper tantrums. You have probably heard them in the past. I have instructed the parents to ignore Billy's behavior at all cost over the next week. As a result, Billy may increase the volume and frequency of his tantrums until he is able to get over them. This should not go on for the entire week. If the volume of a tantrum becomes too loud, do not call the police; instead, call my beeper. I thank you in advance for your kind assistance to the Smith-McArthur family as they address this issue.

As Mr. Smith reads the letter, he looks skeptical. Ms. McArthur asks if this works. The therapist expresses her confidence and explains that she has yet to have a neighbor call the police or disturb the family. In fact, she has yet to be paged by a neighbor. The therapist shares with the parents the importance of letting the neighbors know what is going on.

The therapist ends the session by calling the boys back into the office and saying good-bye to them. Last, she tells the parents to page her should they not feel strong or have any questions. They agree, and a follow-up is scheduled for one week's time. Just prior to leaving, the therapist has the parents sign a limited release of information so she can talk to the neighbors should they call her.

Session Five

The family arrives at the session in good spirits. The parents report that Billy had a temper tantrum five days ago but has had none since. They report with great pride that they were able to ignore his fit. They report that when Billy was ignored, he quickly increased the volume of his tantrum. However, when his parents left the room, he continued his fit for only about 10 minutes. Mr. Smith interjects that the tantrum lasted exactly 8 minutes and 30 seconds. After this, Billy was able to calm himself and behave more appropriately. When Billy asked for a bedtime story that night, his dad refused and Billy started to become upset. His dad simply and calmly asked him if he was going to pitch another fit. Billy said no and went to bed. A few minutes later, Mr. Smith went into Billy's room and asked if, instead of having a story read, might he like to hear a made-up story? Mr. Smith then proceeded to tell Billy and Max a story about his own childhood.

The parents are given positive feedback for their handling of the situation. Billy is also congratulated for being a bigger boy and getting past the tantrum. The therapist asks the parents if they now know how to address any future tantrum Billy may have. They state that they are prepared, but feel confident that Billy is through with that phase of his life. The therapist agrees and suggests that it might be good if the family touches base with her over the phone in two weeks, just to make sure everything is going well.

Follow-Up

In three weeks, the therapist receives a call from Ms. McArthur. During the call, she reports that all is well. Billy is doing better at school. He has had no temper tantrums and in fact has become easier to manage. She reports that Ron, Billy, and Max now spend most bedtimes telling each other made-up stories. The therapist congratulates Ms. McArthur for her hard work and for having the courage to face the problem. She ends the call by telling Ms. McArthur she will be available to work with them again should anything come up in the future.

Case Discussion

In the first session, the therapist is struck by how mature Billy is in his appearance. He looks like a seven-year-old. She is also struck by his vocabulary and how mature he is in his speech. However, she has some concerns about his emotional maturity. Since the family is late, this is a brief session; the therapist is clear to stop on time to provide a boundary for the session itself.

The second session is mostly a diagnostic interview. The therapist establishes the frequency as well as the context of the tantrums. It appears that the parents have anxiety about their neighbors and the father's history of being arrested. In this session, the therapist notes the parents' history of illegal activities but chooses not to bring it up in front of the children. The therapist requests a session with just the adults to work on a plan and to further explore the history of illegal behaviors.

The third session serves to accomplish several tasks. First, the therapist is able to complete a substance abuse assessment. Had the parents been abusing drugs, the therapist would have had to increase the intensity of the therapy to help the family address the issues. Second, she accesses the parenting schema and finds some minor distortions. They are quickly confronted and alternatives are suggested. Finally, the therapist shares with the parents her conceptualization of the role of anxiety in Billy's life. Here she serves as a coach, providing guidance on how the parents can talk to their son about his adoption. Rather than having the discussion in the session, she decides the parents are capable of handling the discussion at home. She assures them that, should the family have difficulty with this, they can talk about it further in future sessions. Finally, she addresses the parents' anxiety about addressing the issues.

The fourth session serves to set up the intervention to extinguish the temper tantrums. By writing the letter and having the parents give the letter to the neighbors, the therapist supports the parents by addressing their anxiety about solving their problem with their son. She establishes rewards for each day he does not have a tantrum.

The last session and the follow-up call serve to reinforce the change the family has been able to make. The therapist is clear to give the family credit for the change, thereby increasing the likelihood that their success will be more general. The therapist ends by welcoming the family back should they need help in the future

Evaluating Behavioral Family Therapy

Behavioral family therapy has had a pivotal impact in transitioning the helping professional from an insight-oriented approach to a problem-solving enterprise. Because it makes no inference as to the intrapsychic process, it is clearly a scientific technique of change. Given this, almost all other schools of marriage and family therapy freely borrow behavior interventions as part of their approach. Likewise, behavioral therapy has paved the way for the acceptance of the brief approaches that place emphasis on changes in behaviors.

In 1978, Gurman and colleagues (Gurman & Kniskern; Gurman & Knudson) published pivotal theoretical and empirical critiques of behavioral marital therapy in the journal *Family Process*. One theme in both of these articles is a concern that behavioral marital therapy would be reduced to mere technique applied without consideration of the unique problem of the client or the uniqueness of the therapist. In response to this critique, Jacobson and Weiss (1978) state, "The condition under which therapeutic change occurs includes the values held by the therapist, the technology available, and the compatibility of the first two with the potential consumer" (p. 154). Thus they argue that a behavioral marital therapist should consider contextual and therapeutic relationship issues when addressing a client's problem.

Of all the approaches discussed in this text, behavioral family therapy has been by far the most researched. This is due, in part, to the fact that behavioral family therapy can trace its origins directly from the behavioral psychology laboratory in universities across the nation. Indeed, the structure of behavioral family therapy is similar to a quasi-experimental design study with pre- and post-treatment behavioral measurement of functioning. Let us review some of the literature that summarizes the findings regarding behavioral family therapy.

Behavioral family therapy has been shown to be effective in producing positive changes in parent training (Gordon & Davidson, 1981). Behavioral treatment for sexual dysfunction has been shown to be effective in large real-world clinical trials (Sarwer & Durlak, 1997). Behavioral approaches have also been shown to be effective for marriage therapy (Baucom & Hoffman, 1986; Gurman & Kniskern, 1981; Montag & Wilson, 1992). Specifically, improving communication skills has been shown to be an effective ingredient in couple therapy (Jacobson, 1978; Jacobson & Margolin, 1979). Likewise, an interesting longitudinal study of behavioral marital therapy (Jacobson, Schmaling, & Holtzworth-Munroe, 1987) found marital behavioral therapy to be effective, but a significant number of clients showed a significant loss in marital satisfaction during the two years after therapy was terminated. While these results are interesting, there is no insight as to what caused the decline in satisfaction in this study, and further longitudinal studies on all types of therapy are needed to understand this phenomenon.

Learning Exercises

1. Declare a "caring day" for someone you are close to. It can be a partner, friend, or even a roommate. Without telling her you are doing this, select a dozen things to do for her that day. When you do these things, notice her response. How does what you do affect the way she acts toward you? How does it affect the way you feel toward her? Does she talk to you about what you have been doing for her? How does she say she feels about you? Discuss this exercise in small groups with your peers. Do any patterns emerge?

2. This exercise is designed to help the therapist become better able to recognize patterns of reinforcement. Go to a playground at a time when you can watch young children playing with their parents. Watch how the parents and children interact. What techniques do parents who have well-behaved children use to shape and control their children's behavior? What techniques do the parents of problem children use in trying to shape behavior? Can you see why these techniques are failing? After you have made your observations, discuss this exercise with a group of your peers.

Discussion Questions

1. Do you think behavioral family therapy's lack of explanation as to how change occurs makes it a less desirable theory to practice, or are you comfortable with its emphasis on the production of therapeutic change?

2. What elements do you think need to be present in the relationship between the client and the therapist for behavioral therapy to be effective?

3. In behavioral couple therapy, what do you think would happen if the therapist's relationship to the respective members of the couple was perceived as unbalanced?

Suggested Readings

Dattilio, F. M. (2001). Cognitive-behavioral family therapy: Contemporary myths and misconceptions. *Contemporary Family Therapy*, 23(1), 3–18.

Ellis, A. (1978). Family therapy: A phenomenological and action directive approach. *Journal of Marriage and Family Counseling, 4*(2), 43–50.

Falloon, I. R. H. (1991). Behavioral family therapy. In A. S. Gurman & D. P. Kniskern (Eds.), *Handbook of family therapy* (Vol. 2, pp. 65–95). New York, NY: Brunner/Mazel.

Huber, C. H., Baruth, L.,G. (1989) Rational-Emotive Family Therapy: A systems Perspective. New York: Springer.

Jacobson, N. S., & Margolin, G. (1979). Marital therapy: Strategies based on social learning and behavioral exchange principles. New York, NY: Brunner/Mazel.

Kaplan, H. S. (1974). *The sex therapy.* New York, NY: Quadrangle Books.

Thibaut, J., & Kelley, H. H. (1959). *The social psychology of groups.* New York, NY: Macmillan.

Web resources

Wikipedia's Summary of CBT
https://en.wikipedia.org/wiki/Cognitive_behavioral_therapy

Beck Institute Homepage

http://www.beckinstitute.org/

Cognitive Behavioral Family Therapy: key terms/concepts flashcards

https://quizlet.com/2590896/mft-terms-cognitive-behavioral-family-therapy-flash-cards/

CHAPTER

5

PSYCHODYNAMIC FAMILY THERAPY

Thinking about this Approach

At the start of the 20th century, until well into the second half of the century, Freudian psychoanalysis was the dominant approach to helping people with their emotional issues. Freudian psychoanalysis ultimately evolved into psychodynamic theory, and has continued to be a viable technique. As such, it will remain in practice going forward. A powerful aspect of this approach is its ability to describe normal and pathological development. Many of the early family therapists were trained in psychoanalysis; leading Bentovim and Kinston (1991) to assert, "Family Therapy arose out of psychoanalysis and psychoanalytically informed thinking" (p. 284). It is the universal theory underlying many of the key psychodynamic terms that are utilized in the helping professions. In fact, many of the popular notions about mental health have their origins in psychodynamic theory.

At its core, psychodynamic theory is a theory of individual pathology. Family therapy and systems theory focus on relationships, and as a result have somewhat glossed over psychoanalytic insights. Furthermore, since psychoanalysis postulates intrapsychic process as internal to the individual, it may appear that psychodynamic theory is lower level focused in comparison to that of family therapy. However, the depth and eloquence with which psychoanalytic theory explains humans is too powerful to ignore. This chapter explores how psychodynamic theory has influenced family systems theory. Since systemic theory explores the circular nature of reality, this chapter also explores how the insight of systems theory has influenced psychoanalytic theory.

The psychodynamic approach is a structural functional type theory. As a modern theory, it postulates that interpsychic unconscious structures influence current emotional regulation and adaption. It may be useful to think about the psychoanalytic approach as being the root language for the helping professions. While no longer the exclusive dominate theory in the helping professions, it still is a vital and dynamic theory. This chapter will trace psychodynamic thinking starting with Freud. We will then discuss the work of Alfred Adler, a fellow founder of the inter psychic approach. Next, we will explore Nathan Ackerman and the Ackerman Institute's contribution to the development of Family Therapy. Turning to the research based attachment therapy and the closely related Object Relations Theory; we round out our discussion of this psychodynamic theory. After exploring the more specific, we will explore how psychodynamic ideas have been incorporated into psychodynamic informed practice.

Sigmund Freud (1856–1939)

Sigmund Freud was influenced by thermodynamic theory, and utilized the term "psychodynamic" to describe how mental process of the mind flow with psychological energy. Freud placed libidinal drive at the center of his explanation of human behavior. Libidinal drive can simply be understood as our sexual drive and desire. In the historical context of Victorian modesty these drives were repressed, and by many cross-cultural standards, continue to be repressed. Repression appears to give rise to intrapsychic conflict. This conflict then builds internally until it is leaked out in the form of symptoms. In psychodynamic theory, symptoms present as outward expressions of unconscious conflict. Since this conflict is located in the unconscious mind, the goal of therapy is to help the client gain insight into their internal conflict.

Freud's view regarding the unconscious mind is made up of three interrelated structures: the id, ego and super ego. Freud's description of unconscious structures in the mind makes this a structural theory. However, unlike structural family therapy (see chapter 9), the structure of psychodynamic theory focuses on the internal and the unconscious rather than external family structure. This theory is also dynamic in terms of its view regarding process. Freud believed that the energy flowing throughout the unconscious mind is that of sexual energy, or sexual drive, and the desire to survive.

At the most basic level, Freud labels the libidinal drives as the id. This portion of the unconscious mind is the first to develop and is responsible for our desire and natural instincts. The id seeks a wide variety of pleasures, including both the sensual and the sexual. The id is balanced by the ego, which decides what pleasures we seek, while also balancing the need for safety in the context of the real world. Being the second to develop, the ego is where we carry our self-concept and ideas of self. The superego, last to develop, is where internalized societal values and morals are stored.

The dynamic unconscious relations of these three theoretical constructs—the id, the ego, and the superego—are the focus of psychodynamic theory. Starting in the 1930's, Anna Freud, Sigmund Freud's daughter, began studying the development of the ego in the relations between child and mother. The ways in which the child and mother attach, or do not attach, is seen as pivotal to one's ability in developing and maintaining heathy relationships throughout life. Attachment is an important contribution to the helping professions from Freud's psychodynamic theory.

Anna Freud (1895-1982) further advanced the study of defenses, which was another important concept that her father, Sigmund, developed. Defenses are psychological patterns of interaction that serve to protect the current state of the ego. Common examples of defenses include: repression, denial, regression, rationalization, and projection. Let us more closely consider the common defense mechanism of denial. With denial, one simply denies that they are in a less than optional state of functioning, thus protecting their current state. Defenses are necessary to maintain integrity of the person. However, over time they can become abused, ultimately working to maintain an ego state that is no longer functional. It is at this point that dysfunctional defenses may trigger the development of neurotic symptoms. Some of the early works in psychoanalysis involved cataloguing the various defense mechanisms clients utilize to protect their ego. It is a mistake to believe that defenses are dysfunctional entirely by themselves. The dysfunction is in not in defending your ego, but when and how you defend it. In fact, healthy functioning people have a wide variety of defense mechanisms they may utilize when needed. Unhealthy functioning people, however, tend to have one defense mechanism that they utilize time and time again to prevent growth of their ego.

Overcoming these defenses has become a universal goal in modern psychotherapy. The therapeutic relationship is often seen as the core mechanism that helps clients overcome their defended position that is causing their psychopathology. In psychoanalysis, the client is seen as projecting their anxiety and fear onto the therapist. This projection, perceived as a natural part of the therapy process, happens when the client transfers their unresolved emotional energy and issues away from himself or herself, and onto the therapist. This phenomenon is referred to as transference. The therapist then interprets this and guides the client towards insight regarding the nature of the unresolved issues. Feelings and issues the therapist develops for clients are understood as countertransference. In psychoanalysis, this is seen as counterproductive, and the therapist is encouraged to resolve countertransference in his or her own psychoanalysis or supervision.

If you take the two concepts of transference and countertransference together as a whole, you will see we have the concept of the therapeutic relationship. Each concept is part of a circular arch that connects the client to therapist: transference, or therapist to client: countertransference. The therapeutic relationship may be best understood as the vessel containing what is essential for therapeutic change to transpire. In fact, this idea cuts across all of psychotherapy. To the structural family therapist, the development of a positive therapeutic relationship with all family members is referred to as joining (see chapter 9). In solution-focused brief family therapy, the therapist develops the power struggle, often seen in overcoming resistance, by developing a collaborative relationship (see chapter 12). Also, experiential therapists, like Carl Whitaker, utilize the therapeutic relationship with the client in the here and now to resolve their emotional issues (see chapter 7).

While the history of psychotherapy and family therapy itself can be traced back to Sigmund Freud, Freud himself was a reluctant supporter of the idea of working with whole families. On one level, Freud was the first family therapist. In the case of Anna O., he was able to treat the young lady by coaching her parents through their daughter's psychoanalysis. Freud was also among the first to recognize "The importance of early familial relationships in shaping personality" (Broderick & Schrader, 1991, p.17). A critique of psychoanalysis focuses on the belief that it puts too much emphasis on early issues, and not enough emphasis on issues in the here and now.

Freud was also largely responsible for working with families being suppressed. Because of dissatisfaction with the outcome of the case with Anna O., and other personal reasons, Freud did not perceive family therapy to be useful. Over time, particularly in America, this view became intensified. So intensified, that some saw family therapy as unethical, and psychologists and psychiatrists alike saw family work as undesirable. Fortunately, the social psychiatric movement in America refocused the helping professions towards the importance of social forces, including that of familial relationships, in treating psychopathology. In order to understand psychodynamic family therapy, we will first discuss the various psychodynamic family therapists who have helped shape the current state of the theory.

Alfred Adler (1870–1937)

Alfred Adler, a former associate of Freud, was among the first to challenge the psychodynamic approach. Being among the first to work with couples and families, he helped change the structure of therapy. Adler believed family dynamics were essential for a person's wellbeing. During sessions, he had his patients sit in chairs, moving them off the couch and upright. Additionally, he worked with his patients to set goals, ultimately making his psychotherapy more focused than was the non-directed exploration of the unconscious mind, which was the hallmark of traditional psychoanalysis. Adler is credited with being the founder of both individual psychology and Adlerian Family Therapy. In contrast to Freud's focus on early experiences and libidinal drives, his approach was centered on the belief that we all have basic feelings of inferiority, and the motivation to overcome them. A person's inferiority came out of one's early perception that their parents had significantly more life skills. These feelings of inferiority produce an identification with the family. This identification leads to a person feeling pressure to conform and internalize the roles and rules of society. Adler also focused his work on the understanding of social interest that connects us to our families and motivates us to start families of our own.

Adler was among the first to recognize the role that context plays in shaping the life of an individual. For most of us, the most significant context is the family. This is especially true for children who are dependent upon their families. Snown, Crethar, Robey, and Carlson (2005) summarize: "Adlerian family therapists perceive family problems to be the result of discouragement and faulty private logic within the family" (p. 120). This can lock all parties into negative patterns of interaction based upon distorted goals. To Adler, effective parenting lies between being overly harsh and autocratic, and being soft and permissive. This is one of the first conceptualizations of understanding healthy functioning as falling between two extreme positions. Younger children need more structure, but as they mature they can handle more autonomy.

Out of interest for child development, Adler's ideas greatly influenced the Child Guidance Clinic Movement. The movement focused on establishing clinics to provide care to children with difficulties, and offering parenting assistance to families with these children. These clinics were often attached to research universities where students from various fields including psychiatry, psychology and social work, worked to help both the children with difficulties and their families. As part of the training, residents and interns observed therapy sessions and conducted therapy sessions under clinical supervision. An additional function of the clinics was to support the public. Later in his career, Alfred Adler became a popular speaker on issues of parenting and mental health.

John Bowlby (1907–1990)

British psychoanalyst, John Bowlby, also interested in child development, developed the Theory of Attachment. He conducted research in the Tavistock Clinic in London. Building upon the work of Anna Freud, he was interested in how relationships in one's family of origin impact personality. Ultimately, this interest grew to become known as Attachment Theory, which describes different patterns of attachment that shape a person's style of relating. Bowlby researched ways in which early maladaptive relationships give rise to psychopathology in adulthood. Furthermore, he investigated how families projected their attachment issues unto the next generation. His student, and later colleague, Mary Ainsworth, further researched attachment and refined the initial principles. Additionally, she is credited with empirically validating much of the theory.

Attachment therapy is an alternative name for holding therapy, an approach to treating children with reactive attachment disorder. Holding therapy involves holding or wrapping the child in a blanket for extended amounts of time in an attempt to recreate early experiences. This approach was popular towards the end of the 20th century. However, Hanson & Spratt (2000) have found no evidence that it is as effective, or more effective, than conventional approaches. In fact, there have been occasional accidental deaths associated with this approach, so the possible injuries do not merit the utilization of holding therapy. More mainstream and legitimate approaches to working with clients struggling with attachment issues are referred to as Attachment Based Approaches or Attachment Theory informed practices (Lopez, 1995; Ng & Smith, 2006; Werner-Wilson & Davenport, 2003).

Bowlby (1988) saw humans as possessing an evolutionary predisposition to develop emotional and pragmatic attachment. "The foundational assumption of attachment theory is that human beings are inherently programed to seek and form attachments, or enduring affectional bonds with others" (Lopez, 1995, p.11). As children we develop relationships with our caregivers in patterns which provide an internal working model of how relationships work. Ultimately, this serves as a map of relationships and emotional regulation, which the child will project and seek out in current and future relationships as an adult. It is here that we see the significance of attachment to family therapy. This process is what family therapists would call intergenerational transmission.

While attachment theory places emphasis on the mother-child relationship, it has expanded to include other early relationships in a child's life. It is now understood that as important as it is for a child to have a secure attachment to their mother, they can have additional attachments to others in their lives. In fact, the current thinking is that the more people a child is attached to, the more adaptive their system is. A child can be attached to other people in a variety of ways, depending upon their relationship with the person. The relationship is determined by the interaction of the child's temperament with the relationship style and temperament of the other that they are in the relationship with. Temperament refers to the genetically pre-determined character traits a person is born with. Let us now look at the styles of attachment this theory postulates. Based on observations of children and their mothers in psychology labs, Ainsworth, Bhehar, Wathers, & Wall (1978), identified 3 styles of attachment.

Secure attachment is identified as a style of relating in which enough of the child's needs are being met that the child has relatively little anxiety. A child with a secure attachment style is not anxious when their parent leaves them for a period of time, as they are confident that the parent will return to meet their needs when necessary. This style of attachment is seen as most adaptable, and in adulthood this person will be well adjusted and able to regulate his or her own emotional wellbeing. According to Lopez (1993): "Consistent and sensitive caregiving by early attachment figures promotes an 'internal working model' of the self as worthy and competent" (p.12). This is seen as essential to the development of personal mental health.

Anxious-ambivalent attachment is created through a consistently unhelpful caregiver.

The child has their needs met, but only on some occasions. The needs are met only after the child becomes anxious. According to Lopez (1995), "This pattern promotes the formulation of a 'working model' of self as uncertain and fearful, and others as desirable and potentially affirming, yet unreliable" (p.12). People with this style of attachment need and seek almost constant approval from others. They often feel lonely without others. Additionally, those with anxious-ambivalent attachment find themselves in disappointing relationships in which they feel helpless in leaving.

Avoidant attachment is the result of a caregiver relationship that is mostly absent. No matter what the child does to elicit support and contact from their care giver, they are denied. As stated by Lopez (1995), "These conditions give rise to an internal working model of self as essentially alone and unwanted, and of others as rejecting and untrustworthy" (p.12). This pattern may give rise to delinquency and antisocial behavior in some situations. In other situations the person with this attachment style compensates by becoming compulsively self-sufficient and isolated. Those with avoidant attachment will maintain greater social distance than others may prefer, and will be unable to move closer at their request.

Bowlby's (1979, 1988) hypothesis about the nature of attachment and its impact has been verified in a wide variety of empirical studies. In the review of empirical findings from Mikulincer, Florian, Cowan, & Cowan (2002), 5 personality traits associated with one's sense of attachment security were identified. These personality traits include: 1) Attached people are less distressed by stressful events; 2) Attached people seek support when stressed; 3) Securely attached people have more positive expectations of relationship partners; 4) Securely attached people have more positive self-views of themselves; and 5) People with secure attachment seek more affection from others, and are more sensitive and responsive to a partner (Mikulincer, Florian, Cowan, & Cowan, 2002). Because of how well validated and how rich a theoretical explanation attachment theory provides, it is likely to be an increasingly influential theory in the future.

Nathan Ackerman (1908–1971)

Psychiatrist, Nathan Ackerman, is considered one of the founders of family therapy. He spent much of his career in New York City, and in 1960 established the Family Health Clinic and the Family Institute. Upon his death, the institute was renamed The Ackerman Institute for the Family. The Ackerman Institute has been a significant training and research center for over 50 years.

Currently, the Ackerman Institute has centers that provide services and trainings in various programs, including:

The Center for the Developing Child and Family

The Center for Family and Health

The Center for Work and Family

The Center for Substance Abuse and the Family

The Center for Children and Relational Trauma

Over the years, the center has conducted some pivotal research and attracted well-established faculty, making the Ackerman Institute a central research and training center.

As a young child psychiatrist, Ackerman became involved in a study on the effects of extended unemployment of miners during the depression of the 1930s. As Broderick and Schrader (1991) summarize: "This experience, plus others, convinced him that emotional problems could be generated by the immediate environment, as well as by the dynamics of the psyche" (p. 23). This study and the knowledge it gathered are considered a vital piece of the general shift in thinking regarding mental disorders in children. Prior to this, the idea that mental illness was entirely the result of internal conflict was dominant. In part from this experience and others, Ackerman came to see that mental disorders may be created by the social environment, relationships within the family, as well as internal conflict.

Originally working at the Menninger clinic in Topeka Kansas, Ackerman first worked with families as part of Ortho-Psychiatric practice. In orthopsychiatry, the psychiatrist works with the identified patient, the child, while social workers work with the child's parents. Recognizing the benefits of meeting as a whole family, he experimented with working with the entire family system to help the child past a therapeutic impasse. Seeing a child's difficulty as largely a result of the relationship with their parents, he saw the family as the proper unit of diagnosis and treatment of the child's problems. In 1955, Ackerman chaired and organized the first session of the American Orthopsychiatric Association on family diagnosis (Broderick and Schrader, 1991), in an attempt to describe family structures and processes that are unhealthy. While the original goals of relational diagnosis remained unachieved, this work ultimately changed how families were thought of in relationship to mental illness. Currently families are seen as having an important impact on the development of mental illness.

Nathan Ackerman was an important figure in the bridging of systems theory and psychoanalysis. He worked with Don Jackson and Jay Haley, both from the Mental Research Institute (see chapter 8), to co-found the journal, *Family Process*, in 1961. *Family Process* has remained a top tier journal, and continues to be instrumental in presenting cutting edge research in family therapy.

As early as 1970, Ackerman called for the inclusion of children of all ages in family therapy. An interesting review by Ruble (1999) of research on the inclusion of children by family therapists almost 30 years later found that while there were multiple calls by a wide variety of theorists, few actually included children regularly. Therapists seemed to exclude children from therapy because they felt unprepared and untrained to work with them.

Contextual Family Therapy

Ivan Boszormenyi-Nagy (1920–2007), a Hungarian born psychiatrist and psychoanalyst developed an approach to family therapy that paid particular attention to relationship ethics between family members. He based his therapeutic approach on two assumptions: 1) The consequences of one person's decisions and actions can affect the lives of all people related to him, and 2) Satisfactory relating for one person is inseparable from responsible consideration of consequences for all of the people with whom he or she is in significant relationship (Boszormenyi-Nagy & Krasner, 1986). Contextual family therapy focuses on the dynamic ethical connections that exist between people in the past, present, and future. Since the theory is also concerned with responsibility, it encourages clients to consider their life priorities and the well-being of future generations of family members.

Boszormenyi-Nagy (1972) introduced the concept of loyalty, which he defined as a preferential commitment to a relationship, based on indebtedness born of earned merit. Parents have children whom they care for in ways that their children can never repay. This loyalty can come under conflict when a person has other obligations. For example, a husband may have a loyalty conflict when his job wants him to work nights, or a teen may have a loyalty conflict when they have to choose between spending time with their peers and going to an extended family gathering.

Boszormenyi-Nagy proposed that an ethical accountability between family members governs family interactions. This sense of fairness cuts across roles, rules, and power and communication patterns. Ethical practices and relationships between members are essential for families to meet the needs of members and fully develop. Boszormenyi-Nagy believes that family members keep ledgers of whom they are indebted to and who is in debt to them. For example, a family member may feel like their sibling owes them for taking care of an aging parent that they live with. At the same time, the sibling may feel like their parent is favoring this sibling by letting them live with them rent-free. We can see that a balance between the rights and responsibilities of the individual needs to be balanced by relationship needs. Additionally, invisible loyalties are the result of attempts to balance the ledger from prior generations.

In contextual therapy, the therapist focuses on four dimensions of relational reality: facts, individual psychology, systemic transitions and relational ethics. By having family members share their individual perspectives and engage in empathic listening, families come to acknowledge each other and develop a more realistic sense of expectations.

Object Relations

Object relations came into play in the 1940's as a result of Melanie Klien's study of object relations in primates. At this time, the psychoanalysis that was practiced in Europe differed in its focus of children's emotional development. In particular, object relations focuses on the child's attachment relationship with the mother. This relationship ultimately sets the pattern in which the person relates to others as objects. This notion is carried through each of the various psychodynamic formulations. In 1988, Sam Slipp published his classic work, *The Technique and Practice of Object Relations Family Therapy*, which integrated ideas from psychoanalysis and attachment theories.

Object relations theory is a very well developed and complex theory. The basic ideas are rather straightforward and intuitive. The way in which we attach to our caregiver in childhood is the most salient component in the development of our personality. In object relations terms, 'mother' refers to a child's primary care giver, not mother as the person who gave birth to the child. In a child's early development, they are fully dependent on their mother for survival. In normal development, the child and mother develop a relationship. In an ideal situation, a child will call out to its mother, who responds with appropriate care and nurturing. In this primary relationship, the child sees others as objects, and thus develops a set of ideas about the nature of relationships. These experiences provide our basic expectations of what sort of world this is. You will notice the similarity here to systems theory's concern with epistemology. Once the pattern of object relations is set, a person goes through their life engaging in relationships where these patterns are repeated.

The concept of "good enough" mothering is also part of normal development. Within this theory, an inadequate mother is seen as abandoning her child. This can lead to a dependent personality type, and/or a personality who tries to cut off from others and socially isolate themselves. If on the other extreme the mother confuses her child's needs with her own anxiety and she meets all of her child's needs, and in some cases more, the child develops incompetence, and in extreme cases, narcissism. "Good enough" mothers will allow the child to develop some level of autonomy and security. They also provide the child with an opportunity to learn to self-sooth. Self-soothing refers to the ability to emotionally regulate oneself during times of stress. Without this ability, people can become impulsive and/or reactive. While the techniques for self-soothing change throughout the life cycle, the use of self-soothing is a lifelong adaptation. For example, babies rock themselves, while adults tend to self-talk when stressed.

Abandonment is an important and often misunderstood concept. The point of reference for abandonment is from the person who feels the loss. In this sense, abandonment occurs whenever I want someone to be there and they are not. It is important to recognize that this makes no reference to the intention of the person who is perceived as abandoning. For example, when a parent dies from a terminal illness, the child experiences abandonment, even though the parent may have fought heroically to beat their illness. From the child's perspective, they want the parent to be there, but they are absent, so the child feels abandoned. It is at this point, the concept of self-soothing comes into play because the child needs to engage in self-soothing and mourn the loss of their parent.

People who have a good deal of hurt or abandonment in their development begin to identify object relations as either all good or all bad. However, since no mother is perfect, we all have early negative feelings about our mothers. In order to process this hurt and rage, children engage in projective identification. Klein (1956) defined projective identification as a splitting of parts of the self and projecting them onto others, including feelings of identification with that person. From here, this thinking is projected onto other individuals and the environment in a projection process referred to as *splitting*. This splitting provides for a predictable, if not favorable, environment. This predictability provides some relief in the short term from the anxiety the person may be feeling. However, this can lead to problems later in life when they fail to make realistic assessments of others, and repress negative aspects of relationships. These repressed object relations can get projected onto partners and children later on in life. In his description of object relations, family therapist Dan Siegel (1991) states: "ORFT puts the projections back in the projectors, makes the conflict ego-alien, and then works on an intrapsychic level to resolve the individual conflicts" (p. 277).

There are notions that as things are on the inside, things are on the outside. Clients with poorly resolved object relations tend to migrate into black and white thinking and/or all or nothing thinking. This is an attempt to resolve their inner conflict by moving to the comfort of absolutes. You may see this in couples when they use words like 'always' and 'never.' Thus, there is a systemic interaction between interpsychic structures and relationships. A person's primary relationship with their caregiver shapes how their interpsychic structures develop. Once developed, the structures are carried forward into adulthood, and ultimately shape one's ability to be successful in adult relationships. Object relations theory predicts that a person will continue to have a pattern of difficulties in relationships until they resolve their conflict. An example of this situation might be a person who comes from a broken home. Despite their good intentions, they find themselves middle aged with multiple failed marriages. They take little or no responsibility for making poor choices or contributing to their failure.

Psychodynamic Informed Family Therapy

Now that we have a basic understanding of how intrapsychic process influences our understanding of individuals and their families, we turn to exploring psychodynamic informed family therapy. In this section, we look at this individual theory and how it influences our understanding of individuals in relationships. Specifically, we are interested in how individuals relate to their families. Understanding the family as being the context in which most individuals live and develop in, may help in this exploration.

Questioning

In psychodynamic family therapy, the emphasis is on helping the client to develop insight into how their developmental history is impacting their current relationships and functioning. Questions are designed to assist in the process of exposing more of the unconscious mind to consciousness. The longer something is repressed, and the more anxiety one has around the repressed information, the deeper one will have to go in therapy to gain access to their unconscious.

Unlike the more action-oriented approaches, the psychodynamic approach does not place emphasis on behavioral change. Instead, psychodynamic therapists seek to describe the underlying psychological factors that give rise to behavioral problems. Clients are encouraged to *free associate* during the session. *Free associations* involve the client voicing whatever comes into their mind. This technique allows the therapist access to the client's unconscious mind. Another important part of the psychodynamic approach is the analysis of dreams. In this theory, dreams are seen as a symbolic reflection of what is going on in the client's unconscious mind. When the client shares their dreams, the therapist interprets the meaning of them, and ultimately helps the client gain insight into their conflicted, and often repressed, inner world.

Structuring

The structure of psychodynamic approaches varies wildly. In most instances, psychodynamic and object relations psychotherapy are open-ended. However, as testimony to the strength of the model, it has also been applied to a brief 12-session model. For example, Kupnick (2002) follows a brief approach to the treatment of PTSD that limits therapy to 12 sessions. Since the relationship between the therapist and family is so vital, therapists often negotiate frequency and duration of sessions with clients. The sessions are structured so that clients are working on releasing repressed emotions from their unconscious, and processing those emotions as well. Most often therapy is structured around weekly or bi-weekly 50 minute sessions.

Responding

In psychodynamic family therapy, it is assumed that the client will project unresolved emotions onto the therapist. This transference in turn produces a countertransference response within the therapist. However, since the therapist has been in therapy themselves, and are often in ongoing supervision, they are able to remain objective.

Insight is the tool by which clients reduce the amount of unresolved unconscious material. Mallouk (1982) eloquently states: "The organizing principal, then, of the therapeutic relationship is for the therapist and patient to plumb the depth of the patient's psyche" (p,430). This process has been described with a variety of terms over the course of development of this theory. Greenson (1965) utilized the term *working alliance* to describe the client-therapist relationship. More recently, Pinsof and Catherall (1986) developed the concept of the *therapeutic alliance* in family, couple, and individual therapy. Additionally, they developed a scale to measure the alliance. Patalano (1997) in his work on marital therapy, describes a successful working alliance: "In marital therapy, a good working alliance is one in which both partners are working with their therapist in a serious and cooperative manner; actively collaborating in the treatment process and experiencing it as an important vehicle to resolving their problems" (p. 498).

It would be ill-conceived to think of the working alliances as being developed at the start of therapy and continuing throughout the relationship. Typically, there are "breaches," or injuries to the relationship, as it develops and continues through the therapeutic process. Beginning therapists make the mistakes of seeing this as a distracting from therapeutic process. Hoverer, it is the pattern of working through these breaches that drives therapy. For example, Kohut (1984) describes an "empathic failure," in which the client temporarily loses trust in the therapist. Safran (1983) uses the term "therapeutic alliance rupture" to describe such breaches in the relationship.

Regardless of what these breaches are labeled, it is within the context of the client-therapist relationship that the client is able to learn about the nature of healthy relationships. As is the case for many families, they are lacking both emotional and physical boundaries. In healthy families, connection is balanced with boundaries. These boundaries and connections occur between people within generations and across generations. The therapist and client explore the nature of healthy relationships together throughout the therapeutic process.

Applications

The applications for psychodynamic family therapy are universal. Since psychoanalytic theory is the universal language for psychotherapy, it has been utilized in all treatment settings. If we consider the relationship of the social psychiatry and Orthopsychiatry models, we see evidence of its utility in almost all situations. Adler included families in his conceptualization of mental health, including families in his seminars and lectures. Ackerman invited young children into family psychotherapy when it was not the typical approach. As can be seen, attachment and object relations theories both inform couple and marital therapy.

Case Study: Phil and Mary

Phil and Mary, a married couple, were referred to a psychodynamic family therapist. They were referred to the therapist because she has a reputation for applying psychodynamic insights to her family therapy clients. In addition, the therapist was selected because of her experience working with clients who have a history of childhood trauma. The couple sought therapy because they have an issue with their five year old daughter, Ashley. Due to trauma from their own childhoods, both Phil and Mary practiced a unique style of parenting, where they set practically no limits with their daughter. From an attachment theory perspective Ashley was anxiously attached to her mother. Mary had periods of deep depression and would sometimes be emotionally unavailable to her daughter. She also suffered from rheumatoid arthritis that would flair up as she became physically or emotionally stressed. Ashley had a significantly more securely attached relationship with her father. However, Phil was more of a playmate than a parent to his daughter. Ashley also had a great Aunt Betsey who was an additional primary caregiver of hers. This aunt originally came to live with the family when Ashley was an infant as temporary help. Since then she has become a permanent part of the family, living quasi-separately in the guest cottage on the family property.

Ashley's parents have two major concerns about their daughter. For starters, she has separation anxiety from her mother whenever she is not around. Ashley also has never been successful in making a bowel movement into the toilet. She evacuates her bowels at exactly the same time in the evening in a pull up diaper, after which she cleans herself up and then takes a shower to get ready for bed. As a result of this behavior, she has withdrawn from any kind of social engagements with peers involving an overnight stay. This particular concern is a family secret that has been kept from Aunt Betsey.

The family wants Ashley to attend a Montessori school that has frequent overnight fieldtrips scheduled in the curriculum. The referring therapist is Phil's primary therapist, who has been working with Phil for a numbers of years. At the same time, Mary has been being seen in the same practice by a fellow analytically trained psychotherapist. The therapy length is limited by time, as

Phil is an author in residence at a local university and resort town, so they will only be available for therapy over the summer. They are planning to return to the city in the fall.

Phil and Mary met 10 years ago in rehab and have been married for 7 years. They started out as friends, with each having the idea that they were "too damaged" by their childhoods and addiction to engage in a deeper relationship. Their friendship evolved into a "friends with benefits" relationship. After living together for a couple of years, they decided to marry and be childless by choice. However, fate interfered with their plan and due to a failure of birth control, the couple was surprised with their daughter, Ashley. Both Phil and Mary were surprised to find that along with the fear they had about being parents, they also found joy in being parents. The couple reports that they enjoy nothing more than being parents, for it provides them with meaning in their lives.

Phil's History

Phil's parents always had a difficult relationship. The couple met shortly after college, became "drinking friends," and then became pregnant after a binge-drinking episode. They married under pressure from both families to "do the right thing." Phil's mother became sober when she found out she was pregnant and was an engaged and loving mother. However, his dad's drinking became more intense and he moved rapidly out of binge drinking and into dysfunctional alcoholism. When Phil was two a developmentally significant event occurred, his paternal grandfather passed away suddenly of a heart attack. His Grandfather's death was a shock to the entire family, and Phil's dad took over the family business.

Within two years of inheriting the business, Phil's dad "Took the company public and started to make fists full of money." However, his parents were unable to adjust to the changes in their lifestyle. His mother became depressed and withdrawn, not fitting in with her new status. His father slipped deeper into his alcoholism, seen now as a raging drunk, and "rageaholic" under the pressure of work. The couple split when his rage turned violent and he beat his wife when Phil was only 7 years old. About two years after the separation, the couple divorced. Phil describes his parent's separation and divorce as "the most dysfunctional ever." After their divorce, the two fought about everything and sharing custody of Phil was very difficult. As a result of the conflict, Phil acted out in school and was sent to therapy at the age of 10. His therapist recognized how toxic his parents were to him and suggested Phil go to a boarding school so that he would grow up in a safer environment. When he was 12 years old, he finally was sent to the boarding school to escape the conflict, and he never looked back.

According to Phil's report he had his first drink at 13. By age 14, he was drunk every day. While he was away at boarding school, his mother became addicted to pain medication that she was prescribed when she threw her back out. Phil reported that his mother never fully recovered from this and she "took to the bed." She remained hurt, angry, and medicated until she passed away from an accidental overdose when Phil was 17. While the cause of death was designated as an accidental overdose, Phil states that she died of a "broken heart." At the same time, Phil's father was continuing in the cycle of on again, off again sobriety. Having been to several residential treatment facilities, he would have brief periods of sobriety, but they were followed by periods of binge drinking that quickly descended into an out of control rage. Phil believed that the most consistent thing about his father was his anger and abuse. He would maintain that in fact, his father was easier to deal with when he was drunk. His rage was more verbal and less physical, and he would often pass out before he could hit Phil. This pattern continued until Phil was 18 years old. His dad passed away from a massive heart attack when he was playing golf at the country club.

After his father's death, Phil slid into a deep depression and even deeper relationship with addiction. He reported that he was profoundly depressed and suicidal, trying for a number of years to kill himself with his addiction. His father's estate had provided a trust to provide for him and his family financially. However, Phil with few emotional resources to help him cope was ill equipped for life. Phil describes his relationship with his father's long-time friend, and now trustee of his trust, as the only long-term positive relationship he has ever experienced.

Phil continued to be in an out of trouble after the death of his father. He attended three different private universities, and eventually found himself spending 28 days in an inpatient treatment facility for his substance abuse. It was here that the sobriety seemed to finally stick, at the age of 24. He became a daily patron of a 12-step group and started psychoanalysis. It was also in the 28-day program that he met his wife, Mary. Phil went back to school to study literature after discovering his love of writing while journaling as a part of his recovery. He has since become a successful writer, publishing several award-winning books.

Mary's History

Mary's parents were childhood friends who got married to meet "expectations of polite society." While an arranged marriage, her mother would joke that she married out of her family's love for meeting expectations, not for her husband. Her mother would also tell her to marry for love, not to please others. Mary's was conceived on the night her dad proposed to her mother. Because of the pregnancy, they had a "short engagement" and then a summer-long honeymoon in Europe to hide the pregnancy from society. They returned to her native New Orleans, with Mary in the fall. At this time, Mary was 12 weeks old, but the parents told everyone that she was just 4 weeks old. Mary did not find out her true birthday until she needed her birth certificate to apply for her passport as a teenager. When Mary was 3 years old, her mother lost a baby sister who was stillborn at 9 months. After that traumatic incident, her mother fell into a deep depression. She attempted to cure her grief by having another child. However, over the next 4 years she would have 3 miscarriages, all in the second trimester of pregnancy. Ultimately, this lead to an increase in her level of depression and she "took to the bed." After that Mary describes how her mother seemed to fade away into her addiction to pain medication. This resulted in further attachment injury to Mary as she was left ill-equipped to manage her emotions or cope with her feelings of abandonment.

Mary reported that she was emotionally raised by her paternal grandmother. For periods of time the grandmother would stay with the family and provide Mary's care, while Mary's mother recovered. Mary's mother seemed to always be suffering from a physical symptom that would need to be treated with pain medication. This worked well for her grandmother, for she was looking for purpose in her life after losing her husband to a boating accident. Mary and her grandmother became very close emotionally, and Mary was provided a somewhat secure attachment figure until was 4 years old. At that age, her grandmother fell and needed assisted care for the remaining 4 years of her life.

After this, Mary saw her less and less, and by the time she passed away, Mary reported missing her deeply and feeling guilty that she did not see her more after she went in the home. Mary has a history of sexual trauma at the hand of her father. Her father practiced obstetrics/gynecologist for a living, and he would "practice his technique" on her. Starting at the age of 6, he would frequently give her exams to see if she was "healthy" or to "test his new equipment." This would occur in their basement exam room in the family estate. Mary reports that there would frequently be "students" of her fathers, who would observe the procedures. Afterwards, he would utilize fear, shame, and guilt to keep their "secret." Mary reports that she could not identify the other spectators. These "examinations" continued until her father experienced a stroke when she was 12 years old. His stroke left him wheelchair bound and nonverbal for the last 5 years of his life. Additionally, Mary reports that she was not connected to her mother, who was struggling with an abusive relationship with her husband. Mary reports that her mother would often oscillate between kind and caring and angry and rejecting. Mary reports that in her own psychotherapy she had decided that her mother was psychotic from her depression and addiction.

Mary reported that after her father's stroke the family was sent into chaos. She utilized that chaos to escape to catholic boarding school. The term escape fits because she simply applied for admission on her own and when the acceptance letter came her mother simply enrolled her without having a conversation about her attending. There she thrived academically and retreated into literature, ultimately leading her to seek a career in language arts. There she struggled with multiple, deep depressive episodes and "experimented with cutting and women." Mary kept the secret of her sexual abuse to herself until well after her father's death. At first, she had dreams about the abuse, and over time she became flooded with memories. Because of this, she suffered a major depressive episode and needed to withdraw for a semester her senior year. Mary also became addicted to drugs during this period, starting with alcohol and then moving to pain pills, and ultimately heroin. She reported that her addictive behavior escalated until she went to rehab and there she met her future husband, Phil.

Psychodynamic Family Therapy

At the start of therapy, Mary was insistent that Ashley would not attend any of the sessions. The therapist agreed to start with that arrangement, but stated that she reserved the right to renegotiate that if they felt the need. In the intake interview, she observed that Mary has limited movements due to her arthritis and that she appeared to be in physical pain most of the time. Phil is able to move freely and seems to be quick to smile and tell a joke. Mary reports that she is receiving high doses of steroids, which have severe side effects on her mood. She is continuing her individual psychotherapy with her analyst. She has sessions via phone three times a week. Phil works with his individual therapist weekly by phone and attends AA meetings 6 days a week. During the discussion, it is clear that in the relationship Phil feels bad about Mary's physical difficulty so much that he defers to her and does not confront her. She is just overwhelmed with fear that they will "ruin" their daughter, Ashley. In fact, her fear is so deep that she is convinced that she is already ruined by her difficulties. However, per Phil's report, the therapist learns that Ashley is a delightful and well-adjusted child in all areas, except for her difficulty in using the bathroom.

It takes until well into the third session before the couple is able to focus on problem solving about Ashley's "bathroom issues." It is clear that the parents have a difficult time setting expectations with their daughter. Phil believes that he and his wife were blessed to have a daughter who has a temperament of wanting to be helpful and accepted by her parents. They reported that they have never had to punish her, except for an occasional time out. For the most part she appears to respond to redirection. People find Ashley fun, easy going, and eager to try to please.

Slowly, the idea of a stress free life for Ashley is confronted. For the most part, metaphor is utilized to introduce the therapist's concern. At one point, Mary talks about how difficult her 12 hours of labor were when birthing Ashley. The therapist uses that as an example and calls attention to the impact of that stress on Ashley. The therapist describes how babies, who experienced a vaginal birth, rather than C-section birth, meet development milestones sooner, grow more quickly, and have less illness. Utilizing the fact that Mary was currently getting physical therapy to recover from a broken ankle the therapist introduces an analogy. Comparing the pain of physical therapy, necessary for recovery for her ankle injury, as similar to emotional pain necessary for some normal development, the therapist confronts the parents approach of being unable to tolerate any stress on Ashley.

In the next session, the sixth, Mary herself relates the emotional pain of her psychotherapy to the physical pain of physical therapy. She tearfully reflects that she and Phil are damaged from their childhoods, and that they have to endure the pain of psychotherapy to recover. At this point in the session, Mary is sobbing and Phil is very tearful himself, wiping the tears from his eyes as he tries to hold it together. Phil introduces the idea that pain and anxiety in life are unavoidable, but that the pain from life is different that abuse. The therapist and parents discuss this in relationship to the Buddhist teaching Phil was exposed to in a recovery program. The therapist goes on to describe, "good enough parenting," parenting that does not shield the child from the pain and/or anxiety of life, but supports children through it. The therapist describes how supporting children through stress is part of good parenting. Phil goes on to state that he would rather teach his daughter to protect herself than to shelter and rescue her.

This is discussed for several sessions, and by the end of the eighth session, both parents were able to see the necessity of supporting Ashley through her toilet training. In fact, calling it "Ashley's toilet training" was what helped shift the parent's thinking. The therapist points out that when Ashley is older, others will see this as her failure rather than her parents. In a panic, Mary turns to the therapist and asks directly "How much time before this may start to happen?" The therapist holds her position and simply states, "Time is short, it may already be happening." The therapist states that she would expect that Ashley keeps her bathroom issues secrete from her friends. She further emphasizes that this will not be a secret her parents make her keep, but will be one she wants to keep herself.

At this point, Phil becomes angry, while Mary becomes very tearful. The therapist suggests that they start to talk with Ashley about it directly. The therapist states that the emphasis will be on taking responsibility rather than assigning guilt. Mary looks grateful at the therapist's statement, and the therapist recognizes that guilt must be an issue for Mary. Mary responded that she was blamed for her her sexual assault and made to feel guilty. The therapist listens as Mary describes how her father blamed her for needing to be examined and being a "dirty girl." The therapist apologizes for this, stating what she endured is not appropriate for anyone to endure.

The therapist provides time to let that sink in for a little bit. Since time is up, the parents are asked if there is any way that they can invite Ashley to be responsible without the use of guilt. Additionally, they area asked to reflect on that before the next session, and are reminded of their appointment the following week.

Before the next session, Phil calls to cancel because Mary has gone back to their home in the city 4 weeks early. She had a severe reaction to her medication and needed to be hospitalized. Since Phil was going to join her in a few days, he requested that they suspend therapy. The therapist expresses her understanding and asks him about their plans for Ashley. He shares that prior to her mother's reaction, they had a brief but supportive talk with her. He also said that he, just in passing, stated that she would need to able to use the bathroom for "number 2" before she can start Montessori school. A couple of weeks later, the therapist is provided an update from Phil. He reports that Mary is recovering from her reaction to her meds and that Ashley has overcome her issue. He shares that one night, when left in aunt Betsey's care while her mother was in the hospital, she just started to use the bathroom. The family is given the option of returning to therapy in their future if needed, and Phil states that he would be happy to contact the therapist if they are in the area again and need further assistance.

Case Discussion

This case involved two people who have and currently undergo a good bit of psychotherapy. This is due to the difficulty of each of their histories and the family's significant amount of resources. Although the identified patient was never seen in therapy, the therapist was still willing to work on this case. This was because the therapist saw the difficulty as lying in the parents and their difficulty in setting limits and challenging their child. The parents are very loving and supportive of their daughter. The degree that they do this is quite remarkable, given how little the parent's families were able to express love and connection. The parent's failure was in setting expectations for their daughter, Ashley. For the parents, setting expectations was viewed as abusive. While this distortion makes sense in the context of their history, it was dysfunctional in the current situation. While the change occurred outside of the therapy, it is reasonable to speculate that the therapy made room for the change to occur.

In this case there were certainly many issues that could be addressed. However, both parties had their own therapists. With therapists of their own, the family therapist focused on parenting and the intergenerational effect of trauma. However, the therapist did consult with both Phil's and Mary's therapists throughout the case. Since Mary could not identify the spectators of her sexual abuse and that her father was deceased, no report was made to the authorities regarding the sexual abuse. The therapist's goal throughout was to address the underlying psychopathology, so that the system would continue to develop, and ultimately Ashley would develop. As therapy progressed, it became clear that the family's unresolved trauma played a significant role in the anxiety the family felt.

Evaluations

Many of the components of psychoanalytic informed family therapy have been empirically validated. Attachment theory was created in a developmental psychology laboratory, and insight from this theory was applied to treatment of hospitalized children. The psychoanalytic model itself has been modified and continuously refined for over one hundred years, so it has stood the test of time. In part, because this theory is a major part of the "language of therapy," I would expect this to continue to be a central theory in the helping professions.

Learning Exercises

1. Go to a park and observe parents interacting with their young children. What can you observe in the interactions between caregivers and their children? What patterns can you notice about relationships between the adults and their children, and the patterns between children interacting with other children?

2. Divide the class into small groups. In the small groups, discuss how your family talked about your birth story and the story of your early development. How do you think these stories relate to your current personality? If you can, describe shifts in your personality. What experiences are associated with these shifts?

3. The case discussed has some ethical and legal issues around the reporting of child abuse. Research your state's legal requirements around the reporting of child abuse. Many states currently mandate reporting in certain situations. What are they in your state?

Discussion Questions

1. In what ways does culture shape parenting practices, and how does that affect early development of personality?

2. Discuss how current trends in care for young children impact the development of self.

3. In what ways do you think increased use of media by young children is shaping their emotional and personality development?

Web Resources

American Psychoanalytic Society

http://www.apsa.org/

Brief Overview of Adler's theory

http://alfredadler.edu/about/theory

Wikipedia page on Attachment Theory

https://en.wikipedia.org/wiki/Attachment_theory

Wikipedia page on Ivan Boszormenyi-Nagy

https://en.wikipedia.org/wiki/Ivan_Boszormenyi-Nagy

Ackerman Institute

https://www.ackerman.org/

Wikipedia pages on Object Relations Theory

https://en.wikipedia.org/wiki/Object_relations_theory

Suggested Readings

Ackerman, N. (1970). Child participation in family therapy. *Family Process, 9(4)*, 403–410.

Bowlby, J. (1988). *A secure base: Clinical applications of attachment theory.* London: Routledge.

Boszormenyi-Nagy, I., & Krasner, B. R. (1986). *Between give and take.* New York, NY: Brunner/Mazel.

Pinsnof, W.M., & Catherall, D.R. (1986). The integration psychotherapy alliance: Family, couple, and individual therapy scales. *Journal of Marital and Family Therapy, 12*(1), 137–151.

Slipp, S. (1988). *The technique and practice of object relations family therapy.* North Vale, NJ: Jason Aronson.

CHAPTER

BOWEN FAMILY SYSTEM THERAPY

Thinking About This Approach

Murray Bowen's approach can be thought of as a first-generation approach. At its core, it is a classical psychodynamic approach that has been updated and informed by systems theory. To develop the early theories of family therapy, theorists frequently simply modified older theories to fit their newly developed systems paradigm. These modifications changed their unit of analysis from the individual to the family. Kerr and Bowen (1988) summarize this by asserting, "Family systems theory radically departed from previous theories of human emotion functioning by virtue of its conceptualization of the family as an emotional unit" (p. viii). Bowen's theory was a grand theory that sought to describe the interrelationship of biological, psychological, and sociological levels of understanding.

Bowen's theory not only has been important to the development of the field, but it serves as a primary theoretical orientation for many therapists. It also has had significant influence on the theories of therapists who have developed an integrative approach (Miller, Anderson, & Keala, 2004).

Bowen started his theoretical journey at the Menninger Foundation in Topeka, Kansas, in 1946, but as his interest shifted from psychoanalysis to more systemic theoretical approaches, he left in 1954 to become a researcher at the National Institute of Mental Health. There Bowen's ability to observe whole families on the research ward pushed his theoretical understanding of families past a Freudian perspective (Kerr & Bowen, 1988). In 1959, Bowen moved to Georgetown University's Department of Psychiatry, where he taught and further refined his theory until his death in 1990.

PHOTO 6.1   Murray Bowen

Bowen's theoretical approach to family therapy is in the style of a grand theorist seeking to develop a theory that explains all social phenomena. As Friedman (1991) points out, "Bowen theory is really not about family per se, but about life" (p. 134). Bowen's work can be understood as an attempt to explain natural evolutionary emotional process. That is, it seeks to establish a model of how animals in general and specifically the human animal adapt to their environments. As Friedman goes on to declare,

> it is thus not really possible to comprehend the thrust of the Bowen approach without considering the nature of our entire species and its relationship to all existing life, and indeed to all previous life (and other natural systems) on this planet, if not throughout the cosmos. (p. 135)

This is in stark contrast to other more recent theories that seek to focus only on therapeutic change and offer no explanation of the human condition. Thus, Bowen's theory has greater appeal to theorists who have an intellectual attraction to understanding rather than to being facilitators of symptom reduction.

The focus of Bowen's work is developing an intergenerational model of psychopathology based on the notion of a universal continuum rather than discrete categories (Friedman, 1991). Thus the occurrence of mental illness is the result of the degree one possesses certain universal traits, not an anomaly of genetic makeup. For example, this position postulates that schizophrenic processes exist in all of us in varying degrees. People who develop schizophrenia simply express a greater degree of the universal schizophrenic trait. Unlike some of his early contemporaries, Bowen was willing to view psychopathology as occurring in both adults and children as well as in relationships between people. Regardless of the apparent locus of the difficulty, the same universal multigenerational transmission forces create the symptoms.

Unlike later models of family therapy, the goal of this approach is not symptom reduction. Rather, a therapist trained in Bowen's theory is interested in improving the intergenerational transmission process. Thus, the focus within this approach is consistent whether the therapist is working with an individual, a couple, or the entire family. It is assumed that improvement in overall functioning will ultimately reduce the family member's symptomatology.

Eight major theoretical constructs are essential to understanding Bowen's approach. These concepts are differentiation, emotional system, multigenerational transmission, emotional triangle, nuclear family, family projection process, sibling position, and societal regression. These constructs are interconnected. One is unable to understand each of the terms without understanding the other terms. To more fully understand the theory, let us look at each of these terms. However, before considering the key terms, we need to first consider the emphasis Bowen puts on the concept of chronic anxiety.

The concept of chronic anxiety holds these constructs together. An underlying assumption in Bowen's work is that anxiety is a natural product in the process of living. Friedman (1991) argues that chronic anxiety can be likened to Freud's notion of libido, which is the drive that powers his theoretical model. However, unlike libido, which is unique to mankind, Bowen found chronic anxiety to be universal to all life. It is an automatic or genetic response, not a cognitive response. When anxiety is low, we are able to think about our situations and our very existence. However, as

| PHOTO 6.2 | Michael Kerr |

anxiety increases, we become less able to think and more reactive to our situation. This pushes the balance between emotionality and thoughtfulness toward emotionality.

This can lead to a situation where the person is likely to be emotionally reactive. That is, he or she will respond to an event with an overly powerful, possibly overwhelming flood of emotion. Emotional reactivity usually results in the expression of powerful emotions, such as anger or rage. Over time the emotionally reactive person becomes conflicted, distant, and emotionally cut off.

Differentiation

Differentiation is the core concept in all of Bowen's theoretical work, and at the same time its definition is the most elusive. Differentiation is related to the psychodynamic concept of ego strength. However, it has been expanded to include interpersonal dimensions. Differentiation refers to how one functions in response to one's level of anxiety. Kerr and Bowen (1988) assert, "The more differentiated a self, the more a person can be an individual while in emotional contact with the group" (p. 94.). This allows the individual to think through a situation without being drawn to act by either internal or external emotional pressures.

The concept of differentiation is best understood in contrast to its opposite counterpart, emotional fusion. Emotional fusion refers to the tendency for family members to share an emotional response. This is the result of poor interpersonal boundaries between family members. In a fused family, there is little room for emotional autonomy. If a member makes a move toward autonomy, it is experienced as abandonment by the other members of the family. If one person in such a family feels anxiety, all members must feel similar anxiety. Often other negative emotions co-occur with this anxiety. Thus, when a member of an emotionally fused family experiences anxiety, an escalation of the emotional process occurs. A member of a differentiated family is able to contain his or her anxiety, allowing emotional issues to be addressed. He or she is able to balance the demands of being both autonomous from and connected to others.

Bowen postulated that the level of differentiation in a family tends to be stable over time. This view sets the goal for Bowen's therapy, which is to increase the level of differentiation in family members. Not only does differentiation play a part in family functioning, but Bowen saw it as playing a major role in mate selection (Kerr & Bowen, 1988). This theory postulates that we select mates who have about the same level of differentiation as we do.

Like a fused family, the thoughts and feelings of an undifferentiated person are fused. This results in a state of unbalance where the undifferentiated person is left to have only emotional or only intellectual responses to anxiety-producing situations. Since the person's emotional processes are cut off from his or her intellectual processes, it is difficult for such a person to find balance.

The confusion about the difference between thought and feelings is in part cultural. Our culture and media often confuse thinking and feeling with each other and use these terms interchangeably. Part of the approach involves helping the client understand the difference between and value of both emotions and thoughts. The therapist serves as an objective observer who provides clients with feedback as they learn to differentiate.

Since emotional fusion leads to people's having a difficult time managing their emotional connection with the people they are fused with, it sets up a need to see relationships in terms of "all or nothing." When the "all" becomes unbearable, an emotionally fused person will cut off the relationship. This often involves a geographic change as well as a cessation of contact. However, this does not resolve the conflict and anxiety. In fact, in some ways it makes it worse. Paradoxically, cutting off relationships fixes the anxiety in fused individuals' minds, and they continue to carry pain, anger, and often resentment. Since they have cut off contact and often placed real geographic distance between themselves and the person they are fused with, there is little chance for resolution of the conflict. One of the key tasks of therapy involves reestablishing contact and resolving issues with people whom clients have cut off.

Differentiation must be considered in its developmental context. Infants are born helpless and fused with their primary caretaker, often their mother. They are dependent on her for meeting all of their needs. At the same time the mother, especially if she is inexperienced, has much to learn about meeting the needs of this particular baby. This relational interaction can produce anxiety in both mother and infant. Over time the child and then the adolescent must develop his or her own separate personality composed of thoughts and feelings and ways of managing both. Ideally, the child develops to be successful and independent and moves out to start his or her own family. According to Kerr and Bowen (1988), "parents function in ways that result in their children achieving about the same degree of emotional separation from them that they achieved from their parents" (p. 95).

Kerr and Bowen (1988) developed a scale of differentiation of individuals ranging from a low of 0 to a high of 100. They saw it as a theoretical scale, but argued that the more differentiated you are according to the scale, the less likely you are to become ill or irrational as a result of stress. Items to be administered as a test of personality profile have never been developed for the scale. Rather, descriptions are provided for broad ranges of scores. Points on the scale are determined by "the degree to which [people] are able to distinguish between the feeling process and the thinking process" (p. 97).

Since differentiation is an issue of self, Kerr and Bowen (1988) have identified additional styles of self. These are referred to as "pseudoself" and "borrowed functioning." Pseudoself is an intellect style based on knowledge and beliefs taken from another. People with a pseudoself often seek validation from others by "talking themselves up." They try to act more mature, strong, smart, or wise. This is done to hide their true self and their fears about their true self.

Borrowed functioning refers to the need to have an appearance of functioning at a higher level than one's partner. It is the result of an unconscious attempt to manage anxiety by focusing on one's partner. The person who is borrowing functioning has a vested interest in maintaining a focus on his or her partner's problem. A person who borrows functioning is operating from a pseudoself position.

For example, a client may need his partner to stay depressed so he can maintain the appearance of superior functioning. This occurs despite his appearance of being willing to participate in therapy with his partner. However, as his partner improves, he will increasingly provoke her to regress to her original level of functioning. Thus, he is willing to participate in therapy as long as it is about someone else. During couple therapy, a spouse who is borrowing functioning might say something like, "Tell the doctor about your self-doubt with asking for a raise."

Like most of Bowen's theoretical constructs, borrowed functioning is seen as an unconscious attempt to deal with anxiety regarding potential exposure of one's true self. If the partner of someone who is borrowing functioning improves, the borrower's difficulty will be exposed or become the focus of therapy and the relationship.

Emotional System

In Bowen's theory, the emotional system is the context in which an organism must exist. It connects members of a system to each other through predictable principles of organization. According to Friedman (1991), "a family emotional system includes the members' thoughts, feelings, emotions, fantasies, associations and past connections, individually and together" (p. 144). In simple terms it is the sum total of all experiences, wants and desires.

The emotional system includes both sides of the classic "nature versus nurture" debate. Aspects of nature captured by this concept include genetics, physical limits and abilities, and physical health. Issues of nurture include sibling position (defined below) and issues resulting from emotional cut-off and fusion transmitted from previous generations. The emotional system is a broad concept and synonymous with what other theorists would simply call a family system. It is viewed as an intergenerational phenomenon and takes into account the mutigenerational transmission process (discussed below).

Multigenerational Transmission

The multigenerational transmission process gives Bowen's theory its multigenerational emphasis and perspective. To Bowen, the connection of current generations to past generations is a natural process. As Friedman (1991) states, from this perspective, "not only can the future be predicted on the basis of the past, but the past can be reconstructed on the basis of the ever-evolving present" (p. 148).

Acknowledging the mutigenerational transmission process involves more than recognizing patterns in a family's history. Multigenerational transmission gives the present a context in history. This context can focus the therapist on the differentiation in the system and on the transmission process.

Bowen places little emphasis on the immediate source of a symptom. Rather, symptoms are seen as a natural expression of anxiety that has been carried forward by the family's emotional system. Here emotional and physical forces come together to allow for the expression of a symptom. Given this idea, the therapist has little interest in just symptom relief. Their emphasis is resolving the root cause of the symptom the client is seeking relief for. If symptom relief is provided the client will quickly develop a different symptom that a therapist might be willing to help they address. The multigenerational transmission process predicts that symptom relief will be short lived. Unless the level of differentiation is increased, a symptom will reappear or a new symptom will appear in another family member.

Emotional Triangle

A triangle is the network of relationship among three people. Bowen's theory "postulates the triangle as the molecule of any emotional system and the total system as a network of interlocking triangles" (Bowen, 1988, p. 216). Anxiety, the compelling factor in much of Bowen's theory, is seen as what motivates people to participate in a triangle. It is postulated that a two-person relationship can remain stable until anxiety is introduced. However, when anxiety is introduced into the dyad, a third party is recruited into a triangle to reduce the overall anxiety (Kerr & Bowen, 1988). It is almost impossible for two people to interact without triangling a third. For example, in couple therapy a common homework assignment is to ask couple to date one another. Typically, couple with children will spend the date talking about their children, or work , or finances. More specific instructions asking the couple to focus on things like art, music, their next vacation, help the couple not triangle anxiety.

Few persons in dyadic relationships have a high enough level of differentiation to avoid participating in triangles. This accounts for the stability of triangles over time. Focusing on triangles supplies a therapeutic strategy in itself. As Friedman (1991) explains,

> if you, as a therapist, allow a couple to create a triangle with you, but take care not to get caught up in the emotional process of that triangle either by overfunctioning or being emotionally reactive, then by trying to remain a non-anxious presence in that triangle, you can induce a change in the relationship of the other two that would not occur if they said the same thing in your absence. (p. 151)

In families, children become triangulated in the parents' relationship and remain there for their entire lives. The patterns of interaction become stable in their structure but are dynamic in terms of their ongoing interaction. Bowen's attention to triangles is common in the first generation of family therapy theorists and has guided the marriage and family therapy movement away from psychoanalytic thinking. The focus has shifted from the interpretation of unconscious processes to observable interpersonal phenomena such as triangles.

Nuclear Family Emotional System

Bowen saw the nuclear family as the most basic unit in society. His concern was the total degree to which emotional fusion can occur in a family system. Chronic anxiety over time was seen as inevitably generating a symptom in the relationship system. This perspective is significant in the development of the field, for this theory can place a symptom inside the system rather that in an individual. Bowen (Kerr & Bowen, 1988) identified three categories of clinical dysfunction resulting from chronic anxiety in a nuclear family emotional system: dysfunction in a spouse, marital conflict, and dysfunction in a child.

As relationships form, people tend to select a partner who has a similar level of differentiation. If chronic anxiety is present in the family, there is a tendency for one of these patterns of symptoms to emerge. Once this emerges, there can be a shift in the locus of the symptoms as the family develops. For example, early in a marriage a husband may express the symptoms, but over time the anxiety gives rise to a pattern of marital distress. Over more time, the marital distress may give rise to a teenager's acting out to resolve his parents' ongoing conflict.

Bowen's interest in the nuclear family as the most basic unit in society is clearly a function of the historical period in which Bowen was writing and developing his theory. More contemporary authors have criticized family therapy for its focus on the traditional nuclear family (see Chapter 3). Bowen's theory is flexible enough to be applicable to a wide variety of family types.

Sibling Position

Bowen emphasized sibling position as a factor in determining personality. He based his conceptualization of the importance of sibling position on the work of Toman (1961). Toman's work described 10 different personality types for each sibling position. This was based on the idea that where a person is in birth order has an influence on how he or she relates to parents and siblings. Remember that Bowen considered the triangle the basic unit of families, so by and large, birth order determines the triangles you grow up in. For example, parents often have higher expectations of oldest children, who as a result often function as mini adults. They often assist with the raising and sometimes the discipline of younger siblings.

Bowen saw sibling position as a way to assess the degree of differentiation and the nature of the multigenerational projection process. He asserts that "the degree to which a personality profile fits with normal provides a way to understand the level of differentiation and the direction of the projection process from generation to generation" (Bowen, 1988, p. 385). For example, a family that has an oldest who acts like a youngest can expect a good deal of triangulation with that child.

Societal Regression

Since Bowen's theory is general and universal, it is logical that it would be used to describe process on a societal level. As Friedman (1991) points out, Bowen "viewed society as a family, that is, as an emotional system complete with its own multigenerational transmission, chronic anxiety, emotional triangles, cutoffs, projection processes, and fusion/differentiation struggles" (p. 165). This unique perspective views society as being influenced by emotional processes. Historically there are ebbs and flows in the amount of anxiety in given societies, and we see the co-occurrence of social problems during times of high anxiety.

If one considers the level of anxiety in our society since the attacks of September 11, 2001, one sees the influence of societal regression. If Bowen were alive, he would likely argue that the appropriate response would be to remain differentiated as a society. He would support our shared grieving but warn us against being emotionally reactive in our response.

Bowen also became concerned with societal regression in the profession and was concerned that family therapy's rapid expansion and popularity could result in its becoming a mere fad. Friedman (1991) argues that the field is regressing in two serious ways. First, it has become overly focused on administration, managerial techniques, and pursuing data indiscriminately. Second, family therapy is increasingly focusing on symptoms and new hot button issues. In summary, Friedman is concerned for the field because

> there is little focus on the emotional well-being of the therapist. Indeed, Bowen theory might say that the pursuit of data and techniques through books and

conferences resembles a form of substance abuse, binding the anxiety that will never really be reduced until the field focuses more on its own differentiation. (p. 166)

Innovations in Practice

By far the greatest innovation of this approach is its provision of a theoretical description of family therapy. The theoretical work of Bowen served as some of the earliest conceptualization of how families could be worked with. This approach, which operated from a psychodynamic

---

FIGURE 6.1 **Key Symbols in a Genogram**

Monica McGoldrick and Randy Gerson, "Key Symbols in a Genogram," Genograms in Family Assessment. Copyright © 1985 by W. W. Norton & Company, Inc.

Source: McGoldrick & Gerson, 1985.

origin, made a smooth shift in the psychiatric community. Unlike the challenge to the mental health establishment from behavioral therapy and experiential therapy, this challenge was internal rather than external. Bowen was a trained psychoanalyst at the start of his career. However, he became less interested in psychoanalysis after reading a report that this approach was not as scientific as previously reported (Kerr & Bowen, 1988). Systems theory provided the bridge to make the study of psychotherapy more scientific.

Part of the difficulty in making family therapy scientific is dealing with the volume of data. Adding a family member to an interview exponentially increases the amount of data the therapist is presented with. To process the data and keep track of the intergenerational patterns, Guerin and Pendagast (1976) developed the genogram. McGoldrick and Gerson (1985) & Gerson, McGoldrick & Petry (2008) expanded on this technique and made it nearly universal in marriage and family therapy. A genogram is a pictorial representation of family structure along with specific information such as dates of births, deaths, and marriages as well as descriptions of relationships. Generations of family therapists started their careers by either developing their own genogram or taking genograms of clients.

Let us walk through the basics of a genogram using the conventions developed by McGoldrick and Gerson (1985; see Figure 6.1). A basic genogram starts with a circle to represent a woman and a square to represent a man. Inside the figure, important information such as age, birth date,

FIGURE 6.2 **Winek-Chute Genogram**

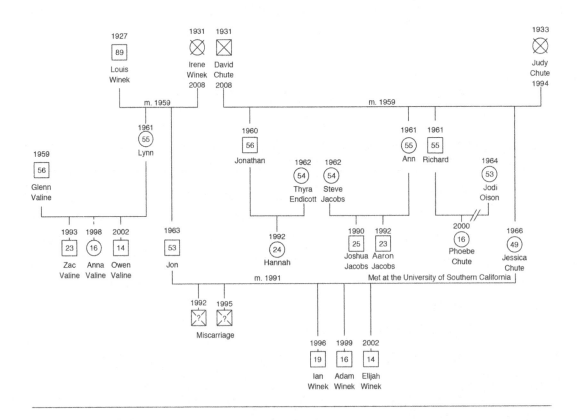

FIGURE 6.3   **Genorgam Symbols Describing Relationships**

Monica McGoldrick and Randy Gerson, "Genogram Symbols Describing Relationship," Genograms in Family Assessment. Copyright © 1985 by W. W. Norton & Company, Inc.

Very close or fused

Fused and conflictual

Poor or conflictual

Close

Estranged or cut-off

Distant

Source: McGoldrick & Gerson, 1985.

addiction, medical issues, and other relevant information can be included. Deaths are marked by an X drawn through the figure, accompanied by information such as date and cause of death. Marital relationships are symbolized by a line between a circle and square. Additional information can be added about the relationship, such as date of marriage if the couple cohabitated prior to marriage or length of courtship if this is significant. If the marriage has ended, the line is broken by two slashes. A common-law marriage is signified by a dotted line connecting the circle and square.

A couple's children are signified by circles and squares that hang down from the marriage line, from oldest on the left to youngest on the right. Again, it is important to fill in important information about each child, such as date of birth and special issues such as addiction or health concerns. Adopted or foster children are connected to their parents by a dotted line. Pregnancy is signified by a line with a triangle, and stillbirths are signified by a smaller circle or square with an X drawn through it. Since abortions are important events in a family, they are signified by a small darkened circle if spontaneous or an X if induced.

As an example, I am presenting a genogram of the Winek-Chute family showing three generations of our family (see Figure 6.2).

A genogram can be used to focus on a variety of issues and factors, depending on the focus the therapist is interested in. McGoldrick and Gerson (1985) developed the symbols in Figure 6.3 to represent styles of relating between family members.

David Schnarch applied Bowen's theory and in particular the concept of differentiation to provide a theoretical link between the treatment of sexual dysfunction and issues of intimacy in conjoint couple therapy. In his book Constructing the Sexual Crucible, Schnarch (1991) develops what he calls the quantum model of sexual functioning. This model is defined as "a systemic framework integrating physiologic and psychological aspects of sexual functioning" (p. 21). This approach moves past a hydraulic view of sexuality, which constructs sexual response as the result of building sexual pressure and increased blood flow to specific organs. In Schnarch's view, sexual dysfunction is a result of emotional fusion between partners. In this approach, intimacy is a natural byproduct of sexuality. Intimacy involves a process of taking risks to grow and deepen emotional connection in the context of a committed relationship. Schnarch expands the discourse of intimacy further than other authors in the field.

From Schnarch's (1991) perspective, difficulty in sexual response and function is related to a person's level of differentiation. In his popular book *Passionate Marriage*, Schnarch (1997) provides examples of couples in therapy who, through increasing their level of differentiation, had spontaneous improvement in their sexual difficulties. From this perspective, we see that sexual problems can be spontaneously resolved by addressing differentiation in the individual as well as in the couple's dynamics.

Questioning

When conducting a therapeutic interview the focus is on the therapist's level of differentiation. According to Friedman (1991), "maintaining a non-anxious presence, or being objective, or even promoting differentiation in others, is connected to the being of the therapist" (p. 138). The therapist's level of differentiation is the key issue in the training of a new therapists. In keeping with the theme of being continuous rather than seeing issues as discrete, the boundaries between supervision and therapy seem to blur. In a famous early paper that Bowen published anonymously (1972; Bowen, 1978), he describes how he worked on his own differentiation. This was done during a family vacation to the area where most of his family lived. Before making the trip, he corresponded with several family members and revealed secrets that he had been holding. He also let them know his travel plans and made himself available to talk with each of his family members during his visit. This action removed him from a number of emotional triangles.

At its core, this approach is an insight-based approach, and many of the questions in therapy are designed to provide the client with insight. They start on the factual and structural level and move to the emotional level. Initially in therapy, the therapist obtains information on the membership of one's family. As therapy progresses, the emotions of the client are explored in depth. As this occurs, the emotional intensity of the session often increases. The therapist maintains firm boundaries as transference and countertransference issues are addressed and resolved. Thus, questions are used to discover the issues and secrets that exist in the client's unconscious mind and extended family.

It is during this assessment phase that the genogram is often used. Factual questions are used to complete the genogram. The genogram serves to provide both client and therapist with an understanding of the problems. It allows clients to understand how issues such as cutoff, fusion, chronic anxiety, and the intergenerational progression impact their current symptoms.

Structuring

Bowen family therapy is structured around the weekly 60-minute session. Family members can be invited for the interview. Unlike some of his founding peers, Bowen was willing to see fragments of whole families and individuals. It is rare that this modality of therapy is delivered in settings other than the professional interview room. It is difficult to remain objective in a client's home, and therefore this theoretical approach does not lend itself well to the family preservation model, in which the therapist will go to the home of a highly dysfunctional family to work intensively with the client.

The interview revolves around a calm discussion of the client's struggles and situation. The question and response sequence provides the structure of the session. In this approach, the therapist's responses to the client become the intervention that moves the client and his or her family to a more differentiated state, so we must consider the responses of the therapist part of the questioning process.

Responding

In a Bowen-style interview, the hallmark of the therapist's response to the client is thoughtful objectivity. When working with a family, the therapist forms a new triangle with the client's family. The therapist's not being emotionally involved in the triangle and remaining objective lets clients become more aware of their own responses. In this way, the anxiety in the room becomes more conscious and gives the client an opportunity to address it directly.

One of Bowen's interview guideline is based on the assumption that "objectivity is inversely proportional to reactivity" (Friedman, 1991, p. 153). To remain objective, the therapist must be able to manage his or her own anxiety. As we remember from our prior discussion, a person's ability to manage anxiety is a function of his or her level of differentiation. For this reason, Bowen places emphasis on differentiation of the self of the therapist. In therapist training, trainees are encouraged to engage in their own personal therapy to increase their level of differentiation. Therefore, the focus of supervision is not on changing the client but on increasing the level of differentiation of the therapist. This creates an isomorphic increase in the client's level of differentiation.

A therapist's objectivity, if understood superficially, would seem to cut him or her off emotionally from the client. This is far from the truth; the therapist feels and is able to express emotional connection with the client. However, when therapists remain objective, they do not get lost or sucked into the emotion around the client's issues. They have empathy for the client's level of anxiety and at the same time manage their own anxiety.

In a similar fashion, Bowen rejected the interpretation of transference as an integral part of the therapeutic process. Rather, he advised therapists to stay out of the client's transference by remaining objective. By remaining detriangled, Bowen invented the now-popular position of coaching. By remaining invested in the client but not overly emotionally involved, the therapist can remain connected with the client but outside of the client's conflict. Acting as a coach, the therapist provides the client with gentle guidance.

The therapist warns the client about the natural consequences of emotional conflict and encourages clients who have been cut off to reconnect. By helping clients reconnect with others in a rational as well as emotional way, therapists provide clients with an opportunity to build real and healthy relationships with their extended family.

It is common for clients to use written expression to make contact with relatives who have been cut off prior to therapy. In these situations, the therapist can help edit letters to family members. When clients are encouraged to set realistic goals that are not emotionally loaded, they are made able to establish a limited but connected relationship with their family.

When people are not able to get all they want from a relationship, they often provoke a cutoff instead of trying to maintain a limited but real relationship. Psychologically, it would seem that we often choose no contact with a relative rather than deal with the implicit anxiety produced by a real relationship. We could simply say that undifferentiated people often decide that nothing is better than something.

Applications

One of the most exciting applications of Bowen theory is in the development of the currently popular approach of coaching. This is defined as "the process of 'coaching' individuals in their efforts to change themselves in the context of their nuclear and parental family system" (McGoldrick & Carter, 2001, p. 281). This approach differs from individual therapy by placing the emphasis not on change in the individual's intrapsychic processes, but rather on changes in actions in a person's network of relationships. Unlike the solution-focused and narrative approaches to working with the individual, the past is emphasized. From this perspective, it is assumed that an exploration of historical process as they influence the family system is essential to changes in the present.

Coaching focuses on several processes that assist individuals in making changes in their family system. In essence, it is psychotherapy in clients seeking to simply maximize their mental health. When a client becomes less anxious, therapy is refocused on the process of planning action with family members. This often involves empowering clients to remove themselves from dysfunctional triangles. From here, clients differentiate by developing an emotional connection with others. They strive to see people for who they are, not for their idea of whom they should be. This means that the differentiated person sees his or her mother as a woman with thoughts, feelings, weaknesses, and strengths in her own right, not as simply one half of the person's dysfunctional parental system. The process of change is a circular process of three steps: "(1) the change; (2) the family's reaction to the change; and (3) dealing with the family's reaction to the change" (McGoldrick & Carter, 2001, p. 291).

Bowen family therapy has been applied to several settings. Hayland (1990) has applied Bowen's theory to her work with hospitalized children and adolescents. Nims & Duba (2011) explore the use of the play therapy techniques of art, sand tray and puppets from a Bowen Systems Family Therapy theoretical framework. In an interesting article, Gibson (1993) builds on Bowen's (1974) article and applies his theory to the systemic treatment of codependence. In this approach, codependence is seen as an issue of emotional fusion. Hertlein and Killmer (2004) made interesting use of Bowen's concept of differentiation in applying it to their treatment of homeless clients who were not mentally ill. More recently Sauerheber, Nims, Carter (2014) explore the utility of Bowen Family Systems Therapy. They argue; "The Bowen Family Systems therapist, in a way that seems consistent with the Islamic tradition, acts as an arbiter for understanding the dynamics of the system without takin sides . p. 232. These authors explore how the key components can help families in ways that respect their cultural believes.

Acting as a Bowen Family Systems Therapist

The hallmarks of Bowenian therapy are anxiety reduction and insight into family dynamics. This occurs by the therapist's maintaining an objective stance, as described above. As therapy progresses, the client is able to become more differentiated—that is, able to remain objective regarding the conditions of his or her life circumstances while staying emotionally connected to extended-family members. Intimacy and sexuality are linked to each other in an emotionally secure manner, and the family is able to promote separation as well as connection in all members. Therapy is often a lengthy process where the family might come into and out of therapy as new issues arise.

Case Example: The Case of George's Anxiety

Session One

George, a 42-year-old Caucasian male, is referred by his psychiatrist for psychotherapy around his depression and anxiety. George is a bright and articulate doctorate-level manager in a grant-funded educational foundation. He has been depressed for two years and relates the onset of his depression to being promoted to a "high-pressure, low degree of autonomy, middle-management position." He has worked with his employee assistance counselor for the past year. He reports that this has provided some relief of his depressive symptoms, but he remains anxious. He further reports that he has difficulty not taking on the problems of his employees.

According to George, he is happy and secure in his marriage. He has been married for 12 years and has two daughters ages nine and five. He reports that the children are doing well and that he has a supportive wife. However, he reports that in recent months he has had difficulty maintaining the boundary between work and home. He brings stress to his home, which he does not like, and he often finds himself so concerned about a detail of his job that he returns to his office in the evening to work on projects and to calm his anxiety.

There is no history of anxiety disorder in his family. However, he describes his mom as an unhappy person. He further reports that during his childhood, he had an overinvolved relationship with his mother. He reports that at some point when he was a teen, his father started to withdraw to his workshop in the garage. When this happened, George became closer to his mother. He has two younger brothers, ages 34 and 32. He reports that they are all doing well, have all graduated from college, and are all in stable relationships.

Toward the end of the first session, the therapist begins to negotiate a therapeutic contract with George. George has been started on a course of antidepressant medication. He also has been prescribed a benzodiazepine to take when his anxiety gets out of control. George recognizes that he needs the meds in the short run, but he is requesting therapy to address issues in his personality so that he can get off the medication in the long run. He reports another depressive episode when he first moved out of the house during his junior year in college.

Session Two

This session is spent developing a detailed genogram. George's genogram is taken as follows.

A couple of significant patterns emerge as the genogram is developed. These patterns revolve around George's relationship with his parents. He feels that his father withdrew from the family when he became a teenager. He recalls that his father would spend more and more time away from the family. This took the form of working overtime and tinkering in his workshop. George reports that at a young age, he had the feeling that his father was avoiding his mother.

This pattern set up the next dynamic apparent in the genogram, which is George's overinvolved relationship with his mother. George reports that he felt he was elected to serve as his mother's companion when his father became less involved. This continued throughout his high school years and into college. George initially reports that he spent the first two years of his college career at a local community college because he was not ready to move out. Then he corrects himself and states that he stayed at home because his mother was not ready for him to move out. His therapist suggests that neither he nor either of his parents was ready for him to move out.

FIGURE 6.4   **George's Genogram**

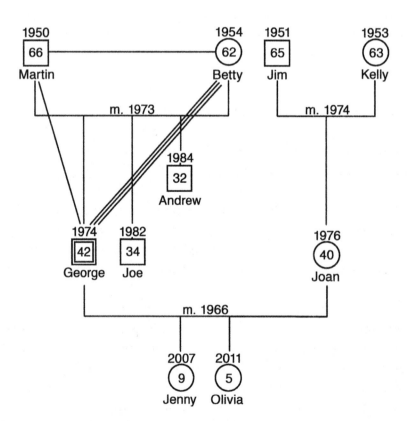

When asked about his current relationship with his mother, he reports that at times it is strained. When asked for more details, he reports that when he calls his parents, his mother always adds "helpful advice" or encourages him to attend the church he grew up in. He reports that while he has a strong faith, he and his wife have chosen a different denomination in their religious practices. He reports that his mom sometimes tries to make him feel guilty for not raising his daughters in the "right church." When asked, the client reports that whenever he calls his parents, he talks to both of them at the same time on the phone. This is taken to indicate that there is a strong triangle with him and his parents. At this point, the client is engaged in a discussion on the nature of emotional triangles and encouraged to write letters to each of his parents, not one letter to both of them.

Session Three

George comes to the third session reporting a significant decrease in his anxiety. He reports that he has been much less stressed at work. When asked how he has been able to do this, he reports that he has been able to stay out of employee conflict. In the past, he would be sucked into a conflict, but over the past week he has been able to stay out of it. When asked what happened when he stayed out of it, he laughs and reports that "no one died." When asked further, he says that the employees were able to resolve the conflict themselves. He reports that when he tried staying out of the conflict, he was anxious at first, but after he calmed his anxiety he was able to stay out. This leads to a discussion on his self-soothing skills. George reports that he was able to talk to himself with a supportive voice. When asked whose critical voice he heard before, he says it was his mother's.

The remainder of the session is spent exploring George's relationship with his parents. He reports that while he was able to write each of his parents their own letter, he was unable to send them. He reports that he found them too superficial to mail. He was concerned that if he confronted his mother, she would slide deeper into a depression she was experiencing.

George is asked how his father handles his mom's depression, and he talks about how his father continues to withdraw. Currently, he is very active with the local volunteer fire department and his radio club. George laughs and says, "He talks to people on the other side of the world but won't talk to his wife." George is then asked to discuss how this abandonment by his father makes him feel.

George is unable to express his anger despite looking angry. When the therapist tells him he looks angry, George states he probably is but is unable to own this feeling. He relates how, when he was a teen, his parents were unable to accept any negative feelings from him. He describes how they would interpret any such expression as his being ungrateful for all they had done for him. He then goes on to describe how he withdrew into music as an expression of his feelings.

His therapist discusses setting boundaries with his parents, especially when it comes to his mother and her constant giving of advice. George becomes somewhat anxious and his eyes fill with tears as they discuss these issues. The therapist asks if he feels such a move would be an expression of his lack of gratitude toward his parents. George affirms this, then goes on to say that while he knows intellectually that it is not an expression of his ingratitude, he feels as if it is. The therapist asks George if he could write and send a separate letter to each of his parents expressing gratitude toward them, then in the future write a second letter to each of them attempting to set some boundaries. George agrees that this would be a good idea but says it would be hard. He also thinks the expression of gratitude and the limits should come in the same letter. The therapist agrees, and George says he will bring a draft to the next session.

When it is suggested that he talk to just one of his parents the next time he calls on the phone, George becomes anxious and states that he is unable to do this. When asked if he could write a letter to each of his parents separately rather that writing them both at the same time, he is open to this idea. The therapist then asks George to write the letters for a homework assignment.

Session Four

George arrives at the next session with drafts of letters to each of his parents. He is visually brighter and reports that between sessions he has been significantly less depressed. He wonders if his medicine is starting to work. The therapist states that he is setting better boundaries in his life and taking better care of himself emotionally, so that this and the medicine are probably helping.

At this point, George shares his letters with the therapist. He describes how difficult it was to write them and reports that he was tearful at several points while writing the letters. However, he reports that rather than holding back his tears and feeling ashamed of his feelings, he let them flow. He also reports that as he wrote the letters over several days, he felt his anxiety diminish.

At George's request, his therapist reviews his letters. His letter to his father discusses his dad's abandonment and talks about his loss over not being closer to him. The letter ends with a request to be closer to him in the future, along with an open invitation to talk in person should he want too.

The letter to his mother is considerably longer. In this letter, he also discusses his feelings of abandonment. He then discusses his feelings of inadequacy that result from his mother's advice giving. He further confronts her for her pattern of offering praise and then adding a *but*. When the therapist asks for an example, George reports that she might say, "Good job," when he got an A– in a class he struggled with, "but if only you worked harder, you could have gotten an A." Another example is, "Your girls are wonderful, but don't you think you should be raising them Baptist rather than in the Presbyterian Church?"

When asked how his parents would respond to receiving these letters, George becomes fearful and states that he thought the letters were for his benefit and not actually to be sent. The therapist then asks what he is afraid of. George answers that he is afraid of losing his relationship with his parents. The therapist states that in healthy relationships, you can say what you need to say to another person at any time. This makes George tearful and quiet.

As the session time ends, the therapist requests that George think about what it would take for him to be able to send such letters. George shakes his head and states that he's not sure. He does say that he feels he can tell his wife his feelings at any time. He also says he feels he could hear what his daughters have to say to him about their relationship. He goes on to describe how they have family meetings to discuss issues in the family as needed. The therapist points out that it's great that he doesn't need his parents to be emotionally mature in his relationship with his daughters.

Session Five

The next session is held three weeks later after George returns from work-related travel. At the start of the session, George talks about a conflict he and his wife had over expenses related to renovations to their living room. He relates the conflict to a miscommunication, and both ended up being hurt by the argument. The therapist asks him to reflect on his feelings during the argument, and he relates that he was feeling abandoned and unappreciated because of his wife's concern about how much the project was going to cost. He thought they had an agreement to start the project, but she didn't see it that way. He had started the project when she was away, as a surprise, and when she returned and raised concerns over the cost, he was hurt. As a result, he withdrew from her for a number of days and felt a slight increase in depression and anxiety.

When asked how he pulled out of his depressed mood, he reports that because of his medication and his ability to calm himself with positive self-talk, he was depressed and withdrawn for only a few days. He reports that six weeks ago he would have been in his bed crying for a week, possibly two.

George also reports that this time when he withdrew, rather than dwelling on the negative hurt feelings, he decided to take responsibility for his feelings and try to find a way out. It was with this spirit that he had the insight that he was experiencing the same kind of feelings he had had in his adolescence when his mother would criticize him. He reports that intellectually he knew his wife was not trying to be critical; she was only surprised and concerned over the family's finances. However, George recognized that he felt hurt and abandoned.

He was able to regroup and talk about the conflict with his wife. They had a productive conversation, and both were able to take responsibility for their own emotional reactivity. Both were concerned that the other had become their parent. George and his wife were able to say that neither of them wanted to be the bad parent. They decided they would be peers rather than take a parental role during an argument. The therapist gives George positive feedback for this innovation and change in their relationship.

In the last few minutes of the session, George discloses that he has decided it would be better if he discussed his relationship with his mother with her in person. The therapist offers to invite her for a session, and George replies that she would never see a secular therapist. He states that he feels he could talk to her on his own and would like to have a session to plan their conversation. A family reunion is coming up in three weeks, and George feels he will have a chance to talk to her then. Since George is feeling so much better, he requests a follow-up in two weeks.

Session Six

At the start of the session, George reports that he has not felt at all depressed or anxious between sessions. He attributes this to his newfound ability to not be drawn into conflict at work. He reports that he does not need the immediate approval of his staff to feel good about himself. He also reports that he has been able to relate to his wife on a deeper level. They have had several long talks about their wants and desires for the future of the family, and they have made some decisions based on these conversations. They have decided that his wife will cut back work to half time to have more time available to be with their children. While this would be a financial burden, they feel good about the decision and how it fits their view of how their family life should be.

As a result, George reports having a better relationship with his daughters. He has made it a point to take separate outings with each one and work on developing a better relationship with each. George becomes tearful when describing how he has sometimes felt self-conscious when with his daughters. He reports that this has shifted and he is able to feel more at ease with them. He recognizes that his uneasy feelings were the result of his fear over being unable to control them. He states that he no longer cares what others think about his daughters; he has decided that what they think of him is more important.

George spends the last half of the session preparing for his talk with his mother. He has thought about the issues a good deal between sessions, and the therapist mostly supports his approach. He has decided to approach his mother from a position of love. He states that his goal is to have a closer relationship. He decides that he does not want to approach his mother out of anger or to seek an explanation for her past behavior.

He has decided that he should approach her alone, without his father present. To lay the groundwork, he wrote her and requested that they spend some time alone. She responded with a phone call inquiring what was wrong. He responded by saying nothing was wrong, just that he would like to talk to her about their relationship. When pressed, he successfully set a boundary and told his mother they could talk more in person. At first his mother was angry; however, when he did not buy into her anger, she apologized for her anger and said that she was looking forward to talking.

Session Seven

George arrives for this session in good spirits and discusses the reunion. He states that it went better than he could have imagined. While he was anxious about the conversation, he reports that he and his mother had a long talk. After she twice denied her tendency to criticize, she was able to talk to him about her struggles with perfectionism. She also started to talk about her emotional abandonment by his father. When George set a limit by telling her that she would have to work that out with his father, she was able to take responsibility for her relationship with her husband.

George and his mother agreed that they wanted to be closer, and his mother agreed to try not to criticize him. They both expressed some concern that she might not be able to do this. They agreed that if she fell into the old pattern, George was to confront her. She also stated that she wanted to be closer to her grandchildren. George admitted that perhaps he was avoiding her to avoid her criticism. To this, she broke down in tears and stated that she thought he was a good father and that Jane was a good mother. She discussed how her mother had criticized her when she was a young mother and was sad that she had repeated the pattern.

During this part of the session, the therapist mostly listens and at a few points gives some positive feedback to support this change in George's relationship with his mother.

George goes on to report that he is feeling no depressive or anxiety symptoms. He states that his job is still stressful, but he is able to maintain a healthy perspective. He talks about stopping his medication someday, but for now he is comfortable taking it. He is grateful for the "coaching" he has received in therapy. He states that he would like to follow up in four weeks for a wellness check and to possibly work with his wife to develop a way to talk to her about their finances. He states that while they share goals for the family's future, they have different views about how they can achieve these goals.

A few minutes are spent reviewing the course of therapy and reinforcing the positive changes George has made in his differentiation. He is also encouraged to continue to set boundaries in his relationships. The option of returning for a session sooner than four weeks is offered should he feel the need. The therapist says good-bye, and George thanks the therapist for helping him.

Case Discussion

The first two sessions are focused on developing a therapeutic relationship and assessing the client's situation. Since George is in a secure and satisfying marriage, his wife is not brought in as part of the assessment. George seems to be having a difficult time with his anxiety at work. He does, however, have difficulty with issues in his relationship with his parents. He is somewhat fused to his mother and is involved in a triangle with her and his father. The therapist ends the second session by educating George on triangles.

In the third session, the client reports that he has made progress in removing himself from triangles at his work. While he has been quick to make progress in his work relationships, he is still stuck in a triangle with his parents. Noting that George has cut off some feelings, the therapist gently makes George aware of some anger that he has related to abandonment from his father and criticism from his mother. In addition to coaching about triangles, the therapist provides coaching regarding setting boundaries with his parents, while encouraging George to develop a more healthy relationship with them.

In the fourth session, George is feeling better and enjoying the early gains of therapy. George has made significant strides in addressing the relationship with his parents and feels somewhat relieved by writing to them. Although happy about the early progress, the therapist is concerned that George was unable to send the letters to his parents. This is taken to indicate that there is still work to be done.

After a long break between sessions, George reports some regression in the fifth session. In some ways he has become his father by withdrawing from his wife. However, since George is bright and really understands what he is learning about emotional reactivity, he was able to talk with his wife about their relationship rather than simply repeating the pattern his parents established.

The sixth session is spent coaching George on ways to improve his relationship with his family of origin. He is actively working to have a different family than the one he grew up in. He is also interested in changing his relationship with his parents and is working hard preparing to approach them in a productive manner.

The seventh session is spent mostly reinforcing changes George has made. The therapist is happy with the level of success to date. Since George requests a follow-up with his wife, the therapist is willing to coach the couple to improve their relationship and further disrupt the intergeneration transmission process.

Evaluating Bowen Family Systems Therapy

A comprehensive review of literature on outcomes, published by Miller and colleagues (2004), concluded that clinical research provides evidence that Bowen's theory is a valid and effective theory of marriage and family therapy. It is surprising that such an influential theory in the field of marriage and family therapy has lacked empirical validation for so long. However, the relevance of Bowen's theory and the power of anecdotal reports of clinical change have long been enough to provide for the long-term acceptance of the theory. If this were not a foundational theory, it is doubtful that it would be so well accepted with so little empirical verification.

Despite the lack of direct evidence, Miller and colleagues (2004) have provided some evidence of support for Bowen's theory by testing the empirical validity of several of the concepts underlying it. They looked at the theoretical constructs of marital similarity, chronic anxiety, marital satisfaction, triangulation, multigenerational transmission of emotional processes, sibling position, and universality. After an exhaustive review of the literature, they concluded that, "in support of Bowen theory, differentiation and anxiety were found to be significantly associated with psychological adjustment and marital satisfaction" (Miller et al., 2004, p. 462). However, there was no valid evidence that people marry someone of the same level of differentiation and little support for Bowen's specific theory of sibling position. Likewise, there was little support of Bowen's theory of triangulation, and his concepts of multigenerational transmission and universality remain untested.

Bowen clearly spells out the relationship between anxiety and differentiation when he states that "chronic anxiety increases as level of differentiation decreases" (Kerr & Bowen, 1988, p. 117). It is further hypothesized that anxiety leads to psychological distress, and studies have indirectly tested the link between the two. Miller and colleagues (2004) have located eight studies that find the predicted relationship between differentiation and psychological distress.

Miller and colleagues (2004) have extrapolated that "Bowen's theory hypothesizes that differentiation is positively correlated with marital satisfaction" (p. 457). Based on their extensive review of the literature, they conclude that "several studies have examined this proposition and have found a strong, positive relationship between differentiation and marital quality" (p. 457).

Learning Exercises

1. Practice creating a genogram by interviewing members of your family. Be sure to provide as many details as possible over three generations. What significant events have occurred in your family over the past 50 years? More important, what has been the family's response to the anxiety that these events have created? Try tracing the intergeneration projection process that occurs in your family. Are there any cutoffs from members of your family that have produced any "outcast" or "lost" members?

2. Divide into groups of three, each consisting of a therapist, a client, and an observer. Have the therapist conduct a 15-minute interview with the client

about a conflict-carrying situation the client was in recently. While the interview is going on, have the observer watch the therapist to see how she processes the client's anxiety and feelings about the conflict. At the end of the time, have the observer provide feedback to the therapist about her objectivity. When did the therapist seem least and most objective? Have the client also provide feedback about how supported he felt, especially when the therapist was objective.

3. Divide into groups of two or three and discuss the level of differentiation in your family of origin. How did that level of differentiation change over the period of your development? Were there any members who borrowed functioning?

4. Divide into groups of two or three and discuss how you process the anxiety in your lives. Discuss periods of your life where you experienced the most anxiety. How did you cope with your anxiety? Since Bowen saw sanity–insanity as a continuum and believed that chronic anxiety results in emotional difficulty, describe how you would become crazy if you became overwhelmed by anxiety. In other words, what kind of crazy would you go if you went crazy? Are you more likely to implode (turn inward with anxiety) or explode (act outward with anger)?

Discussion Questions

1. A superficial understanding of objectivity sees it as a cold, uncaring, almost antiseptic position to take during an interview. Discuss ways objectivity can be presented to the client in a caring, compassionate, and empathetic way.

2. Discuss how anxiety prevents you from being differentiated during times of crisis. What techniques do you use to manage anxiety? How do these techniques allow you to remain differentiated during times of crisis?

3. In your family of origin, what themes have been repeated over several generations? Are there members of your family that you have cut off? If so, what is the family's explanation of why and how this happened? What would be different in your family if you reconnected with the members you have cut off?

4. Talk about the current level of anxiety in your class regarding being successful in your training. As you take positive steps to decrease your anxiety, what happens to your ability to be clear in your thinking and in touch with your feelings?

5. If we define "closeted" as withholding information about yourself out of fear of rejection. How is "coming out" part of a differentiation process. Can you describe a successful experience of coming out?

Web Resources

The Bowen Center for the Study of the Family Home Page

https://www.thebowencenter.org/

Wikipedia's page on Murray Bowen

https://en.wikipedia.org/wiki/Murray_Bowen

Suggested Readings

Bowen, M. (1978). On the differentiation of a self. In M. Bowen, *Family therapy in clinical practice* (pp. 467–528). Northvale, NJ: Jason Aronson.

Friedman, E. H. (1991). Bowen theory and therapy. In A. S. Gurman & D. P. Kniskern (Eds.), *Handbook of family therapy* (Vol. 2, pp. 134–170). New York: Brunner/Mazel.

Gerson, R., McGoldrick, M. & Petry, S. (2008) *Genograms: Assessment and Intervention.* 3rd ed New York: Norton.

Kerr, M., & Bowen, M. (1988). Family evaluation: An approach based on Bowen theory. New York: Norton.

Miller, R., Anderson, S., & Keala, D. (2004). Is Bowen theory valid? A review of basic research. *Journal of Marital and Family Therapy, 30,* 453–466.

CHAPTER

SATIR TRANSFORMATIONAL SYSTEMIC & SYMBOLIC-EXPERIENTIAL FAMILY THERAPY

With Laura Eubanks Gambrel, Ph.D.

| PHOTO 7.1 | Laura Eubanks Gambrel & Jon Winek |

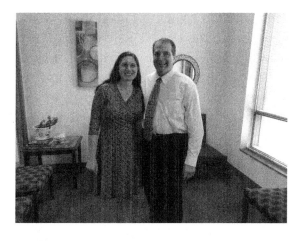

Thinking About This Approach

Experiential Family therapy is a foundation approach to Family Therapy. Influenced by ideas from gestalt therapy the focusing on emotional responses in the here and now of the therapy session experiential family therapy was and remains an influential approach. Virginia Satir and Carl Whitaker are two of the most influential developers and practitioners of this model. Both were central in the development of family therapy. Satir (Transformational systemic therapy) was noted for her training and clarity of techniques that assist clients in being emotionally available for each other. Whitaker (Symbolic-Experiential) was noted for his playful yet provocative approach to promoting change in his clients.

Virginia Satir (1916–1988)

Virginia Satir, who has been referred to as "the mother of family therapy," developed an approach to therapy based on humanistic principles and grounded in the experiential framework. She was among the first women to be leaders in a field that has a significant majority of women practitioners. Her clinical work was also impacted by her time in the 1950s and 60s at the Mental Research Institute (see chapter 8) in which she focused on communication patterns. The foundation of the Satir Model brings together these three influences making it a form of therapy that believes in the inherent goodness of people and their ability to tap into inner resources to solve their own problems (humanistic), that experiences in the present can lead to increased awareness and growth (experiential), and that communication patterns (MRI) can be understood to help people live more congruent lives. This approach was called a communication model because of this focus on congruent communication, and was also referred to as the Human Validation Process Model because of the focus on humanistic principles. The approach is now usually called the Satir Model which focuses on the founder herself, and more recently has been named Satir Transformational Systemic Therapy and Satir Brief Transformational Therapy—which focus on the transformational aspects of the model that have become highlighted in recent developments. Her work was influential and groundbreaking to the field of family therapy, writing one of the earliest books (1964) about family therapy—*Conjoint Family Therapy*. Her contribution has been undervalued at times perhaps because of her focus on teaching experientially instead of academic writing and research of her model. The Satir Model has been less popular in the United States as there are few training program specifically teaching this approach. However, her work is still strong in Canada and is widely used in Asia where the Satir Model is currently very popular.

Satir used very emotionally evocative techniques which made her popular among wide audiences. Her humanistic/experiential approach made her a guru in the growth human potential movement. She traveled extensively across the country presenting workshops where her ability to provide clarity to developing clinical techniques. Her interests evolved into having concern for communities and she became involved the Esalem institute in California. This is an intentional community focused on humanistic education.

Meditations and Spirituality

Virginia Satir increasingly included spirituality in her approach to therapy as it developed. The self portion of the iceberg metaphor was described as how people felt not only about themselves but also their connection to life giving energy from a higher power. Though Satir did not have a specific religious background to her approach, she felt that helping clients to connect with a higher power was an essential part of healing. Satir would often use guided meditation in her experiential workshops to help people to tap into their inner resources and life force energy. The book *Meditations and Inspirations (1986)* has a collection of these meditations.

Foundational Concepts

Satir believed people were motivated by two main drives—safety and love—and that as children we tend to adopt coping mechanisms that help us to meet these two needs. However, as we age at time these coping behaviors become maladaptive and yet we have difficulty learning new ways of being. By helping clients to understand the motivations of their behavior from this perspective it can be very nonpathologizing and help family members (and therapists) gain empathy towards individuals that are presenting with coping behaviors that may be difficult to relate to. The Satir Model is growth oriented and related to helping people to become fully human. She describes this as: "people who understand, value and develop their bodies, finding them beautiful and useful. They are real and honest to and about themselves and other; they are loving and kind to themselves and others. People living humanly are willing to take risks, to be creative, to manifest competence, and to change when the situation calls for it. They find ways to accommodate what is new and different, keeping that part of the old that is still useful and discarding what is not. When you add all this up, you have physically healthy, mentally alert, feeling, loving, playful, authentic, creative productive responsible human beings," (Satir, 1988, p. 3).

Satir focused on the coping with a problem instead of the problem itself, believing that individuals could solve their own problems once they could be in touch with their genuine, authentic selves and tap into their own resources. She also believed that behaviors such as coping were not necessarily good and bad, but should be chosen instead of automatic and defensive. Problems arise when people have too few options in how to respond, not necessarily because of what they are doing. Satir believed in helping people to change through adding new options, not taking them away. She would encourage her clients to keep all aspect of themselves and add on new ways of responding. She related this process metaphorically to a fountain, if certain options or parts of the self are cut-off then it becomes like a fountain where spouts are shut off and it is out of balance. Then, some areas are clogged up, others dribbling, some shooting out at weird angles. When all pathways are open, and all options are available, the streams of water can flow freely and it creates a fountain as a whole—symmetrical and in balance. For example, a women who is wanting to be more assertive in her relationships might say "I used to be passive and now I want to take control. I don't like who I used to be." A Satir therapist would encourage her to keep passivity as a choice for when it might fit and embrace confidence as a new skill to use when that was appropriate—instead of never allowing herself to be passive again. In this way, the client can add options and make her fountain fuller, instead of just lopsided in a new direction.

Satir also felt it was important for people to have at least three options at any given time, this would bypass an either/or stance that can lead people to be stuck. This way—through adding new choices—people can change and move towards more congruence. The Satir Model is focused on guiding people to have new experiences, so that they can be free of the constraints and rules from their family of origin that may no longer fit them. In session, this is done through enacting new ways of being with the body, mind, and self. Overall, this method of conjoint family therapy includes paying attention to many aspects of family therapy that were common at the time, for example communication patterns, hierarchy, boundaries, and family rules. What makes the Satir approach unique is the focus on the wholeness of self within a system, and guiding the client to experience self-worth in the therapy room.

Coping Stances

When people are not congruent in their communication, they follow established patterns to cope with a particular situation. Satir identified four common ways of coping with stress, or surviving in environments when one cannot be him/herself, called coping or survival stances. Though people can use any of these stances and many people use all of them at different times, each person has a primary coping stance that is their default when stress arises. These stances are: placating, blaming, super reasonable, and irrelevant (Satir, 1988). Each of the four stances also has a body sculpt (posture)and phrase that illustrates it. The placating stance is when a person sacrifices him/herself to make peace. This person is focused on pleasing others, often at his/her own expense. The blaming stance is not taking responsibility and making everything someone else's fault. The super reasonable stance is focusing on details and facts, and not acknowledging emotions. Someone in the irrelevant stance will do and say anything to cause distraction and change the subject. This stance is cutoff from self, other, and the environment. Though congruence, instead of one of the coping stances, is usually a preferable communication choice none of the coping methods are inherently problematic as long as they are chosen consciously instead of as a default reaction. For example, someone may choose the placating response with a police officer after being pulled over for a speeding ticket as this may help to not escalate the interaction.

Primary Triad

The family of origin in the primary triad, which includes and individual and his or her parents. By highlighting the primary triad, Satir was giving emphasis to how our relationship with our parents continues to impact our future relationships and feelings of self-worth. Satir also discussed how the coping stances in the primary triad can have a lasting influence on an individual, as can the rules and expectations of the family of origin. Whether or not both of parents were involved in parenting, there is still an impact on a child from both because even in absence the parent influences the child.

Carl Whitaker (1912–1995)

| PHOTO 7.3 | Carl Whitaker |

Symbolic-experiential family therapy is an approach to therapy that Carl Whitaker (1912-1995) began to develop in the 1940s and continued to expand until his death in 1995. He worked at the same time other founders of family therapy independently began to study working with whole families. Whitaker's early model focused on working with families who had psychotic members in inpatient settings. However, as early as 1953, when Whitaker published his first book with Thomas Malone, *The Roots of Psychotherapy*, Whitaker shifted his epistemological view of psychiatry. He abandoned his analytic view that problems are caused by internal conflicts for a view that placed emphasis on external conflicts in relationships.

Two major experiences in Whitaker's early career influenced the development of his theory. First, he was trained as a child psychiatrist at the Bingham Child Guidance Clinic and Ormsby Village in Louisville, Kentucky. Second, he was involved in the treatment of posttraumatic stress disorder in Cold War scientists (Roberto, 1991). These experiences led him to develop a therapy in the "here and now," typical of play therapy and emotionally responsive to the needs of trauma

Video Call Out 7.1: Experiential Family Therapy

In the video Dr. Mulgrew is engaging the client playfully, using humor and wit. If you watch his eyes their playfulness is almost flirtatious. His use of eye contact communicates that he cares for the clients and their relationship on a personal level. This process puts energy and laughter back into the relationship. Here the playful process of therapy replaces the play that is missing for the relationship. In the discussion Dr. Mulgrew describes how play is freeing, allowing for spontaneous emotional expression of feelings.

survivors (Roberto, 1991). These two positions have become the trademarks that distinguish this theory from more psychodynamic or behavioral approaches.

Since in this approach the therapist becomes directly emotionally involved with the client, therapists using this model prefer to work in co-therapy teams. One member of the team is free to engage with the family directly and become a temporary part of the family. While this occurs, the other therapist takes more of an outsider role and is more emotionally disengaged from the family, which allows her or him to be an observer of the therapeutic process. The roles are switched several times during a session, modeling role flexibility for the family.

While Whitaker's theory predates the concept of postmodern or second-order epistemological approaches, it clearly can be classified as a second-order approach. The therapist's emotional participation is seen as the engine that drives the therapy. Without subjective involvement and emotional connection, there would be no inducement for the client to change. Students in this school of family therapy, like those studying Bowen's approach, are encouraged to undergo their own therapy. As Roberto (1991) argued, receiving therapy as part of training "has profound effects on personal maturation as well as on the ability to form effective alliances with the families that come to us in distress" (p. 446).

In fact, an emphasis on the self of the therapist is central to this approach. While this type of therapy is personal in nature, it is important to recognize that it is not about rescuing clients from their families or relationships. Therapists working from this perspective often caution against missionary zeal in saving clients, asserting that missionary is the favorite dish of cannibals (Whitaker & Bumberry, 1988). Thus, there is an emotional connection with one's client at the same time that there is a boundary. On the surface this seems paradoxical, but on an emotional level it is a healthy perspective. This process is similar to what occurs in good parenting. Good parents are clear that they care about their children while they empower them to make their own good choices and live their own lives.

During the first portion of his career, Whitaker avoided clearly articulating his theory of family therapy. In 1975, he published a widely read article titled "Psychotherapy of the Absurd," followed by "The Hindrance of Theory in Clinical Work" in 1976. In these articles he emphasized his view of the client–therapist relationship. He argued that paying too much attention to theory could prevent therapists from developing a relationship with their clients. We will discuss this issue in greater detail later in this chapter.

In Whitaker's later books, *Dancing With the Family* (Whitaker & Bumberry, 1988) and *Midnight Musings of a Family Therapist* (1989), he more clearly lays out his assumptions and techniques of his approach to therapy. First, he takes a radically family systemic view and recognizes the family as the basic level of mental functioning. Whitaker and Bumberry (1988) clearly assert, "There is no such thing as an individual" (p. 36). Here he argues that what we think of as individuals are simply a fragment of a family. In this belief, Whitaker differs from some of his contemporaries.

Whitaker also believed that families are resilient and stronger than they first appear. He observed over his long career that families are powerful systems with a complex web of emotional and practical roles. These roles are assigned to individuals as well as volunteered for by members of the families. In this theory, the family member who presents with the problem requiring treatment is a scapegoat. This person is the one that the family views as having the problem: mental illness, disease, disobedience, badness, or some other malady. This view gives the therapist the freedom to confront both the scapegoat and the family. Whitaker assumes it is the therapist's role to push a family to grow and expand emotionally. To be gentle and unchallenging to a family would be a disservice to that family.

Whitaker also assumes that the therapist does not effect growth or change in a family. In essence, you cannot give the family advice or even tell them what to do. Families grow only as a result of the process that they engage in with you, the person of the therapist. As Whitaker put it, "it's not the family *or* the therapist, but the family *and* the therapist that make up the vehicle to growth" (Whitaker & Bumberry, 1988, p. 38).

This view puts us, the therapists, on the same playing field as the client. Therapist and client are similar and connected by a mutual need for growth. This theoretical position takes the therapist out of the expert, guru, or even savior role. The expert role position is appealing to some, but it is

Video Call Out 7.2: Experiential Family Therapy

Dr. Mulgrew confronts the couple at several points. When he does this he smiles with very bright eyes and sometimes a chuckle. This meta communicates his empathy implying that they can do better. Here he is communicating on several levels. While he is critical of their behavior, his playfulness is supportive of the relationship. One could assume that when the couple confronts each other they are serious and anxious which creates distance. This can be described as leaning in and giving caring/constructive criticism, versus leaning away and being critical.

not helpful in the long run. Whitaker sees it as the therapist's responsibility to dispel clients' projection that the therapist can save them (Whitaker & Bumberry, 1988). This can be done simply by letting the family catch a glimpse of your humanity. Thus it is considered necessary for experiential therapists to be able to talk about themselves in the therapy session. While the self of the therapist is open for discussion, it is not the focus of the therapy. Self-disclosures serve to level the playing field and make the client a fellow human interested in growth.

Whitaker is one of the few theorists who talk about the therapist's emotional caring for the client. This is distinguished from caretaking for the client. In caretaking, you try to help clients solve their problem, situation, or even their life. It is between the extreme positions of rescuing the family and being a tough director to get them to rescue themselves that caring exists. As Whitaker and Bumberry (1988) put it, "excessive nurturing typically falls into the trap of 'helping' while exaggerated toughness often is sadistic" (p. 39). Caring is the result of solving the dichotomous dilemma of what level of involvement you should pursue with your clients.

Given this position, we see that our view of confrontation shifts. It is not from a higher position of knowledge or morality; it is part of nurturing. Whitaker and Bumberry (1988) assert, "You can only confront to the extent that you can nurture" (p. 39). Confronting others seems to increase our emotional awareness of how people are emotionally impacted by us. It can be done in a caring manner rather than in an angry or hostile manner. In our society, the need for confrontation is often suppressed for so long that when it is acted on, so much pent-up feeling is released that it turns into an angry attack on the person confronted.

As Whitaker pointed out, the process of therapy is metaphorically similar to the process of parenting (Whitaker & Bumberry, 1988). Your ability to support and encourage your children must be balanced against your ability to challenge, confront, and discipline them. Thus, being a good parent or therapist is a process, not a state of being; it is in striving to find balance that success is achieved (Whitaker & Bumberry, 1988).

Healthy People Marriages and Families

Both of these theorists had developed theories of what mental health looked like in persons marriages and families. Satir had more focus in the development of personality traits and defenses that inhibit healthy communication. Whitaker focused more on the development of healthy marriages and families.

The iceberg metaphor of personality is a central part of the Satir model. It starts at the surface in terms of what you can see clearly with behavior, at the waterline is coping (sometimes visible, other times not), and below the surface with increasing depth is: feelings, feelings about feelings, perceptions, expectations, yearnings, and self. Each aspect of the iceberg is an intervention point. This metaphor can help to guide a therapist with questions to lead clients towards transformation and greater congruence at different levels of their personality. This model helps structure therapy sessions and guide the therapist to where a client may be stuck and needing change. For example, a client may discuss feelings of anger towards an ex-boyfriend because of infidelity. The therapist could then guide the client to greater awareness at each level by asking the following questions: How do you feel about feeling angry? What beliefs and values do you hold related to infidelity? What expectations did you have toward your boyfriend related to commitment? What expectations do you think he had of you? What does your deepest self want in regards to romantic relationships? How do you feel about yourself (i.e., how is your self-esteem) when you reflect on this infidelity? Through this process, the therapist can help the client to be able to meet his/her own yearnings and feel good about him/herself not dependent on the relationship.

FIGURE 7.1   The Personal Iceberg Metaphor

John Banmen, "The Personal Iceberg Metaphor," from "The Satir Model: Yesterday and Today," Contemporary Family Therapy, vol. 34, no. 1, pp. 7-22. Copyright © 2002 by Human Sciences Press.

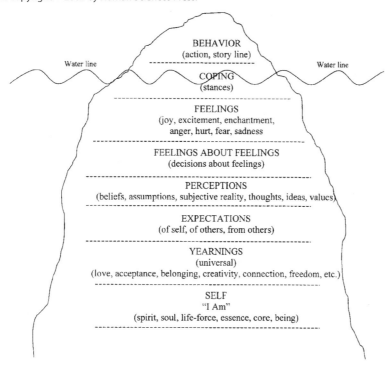

Whitaker (1977) describes healthy families as having traits that differentiate them from unhealthy families. From this perspective, rigidity over time would lead to maladaptation. Whitaker describes a healthy family as "one that maintains a high degree of freedom of inner unity and a high degree of individuation" (p. 4). This is not a contradiction, because a family needs to maintain its cohesion but at the same time allow members to connect within it and to become intimate with members outside of the family. This needs to occur without threatening the identity of the family.

Healthy families also display a high degree of role flexibility. This is expressed not only in times of high stress, but also in day-to-day interactions. For example, parents should be able to play with their children, and children can occasionally parent a parent. This occurred in my family one day while I was driving. I was playing with my 10-year-old, racing the engine and telling him I was going to drive at a ludicrous speed. My seven-year-old was not amused by this and warned me about the risk of receiving a ticket for speeding. Hearing the anxiety in his voice, I agreed and stopped racing the engine. Flexibility allows for spontaneity and creative response to situations.

Whitaker (1977) saw families as part of an extended family and friendship network. This anticipates the notion of a global village that is currently popular. Whitaker recognized that nuclear families do not have all of the resources necessary to function as autonomous units. Rather, they function best in a mutually supportive and dependent network. Whitaker was willing to call these supports directly into the therapy session. During his years of consultation, he would work with the family and their therapist. He would treat this unit as a single-patient system and seek to induce creativity and spontaneity in this system.

The Symbolic-Experiential View

Central to Whitaker's view of therapy (Whitaker & Bumberry, 1988) is the notion that humans use a small number of constructs to filter and organize emotional experiences. We use internal constructs to make sense of our external experiences. As Whitaker and Bumberry state, "it is the richness or poverty of these constructs that goes a long way in determining the subjective experience of living" (p. 75). For example, I have friends who are artists, and they have hundreds of ways to describe color and light. I have significantly fewer ways to talk about different colors and light. As a result, my artist friends have a deeper experience of color and light in their lives than I have.

Given this simple but profound fact, growth-oriented therapy is centered on increasing the richness of clients' internal constructs. Or, simply put, "the richer and more diverse this world, the more freedom and creativity we have" (Whitaker & Bumberry, 1988, p. 75). Thus, therapy is focused on increasing the richness of clients' lives. Since therapists have only indirect contact with their clients' inner life, it is important that they have a good sense of their own internal lives. They recognize that their clients can grow only if they themselves are in the process of growing.

Experiential therapists believe in universals of the human condition. However, these universals, while from a common evolutionary past, are not viewed as appropriate for "polite society." These include but are not limited to anger, rage, hurt, abandonment, jealously, and loneliness. We also share homicidal, suicidal, and primitive sexual impulses. Although society calls on us to keep these emotions in check or repressed, they have an effect on our day-to-day functioning.

One of the ways families cope with and control these primitive impulses in the context of a broader society is to express them in a symbolic manner. The symbols for these intrapsychic processes can be universal or unique to each family. All family members participate in this process. For example, a couple who had difficulty connecting on an emotional level were asked to bring their five-year-old son in for a session. The parents initially objected to bringing their son to the session, stating that he knew nothing of their issues with intimacy. When the son came in for a session, the therapist asked if his parents had talked to him about why they came for therapy. He said that they hadn't, but added that he thought he was there to talk about his parents getting a divorce. When asked why he thought that, he stated, "Mommy doesn't kiss Daddy like in the movies anymore." This phrase became a metaphor for the couple's issues with intimacy.

In this way, symbolic-experiential family therapy bridges the intrapsychic view of psychoanalysis and the relational view of systemic therapy. While psychoanalysis seeks to interpret the dark parts of humanity residing in a patient's unconscious, experiential therapy seeks to allow patients to connect with their family through the symbolic expression of these impulses and feelings. As Whitaker and Bumberry assert, "symbolic therapy, therefore, focuses on helping people become more comfortable in their impulse living, to be less frightened by it, and to integrate it more fully into their concrete living" (p. 79).

Thus life, death, and the abandonment caused by death get played out in the symbolic experiences of therapy. Much like young children often act out life-and-death issues in their play, symbolic-experiential therapy plays out life and death through the expression of symbols. As Whitaker and Bumberry (1988) state, "the idea that it's only by facing your own personal death that you're free to live is hauntingly accurate" (p. 80). Thus, helping people express their emotions about these "dark" issues helps free them to fully live.

In large part, our society deals with issues of life and death by depersonalizing them. When human tragedy strikes, rather than spending our efforts in grieving and caring for victims, we spend time assigning responsibility and blaming those whom we hold responsible. It is as if we as a society cannot deal with a negative outcome. While anger is part of the grieving process, we seem to often get stuck in it. For example, I know a family who became angry with the medical establishment for not yet finding a cure for their young son's diabetes. Once they had grieved the loss of his "normal" development, they became grateful for the degree of treatment available that allows their son to live a "modified" normal existence. Symbolic-experiential therapists help clients move past their anger and grieve the loses in their lives.

In a similar manner, issues of sanity and insanity are addressed symbolically in this approach. It is common for clients to become fearful that they will become insane and lose all touch with reality. To insulate themselves from this fear, they often develop symbolic ways to express their concerns about their mental health. Therapists using a symbolic-experiential approach normalize clients' concerns about losing their mental health. They might do this by describing how they themselves might go crazy or even describing an incident where they went crazy. For example, I saw a colleague describe to a client how she went crazy one time. She had just been knocked off her bike by a careless motorist. When the motorist got out of the car, she was more concerned about her car than she was about whether the biker was okay. This triggered a rage response in the therapist, who "cussed out the driver." After the therapist shared her story, the client saw her as less than perfect herself and as a result became more open with her. The client described how she also lost her mind with her partner and how they got into physical fights.

Thus, this approach builds on the idea that mental illness is a continuum. However, it also embraces the notion that on occasion we cross the boundary into insanity. This crossing over and back is part of the process of living and growing. By being in touch with their own process, therapists can support others in their struggles with these issues. Their empathy can be a perch from which the therapist can call clients back to sanity when the client crosses over.

Again, the therapist is required to lead by example. To encourage people to enter their symbolic world, therapists must be able to enter it themselves. This can be done in a variety of ways. They can talk about their human frailty, insecurities, fears, and anxieties. As the therapist becomes less than perfect, the client is more likely to become vulnerable. With vulnerability comes openness to change.

Therapists can also enter clients' symbolic world by offering a metaphor to describe their experience of the clients. For example, I once accused a husband who had ruined his family's finances and lost their home of trying to provoke his wife into killing him. I further accused him of having suicidal impulses that he was trying to get his wife to act on by proxy. Later in the session, he recalled how his parents would fight violently. He further recalled how, during a particularly violent argument, his father coughed up blood at the dinner table, collapsed, and later died. This opened therapy to a new deeper level. This client was able to admit that he sometimes had suicidal impulses and that he had the rough outlines of a plan.

When entering the symbolic world of a client, it is important not to explain your symbols. If you do that, it will take the client out of the symbolic world into the literal world. The therapist must simply wait to see if the client will respond with his or her own metaphor. At this point, a common mistake is to discuss which metaphor is correct. That will also push the client into the literal world. The best response is to simply respond with a new metaphor based on a synthesis of the two—to which the client will most likely have an emotional response, offer a countermetaphor, or both. With each of these responses, you are entering the client's symbolic emotional world.

Goals in Satir Transformational Systemic Therapy

Satir was person-centered and adapted her work to meet the needs of the individual and family she was working with, and there were metagoals for therapy that were always worked towards no matter the client's individual goals. Satir's metagoals for therapy are: congruence, self-esteem, choice making, and responsibility. Overall, the approach is growth oriented, seeking to help clients to feel worthy and energized, as opposed to curing pathology.

Though all four metagoals are important, congruence is at the core of the Satir model. When individuals are able to be more of their authentic selves, they are less defensive and more receptive to others therefore leading to more healthy relationships as well. As this process unfolds, it leads to a transformation of family rules that prevent people from living according to their true nature. According to this model, congruence is what allows people to connect to their own life force energy and therefore feel energized and fulfilled in their lives and relationships.

Congruence is when what is inside matches with what is outside—one's feelings are able to be expressed in a straightforward way. Satir said that congruence is about saying your true yeses and true nos—when you say yes, you mean yes and when you say no, you mean no. It is also important for congruent communication that the message that is being sent verbally is in tune with nonverbal cues. In a more general sense, congruence also includes being aware and accepting of self, other, and context, so that you can respond instead of react to a situation. Incongruent communication can be especially difficult for children who may become confused about how to understand the messages being sent by their family members. Helping families to support freedom of expression is an important aspect of this model.

Satir also focused on improving client's self-esteem, choice making, and responsibility. Self-esteem is how people feel about themselves and is central to our relationships with others. Satir explains: "Self-esteem is the ability to value one's self and to treat oneself with dignity, love, and reality…I am convinced that the crucial factor in what happens both inside people and between people is one's self-worth…" (Satir, 1988, p. 22). When self-esteem is high, individuals feel worthy and valued, and can be more Congruent in their lives because they do not feel they need to hide who they are in order to receive love. Choice making is important for people to feel they have agency in their own lives and can authentically choose what is best for them. This shifts people from doing what others want to doing what is in line with their own true desires. Personal responsibility relates to people taking accountability for their behaviors, instead of blaming others or feeling like a victim.

Whitaker's Symbolic Experiential Therapy

A key innovation of this theory, like that of other early theories, is a shift in the perceived locus of the problem. In this view, emotional difficulties are seen not as an intrapsychic problem but an interpersonal problem. That is, people do not suffer as the result of a psychological dysfunction; rather, human suffering is the result of disturbed interpersonal relationships. It is assumed that the disturbance most often occurs in the family, since family relationships tend to be the most emotionally significant relationships. It is also in your family that you are socialized. This led Whitaker to work with multiple generations of families.

As the locus of the problem shifted, so did the goal of therapy. Rather than repairing a person's intrapsychic conflict, thereby relieving the person's symptoms, the symbolic- experiential approach seeks to provide a forum for clients to resolve ongoing interpersonal conflicts. You could say that this approach helped shift psychotherapy "out of your head and into your heart." The goal of therapy from this perspective is to promote personal growth. Growth is seen as the natural product of emotional connection.

While this theory predates the theoretical discussion of second-order cybernetics, it clearly embraces its tenets. Rather than seeking to develop an objective model of therapy, the symbolic-experiential approach is driven by the subjective experience of the therapist. From this perspective, the therapist joins with the family as a temporary member. By embracing the family's biases through openly discussing them with the client, the therapist enters the client's system. Once inside the client's family, the therapist is able to provoke change. From here, the therapist then disengages from the family. A postmodern epistemological perspective can be developed from this line of thinking.

Given its emphasis on the therapist–client family relationship, this approach also helped develop an emphasis on the self of the therapist. The call for the therapist to be emotionally healthy and stable is implicit in this theory. Likewise, emphasizing a stable and secure co-therapist relationship helps keep focus on the self of the therapist. This helped the field move away from viewing the therapist as an objective, nonemotional, disconnected provoker of change to a view that is more collaborative.

The process of subjectively connecting with the family and disconnecting is repeated time and time again. Since the therapist joins the family and seeks to have a subjective connection, a co-therapist is often employed. The co-therapy team's mandate is to have a greater allegiance to each other than to the family. This emphasis on the co-therapy team's connection not only models for the parents successful collaboration and co-parenting, but also allows the therapist a way out of the system at the end of the session and at the end of treatment. This also prevents the therapist from having fantasies of rescuing the family.

Questioning

Process of Therapy

Similar to other humanistic therapists, Satir believed that safety is what allows people to grow. She used touch, genuine contact, acceptance, and other clinical techniques to create a safe environment for clients as the initial stage of therapy. The experiential nature of her work focused on asking people to sculpt, inhabit, feel, and behave in new, more congruent, ways in the therapy room. This experiential model focuses on change in the present moment. One way a Satir therapist would do this is through guiding clients into the experience of their own bodies. This body focus could lead a client into a deeper experience in the moment, and create an opening for transformation.

The steps in a session of therapy following the Satir model are: preparing self, making contact, listening to the problem, setting positive direction goals, committing to change, working towards change, anchoring change, and giving homework to practice change (see Banmen, 2002 for additional details). Satir therapists initially center themselves and connect with their own resources before meeting with clients so they can be fully present. This is always the first step in the therapy process. Then the therapist connects with all of the clients in the room, this is the step of building rapport or making contact. Next, the therapist would ask the clients to speak about what has brought them to therapy and what they would like to work on. In the Satir model, this story about the problem is only discussed briefly to allow more focus on the change process. Then the therapist would help clients to set goals for the whole person and ask the client "Are you ready to commit to working on that goal?" (Banmen, 2002, p. 20). In the Satir approach instead of assuming a commitment to change, it is specifically addressed with the client. The major task of therapy is then working towards that goal, and the higher order meta-goals as discussed previously. To anchor change in session, the therapist may guide a client through a body awareness activity or a visualization of imagining how being different may impact a variety of aspects of his/her life. Finally, the therapist and the clients will work together to plan homework to practice the change that has occurred in their lives throughout the week until the next session. Overall, this process helps clients to connect with their own inner resources to make life affirming changes—leading them to greater freedom of expression and congruence.

From the symbolic-experiential perspective, the therapeutic interview is a conversation that is always emerging. Therapists seek to have the interview driven by their unconscious mind. Here they endeavor to develop a genuine connection with all of the family members. By being in touch with a shared sense of your client's humanity, you can allow your unconscious mind to guide therapy. Therefore, therapy is not based on a theoretical line of questioning.

From this perspective, questions serve to help the therapist establish a genuine relationship with the patient. The therapist asks questions to learn personal information about clients, not to provide clients insight into their process. Insight is not seen as essential to mental health; rather, openness and spontaneity are considered vital. Since the questions are not meant to provide insight, it is not appropriate to ask questions you think you already know the answer to. Observations are simply shared as statements, to which the client can respond. For example, rather than asking an adolescent client, "Do you feel like sometimes your father babies you?" you might simply make the observation that "it seems like your father babies you." This is more likely to provoke an emotional experience and motivate the client to speak with his father about this issue.

Since therapy is driven by the therapist's unconscious process, therapists operate under the assumption that their thoughts, feelings, and fantasies that come up in session belong to the client. Given this assumption, the therapist should be able and willing to make associations freely during the session. If the therapist thinks of a line from a book or even a movie, he or she shares it. Here again, the assumption is that the therapist's unconscious mind brought it to consciousness for a reason. Talking about it with the client makes it more likely that the therapist's unconscious mind will have an emotional response. Thus, rather than thinking about what they are going to say, symbolic-experiential therapists say what they are thinking or feeling. They might even go to the extreme of falling asleep during a session and waking up to share their dream.

Since a genuine relationship between client and therapist is the goal, there is more room for personal disclosure from the therapist. Again, shared connection and being real is the goal of disclosure. While some disclosures place the therapy at risk of blurred boundaries, the function of the co-therapist alliance is to help bring the focus of therapy back should it stray too far toward the therapist. The client's response will also keep the therapist focused on the client rather than on the therapist's issues. In addition, ongoing peer supervision will help keep the boundaries clear.

Structuring

Role of the Therapist

The self of the therapist is central to Satir's work, as it is in experiential therapy in general. The therapist is a model for congruence and needs to be able to demonstrate this in session. Thus, this form of therapy could look very different depending on who is enacting the therapy since being true to who the therapist is as an individual is essential.

In terms of the structure of the course of therapy, symbolic-experiential therapists are flexible. They are willing to meet every week for longer than one hour. Therapy should be long enough to build sufficient emotional intensity to produce the desired change. The longer sessions are appropriate also because multiple generations are often included in the interviews.

Theoretically, the course of therapy is divided into four distinct stages or segments: battle for structure, battle for initiative, therapeutic alliance, and termination (Whitaker & Bumberry, 1988). Each of these stages involves critical issues and substages to be negotiated. To understand the process of symbolic-experiential therapy, we will look at each stage in detail below.

Responding

Since this is a second-order epistemological approach and the perspective of the therapist is considered essential in the therapeutic process, responses to clients are based on being open and honest. Therapists are granted permission to speak honestly and openly as ideas and feelings come to them. A symbolic-experiential therapist might cry with a client who is grieving a loss or express anger at a client who is being manipulative. Being emotionally available to your clients allows you to serve as a role model for the family in letting them see a range of emotional response.

This position makes this approach somewhat controversial. A critic might argue that it can become hard to distinguish therapist from client. However, two factors help guard against the therapist's simply becoming another client and not challenging clients to address their issues. First, this approach is often conducted by a co-therapy team. As one therapist enters into a deeply emotional interaction with the family, the second therapist remains more detached and distant. This allows the second therapist to pull the first therapist out of the interaction if the therapist loses his or her connection with the therapy team. Second, there is an implicit mandate that symbolic-experiential therapists have worked on or are currently working on their own issues in therapy. If they are secure in their emotional well-being and have their emotional needs met in their personal relationships, symbolic-experiential therapists are less likely to blur the professional boundaries.

Part of the therapeutic response comes from the co-therapist team's responding to each other in front of the family. When needed, they will have a conversation to address issues in the treatment team. This not only makes the treatment team a self-corrective, higher-order system, but it allows the team to model healthy executive functioning. For example, in a couples session one co-therapist might talk about feeling abandonment by her co-therapist when he overly focuses on the wife's feeling of abandonment by her husband. In this way, the treatment team becomes isomorphic with the family system. Isomorphism is the tendency for similar patterns of interaction to occur at different levels of connected systems.

As you recall, central to this approach is the belief that mental illness is on a continuum and that we all have periods of insanity, rage, anger, hurt, and fearfulness. From this perspective, if you, the therapist, recall one of these moments of your insecurity, it would be appropriate to share your struggle. The assumption is that clients are entitled to your emotional response during a session and therefore that you should share it with them. This might take the form of a story about yourself. Likewise, you might share a story about another client who worked on a similar issue, if you recall that client while meeting with your current client.

Another way to respond to your client's concern about an issue is to extend the symptom. For example, if a client states that he is afraid he is losing his mind, you could ask him to describe what that would look like. Does that mean he will start hearing voices? Does that mean he will not recognize loved ones? Does that mean he will be pushing a shopping cart down the street yelling at everyone? Probing for details can prompt clients to enter the metaphoric world and deal with their fears metaphorically.

Applications

Sculpting

Unlike Whitaker, who avoided describing techniques, Satir developed several techniques for working with her clients and their families. Sculpting is one of the most popular techniques of Satir. It involves moving the body in a variety of postures—self-directed or by the therapist—to help one to embody a variety of emotions and situations in the present. Sculpting is done in relationship to coping stances and family reconstruction, or may be a separate intervention done spontaneously in session. In family sculpting the therapist may ask each member of the family to move others around to highlight different perspectives about a particular issue. For example, if parents are in conflict about how to address a teenager's alcohol use, the therapist may ask the teenager to place both parents in the room in positions and a body posture of what they look like when they argue. Then, each parent would do the same and the various sculptures would be inhabited and discussed. Additionally, the therapist may ask the family to sculpt how they would each like the family to be interacting or what the dynamics are as positive, more healthy relationships are being formed in the family as therapy unfolds.

Each of the four coping stance also has a body sculpt that accompanies it. The sculpt for placating is down on one knee with the right arm over the chest and the left arm up in the air. The phrase associated with this stance is "I'll do anything if only you'll love me." In blaming The body posture is standing with the left foot in front of the right, the left hand on the hip, and the right arm pointing straight ahead. The phrase associated with this stance is "It's all your fault." For super rational this stance is standing straight up almost on your toes with arms crossed in front of your body looking down your nose. The phrase associated with this stance is "Just the facts." The irrelevant stance is always moving, in constant motion. Congruence is not a coping stance, but is a form of communication that also has a body sculpt associated with it. The congruent posture is standing straight and relaxed, shoulders firm but not straining, with arms bent and palms up in the air, and making eye contact with the person across from you.

A Satir therapist may use these stances to help sculpt individuals in session who are using a coping mechanism without awareness. This can be especially helpful in couple and family sessions to see how family members see each other and to bring awareness into patterns of interaction. For example, if two members of a couple are constantly arguing and blaming each other for their problems, the therapist may have them stand facing each other in the blaming posture. This intervention would serve to bring awareness to a pattern of incongruent of communication in the relationship and therefore help people to break this pattern of interaction. This could help to shift the communication from one of incongruence to congruence.

Family Reconstruction

Another intervention used by Satir was family reconstruction. This was done through an individual having multiple people reenact his/her family patterns. This method of sculpting was often used with large groups in Satir workshops. This allowed individuals to gain awareness into past family patterns and then transform outdated patterns and rules from their family of origin that may be negatively impacting them in the present.

Acting as a Symbolic-Experiential Family Therapist

Symbolic Experiential therapy's main technique is the therapist's use of self in the therapeutic relationship. This produced a cybernetic of cybernetic system of therapy. When a co-therapist was utilized Whitaker would talk with the co-therapist in from of the family. In these situations this was utilized to provoke an emotional response in the family. Symbolic-experiential therapy has direct applications in marital therapy. From this perspective, marriage is an attempt by each family to reproduce itself. This view sets up an inherent power struggle. In a couple interview, all aspects of their life are explored, including issues of intimacy and sexuality. The purpose here is not to downplay tensions but to focus on the family of origin. As Roberto (1991) has stated, "the underlying message to spouses is that the marriage is a crucial vehicle for self-expression and differentiation from one's family, and that its future welfare cannot be taken for granted or discarded lightly" (p. 469). If there are children present in the family, they are brought in to help make boundaries between the couple and the children.

As stated above, symbolic-experiential therapy has been conceptualized as occurring in four overlapping phases: battle for structure, battle for initiative, therapeutic alliance, and termination (Whitaker & Bumberry, 1988).

The battle for structure starts during the first contact with the therapist, usually through a phone call. In this phase, therapists set minimum standards for what they will accept as necessary for therapy to be successful. In most situations, symbolic-experiential therapists see only the entire family residing in the home; this can involve at least two but often three and even four generations.

This position is not a technique or power play. Rather, it gives the therapist clarity on what will be required for therapy to be successful (Whitaker & Bumberry, 1988).

| FIGURE 7.2 | Whitaker Stages of Therapy |

Since the emphasis is on whole families and since Whitaker denies the existence of individuals, the whole family is required for therapy to begin. If less than the whole family shows up, the therapist cancels the session and sets a new date when the family is sure all members will be present. This position makes sense when you consider that in systems theory, the whole is greater than the sum of its parts. It also helps define the problem as an issue for the whole family. Since all members are present in session, it becomes more difficult for family members to undermine change between sessions.

Attention in this stage of therapy is focused on the process of joining. Here again, the second-order perspective of this model comes through. Joining is the mutual process of getting to know each other. Clients need to feel that the therapist is able to understand them and is able to consider their needs. Whitaker takes a unique position in the field on burnout, stating that "giving up or compromising your own beliefs, standards, and needs leads only to therapist burnout" (Whitaker & Bumberry, 1988, p. 57).

During joining, therapists takes a meta position. Here they seek to join the oldest generation and take a position where clients have greater expectations of them than they have of their clients. Part of this stage also involves getting the least emotionally involved person to describe the family. Whitaker (Whitaker & Bumberry, 1988) is clear that his bias is that it is usually the father who is most disconnected. However, this is not always the case, and in some instances the father is not available because of death or emotional cutoff.

The symbolic-experiential therapist seeks to expand the symptom during this stage of therapy. Families come in with a specific problem that is usually centered around one person. By expanding the problem to include all family members, the family's perspective shifts. Members are eased into an interpersonal perspective of the presenting problem. No longer can they hold one individual responsible or worthy of blame.

This stage is concluded as the family and therapist start to engage in a battle for initiative. Here the family must take responsibility for and ownership of their own change. They are often eager for the therapist to fix them or at least provide the correct solutions. It is easy at this point for the therapist to try to save the family. This stage often produces a good deal of tension and anxiety in the family, marked by pauses and awkward silences. This places the therapist on the sidelines in a coach-type role as the family becomes the player in its own therapy.

As the family takes initiative, the therapist forms a therapeutic alliance with the entire family, not just the scapegoat or the hero. By connecting with the family, the therapist becomes personal and creative. The family no longer needs the security of the presenting problem as it risks new behaviors. It is here that the therapist also becomes more spontaneous, provoking a like response from the family.

As family members continue to be flexible and take more responsibility for their lives, the therapy moves to the termination phase. They start to see the therapist as more of a person and often start to ask her or him personal questions. There is often a sense of loss and sadness over the ending of therapy. As part of saying good-bye, the therapist allows opportunity for the family to return in the future for a wellness visit.

Case Example: The Case of Mike's Oppositional-Defiant Behavior

Intake

You receive a phone call from Mrs. Green requesting therapy for her 16-year-old son, Mike. She states that her family physician has referred you to them and that you should be able to help her son. She immediately tells you that he is "out of control." He doesn't come home from school until late at night. In addition, he and his father have hostile and angry arguments resulting in her becoming fearful. When you ask what she is afraid of, she states that she is "afraid that her son and husband might get into a fistfight."

You tell her that you and your colleague, Dr. Rodriquez, would be willing to see her, her son, and her husband Wednesday at 3 p.m. Mrs. Green states that she thought she could just bring her son Mike in for therapy. You apologize that her doctor did not explain that you work with the entire family on these issues. You then ask her if Mike has any siblings, because you would like to see them also. She states that he has a 19-year-old half sister Amanda, who attends a local community college and is doing well. She asks, "Is it necessary to bring in the entire family?" You tell her that in your mind the entire family is affected by this problem and that in your experience, unless the whole family comes in, situations like this have little hope of success. You further state that it is your preference to take on cases you feel you can be successful with. You invite her to talk with her husband and call you back after she has arranged to bring her whole family. You also tell her that if her husband has any questions, you would be willing to talk to him on the phone, but you are not interested in starting therapy without everyone in the family present.

The next day Mr. Green calls you to talk about seeing his son. You restate your preference for seeing the whole family. As he questions you, you state that you see these sorts of situations as family problems and that you feel the presence of the whole family is necessary for you to help them. He reluctantly agrees to set an appointment, and you discuss such logistics issues as the location of the session, fees, and the cancellation policy. You end the call by reiterating that it is imperative that the whole family come for the session.

Session One

Mrs. Green calls 20 minutes prior to the session stating that her son is refusing to come. You inform her that you will be available for the entire session but that, consistent with your cancellation policy, you will have to charge them for the session. However, you suggest that she and her husband do whatever it takes to get Mike to the session. Mr. Green then takes the line, and you restate your suggestion that they do what it takes to get their son to the session.

The family arrives one hour into the scheduled 90-minute session. You warmly welcome the family and introduce yourself and your colleague, Dr. Rodriquez. You notice that Mike, the identified patient, looks disheveled and that he has an angry scowl on his face. His older sister Amanda looks as if she has been crying and also seems to be suppressing some anger. Mrs. Green has a determined look and is hovering close to her son. Mr. Green also looks disheveled. He is dressed in a professional manner, but his shirt is partly untucked and he seems somewhat out of breath. He looks considerably older than his wife.

Mike immediately starts to assert that he is angry at his father for trying to bring him to the session against his will. As he starts to complain, Dr. Rodriquez interrupts and asserts that he would like to start with Mike's father. He simply states that he likes to hear from the parents first, and that since Mr. Green looks most involved in what is going on, he would like to hear from him first. You agree with Dr. Rodriquez and simply tell Mike that you would love to hear from him after his parents speak, and that if there isn't time to check in with him during this session you might be willing to let him start next session.

Mr. Green begins by talking about how he had to chase his son around the house to get him to come to the session. As he describes his failed attempts, you interrupt him and ask him to focus on what worked. Mr. Green then describes how he tackled his son in the living room and held him down. Mike becomes defensive and states that he could have taken his father if he wanted. You respond to Mike by stating, "Yes, of course; then you must have wanted to be captured by your father. Part of you must have wanted to come with your family."

At the end of this exchange, Amanda becomes tearful and complains that it is always about Mike and never about her. As she speaks, Dr. Rodriquez asks, "How would you like it to be about you? Would you like your father to wrestle you down?" She responds dismissively that he is not her father. Dr. Rodriquez says, "Then perhaps it's your mother that you want to wrestle you down." Amanda goes on to describe how she is unable to get attention from her parents, especially her stepfather. You ask Amanda where her father is. Her mother starts to respond, but Dr. Rodriquez stops her by stating, "Amanda was asked that question." Amanda looks down at the floor and states that she has never seen him in her life and doesn't know where he is. You ask her how she feels about this. She quickly states that she feels nothing toward him, but you notice that she is looking at the ground and speaking in a lower voice.

At this point, Dr. Rodriquez notes that time for this session has expired, and he turns to the parents and invites them to bring the entire family back the same time next week. At this point, Mike responds that this session was a waste of time and that the two doctors don't know what they're doing. Both you and Dr. Rodriquez laugh and say to Mike, "Nice try." Mrs. Green laughs at how you and Dr. Rodriquez say this at the exact same time. You tell her that after years of working together, you are like an old married couple. This makes Mr. Green laugh, and he states he would be glad to come back at the same time next week. As you get up and shake both his and his wife's hands, you reassure him that he will probably have a better time getting his family in next time. Dr. Rodriquez reinforces your statement, stating that the important thing is that Mr. Green now knows how to get his family in. As the children each shake your hand, they are unable to make eye contact, and Mike is looking at the floor.

Session Two

The family arrives for the session five minutes prior to the scheduled start time. Both Mike and Amanda seem angry and are unable to make eye contact with each other. Mrs. Green is talkative and seems nervous. Both you and Dr. Rodriquez welcome the family and ask how you can help them. Mr. Green quickly turns his attention to his son Mike and describes his difficulties.

He reports that Mike was diagnosed at age 13 with oppositional-defiant disorder. He states that Mike has been unable to follow simple directions and that he seeks negative attention from authority. You explore in detail what Mr. Green means by this. He describes how Mike has had problems with authority at school and with his mother. It is not until recently that he has had problems with his father and other men.

Dr. Rodriquez asks Mike if any of his teachers growing up were men. Mike reports that all of his teachers in elementary school were women. Dr. Rodriquez asks Mike when he became sexist. Mike gets angry and responds that he is not sexist. You add that he is making progress in overcoming his sexism by not listening to men also.

Mrs. Green laughs and then smiles as she thinks about this assertion. Noticing her response, you ask her to talk about what is going on for her. She states that while on the surface this idea seems funny to her, in part it seems to be true. Dr. Rodriquez pushes her further, asking her if dealing with sexist men is an issue she has struggled with in her life. She tells of how her father would not support her going to college when she graduated from school, despite the fact that he supported her brother in going to college. She states that she resented this because she was a much better student than her brother. You ask her if she has ever confronted her father on these issues.

Before she can answer, Mr. Green interrupts nervously and states that you do not know her father. He is not the kind of man you can talk to about these types of issues. You ask Mrs. Green if her husband always rescues her from her father. Before she answers, Mike angrily states that this session is nonsense. Dr. Rodriquez says to Mike, "I think you would enjoy having the attention placed on someone else for a change." In response to this, Mike gets quiet, and his mother hides her face and starts to cry quietly.

After a little while, Mrs. Green softly begins to describe how Mr. Green rescued her from her father and single motherhood by marrying her. She had been angry at her father, who would not allow her to fulfill her dream of going to college, and when she was 18 she got pregnant with a boy she had just met. She believed that he would provide a means for her to escape her childhood home, but when she told him she was pregnant, he disappeared. He has never made contact with her or her daughter since. Being an unwed mother forced her to continue to live with her parents and take a low-paying job to make ends meet. She met Mr. Green at her work when she was 20, and they started to date.

You ask her how her parents accepted Mr. Green when he started to come around. Mr. Green interrupts and states that he and her mother got along well, but he and her father did not get along. He goes on to explain that because he was nine years older than his wife, his future father-in-law did not like him. You ask how they get along now, and he states that over the years they have developed a good relationship. Dr. Rodriquez asks Mr. Green how Mike's grandfather feels about his behavior. Mr. Green states that they have not talked with Mike's grandparents about their problems with Mike. Turning to Mrs. Green, you ask her why she has not talked to her father about these issues. She becomes tearful and states that she does not want to upset him. She goes on to explain that three years ago she lost her mother and that since then her father has been withdrawn and depressed. Dr. Rodriquez interjects with, "Let me guess: your dad gets angry as part of his depression."

Surprised, Mrs. Green asks Dr. Rodriquez how he knows that her father gets angry when he is depressed. Dr. Rodriquez states that this is just how he feels in his mind. He goes on to ask Mike if he was close to his grandmother. Mrs. Green starts to answer, and you interrupt by stating you would like to hear from Mike himself. Mike starts to get tearful as everyone in the room looks at him. Rather than expressing his emotions, Mike becomes angry and states that therapy is a stupid waste of time. Before you can confront his anger, Mr. Green states that this has struck a nerve and perhaps Mike's anger has to do with the loss of his grandmother. You and Dr. Rodriquez agree, and you further state that Mike is not at all unlike his grandfather.

As Mrs. Green comforts Mike, you and Dr. Rodriquez provide space for the family to grieve by simply being quiet. After a few minutes, Amanda, who has been fighting back tears, starts to cry and talk about how much she misses her grandmother. As she is given space, she starts to become somewhat angry at her brother. She accuses him of being selfish by calling the family's attention to himself. Dr. Rodriquez asks her how she sees her brother as selfish, and she states that because of her brother's problems she feels like she must hide her feelings and grief. You lovingly scold her and state that it is never a good idea to hide feelings. Dr. Rodriquez nods his head in agreement and states that it is hiding feelings that makes many families sick.

Dr. Rodriquez notices that time has almost expired, so he states that this is a good place to stop. Mr. Green asks, "But what do we do about Mike and his problems?" Dr. Rodriquez replies, "I don't know. Why are you asking me? However, after this session I'm going to try to remember to keep expressing my feelings." You state, "This session has reminded me of how important grief is, and I'm going to keep grieving losses in my life." Mrs. Green asks you, "When will you stop grieving?" You answer, "You never get over a loss; you just get more effective at grieving." You end the session here and set a follow-up in one week.

Session Three

The family arrives at the session on time and in good spirits. You notice the change in the appearance of the family members, and you comment that everyone looks as if they are in a good place. Turning to Mr. Green, you ask him what is different. Mr. Green responds that he is not sure, but he has noticed a difference in his children's relationship toward each other. He goes on to describe how they have spent some time together since the last session. He notes that they seem to bother each other less. In fact, they went to a movie together last weekend, and both seemed to have a good time. Both Mike and Amanda go on to talk about what a good time they had at the movie and describe how they enjoyed hanging out together.

Mrs. Green interjects that she is concerned that her daughter is spending too much time away from her studies. She says, "I'm glad their relationship is improving, but I'm afraid her grades will suffer." Dr. Rodriquez asks Amanda if she minds being perfect. She becomes defensive and responds that she is not perfect. You respond by saying you know that, but you're worried that her parents expect perfection. Amanda agrees, looking at her brother, and then asks, "Are you implying that if I'm perfect, that means he has to be a problem?" You agree and ask, "Does Mike ever get to be perfect and you get to be bad, or even just less than perfect?" She says no and seems very sad at this idea, and you notice that Mike is smiling.

Mrs. Green becomes defensive and states, "It's not that we don't care for Mike, but he has always had a hard time following directions." You reassure her that you are not accusing her of not caring for Mike. You state that you know that they not only care for their children, but that they love them very much. You ask her and Mr. Green, "What would you two do with all of your time if your children were fully competent?" Mr. Green asks, "What do you mean, fully competent?" You answer, "Someone is fully competent when they no longer require someone to worry about them." Dr. Rodriquez interjects, "Someone is fully competent when they are given the privilege of suffering for their own mistakes."

Mr. Green states that he cannot imagine that happening and that he will always care for his children. Dr. Rodriquez pushes on him that this is not a good outcome for parents. "You will always care about them, but you want them to care for themselves." You add, "You also want them to be able to care for the grandbabies when that time comes." Mr. Green contemplates your statement, then goes on to say that he never thought of it like that. You encourage him to think of parenting as a job you try to retire from. It is important to expect and work toward getting your children to take care of themselves as soon as possible.

At this point, you become aware of the sadness on Mrs. Green's face. Dr. Rodriquez asks her what is going on with her at this time. As she holds back tears, she talks about her fear that her children will grow up and go away. She talks about her fear of abandonment, and you become aware of the return of grief about the loss of her mother. You sit quietly for a few minutes as Mr. Green starts to talk. You interrupt him by asking him to simply put his hand in his wife's and support her while she grieves. At this point, Amanda becomes tearful and hugs her mother.

Mike, who is sitting alone in a chair, looks awkward and disconnected from the rest of the family, who are embracing on the couch. Dr. Rodriquez calls attention to this by addressing Mike directly: "I notice you are again odd man out, the fourth person looking for a seat on the three-man couch." For an instant, Mike looking as if he is getting mad, but then he softens and becomes sad and somewhat tearful. Fighting back tears, he responds, "Yeah, that's the story of my life; sometimes I feel like they would get along better without me." His sister joins him in his chair, and both his parents reach out and place their hand on him. In response to this, his tears flow more freely. Both you and Dr. Rodriquez allow the family some space by being silent for a couple of minutes.

As the family starts to dry tears and regain composure, you comment that you're glad Amanda joined Mike on his chair. You praise her for trying to be Mike's peer rather than his third parent. Embarrassed, Amanda talks about how sometimes she feels responsible for him and how she tries to take care of him. Dr. Rodriquez asks if she takes care of him out of concern for him or out of concern for her mother. You ask Dr. Rodriquez, "What difference does it make?" Dr. Rodriquez states that siblings should take care of each other to take care of each other. This helps them be ready for the time when they will become orphans.

Mr. and Mrs. Green exclaim in harmony, "Orphans!" Mr. Green adds, "Are you trying to kill us off?" Dr. Rodriquez responds, "But all parents would rather die themselves than bury one of their children, so in effect all parents want their children to become orphans someday. Not someday soon, but someday." You add, "The problem is that few parents help prepare their children for the day that will inevitably come."

Dr. Rodriquez then restates and slightly rephrases your prior question to the parents: "What will the parents in this family do when your children are competent?" Mr. Green notes that the question has changed, and Dr. Rodriquez accepts this but goes on to point out that the question has not been answered. Mr. Green shares that he is afraid his wife would lose interest in him and divorce him. Mrs. Green looks hurt by her husband's response and states that that is not true. You interrupt her and state that her husband was sharing his feelings, not making a prediction. You go on to explain that feelings have a logic of their own. They are not right or wrong; they just exist. In fact, if you argue with an emotion, it doesn't necessarily change but will often go underground and come out as a different feeling. Mrs. Green nods in understanding and then asks, "What can I do?"

You smile at her and nod as you explain, "The best thing to do when someone else talks about their feelings is to talk about your feelings." Dr. Rodriquez agrees and explains that Mr. Green was talking about his abandonment. Mrs. Green is surprised to hear about her husband's abandonment and starts to talk to Dr. Rodriquez. He directs her to talk to her husband, and they spend a few minutes trying to talk to each other about their feelings. In response to her husband's feelings of abandonment over the children, Mrs. Green expresses feelings of abandonment over her husband's career. At this point, Mr. Green becomes defensive and starts to argue with his wife.

You stop him and state that he is in the position his wife was in when he started to talk about his feelings. He sighs and agrees with you. He spends a few minutes listening to his wife talk about her abandonment over his long hours at work. At this point, he becomes angry and talks about how he started to work long hours so his family would have the things they needed to be happy. His wife responds in anger that they needed him present, not things to be happier. At this point, you notice that both Mike and Amanda start to become anxious and lean in toward their parents. Dr. Rodriquez also notices this and cautions the children to stay out. He tells them that their dog does not belong in this fight. Amanda is puzzled and ask what this fight has to do with dogs. You explain that her parents are in a dogfight about how close to be with each other. If she or her brother gets involved, they might not resolve it. You caution her that it is better to save your dogs for fights you need to be in. Mike is nodding in agreement, and you ask him how it feels not to be in the fight. He answers that his feelings are mixed. He goes on to explain that one dog is relieved not to be in the fight and one dog feels disloyal for not being in the fight.

Laughing, Dr. Rodriquez is surprised that Mike has two dogs in his metaphor. He states, "Mike, your problem is you have TDD." Smiling, Mike asks, "What's that?" Dr. Rodriquez states that it is Two-Dog Disorder. You agree and suggest that he should get his dogs to fight with each other rather than rescuing his parents by getting mad or acting bad. Both he and his sister start to laugh, and slowly their parents find the humor in this situation.

As the family prepares to leave, Dr. Rodriquez cautions the children about rescuing their parents by doing something between sessions that might make them feel they need to care for them rather than have a fight with each other. You thank the family for coming and set a follow-up session in two weeks. Everyone seems in good spirits as you remind the parents not to let the children distract them from each other.

Case Discussion

In this case, the battle for initiative started prior to the clients' arrival at the first session. In this instance, the therapist's insistence on seeing the entire family created a crisis in the family. The therapists were delighted that the family was able to solve the crisis. When the therapy team was called, they stuck to their values and would not see a fragment of the family. This led to an innovation on the part of the family. When they did arrive at the session, the therapists jumped into the family's process. Here they continued to both engage the family and set unified boundaries and expectations.

The second session starts out with the therapists' confronting Mike's gender attitudes in a playful way. As they explore this, they stumble across grief issues that seem to be repressed. When Mike is unable to express his grief, the therapists draw parallels between Mike and his grandfather.

In the third session, the therapists again provoke emotional discussion about charged issues. They explore with the family the rigidity of the roles the children play. The therapists help the parents address their feelings of abandonment by the passing of the prior generation as well as their anxiety around launching their own children. Again the conversation returns to loss. However, the family is addressing future loss and seems to be in a better place. The therapists are pleased with the degree that the family has become more emotionally expressive over the last three sessions. They are willing to continue to work with the family until the family feels satisfied with the amount of growth they have experienced.

Evaluating

Symbolic- Experiential Family Therapy and Satir Transformational Systemic Therapy

As a whole, little research has been done to validate either of these approaches empirically. This is in part because the theoretical tenets have been relatively difficult to operationalize. Operationalization is the process of defining core variables in terms of how they are measured in research. Issues that are key to experiential theory, such as symbolic connection, self-worth, and perturbing, are difficult and perhaps impossible to define in a way that can be measured. However, Gurman and Kniskern (1981) have argued that the least broad principles describing interventions can be identified. Likewise, Piercy and Sprenkle (1990) have recommended that practitioners identify the core variables within each approach to marriage and family therapy.

Toward this end, Mitten and Connell (2004) conducted an important study using grounded theory to "derive a conceptual framework for symbolic-experiential therapy inductively" (p. 468). In this study, videotapes of Whitaker's therapy were coded by experts and core variables in his work were identified. Based on their observations, Mitten and Connell concluded, "Whitaker facilitated change in families by accessing and intervening in symbolic processes" (p. 474). Additionally, Lee (2002) developed the Congruence Scale as a way to measure a client's progress on a key component of the Satir Model, which could be useful for future research into effectiveness of this therapeutic approach.

Learning Exercises

1. Get into a group of five or six and form a circle. Have one of the group members start a story and tell a few lines of it, then tap someone else in the circle. Have the tagged person advance the story for a few lines and then tag the next person. As the story unfolds, pay attention to the unconscious connection among members of the circle. What themes emerge? When were you were able to predict the direction another would take the story?

2. Keep a journal of your feelings about various events and people in your life. After a week or two, review the journal and look for patterns in your feelings. Are there times you avoided expressing your feelings? If so, what were you afraid of?

3. In groups three, set up a sculpt of your primary triad—having two people act as your parents, and you as yourself as a child. What new insights do you gain through this process? What did you learn about each of your parents and your role in the family?

1. Think back to your family of origin. What were you taught about the nature of life and death? Has that view changed now that you are an adult? If so, how has that view changed?

2. How do you feel about the idea of expressing your feelings to your clients?

3. How can you be open and honest and at the same time be safe emotionally?

4. In what settings are you more and less inhibited in expressing yourself? In what settings are you able to speak without thinking about what you are saying?

5. What parts of your personality would help or hinder your ability to make deep and honest connections with your clients?

6. What rules are you still living by from your family of origin that you are ready to leave behind? Which would you like to consciously keep?

7. How do you feel about touch in therapy? In what instances is it helpful and appropriate for a therapist to touch a client and when is it not?

Web Resources:

Esalen Institute

http://www.esalen.org/page/our-story

Flash cards to help understand key terms/concepts in Symbolic-Experiential Family Therapy

https://quizlet.com/12635746/experiential-symbolic-therapy-flash-cards/

Wikipedia Page on Carl Whitaker

https://en.wikipedia.org/wiki/Carl_Whitaker

Article on 10 Essential Elements of Carl Whitaker's Theory and Therapy http://www.goodtherapy.org/blog/10-essential-elements-of-carl-whitakers-theory-and-therapy-1212144

Website on Carl Whitaker and his Theory

http://www.mindfortherapy.com/carl-whitaker.html

The Virginia Satir Global Network;

http://satirglobal.org/Satir Institute of the Pacific and Satir Institute of the Rockies (offering trainings on the Satir Model)

http://satirpacific.org/ and http://satirtraining.org/

Suggested Readings:

Banmen, J. (2002). The Satir Model: Yesterday and today. *Contemporary Family Therapy*, 24(1), 7–22. doi:10.1023/A:1014365304082

Satir, V. (1988). *The new peoplemaking*. Mountain View: Science and Behavior Books.

Satir, V., Gomori, M., & Gerber, J. (2006). *The Satir Model: Family therapy and beyond*. Palo Alto, CA: Science and Behavior Books.

Whitaker, C. A. (1975). Psychotherapy of the absurd: With a special emphasis on the psychotherapy of aggression. *Family Process 17*, 1–15.

Whitaker, C. A. (1976). The hindrance of theory in clinical work. In P. J. Guerin (Ed.), *Family therapy: Theory and practice* (pp. 154–164). New York: Gardner Press.

Whitaker, C. A. (1989). *Midnight musings of a family therapist*. New York: Norton.

Whitaker, C. A., & Bumberry, W. M. (1988). *Dancing with the family: A symbolic-experiential approach*. New York: Brunner/Mazel.

SECTION 3

Systemic Models of Marriage and Family Therapy

The theories of family therapy described in this section are examples of second- generation models of family therapy. They emerged out of the practice of systemically oriented therapists and theorists and were among the first theories to develop from a fully systemic paradigm.

Chapter 8 explores the Mental Research Institute (MRI) family therapy model, one of the first approaches to be developed from a systemic paradigm. MRI was the locus of much of the early research that gave rise to the systemic paradigm. The institute uses a brief approach that emphasizes changing the system by modifying communication patterns in the family.

In Chapter 9, we consider the structural approach. This approach focuses on how changing the structure in the family can result in changes in how the family functions. The structural approach attracted a following of practitioners who were drawn to the model's ability to produce maps of the family system as well as relatively easily understood techniques for producing change.

Finally, we explore the strategic model of Jay Haley in Chapter 10. This approach is related to both the MRI and structural models. However, Haley contributes several unique concepts that make his model very important in the development of family therapy.

CHAPTER

MENTAL RESEARCH INSTITUTE
FAMILY THERAPY

Thinking About This Approach

The Mental Research Institute (MRI) was founded in Palo Alto, California, in 1958 by Don D. Jackson, M.D., making it one of the original family therapy schools. In 1962, the center was the first to be funded by the National Institute of Mental Health as a training center for family therapy. They have remained an important Research and Treatment institute. The website mri.org contains information on their therapy and training services. MRI was involved in the foundation of the marriage and family therapy field. Many pioneers were brought to the institute under the direction of Don Jackson. The early staff of the institute included such renowned figures as Gregory Bateson, Jay Haley, Jules Riskin, William Fry, Virginia Satir, Paul Watzlawick, and John Weakland. This was perhaps the first school of family therapy to develop a unique theoretical orientation, making it what we consider a second-generation theory of family therapy. Other schools developed during this period were revamped versions of linear theories. MRI's emphasis on family process makes it one of the first true schools of family therapy.

PHOTO 8.1   **William Fry, John Weakland, Gregory Bateson, Jay Haley**

"The Bateson Team William Fry, John Weakland, Gregory Bateson, Jay Haley," Mental Research Institute. Copyright © by MRI. Reprinted with permission.

The center developed out of the Bateson research project studying communication in families having a member with schizophrenia (Bateson, Jackson, Haley, & Weakland, 1972). Gregory Bateson, a noted anthropologist, brought together a research team that included Don Jackson as a psychiatric consultant; John Weakland, a former chemical engineer and anthropology student; and Jay Haley, also an anthropologist. What began as a study of communication patterns turned quickly into some of the first attempts to conduct family therapy (Weakland, Watzlawick, & Riskin, 1995). As John Weakland describes, the shift from discovering the origins of schizophrenia to assisting the families of people with schizophrenia came about incidentally. Weakland recalls,

> So having got the patients, the families, and ourselves into a room, the next thing that happened was attempts at family therapy. My usual statement about this is: We did this partly to repay the families for their cooperation, partly for curiosity to see what we could do, but in my own case, at least, it was also a means of self defense because the impact of the schizophrenics and their families pulling at you while you were interviewing them was too damned big to stand if you didn't try to do something to change the system. (Weakland et al., 1995, p. 5)

For the most part, the team members were not trained in therapy and were relatively free of the confines of the linear-based psychodynamic theory that dominated the field at the time. Jackson, the only formally trained therapist, was already somewhat on the fringe of traditional psychotherapy. His mentor, Harry Stack Sullivan, had taught him to pay attention to interactions in the family. This experience contributed to a fresh perspective free of biases and limitations on what could be done to treat people with schizophrenia and to help their families.

As the MRI research team began treating families, Jay Haley and sometimes John Weakland would consult with Milton Erickson on his techniques of hypnotherapy. From these consultations, two main ideas came about that influenced the development of the MRI approach and, ultimately, family therapy. First, Erickson was very directive with his clients. Some would consider him manipulative. Not only was he directive, but he would take direct responsibility for effecting change. Second, he used a nonhistorical approach that emphasized change in the present and future, not in the past. This made the MRI approach one of the first to break psychoanalytic tradition by not placing emphasis on the resolution of past trauma.

This approach has been given a variety of different labels, which speaks of the wide influence the institute has had on the field. At times this approach has been labeled strategic (see Chapter 9), referring to its direct involvement in the client's problems and lives. It has also been referred to as a brief or solution-focused approach (see Chapter 10). It is action oriented and moves quickly to address problems. In addition, it has been described as a communication approach because of its original emphasis on communication among family members, with a focus on the pragmatics and behavioral outcomes of communications. Most recently, research at MRI has contributed to the constructionist approach (see Chapter 11) of family therapy. This chapter will focus on some of the more historical writings of the members of this school to provide an understanding of its contribution to the field.

The emphasis on communication at MRI led to the now classic *Pragmatics of Human Communication*, published by Watzlawick, Bavelas, and Jackson in 1967. This work was an attempt to develop an algebra of communication, a language to be used for discussing communication. The goal of this theoretical enterprise was to articulate the rules of communication. These rules were referred to as metacommunication. It was hoped that by establishing the rules of communication, therapists could be more effective.

Therapists at MRI use a multidisciplinary team approach in treating clients. As an institution, the defined purpose is "to conduct and encourage scientific investigation, research and discovery in relation to human behavior and for the benefit of the community at large" (Weakland et al., 1995, p. 1). With such a noble charter and a creative staff association, it is difficult to summarize the institute's approach to the field.

Innovations in Practice

While the MRI approach created numerous innovations that have been incorporated into family therapy as a whole, this review will focus on its key contributions to the field. For an MRI therapist, the locus of the problem lies in communication that occurs in a system. This communication focus shifts the emphasis in family therapy from the past to the present. Communication in this model is described using the black box metaphor. Here the researcher considers only what goes into and out of the system. There is simply no concern for the inner workings in this theory. With this model, the internal (unconscious) structure of the individual in the family became an unnecessary construct. As researchers became interested in the input and output communications of a family, the emphasis shifted to exploring whether the message sent was consistent with the message received by others.

Given the circular nature of communication, the distinction of cause and effect became impossible to establish. The chain of events was not seen as cause and effect, but effect and effect. This led to a description of communication through cybernetics. The cybernetics view is also likened to game theory. Game theory describes, through observation, how a game is played. For example, in the double bind study, the assumption is that schizophrenia is the result of interactions among family members that result in the person's withdrawing from reality. Bateson and colleagues (1956, 1972) laid out six conditions of the double bind that are associated with communication in a family that produces a member with schizophrenia:

1. [There are] two or more persons. . . .
2. Repeated experience. . . .
3. A primary negative injunction. . . .
4. A secondary injunction conflicting with the first at a more abstract level, and like the first enforced by punishments or signals which threaten survival. . . .
5. A tertiary negative injunction prohibiting the victim from escaping from the field. . . .
6. Finally, the complete set of ingredients is no longer necessary when the victim has learned to perceive his universe in double bind patterns. (1972, pp. 206–207)

This situation does not allow the person with schizophrenia to interpret his or her feelings. Over time he or she becomes frustrated enough to draw into madness.

Bateson and colleagues (1972) provide an example that makes the process more tangible:

> A young man who had fairly well recovered from an acute schizophrenic episode was visited in the hospital by his mother. He was glad to see her and impulsively put his arms around her shoulders, whereupon she stiffened. He withdrew his arms and she asked, "Don't you love me anymore?" He then blushed, and she said, "Dear, you must not be so easily embarrassed and afraid of your feelings." The patient was able to stay with her only a few minutes more and following her departure he assaulted an aide and was put in the tubs. (p. 217)

Let's look at the six conditions as they apply to this example. 1. The young man and his mother are the two people who are involved in this example. 2. We assume this is a pattern that is repeated time and time again. 3. The primary negative induction was when the mother stiffens and pulls away from the man impulsive hug. 4. After he pulls away her comment "Don't you love me anymore?" serves as the secondary negative injunction. 5. The mother's comment "Dear, you must not be so easily embarrassed and afraid of your feelings." serves as the third negative induction. This traps the man with it's implications that if he would express his feelings (recall that his expressions was first met with her pulling away)he would be ready to leave the hospital. 6. Finally, his attacking the aide demonstrates that he has learned to act crazy in his universe.

This model generated exorbitant excitement, resulting in a predictable overgeneralization of the construct. In the introduction of their edited monograph on the double bind theory of schizophrenia, Sluzki and Ransom (1976) point out that

> over the years the logical beauty of the concept has created an illusion of concreteness: it gives the impression of being a handy notion that can be plugged

into many different models. But this misunderstanding has led to many intellectual dead ends. (p. vii)

The double bind was not intended to be seen as a causal mechanism that results in schizophrenia. Double bind is simply an observation of a specific communication pattern associated with schizophrenia. It is most likely not the presence or absence of this pattern that leads to schizophrenia, although the intensity and frequency of this pattern may play a part in its etiology. What is interesting here is recognition of the impact of inconsistent communication on family members. Segal (1991) provides an accurate summary of Bateson and colleagues' (1972) paper when he asserts, "Although a novel explanation of schizophrenia, the paper's true importance rests on the argument that disturbed behavior is a function of an interpersonal system rather than an intrapsychic one, wedding cybernetic epistemology to psychiatry" (p. 172).

Analysis of Change

Another important contribution developed as a result of MRI is the publication *Change: Principles of Problem Formation and Problem Resolution* by Watzlawick, Weakland, and Fisch (1974). Their work was based on group theory and a theory of logical types. Group theory provided insight into change within a frame of reference. The theory of logical types provided insight into changes in the client's frame of reference.

According to Watzlawick and colleagues (1974), a first-order change is a change in increments, while a second-order change involves a logical jump or a change in the frame of reference. The discontinuous nature of second-order shifts provides a certain degree of uncertainty that can be experienced by the client as a leap of faith.

> To exemplify this distinction in more behavioral terms: a person having a nightmare can do many things in his dream—run, hide, fight, scream, jump off a cliff, etc.—but no change from any one of these behaviors to another would ever terminate the nightmare. *We shall henceforth refer to this kind of change as first-order change.* The one way *out of* a dream involves a change from dreaming to waking. Waking, obviously, is no longer a part of the dream, but a change to an altogether different state. *This kind of change will from now on be referred to as second-order change.* ... Second-order change is thus *change of change.* (Watzlawick et al., 1974, pp. 10–11)

To fully understand this distinction, we must be clear on the concept of frames and the process of reframing. A frame is a view of the world that a client possesses. Embedded within this view is a statement on the nature of the problem that the family is seeking help with. The therapist may have a different frame of reference regarding the problem. These different, often competing frames are presented in the form of metaphors. For example, the quintessential psychodynamic concern for a client's ability to resolve the Oedipus complex is based on a metaphor. It compares the difficulty of a young boy in relating with his parents to a classic Greek tragedy. Calling attention to the metaphorical nature of frames, the MRI school taught family therapy to use the family's frame of reference. In practice, this is accomplished by listening to the metaphors the family uses to describe problems. By speaking with similar metaphors, the therapist is able to access the client's language and speak more directly to the family.

Theory of Change

Paul Watzlawick developed a structured family interview protocol. This assessment protocol was one of the first and also one of the most widely used assessment procedures. The protocol consists of five steps. The first involves interviewing each member alone to ask, "What do you think are the main problems in your family?" (Watzlawick, 1966, p. 257). After each member has provided a perspective on the problems, the family is left with the instruction to reach a consensus. This portion is observed by the therapist. In step two, the therapist observes the family for five minutes as they plan an activity together. In step three, the parents are interviewed alone and asked, "How, in all the millions of people in the world, did the two of you get together?" (p. 259). In step four, the therapist asks the parents to describe the meaning of the proverb "A rolling stone gathers no moss." The children then return and have the meaning of the proverb described to them by their parents. The final step consists of a game where the family is blamed for a problem. While this structure provides much interesting data, what is most important is the opportunity it gives the therapist to observe a family's process. Once the process is observed the therapist knows where to target their interventions.

An MRI therapist is able to use a change in the way the client's problem is framed as an intervention. By changing how a problem is labeled, the nature of the problem is changed. The essence of a successful reframe is that an impossible or unsolvable problem is reframed as a normal and solvable one. For example, a child's parents see him as "lazy," and they are overwhelmed by this view of their son. They simply cannot get him to do anything because he is "lazy." By reframing the child's laziness as a lack of motivation, the parents are given more options to motivate him.

Many therapists see paradoxical interventions as central to this approach. The presumption is that by prescribing the symptom, the client is miraculously encouraged to give up the symptom. This is far from the truth. A paradoxical directive is more involved than simply prescribing the symptom. It is an advanced intervention that should be used only by an experienced clinician or under close supervision. It would be unwise to prescribe suicidal or even self-destructive behavior.

The first requisite of a paradoxical intervention is a trusting client–therapist relationship. MRI therapists are masters at developing such a relationship almost immediately. This is accomplished by learning to speak the client's language. Once a relationship is developed, the therapist elicits a commitment to therapy. Next, the client is instructed to continue to engage in the symptomatic behavior, yet to do so in a slightly different way. For example, a client who experiences uncontrollable sobbing throughout her day may be instructed to get up an hour early and cry for the entire hour. Such an intervention changes the form of the problem. When the client performs the prescribed behavior, the problem is reframed from being out of control to being controllable. No longer is the client under the control of her tears, but rather she can control the time and duration of her crying, ultimately demonstrating control over the symptom. Gaining control over the symptom may result in giving up the symptom.

Questioning

The MRI approach emphasizes changing the patterns of communication that maintain the client's problem. This emphasis guides the style of the interview conducted by the therapist. The therapist is interested not only in the problem, but also in how clients communicate the problem to each other. Given this, the therapeutic interview is seen as a place to access information from the answers given by the clients. Of equal importance is how the clients communicate with each other and the therapist during the interview.

According to Segal (1991), when collecting data, the therapist usually directs clients to talk to him or her rather than to each other. This allows a specific and concrete understanding of the problem as it is perceived. The therapist facilitates descriptions of interactions presented like a script, complete with stage directions. That is, the description should contain information about how the clients respond to each other.

In this approach, it is also common for the therapist to observe family communication patterns. The therapist may ask clients to engage in an exercise that allows such observations. For example, a couple may be asked to discuss where their next vacation might be spent. This discussion allows the therapist to observe the couple's communication patterns in the context of a problem. It is assumed that this pattern is representative of how the couple communicates at home.

Structuring

The communications interview tends to be structured in the standard 45- to 50-minute therapeutic hour. In most instances, the entire family is asked to attend the interview. However, if it is inconvenient for a family member to attend, he or she may be allowed to remain absent. The family as a whole is seen as important, but it is rare that therapists insist on every member's presence at the interview. In recent years, the MRI group has started to work with individuals, but the therapist usually tries to get at least two members of the family to attend the interview since communication is best observed in dyads. Sessions are scheduled weekly and treatment tends to be brief, lasting, for the most part, less than 10 sessions. It is common to limit the number to 10 or less at the onset of treatment. This aids in framing the problem as solvable and empowers the family.

The interview is also structured so that the therapist takes a less powerful position. This design allows the therapist to be the expert in the therapy process while also allowing the clients to be the experts in their lives. This often takes the form of being honest about one's struggle to understand the client. For example, if a client asks, "Do you understand?" the MRI therapist might respond, "No, but please bear with me as I struggle with understanding your situation. Your situation is unique, and I feel having the details is important."

Responding

Throughout the interview, the therapist tries to model good communication skills. The goal is to respond to the client in a clear and concise manner. MRI therapists emphasize open and honest communication, and they pay attention to nonverbal communication as well as verbal communication. Inconsistencies between verbal and nonverbal communication tell the therapist that he or she is personally overinvolved. This is a sign that the therapist should seek supervision to resolve the inconsistencies or make a referral if they cannot be quickly resolved.

Applications

This approach is versatile and has been applied to clients with a diversity of issues. Since this approach does not see problems as the result of a disorder or psychopathology, it is widely applicable. The assumption that the problem occurs at the interpersonal level and is the result of communication can be explored in a variety of settings. For example, it has been applied to phobic disorders (Nardone, 1995), marital therapy (Soroka,1995), and residential/day treatment (Soo-Hoo, 1995). This approach was also an inspiration for the Italian psychiatric researchers Mara Selvini Palazzoli, Luigi Boscolo, Gianfranco Cecchin, and Giuliana Prata who developed Milan Family Therapy (see chapter 11).

Acting as a Mental Research Institute Family Therapist

When the client makes the initial phone contact, the therapist asks who in the family is involved with the problem for which he or she is seeking help. As the caller identifies different family members who are affected by the problem, he or she is asked if they would be available to come in for the therapy. In this indirect manner, the therapist gathers the family members for an initial session. As the family arrives, they are greeted and introduced to the therapist.

In the beginning, little history is taken. The focus of the interview is quickly placed on the problem. If the problem is seen as carried in an individual, it is quickly reframed as a problem in the system as a whole. For example, if a child is seen as "a bad person," the therapist may reframe the problem as a pattern where the child is being held accountable for all that goes wrong in the family. In this approach, the locus of the problem is not seen as residing within an individual, but as existing among people as they communicate.

Assessment

The interview quickly moves to an assessment phase as the nature of a problem is explored. First, the problem is defined in clear and concrete terms. It is best if as many family members as possible are involved in the definition of the problem. For example, a better definition than that Emily is a bad girl would be that the family is having a hard time rearing a six-year-old. It is desirable to define the problem behaviorally and specifically. To continue with the above example, the family is having a hard time getting Emily to follow directions from her stepdad. Here, the approach borrows from behavioral theory and is linked by the assumption that behavior is communication. It is also desirable to have affirmative goals rather than goals focused on the absence of a symptom. For example, if a client is agoraphobic, the goal of being cured of agoraphobia is marked by the absence of anxiety. An affirmative goal would be for the client to be able to get out successfully twice a week.

Second, previously attempted solutions to the problem are thoroughly investigated. It is often the case that a problem is maintained by repeated attempts to solve it. A teenager runs away in response to being grounded for a month. The grounding by the parents had escalated over several months in response to the teen's truancy. However, the parent's response had not been successful, but only escalated in step with their teen's behavior.

It is also the goal of this approach to offer unique solutions. If a family is simply told by a therapist to do something they have already tried but failed at, they are likely to simply leave treatment without informing the therapist. Finding out what has already been tried increases the credibility of the therapist. It also serves to frame the therapy as experimental and based on trial and error.

Also in this stage of treatment, the therapist seeks to define the change to be achieved in clear and concrete terms. The better defined the goal, the more quickly it will be met. The goal is often a small change that allows the client to be successful. As Segal (1991) suggests, a MRI therapist may ask,

> "Since we only have 10 sessions, we need to define a goal of treatment that would tell us you are beginning to solve the problem. You're not completely out of the woods, so to speak, but you'll have found the trail and can find your way on your own. So, what would be the smallest, concrete, significant indicator of this?" (p. 182)

The definition of the solution is sought in terms of behaviors. Specific statements are better than vague statements. For example, if a client presents with depression, it is better to define change in terms of positive things he would do, rather than as the absence of depression. That is, you would ask the client what he will be doing with his time when he is no longer depressed.

Intervention

In the intervention phase of treatment, the therapist's goal is to formulate and implement a strategy for change. Based on the analysis in the assessment phase of treatment, the therapist develops a plan of action. The plan can be direct, such as contracting, developing, and practicing good communication skills. The plan can also be indirect, such as a paradoxical intervention. The hallmark of the MRI approach is direct involvement on the part of the therapist in solving the problem. Therapists become directly involved in the family system and manipulate and influence people to change. Since this school was the first to describe second-order change, people often think that practitioners are always seeking to establish second-order change with their clients through reframes or paradoxical directives. However, it is often the case that a first-order change is all that is necessary to meet clients' needs. Frequently clients, especially couples, simply need coaching in more effective communication.

Termination

The termination phase of treatment follows shortly after success in the intervention phase. Segal (1991) provides three criteria indicative of the need for termination: (1) a small but significant change has been made in the problem, (2) the change appears to be durable, and (3) the client states or implies the ability to handle the problem without the therapist. Once these criteria are met, the client is given credit for the change and encouraged to take a break or vacation from therapy. The client is also cautioned that the change may not last forever and that the problem may reappear. This is a paradoxical inoculation against a relapse. It is not uncommon for a family to return after the original course of treatment has been terminated. The stages of treatment begin again, and often the clients will attend until the new problem is sufficiently resolved.

Case Example: The Case of Jason's Poor Self-Esteem

Stacey requests couple therapy by telephone for herself and her husband. She complains of arguing a lot and says that her husband, Jason, has low motivation and drive. She explains that shortly after the arrival of their first child, Mia, arguments began between herself and her husband. She reports that just before the birth seven months ago, she quit her job as a paramedic. Jason, a salesperson who formerly made a very comfortable commission, has been in a sales slump for five months. Although the couple have always counted on Stacey's being a stay-at-home mom after the birth of their first child, she is afraid that her husband can no longer support the family and that she'll have to leave her daughter and find another job.

Stacey is concerned about arranging a meeting time, so an evening appointment is scheduled so her husband doesn't have to miss work. She is also concerned about the length of therapy. The therapist responds by saying that it is impossible to tell at the beginning of therapy how long it could take. He further explains that he likes to be as efficient as possible and that he sees clients for no more than 10 sessions. The therapist also requests that the couple find a sitter for the baby so that he and they can talk more easily.

Session One

The couple arrives promptly for the session, but unexpectedly they have their daughter with them. At the beginning of the session, Stacey explains that her mother is sick and, as a result, couldn't sit for Mia. The therapist accepts this without question and begins the session.

The couple look strikingly different. Jason is rather disheveled. He is dressed professionally, but his Oxford shirt is wrinkled and worn. While he is very thin and gaunt, Stacey is vibrant and dressed very colorfully.

The first question the therapist asks is, "How can I help you?" Stacey responds by pointing her finger at her husband and stating, "The problem here is that he has low self-esteem." In response, Jason hunches down slightly and looks at the floor. The therapist tries to interrupt Stacey but finds it very hard to get a word in as she speaks for several minutes about her husband's low self-esteem. During this time, Jason continues to look at the floor. After a while, the baby in Stacey's arms starts to get fussy, and her attention is drawn to her child.

While his wife is distracted by the baby, Jason complains that his wife doesn't respect him. He states that since the baby was born, she hasn't given him the time of day. He mumbles that he's not sure the child looks very much like him. In response, Stacey glares at her husband and states, "You're right, she doesn't."

The therapist tries to interrupt the couple, but they keep arguing, so he wheels his chair between them, holds his hand up more assertively, and calls for a time-out. When they give him their attention, he sets some ground rules. The first rule is that Stacey should speak for herself and Jason should speak for himself. The therapist explains that it isn't fair to speak for someone else or state how another person is feeling, even when you're right. The second rule is that there is to be no dagger throwing.

Both husband and wife look puzzled and ask about dagger throwing. The therapist describes it as statements and looks that are meant to hurt the other. The couple try to look innocent, so the therapist reminds Jason about his comment about the baby not being his. He also reminds Stacey of her response to her husband's comment. She starts to argue, stating that Jason started the argument. The therapist responds by pointing out the unimportance of who began the argument. He informs the couple that they appear to be pretty equally matched fighters. He then states that he is not interested in how well each can fight; instead, he is interested in the two of them getting along.

The therapist then instructs the couple on the use of "I" messages. He tells them that they can talk about themselves only by beginning each sentence with an "I" statement about how they feel. At this point, Jason describes feeling unsupported. He gets up for work alone while his wife stays in bed. Jason describes working a hard day at a "cutthroat job" and coming home to a wife exhausted from taking care of their daughter. Stacey also describes feeling unsupported after a hard day of providing care for her daughter when her "vacant" husband returns from work and provides little assistance.

When the therapist asks about their goal for therapy, they look puzzled. Stacey states that she thought the purpose of therapy was just to talk about problems. The therapist responds by saying that he is more interested in solving problems. Jason states that he would like to have better self-esteem and feel like he and his wife are a team. The therapist responds that he would be most interested in working on Jason's relationship with his wife, and that the problems may be related.

Just before the session closes, the therapist asks the couple if they have any questions. Jason asks if they are hopeless. The therapist assures him that, while each couple is unique, he has worked successfully with clients who had what seemed to be more severe problems. Stacey asks for homework. The therapist assigns them the task of observing each other and noticing when their partner is trying to be supportive. They respond to this with laughter, and Stacey adds that support rarely occurs. The therapist suggests that it might occur more often than noticed and emphasizes that they will be best served if they write down their observations daily.

To close the session, the therapist asks the couple about babysitting. Stacey quickly becomes frustrated and starts to explain all of the difficulties in finding care for the baby. The therapist quickly backs down, offers his understanding of the difficulty, and says that a sitter is not necessary. He states that this difficulty, while frustrating, may be playing a part in the couple's problem. A follow-up session is set for one week.

Session Two

The couple arrives for the session early and without their daughter. They appear to be in good spirits and are both well dressed. As the session opens, the therapist asks how they did with their homework. Jason has prepared a list, while Stacey reports that she was too busy to do much of her homework. She reports that she did it for the first two days but was unable to follow through after that. Jason responds by joking with his wife, and the therapist can't help noting the good mood.

When the therapist inquires about how work is going, Jason reports that he closed a big sale and will receive a sizable commission as a result. The therapist asks him how his self-esteem is. He reports feeling very confident and "on top of the world." However, he has some doubt about being out of his sales slump. His wife responds supportively, but then says that if he had better self-esteem, he would have fewer and shorter sales slumps. In response, he looks at the floor and shakes his head.

The therapist then asks the couple to allow him to talk to them about their history as a couple. They agree, and he starts by interviewing Jason.

Jason vividly remembers how he met his wife, down to what she wore on their first few dates. They met five years ago while in college after being introduced by a mutual friend. Jason reports that he was "dumbstruck" by his future wife's beauty. He reports that as soon as he saw her, he told his friend she was the woman he wanted to marry. He reports being attracted to her "carefree spirit and ability to love life."

Stacey has a much less vivid memory of their early relationship. She reports that, while she liked Jason when they met, she wasn't ready for a "serious" relationship. He started to pursue her and, over time, she came to love him. She reports that he asked her to marry him twice before she said yes. It wasn't until after she graduated that she was willing to accept his marriage proposal. When the therapist asks Stacey when she fell in love with her husband, she blushes and says she doesn't know. She goes on to explain that while she is clearly in love with him now, her love has grown slowly and so she can't say when she fell in love.

The therapist notices that during the discussion of their history, both seem to be in a good mood. They smile and touch each other a lot. The therapist shares his thought that part of the problem is that they don't have much time for their relationship. He recognizes the difficulty in finding time with a young child to care for and encourages the couple to problem-solve by finding time for one date over the next week.

The remainder of the session is spent observing the couple as they arrange a date. The therapist offers little input, since the couple do a pretty good job of listening to each other and communicating their wishes and feelings. A follow-up session is scheduled for one week.

Session Three

As the third session began, the therapist notices that Jason looks much like he did at the first session, tired and disheveled. The therapist asks Jason how things are going. Stacey starts to answer for him, so the therapist quickly interrupts her and states that he wishes to hear from her husband. She seems okay with the therapist's interruption and states that she speaks for her husband too often. Jason agrees with his wife in a neutral tone. The therapist leans in to Jason and says in a low voice, "Ask your wife to let you speak for yourself." Jason looks his wife in the eye and says, "Honey, thanks for your concern, but let me talk to the doctor myself." The therapist smiles at the couple and nods his approval.

Jason starts to discuss his poor self-esteem. The therapist asks him what happened between last week and this week to make his self-esteem a problem again. He states that his client canceled half of his sales and his boss blamed him for losing part of what he had negotiated. At the therapist's request, Jason discusses the situation at work. He discusses how his feeling of worth depends on his sales. At this point, the therapist declares that Jason's work is bad for his "other" esteem.

Stacey becomes curious and asks what other esteem is. The therapist explains it as ideas about yourself that you get from others. He also explains that it is different from self-esteem, which comes from yourself. He explains to Jason that it seems his poor other esteem piled up on his good self-esteem, causing him to feel very down. Jason laughs in relief and describes it as "piled up like a big old pile of shit." Stacey starts to laugh and scolds her husband for saying *shit*. The therapist laughs and comments about their creative use of words.

Stacey becomes sad and admits to contributing to the pile at home. She talks about how the responsibility of the new baby and the unpredictable finances make her stressed. She admits to taking that stress out on her husband. She begins to tear up and states that she feels she has become her mother. After a minute, the therapist asks Jason if he married his wife or her mother. Jason is clear on the fact that he married his wife. The therapist asks him to explain to his wife that she is not her mother. After Jason gives a brief explanation, Stacey appears in better spirits. The therapist then instructs Jason to explain to his wife the difference between her and her mother. He does this, and a follow-up is scheduled for one week.

Session Four

The couple arrives at the session in bright spirits and holding hands. They report that, despite a big fight the previous week, things are going very well. They have even made arrangements for the sitter to stay with their daughter after the session and seem to look forward to a date. They are both excited and share that this will be the first time they've been out alone since the baby was born. The therapist reinforces the date and discusses the importance of spending quality time together. He suggests that, during the date, they set a limit of not talking about their jobs or their daughter.

Jason shares that his work was the source of the previous week's argument. The therapist asks how they finished their fight successfully. They share that they were able to talk about themselves rather than blaming each other. The fight began when Jason introduced the idea of quitting his job to work with his father. While this would mean a cut in pay in the beginning, his father would retire soon, allowing Jason to head the business. He thought he could turn the business into a more successful enterprise.

Stacey reports feeling "freaked out" because of the initial pay cut. But as she thought about it, she began to change her mind. She thought about how her husband would be happier working for his dad. They are very close and he enjoys his father's company. Stacey also points out that she and her husband have been poor before, and amazingly, it was a time when they were happier.

When asked how this affects his other esteem, Jason admits that it is growing by leaps and bounds. He has sold more than ever at work and feels very good about his family life. He reports an incident where his boss wanted him to work overtime, but he refused. He describes his boss as a bully feared by everyone in the office. He says that once he stood up to his boss, the bullying stopped. This made him feel so good about his work setting that he no longer felt like quitting. However, he is still thinking he might want to work with his father.

The remainder of the session is spent planning for the future. Toward the end of the session, the therapist asks the couple if they feel satisfied with the success of the therapy. They state that their goal of learning to get along well by fighting fairly has been achieved. They do want to schedule a follow-up in two weeks to make sure the changes stick. The therapist agrees, and a follow-up is scheduled.

Session Five

The couple arrives at the session in good spirits. Both are well dressed and report that they have planned another date for after the session. Stacey reports positive occurrences since the previous session. The couple have struggled with "normal" stuff such as day care, finances, and family issues. The difference is in how they are getting along with each other. Stacey reports that her husband is her partner again. She mentions how nice it is to have her husband back. She is relieved that his confidence has returned.

The therapist congratulates Jason for his accomplishment in restoring his esteem. Jason says he feels he has good self-esteem and other esteem. He expresses regret for allowing himself to get in such a sad state in the first place. He states that he didn't see it coming. The therapist shares with him that many families experience such problems with the arrival of their first child. Jason agrees and shares that, while the child is a joy in his life, he became more serious when she was born. Now, he is able to see he was too serious.

The therapist congratulates the couple for their success at being a team again. Stacey responds by saying how easy it was once she got started. She also states that it was even easier when her husband felt better. Jason agrees and states that having his wife on his team "makes me feel like a winner despite my loser job." The therapist emphasizes the distinction that he is in a loser job, not a loser himself for having the job.

Stacey shares that the couple has reached a decision regarding her husband's plan to work with his father. They have decided that as long as his current job goes well, he'll keep working there for six more months before leaving to work with his dad. Six months would give them a bit more financial security. However, if things go poorly at his present job, he will go to work with his father sooner. The therapist asks Jason if he will be able to quit in six months if things are still going well. He states that he has already written the resignation letter and that his father has it and will send it in five months, giving four weeks' notice. When the therapist asks if his father will send the letter, Jason states that he is 100% sure. His father is very much looking forward to working with his son.

As the end of the session approaches, the therapist asks the couple about any other issues they might like to address. They state that things are going well and that they are optimistic about the future. The therapist offers to see them again should anything change. He shares that Jason's transition to working for his father could be a problem and offers to see the entire family, including Jason's parents, if need be. The couple is thankful and shares that they will call if necessary. At this point, the therapist suggests ending therapy and charges them for only half a session. They are grateful for the suggestion. All of them say their good-byes.

Follow-Up

The therapist receives a call from the couple seven months later stating that things are going well. Jason is working for his father and really enjoying it. Stacey has taken a part-time job and is enjoying herself.

Case Discussion

While the couple presented in such a manner that the therapist could see either one as the problem, he viewed the problem as residing in their communication pattern. The therapist moved quickly to interrupt the communication pattern between the partners, thereby helping them improve their communication. The therapist was pleased with their success in the negotiation of a therapeutic goal. At the very end of the session, Stacey became defensive about not having a babysitter, and the therapist strategically backed down from that request.

The fact that the family arrived at the second session early and without their daughter was taken to indicate that the couple had bought into therapy. However, the fact that the couple had only partially completed their homework indicated that the therapist still had to further build the therapeutic relationship. While the therapist saw the problem in the present, he used a discussion of the history of the couple's relationship to assess the relationship through an observation of their mood. Given the degree of connection, the therapist encouraged them to arrange a date between sessions. Since they had not completed the last homework task and did not ask for new homework, the therapist decided that encouragement rather than direction in the form of homework would be more likely to produce client follow-through. He hoped that by next session the couple would have actually gone on a date.

In the third session, the therapist was pleased that his first attempt at a reframe resonated with the family. Had the couple not been moved by the reframe, the therapist would simply have moved on. Like a joke someone doesn't get, an explanation doesn't help. Since the reframe had an emotional impact on the couple, especially the wife, the therapist supported the couple in talking about their view of their situation from their new perspective.

In session four, the couple continued to be in a different emotional space. The shifting in their views of the world had allowed them to once again work together. The therapist was pleased that they were able to negotiate a very emotionally charged issue (Jason's employment status) in a relatively constructive manner. During this session, the therapist shifted their focus from promoting change to making the change stick.

The fifth session was similar to the fourth session in that the focus was on maintaining change. Since the couple reported that they were doing well and spent the majority of the time talking about future plans, the therapist moved to closing the case. Since the couple felt comfortable ending therapy, the therapist terminated with an open invitation for them to return at some future date.

Evaluating Mental Research Institute Family Therapy

Theoretical Critiques

MRI's "black box" approach to working with families makes this theory systemically consistent at the level of simple cybernetics. It is assumed that stuck systems can be unstuck by providing information that will move the system forward again. However, MRI's influence on the field cannot be underestimated. It has had direct influence on several schools, including strategic therapy (see Chapter 10), Milan family therapy (see Chapter 11) and solution-focused brief therapy (see Chapter 12), as well as the field as a whole.

This approach is not systemically consistent at the level of cybernetics of cybernetics. The influence of the therapist is not included in the description of the family's process. This is inconsistent with the view of the family as open and responsive to the wider environment. Thus, practice is inconsistent with theory. Because this model is very intellectual and scholarly, it is possible that theoretical understanding outpaces innovation in practice. It is important to note that recent contributions from this school have been more consistent in terms of second-order cybernetics (see Chapter 11). While there are some internal inconsistencies in this theory, it has been proven to be a very effective approach to family therapy.

Empirical Evaluations

The MRI group has been more interested in the advancement of their theory than in the empirical verification of their approach. As a result, there has been only one published study of outcome (Weakland, Fisch, Watzlawick, & Boden, 1974). In 40% of cases, the presenting problem was eliminated without symptom substitution, while 32% reported significant improvement. While this single study is insufficient to evaluate the effectiveness of the approach, it is impossible to doubt the impact this approach has had on the thinking of most practicing marriage and family therapists.

Learning Exercises

1. Get into small groups of three or four. Take turns interviewing each other about the decision each of you made to go to graduate school. As you listen, think about how each person frames the decision. What problem was she trying to solve? Discuss with your peers the frames that they placed their decision in. What does each of the frames in the group allow each person to do? In what way does each frame limit each person?

2. Making "I" statements is a communication technique that goes a long way in helping to de-escalate an argument. In essence, arguing couples begin each sentence with an "I" and avoid talking about the other by making a "you" statement. Practice this technique the next time you get into an argument. Afterward, reflect on how your argument was different.

Discussion Questions

1. Describe ways you are good at persuading people. What techniques do you use when you want to get your way, want connection, or want to do something with someone else?

2. Critics view this approach as manipulative and proponents view it as persuasive. What difference does each of these frames make in your understanding of the MRI approach?

3. Which one of the techniques of the MRI approach seems most comfortable to you, and why do you think that is the case?

Suggested Readings

Bateson, G. (1972). *The cybernetics of "self": A theory of alcoholism.* In G. Bateson (ed.), *Steps to an ecology of mind* (pp. 309–337). Chicago, IL: University of Chicago Press.

Watzlawick, P., Bavelas, J. B., & Jackson, D. D. (1967). *Pragmatics of human communication: A study of interactional patterns, pathologies, and paradoxes.* New York, NY: Norton.

Watzlawick, P., Weakland, J., & Fisch, R. (1974). *Change: Principles of problem formation and problem resolution.* New York, NY: Norton.

Web References

Mental Research (MRI) Homepage

http://www.mri.org/

Don Jackson Memorial page

http://www.mri.org/dondjackson/mri.htm

Flashcards for understanding important concepts in MRI

https://quizlet.com/6319852/mri-mental-research-institute-flash-cards/

Wikipedia's information on MRI

https://en.wikipedia.org/wiki/Mental_Research_Institute

The Facebook group dedicate to MRI

https://www.facebook.com/pages/Mental-Research-Institute/150372734979148

CHAPTER

9

STRUCTURAL FAMILY THERAPY

Thinking About This Approach

Structural family therapy became a very popular and dynamic approach to working with families starting in the 1970s. It came out of the work of Salvador Minuchin and his colleagues, first at Wiltwyck School for Boys in upstate New York and later at the Philadelphia Child Guidance Center. Minuchin is a child psychiatrist by training and became concerned early in his career about the impact of a child's family on her or his functioning. His model came out of his observations of family process and treatment outcomes. In part, the popularity of his approach is just a function of the large number of therapists he trained at the Philadelphia Child Guidance Center. By the 1980s, it was one of the most widely taught theoretical models.

The structural approach was pivotal in the development of family therapy because it was one of the first developed out of research and treatment projects that directly observed families. The concepts and constructs used in this theory came directly from observation of families in family therapy. Here the practice of family therapy provided direct feedback to the development of family therapy theory. This makes the structural approach a first-generation model of family therapy. Like other theories of its time, such as that of the Mental Research Institute (Chapter 8) and the strategic approach (Chapter 10), this theory was developed to deal with families from its first conceptualization. This is in contrast to other theories, such as the behavioral (Chapter 4), Bowen's systems theory (Chapter 7), and experiential (Chapter 7) models, which resulted from the modification of what were originally individualist views of therapy.

PHOTO 9.1   Salvador Minuchin

This approach was important to the development of family therapy also because Minuchin was one of the first theorists to view the whole family as the focus of treatment. In structural family therapy, pathology was seen as residing in three possible locations: inside the patient, in the social context, or in feedback between the patient and the context (Minuchin, 1974). Thus, this approach was one of the first theories to recognize the relationship between the environment and the psyche. Minuchin clearly states that "the individual influences his context and is influenced by it in constantly recurring sequences of interactions" (p. 9). To effect change in therapy, the therapist joins the family system and seeks to alter the family's organization from within that system. The therapist's goal is to provide different feedback between the family and its environment that will support change.

A hallmark of structural family therapy is the attention it gives the relationship of the family's structure to its functioning and process. Structure is patterns of relating, or process, over time. Basing his view of nuclear family on the structural functional sociological theory of Talcott Parsons (Parsons & Bales, 1955), Minuchin explored how emotional, pragmatic, or both emotional and pragmatic needs are met in a family. Emotional needs of family members include such things as love, a feeling of belonging, and connection. Pragmatic needs include such things as food, clothing, shelter, and transportation.

Families that are well organized with clear boundaries and rules for interaction seem to function better in meeting both types of needs for their members. Families that are disorganized, with overly rigid or diffuse boundaries, often do not meet the emotional or pragmatic needs of the family. This structure over time leads to the expression of psychopathology in one or more family member.

Family members often serve multiple roles within the family. For example, an adult male may be husband to his wife, father to his children, and adult son to his parents. These multiple roles have unique responsibilities. Each of these roles has a unique skill set that is often inappropriate to be performed in a different role. For example, while being flirtatious with your wife will help maintain a healthy marital bond, being flirtatious with your teenage daughter is inappropriate.

In the 1950s and 1960s, most approaches to psychotherapy were insight based and focused on individuals. Minuchin's focus on the structure of the family was part of a radical departure from that view of psychotherapy. Early in his career, Minuchin and his colleagues noticed that changes made by the child in such insight-based approaches quickly evaporated when the child was discharged to her or his family (Colapinto, 1991). By addressing dysfunctional processes and structure in the family, the change was more likely to be maintained once the child left the treatment center. If the family could maintain the new structures, then the change was more likely to be stable upon discharge from treatment. In structural family therapy, this is accomplished by practicing new processes both in session and at home until they become the new, healthier structure.

In addition to focusing on structure, this approach was among the first to recognize that development influences the functionality of structure. Failure to recognize the influence of family development had made it hard to describe family function in a way that had clinical relevance. This is because families have different styles of functioning during different developmental stages. Minuchin was revolutionary because he not only considered issues of individual development, but also concerned himself with family development. Minuchin identifies four unique development stages: couple formation, families with young children, families with school-age or adolescent children, and families with grown children (Minuchin & Fishman, 1981).

After his initial work with poor families in New York, Minuchin moved to Philadelphia and transformed the Philadelphia Child Guidance Center into one of the top family therapy research and training centers. He successfully recruited Jay Haley, known for his strategic approach (see Chapter 10), to join the center, and there their models became somewhat blended. Both the structural and strategic models focused on the therapist's taking responsibility for changing the family directly. They also were similar in their interest in the function of hierarchy in family processes.

Since the Philadelphia Child Guidance Center was involved in training therapists, the structural model was further refined by being under observation itself. The center made extensive use of one-way mirrors during therapy as well as live supervision. This allowed therapists to receive feedback in real time. In 1992, Aponte discussed how the person of the therapist is trained in structural therapy. He states, "The structural approach recognizes the central position of the clinician in the therapeutic relationship, and training emphasizes the strategic use of self within the therapist-client transaction" (p. 269). This position makes this approach one of the earliest to incorporate a postmodern or second-order cybernetics perspective. From this theoretical position, the treatment system is conceptualized as a family-plus-therapist suprasystem.

Innovations in Practice

A key innovation of this approach is its emphasis on moving therapy from a passive, insight-driven process to an action-oriented, problem-solving endeavor. This action takes the form of practicing healthier structures until they become part of the family's homeostasis. As structural family therapy shifted the therapeutic process from insight or understanding to action, it also shifted its time focus.

Family therapy became less interested in historical analysis of the origin of the problem and more interested in what action could take place in the here and now to help the family resolve their problem. This was largely a pragmatic position. An understanding of how a pathological structure developed offers little insight into how it can be altered. This moved family therapy out of exploring the past to changing structure in the interview room.

Families as Systems and Subsystems

In structural family therapy, the family structure is given primary consideration. Individual functioning is seen as dependent on the functioning of the broader system, the family. This approach has adopted many of the basic principles of family systems theory, namely, families are seen as the result of the relationship of all of their parts. In this approach, structures are the means by which a system regulates itself, functions are the actions by which the system fulfills its purpose, and operations are the functions performed by each action (Aponte & VanDeusen, 1981). For example, a mother performs the function of disciplining her child through the operation of telling her child to go to bed. This operation serves to regulate sleep in the child. Once established, the system's pattern of interaction maintains a homeostasis through feedback into the system.

Families develop pathology as a result of not having structures that are able to process stressors or day-to-day operations. These stressors can be a result of the wider social context. For example, a father who loses his job may start to drink, while his son may develop difficulty in school. Family pathology also can occur as a result of a developmental change in the family. For example, a single father might have a difficult time dealing with his daughter's reaching puberty and becoming interested in boys. As a result, he becomes overbearing, which leads to conflict with his daughter. She then responds to his attempts to control her by acting out.

Theoretically, the overall structure of a family is divided into subsystems. These are smaller systems that also have functions and sets of interactions. Each subsystem has its own homeostasis and feedback patterns. These subsystems in the family are interdependent. Examples of subsystems are the parental subsystem, made up of the parents. This can be a husband and wife, a father and his second wife, or a single parent and supportive friends. This is contrasted to the sibling subsystem, which might consist of a brother and his older sister.

Related to this theoretical view of a family as a system that drives therapy is an eco- structural approach to therapy. As defined by Aponte and VanDeusen (1981),

> the eco-structural approach to therapy, which is part of this structural therapy movement in therapy, is an effort to include, along with the family, other social systems as contributors to the structure of human behavior, and to work through all these systems to achieve change. (p. 311)

Thus, this approach is broader than just focusing on the family and looks at all systems that impact the family. Representatives from all of these systems are frequently invited to therapy and given full consideration in the treatment, making this a broad systemic approach.

Hierarchies

In structural family therapy, attention is given to the hierarchical relationship of subsystems to each other. In this model each older generation has executive functioning over the younger generation. That is, the parental subsystem has influence over decisions made by the sibling subsystem. While there is feedback in the form of information exchange between the levels of hierarchy, decision making is the function of the higher subsystems. For example, the parents might ask the children what they would like for dinner. However, if the family has good executive functioning, the parents consider their child's wish for candy for dinner but reach a decision to serve a balanced meal.

Healthy families have a clear boundary between themselves and their environment and between each of the subsystems. In unhealthy families the boundaries become blurry. For example, in an unhealthy family a child might be consulted by a parent for her opinion of an appropriate punishment for her sibling, while in a healthy family a child might be given a consequence such as a time-out for trying to parent her sibling. That is not to say that parents should not put an older sibling in charge of a younger peer in their absence. The latter is an adaptive practice as long as the parents are clear that the older child's authority is granted through the parents and is in place only in the absence of the parent.

Detouring occurs when a family member avoids dealing with someone within her or his subsystem. This is often the result of conflicts within that subsystem. For example, a couple may be so angry with each other that they talk only through their child. Over time, some families develop a maladaptive structure referred to as a cross-generational coalition. In a cross-generational coalition, members of two different generations join forces against another member of the family and disrupt the family's healthy functioning.

Roles and Rules

Within each level of the hierarchy is a set of roles and rules associated with each position. *Rules* govern the range of appropriate behaviors for each position. Failure to follow the rules in each position results in breakdown of the system. *Roles* are assigned to each member of a family and modified based on the member's ability to perform them. A balance between roles that are too flexible and roles that are too rigid provides optimal functioning. Overly flexible roles make it hard for the family to maintain a stable process. Overly rigid roles do not allow for creativity, and these families struggle to adapt to unusual circumstances. Roles are also influenced by the developmental stage of the family. Parents take a more hands-on role with their young children, a supportive role as their teens struggle to establish appropriate independence, and a consultative role with their grown adult children.

Boundaries

A boundary is the barrier that separates a system or subsystem from its broader context. Boundaries must be flexible enough to allow for new ideas and processes to enter the system. A healthy system is flexible and is said to have appropriately permeable boundaries. At the same time, it must be strong enough to allow the system to remain intact. Systems with no boundaries or boundaries that are too weak risk disintegrating into the environment. These boundaries are called diffuse. Boundaries that do not allow information to cross are referred to as rigid. For the family system to function efficiently, the boundaries must be strong enough to hold together, permeable enough to allow new information into the system, and clear to all family members.

Minuchin (1974) conceptualizes boundaries as occurring on a continuum that ranges from disengaged to enmeshed. Between these two extremes, most families are able to maintain appropriate boundaries. In a family with disengaged boundaries, the system can have inappropriately rigid boundaries. This style of family allows a good deal of individual variation and autonomy but does not foster a strong sense of belonging. This tolerance for individual variation is allowed to occur until a rigid boundary is crossed.

A family with enmeshed boundaries has a blurring of the boundaries between its subsystems. It is hard to tell when one subsystem ends and another begins. A family with enmeshed boundaries lacks significant distance between family members. This style of family produces heightened feelings of belonging. However, these feelings of belonging come at the price of any sense of autonomy. In such families, the degree to which boundaries are differentiated and enmeshed is a function of a variety of factors in addition to family pathology. Developmental and cultural factors also influence the degree of enmeshment or disengagement in a family's boundaries.

Again, structural family therapy recognizes that developmental factors have a direct impact on the style of boundaries. This is one reason developmental factors became more prominent in a variety of other approaches to family therapy. In general, developmental processes in individuals impact the structure of the family. Families that do not adapt family structures to changes in family development tend to become psychopathological. Families with young children typically have enmeshed boundaries between their sibling and parental subsystems. Likewise, culture has an impact on the style of boundaries a family maintains. For example, a Hispanic family might have boundaries that appear enmeshed to their Caucasian neighbors, while, to the Hispanic family, their Caucasian neighbors seem distant and disengaged.

Joining

Joining is a process of developing a relationship with the family that allows the therapist to observe and ultimately participate in the altering of the family structure. According to Minuchin (1974), in the joining process therapists "[hear] what the family members tell them about the way that they experience reality" (p. 89). Since joining involves becoming a temporary member of the family or developing a therapeutic system made up of the family members plus the therapist, the therapist must become personally available to the family members.

The process of joining involves both the attitude with which the therapist approaches the family as well as the actions in which she or he engages. First, it involves nonjudgmental acceptance of the family's current level of functioning. The therapist seeks to understand, not to judge. If the family members feel judged, they are not likely to be open to revealing their structure, nor will they be available to participate in the change process. Second, the therapist needs to establish an empathetic relationship with the family. As Minuchin (1974) states, the therapist "emphasizes the aspects of his personality and experiences that are syntonic with the family's" (p. 91). In this way, the structural approach parallels experiential therapy in its emphasis on personal connection with clients.

Initially, the therapist joins with the family system as a whole. However, as therapy progresses, the therapist may choose to join with a subsystem (Minuchin, 1974). From that position, the therapist is able to observe the response of the system as a whole. For example, in a case where parents are having a hard time setting limits with their teen, the therapist might talk with the parents about their perceptions of their ability to parent. Or in a case where a single parent is starting to date and the children have concerns, the therapist might join with the children and discuss the qualities they would like to see in their parent's dates.

Enactments

Enactments, the central technique of the structural approach, involve directing the family to interact in a way that brings the family's difficulty into the room. Once this occurs, the therapist has direct access to the family's process. This allows the therapist to observe and even modify the family's problematic structure (Minuchin, 1974). An enactment can start as easily as the therapist's stating, "I want you to discuss with your daughter how you expect her to behave at school." Thus, the implicit goal of an enactment is to encourage the family to have conversations that allow problems to be solved in the therapy session.

The brilliance of this intervention is its straightforward simplicity. However, it is often very difficult to put into action. In their empirical exploration of the use of enactments, Nichols and Fellenberg (2000) point out that novice therapists often choose to avoid using enactments for a variety of reasons, including anxiety on the part of the therapist or the client, clients' memories of past failures, and clients' desire to have the therapist understand their position.

These researchers have also identified a variety of factors in both successful and failed attempts to perform an enactment. In their research project, Nichols and Fellenberg (2000) made observations of successful and unsuccessful videotaped enactments by four experienced structural therapists. They broke each enactment down into three phases: initiation, facilitation, and closing. Based on their observations, they make some recommendations. First, the therapist can speak with clients about their history of discussing the problem, highlighting instances that have been productive. Once the groundwork has been laid, the therapist can invite the clients into a new conversation in the spirit of being productive. The chairs can be moved to face each other and the therapist can set the stage for a productive, collaborative conversation. Furthermore, it is helpful if the therapist is specific in setting the topic for discussion.

Nichols and Fellenberg (2000) have identified three principles for increasing an enactment's effectiveness once it is under way. First, do not interrupt. Letting the family struggle to get through to each other gives them the best chance of effecting change. Interruptions should occur only when the interaction becomes destructive or abusive. Second, it is helpful if the therapist takes the enactment to a deeper emotional level. Nichols and Fellenberg provide several examples: "asking a nagging father to talk about his own growing-up years, inviting an angry and attacking wife to talk about her hurt and loneliness, or asking a brooding adolescent if she thinks her parents understand the pressures she lives with in high school" (p. 152). Finally, it is important to focus on the process of communication rather than taking sides. Process comments are much more useful in keeping the conversation going.

Experienced therapists close enactments in ways that encourage the need for continued dialogues. As Nichols and Fellenberg (2000) conclude, "Clients should begin to learn something about the problematic patterns of their interactions, and they should finish with a clear direction for continued improvements in their ability to communicate with each other." (p. 152).

Mapping

The structural approach's popularity is partly due to its ability to describe complex family patterns and structures. This is accomplished by the development of family maps. According to Minuchin (1974), "The map allows the therapist to formulate hypotheses about areas within the family that function well and about others that may be dysfunctional" (p. 90). Unlike the genogram discussed in Chapter 5, the map does not seek to describe the entire family structure. It focuses on the structure of the family members present in the therapy room. The emphasis in the map is on the therapist's impression of family structure as observed during the process of therapy. It is based on

FIGURE 9.1   **Symbols for Boundaries and Relationships**

FIGURE 9.2 **Detouring**

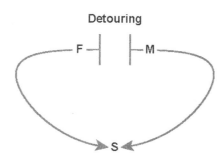

Detouring

a variety of data obtained through the joining process and developed through a combination of observation and self-report of the family.

Maps are based on a simple shorthand for key family members and their relationships. The mother and father are represented by a capital M and F, respectively. Together they make up the parental subsystem. Boundaries between members of a subsystem as well as between subsystems themselves are represented. The identified patient is represented by IP, and T can represent the therapist. Sons are represented by an S and daughters by a D. Multiple children of the same gender are represented by a subscripted numeral after the S or D. Boundaries between individuals and subsystems are represented by the symbols described in Figure 9.1.

FIGURE 9.3 **Cross-Generational Coalition**

Cross-Generational
Coalition

Let's look at an example. If a husband and wife stopped talking to each other and communicated through their son, the map would show the conflict between the husband and wife as follows:

If over time the parents compete for their son's attention rather than addressing the conflict in their relationship, the family is at risk of developing a cross-generational coalition. In this example, let's say the mother wins the son's allegiance through special attention. This family will then develop a cross-generational coalition where the son and mother team up in hostile interactions with the father. This situation would be mapped as follows:

Questioning

Structural family therapy is an action-oriented and present-focused approach to changing families. By and large, it does not concern itself with the past. While the family's current functioning may have been generated in the past, it is viewed as being maintained in the present. It is also in the present that the change will occur. Given this, there is little concern with the history of the dysfunction. Rather, the focus is on how the system maintains the problem.

The development of a problem may have little to do with how it is maintained. For example, a family may have started treating a child with a serious illness as fragile. However, after the illness has resolved, the child may continue to act fragile to continue to get special attention from his parents. This often leads to resentment from the "fragile" child's siblings. In our culture there is a belief that understanding how a problem develops is central to solving it. When the family presents with a need to have the generation of a problem understood, it is useful to spend some time initially getting clarity around the problem. Unless the family members have a good deal of interest in the past, there is little history taken in this approach.

Since this approach is action oriented, the majority of the interview focuses on describing patterns of interaction and structures in the family. Members might be asked to describe how other members of the family function as well as how they themselves function. However, this approach is also sensitive to hierarchy, so a lower level of the family would not be asked to describe the functioning of a higher level. For example, a child would be asked to share her perspective on her functioning in school, as would her parents. However, it would not be appropriate for that child to describe her sister's school performance. In the same manner, it would be inappropriate for the parents and children to discuss concerns about the grandparents.

Joining is a key theoretical contribution of this approach. It is important to consider how it is facilitated by the interview. The goal of joining is to become a member of the family system. Questions are asked from the perspective of a future insider. The therapist takes a neutral, nonjudgmental stance and approaches the family with a natural curiosity. This position of seeking to understand how the family functions serves as the foundation for the development of the therapist-plus-client system. It is this relationship that establishes hope in the family and allows them to follow the therapist's directives. Directives are designed to promote the establishment of more functional structures. As change occurs, the family is supported as it establishes a new homeostatic mechanism to hold the new system steady.

Structuring

True to its name, structural therapy is driven by its ability to help families change and redefine their structure. Given this, the structure of the interview is straightforward and direct. As described above, the therapist quickly joins with the family by establishing a personal relationship with all members. In particular, joining involves establishing a position of leadership with the highest level of the family's hierarchy.

From this position of leadership, the therapist alters and supports the executive subsystem in the family. This is done by enabling its members to clearly establish more appropriate boundaries. The therapist also assists the executive subsystem in making decisions about the family. For example, in a family with a teenager who has violated curfew, the therapist might encourage the parents to agree on the amount of time he will lose his driving privileges. In this situation, the parents are prompted to act as a unified front to reach a consensus about how long the consequence will be applied.

Families with only one parent present a unique situation. It is often the case that, out of the isolation inherent in being the family's sole executive, a parent will allow a child to become parentified. In this situation, the parentified child is treated as a quasi-adult with access to the adult's confidence and decision-making authority. While the child may initially seek out and embrace this position of privilege, over time it becomes a burden. An innovation to address this structural problem might be to allow extended family or single parents from other families to become consultants for the executive subsystem.

In addition to supporting the executive subsystem's position of authority, the structural family therapist helps establish appropriate intergenerational boundaries. For example, suppose that, in the case above, the teen's younger brother interjects that taking the car away from his brother would also punish him, since he depends on his brother for transportation. As a result, his brother's loss of driving privileges would be unfair to him. In this situation, the therapist could help the parents see the manipulation and set boundaries in the younger brother. This could be done by giving the parents a directive. Here they would be asked to tell their younger son to stay out of the discussion.

Video Call Out 9.2: Structural/Strategic Family Therapy

In this video Dr. Edwards has the daughter switch seats with her father. This places the parents next to each other symbolically breaking up the cross-generational coalition. When they sit in this position he encourages the parents to consider drug testing. He also encourages the parents to set limits on their daughter, recommending that she not be allowed to drive until she has a clean urine screen. While the mother is still coming around to this concern about her daughter's drug involvement, Dr. Edwards shares the school's concern that Kara was caught with an amount of drug typical for someone involved in distribution. This further reinforces the parents as an executive system, which functions to support their daughter.

A mistake often made by novice structural therapists is to take too much responsibility for altering the family's structure. It is far better to allow the executive subsystem to make its own correction in structure. A useful way for therapists to think about their role in restructuring the system is that of a consultant to the executive subsystem. The therapist provides directives to that system, and it is up to the system to implement the changes in structure. For example, during a session a child may wander across the room and start to rummage through the therapist's desk. Rather than asking the child to stay out of the desk, the therapist might ask the parents to direct their child to stay out of the desk. This gives the therapist an opportunity to observe how the parents direct their child. If they have difficulty with this task, the therapist can continue to coach and support them as they try to successfully direct their child.

The most common structure of the therapeutic interview is a meeting with the entire family. This is especially true of the intake session. However, structural therapists are flexible in their structure of therapy, often meeting with the family for a significant amount of time to be effective and sometimes doing a long marathon session when such a meeting has the potential to be productive. Meetings are scheduled frequently enough to maximize effectiveness. Since the structural model is informed by the client's environment, representatives from larger systems are often invited to the sessions. If possible, the referral source is invited to attend the first session. For example, when a family is referred by social services, a structural therapist will invite the case worker to attend the session. In session, the case worker can provide clarity for the therapist concerning the family's current functioning and help the family set specific goals for the outcome of therapy.

While the structural family therapist most frequently works with the whole family, sometimes it is appropriate to meet with subsystems. For example, it would be useful to excuse a child before confronting the parents on their inappropriate parenting techniques. This way the therapist creates a boundary between the parents and children. Furthermore, it prevents the children from viewing their parents as less of an authority and further empowers the parental executive subsystem.

Video Call Out 9.3: Structural/Strategic Family Therapy

Toward the end of the session Kara is asked what she would like from therapy. This is after the needs of the executive subsystem have been somewhat addressed. Her request is for independence and use of a car. This is balanced against her parent's need for safety. Her desires are linked to her being able to produce negative urine screens that document her progress. In the post-session interview Dr. Edwards states that he is concerned that she has been experimenting for a while. The utility of the drug test is that it can give knowledge that Kara's word can't. This eliminates denying, lying and minimizations by providing empirical data to the therapist.

Responding

This approach calls for the therapist to join with the family system to effect change from the inside of the family. To do this, the therapist engages with the executive system first. The therapist strikes a balance between being a directive expert in family functioning and being a supportive consultant. As a consultant for the family, the therapist responds directly to any questions they have. The therapist models a caring executive system that helps the family become more comfortable with the changing structure.

In this approach, the therapist seeks to be responsive to clients' need for improved structure. The therapist uses the leverage gained from joining with the family to induce the desired change, taking the position that the clients are directly responsible for change. In situations where the family tries to make the therapist responsible for change, the therapist gently redirects the family. If the redirect fails to allow the family to take responsibility, the therapist can respond by creating a boundary, which entails simply stating that the therapist is not responsible for creating changes for the family and that the family needs to put forth effort during the enactments.

Applications

Since structural family therapy is a foundational theory, it has been widely applied to a variety of settings and presenting problems. It is a core approach for many family therapists who have been practicing since the early 1970s. Given that its influence has been widespread, components of this model have been adapted to many eclectic and integrated models of family therapy. However, for the sake of brevity, let us discuss some of the applications of structural family therapy in its pure form as well as a few recent examples.

Structural family therapy has frequently been applied to culturally diverse families. Examples include Asian American families (Kim, 2003), Chinese families (Jung, 1984), Native American families (Napoliello & Sweet, 1992), ultra-orthodox Jewish families (Wiselberg, 1992), and Italian American families (Yaccarino, 1993). Ethnic families often have issues of deciding where to maintain their unique cultural traits and how to intersect with the broader culture. This often gets expressed in tension between generations, as older generations frequently take a conservative stance in contrast to their children's liberal stance. Structural family therapy and the use of enactment allow families to discuss this tension in a way that can enable the parents and children to move toward a resolution of their ongoing conflict.

A noteworthy application of structural family therapy was suggested by Lever and Wilson (2005) for use in families where grandparents have become primary caregivers in the family. These authors document a 65% increase in the number of grandparent-headed households between 1990 and 2000, and there is reason to expect that this trend will continue in the foreseeable future (Lever & Wilson, 2005). While these grandparents make significant personal sacrifices and are a true innovation in structure, these families face many challenges. The normal family developmental pattern is disrupted, and there is a limited cultural model for how grandparents can be successful in the child rearing task. Often children, parents, and grandparents become angry over the absence of the parent generation, which can result in a loss of boundaries. Structural family therapy can be especially helpful in allowing these parties to resolve their anger issues as they reestablish appropriate intergenerational boundaries.

A well-researched and interesting application of structural family therapy is in working with families who have a member struggling with anorexia nervosa (Fishman, 2006; Minuchin, Rosman, & Baker, 1978; Raymond, Freelander, Heatherington, Ellis, & Sargent, 1993; Stein, Mozdzierz, & Mozdzierz, 1998; Vetere, 2001). In addressing this issue, the family therapist acts within a treatment team that helps the patient's family deal with the identified and often dangerous weight issues. Here enactment helps the family deal with interaction patterns that support the eating disorder.

An advanced type of intervention for families with a member who has anorexia nervosa involves having a session where the therapist and family meet over lunch. As Rosman, Minuchin, and Liebman (1975) relate, "eating lunch with the family provides exceptional opportunities for the therapist to observe family members' transactions around eating as well as make on-the-spot interventions to change the patterns of these transactions" (p. 846). Thus we see that structural family therapy's ability to directly assess and change family structure makes it a useful approach to working with troubled family members. This serves as in example of a structural family therapist have enactments around the families most difficult issues. From here the seek to utilize the emotional energy around this issue to motivate family members to alter the structure of how they relate.

As mentioned above structural family therapy, largely because of it's ability to produce change has remained a popular approach to work with families. Recently some creative work has been done with this theory in a wide range of settings with a wide variety of clients. Messina, Kolbert, Hyatt-Burkhart, & Crothers (2015) utilized structural family therapy to address issues in the relationship between school systems and family systems. In another similar article Kindsvatter, Duba, Dean (2008) explore structural techniques for engaging reluctant parents in counseling with their teens. Laura & Kindsvatter (2014) describe a creative utilization of structural family therapy in working with families experiencing job loss. Recognizing the role of career in structuring one's life authors provide useful intervention for families dealing with this transition. In these examples of applications we see that structural family therapy remains a vibrant and relevant theory.

Acting as a Structural Family Therapist

Structural family therapists seek to see whole families, often bringing several generations of families together for the session. They are comfortable working alone or with a co-therapist during the interview. Since broader systems are included in the treatment, the therapist often strives to include the referral sources in at least the initial intake session.

From the start of the therapeutic process and throughout the entire course of the session, the therapist is active and socially engaging, an active participant in the process of changing the family's structure. She or he makes suggestions and expresses feeling about the family's struggles to resolve their problems. After making a suggestion for the family, the structural family therapist is careful to follow up on the outcome of that intervention. If the family fails, the structural family therapist accepts the failure and uses that information to modify her or his map of the family as well as further interventions. Structural family therapists model patience, for frequently it takes a while for the changes made to become comfortable or natural to the family.

Case Example: The Case of Pablo's Truancy

You receive a phone call from the professional school counselor at the local high school, Ms. Jones, requesting that you see the Gonzales family. The family consists of Juan the father, age 39; Rosario the mother, age 33; Pablo their son, age 14; and Maria their daughter, age 13. Pablo has been suspended from school for numerous absences. He has little interest in his studies and claims that he will drop out when he is 16. He wants to be a truck driver like his father. His father is a high school graduate who works the midnight shift driving a delivery truck. Pablo's mother works in the afternoons at a local store. She did not graduate from high school, having dropped out in her senior year. Pablo's mother is unable to get him up for school in the morning, and as a result he is in danger of failing school. A medical evaluation found Pablo in good health and discovered no medical reason for his inability to get up in the morning. The school is giving the family two weeks to show improvement in Pablo's attendance, or they will refer the case to social services for truancy and neglect.

As you talk to the counselor, you share her concern for the family and ask when she will be able to attend a session with the family. She is surprised by this suggestion, and you state that you would like her to attend the beginning of the first session so she can represent the school's position. You also state that her presence will assist the family in developing a positive relationship with the school. You suggest an early appointment so that Mr. Gonzales can attend after he gets off from work. You assure her that in your thinking it will be key for the whole family to attend as well as her. She sets an appointment and states that she will call to confirm it after she talks to Mrs. Gonzales.

The school is referring the family to you because you have had success in other cases they've referred. While you are Caucasian, you have experience working with Hispanic families. The Gonzaleses are an English-speaking, Mexican American family who have been citizens for two generations.

Session One

The family arrives on time for the session, and as you escort them into your interview room you note that they are all dressed in a neat and casual manner. You make a point to address Mr. Gonzales first, giving him a firm handshake and thanking him for bringing his family to therapy. You next shake Mrs. Gonzales's hand and thank her for bringing her family to therapy. Next you greet Ms. Jones, shaking her hand and thanking her for bringing the family to see you. You ask the adults if they had any problem finding your office and compliment them on their promptness. You shake the hands of each of the children as they enter the room. You invite the family to sit in your interview room by pointing to your chair and saying, "I usually sit here. Please sit where you are comfortable." As the family begins to sit down, you take note that Mrs. Gonzales has the paperwork all filled out. You thank her for having it done prior to the session, and as you briefly review it you ask her and then the family if they have any questions about it. When they all say no, you say, "Great! Let's get started."

You take note that Mr. Gonzales sits closest to your chair on the sofa. His wife sits next to him and their daughter sits down on the other side of her mother. Finally, Pablo takes a seat in the armchair across from you, which places him closest to his sister and farthest from his father. You bring an extra chair next to yourself for Ms. Jones. You then ask Mr. Gonzales if you could start by having Ms. Jones give a report of the school system's view of the family's situation. As Ms. Jones starts to give her report to you, you redirect her to give her report to the parents.

Ms. Jones brings out a folder that has a record of Pablo's school attendance. At the three-month mark in the school year, he has already had his allowed allotment of absences for the whole year. The school is also concerned about his being late to class. Ms. Jones also raises with Pablo the school's concern about his indifferent attitude. When she brings up these issues, he shakes his head and looks down muttering, "Whatever."

This comment makes Mr. Gonzales angry, and he starts scolding his son. He commands that Pablo sit up straight, take his hat off, and start addressing Ms. Jones with respect. As he does this, his wife places her hand on his leg as if to restrain him while at the same time looking at him in support of what he is saying. In response, Pablo sits up, removes his hat, and mutters a weak, "I'm sorry" to Ms. Jones. She seems uncomfortable by this interaction and quietly responds, "That's OK." Mr. Gonzales speaks further to his son in an angry tone in Spanish. After a few sentences, his son looks away at the floor and softly says in a childlike voice, "Sorry, Papa."

In response to this, you address Mr. Gonzales and apologize that you do not understand Spanish. However, you state that even if you do not understand the language, you can tell he was talking to his son about respect and that you see that it is an important value in the family. Mr. Gonzales says that out of respect for you, he will try to remember to speak only English in therapy. You state that while you do not speak Spanish very well you do understand a little, and that you understand that some important things can be said only in the "family's language." You go on to say that you did not feel disrespected when he addressed his son.

You then ask the parents if it's okay that their family therapist can understand only a little Spanish. Mrs. Gonzales reassures you that since you understand the importance of respect, she and her husband will be able to trust and work with you. You further say that you have some understanding of Mexican American culture but will need help understanding how it impacts the Gonzales family. You go on to state that you would be willing to learn about the values of their family in therapy and that you will try to provide therapy that respects those values. Mr. and Mrs. Gonzales agree to this contract. You then address Pablo and Maria and ask if they also agree to help educate you in their family's culture. In response, they simply nod their heads.

You turn back to Ms. Jones and ask her to continue to discuss the school's perspective on Pablo's school performance. She goes on to talk about his potential but states that she is concerned about his recent decline in motivation. She goes on to explain that Pablo's teachers find him capable of completing his work. They find him to be a bright, interesting kid. She states that while he is not the most academically gifted child, until recently he was a hard worker and easy to get along with. While the school does not find any evidence of attention-deficit disorder, they have recently become concerned that he may have an oppositional-defiant disorder.

You ask Ms. Jones if this is a change, based on her experience with him. She states that last year in school Pablo was a very cooperative and concerned child. However, over the summer, his motivation seemed to disappear. She also reports that teachers have tried to approach him but that he has distanced himself from them. She reports that there have been no discipline referrals for Pablo. You ask her if she expects any drug involvement on his part.

This question grabs everyone's attention, and Pablo quickly denies any involvement. Mrs. Gonzales looks her son directly in the eye and tells him he better not be involved in drugs. Mr. Gonzales states that he has friends at work who have children involved in drugs, but he doesn't think his son is. Ms. Jones agrees and states that she doesn't see any drug signs with Pablo. You state that you didn't mean to scare everybody but asked so that you could fully assess the situation.

Ms. Jones goes on to say that Pablo's change in attitude is a mystery to the faculty at his school. While he was not the strongest student last year, this year he seems to be unable to be motivated in any way. The school is concerned because Pablo is not attending school on a regular basis, and if there is no significant change in his school attendance, truancy charges will be filed against him. You ask Ms. Jones to define what the school means by "significant change." Ms. Jones states that Pablo needs to be in school every day until the end of the term, which is two weeks away. Furthermore, he needs to complete all of his work and have no suspensions during the same period.

You thank Ms. Jones for attending therapy and ask her if she has anything to add. You remind her that you have a release to talk to her and ask her if she would be willing to contact you if anything comes up. You also ask her if you can follow up with her in a few weeks for a progress report. When you walk her to the door, you again thank her for her involvement with the family. As you escort her outside, you remind her that she should feel free to call you should anything come up.

After Ms. Jones is gone, you return your attention to the family. You again address Mr. Gonzales, this time asking him how he and his wife can make sure Pablo gets to school over the next two days until you can see them back for a follow-up session. Mr. Gonzales suggests that since he has the next two days off from work, he can be the one who gets Pablo ready for school. You ask if they think that will work. Mrs. Gonzales points out that her son has less of a problem following her husband's directions.

FIGURE 9.4   **Gonzales Family**

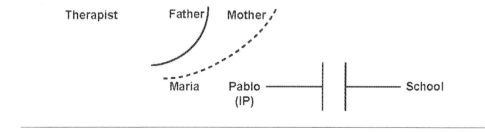

As you point out that time is almost over for this session, the parents start to talk to you and their children about the importance of education. You let this go on a few minutes, then clarify that the parents' goal is for their children to graduate from school, not just attend until they can legally drop out. The parents quickly agree, but Pablo shakes his head and states he does not think he wants to graduate. You tell him that you hear and respect his opinion but that you are not sure being a dropout is in his best interest.

You tell the family that you need to end the session here and get up to escort them out. As they get up, you look directly at Mr. Gonzales and emphasize that it is very important that he get his son to school over the next two days. He agrees, and you walk with the family out of the office, thanking them for their participation.

Between sessions, you develop a map of your hypotheses of the family's structure. You draw diffuse boundaries between the mother and both of her children. The father has a detached relationship with the family, who are at risk of developing a cross-generational coalition. You draw the school as being in conflict with the son, who is this family's identified patient. You draw yourself as a member of the parental generation who is trying to join with the family and the executive system and attempting to break down the detachment between the father and the family.

Session Two

The family arrives promptly for their second session, and you ask the parents to sit on the sofa and the children to take seats in armchairs across from their parents. You sit off to the side between the two subsystems. Mr. Gonzales seems less stressed and starts the session by stating that he was able to get Pablo to school on time the past two days. You congratulate him on his success and notice that Mrs. Gonzales is smiling brightly and looking directly at her husband. Mr. Gonzales describes in detail how he got his son up and off to school. When Pablo would complain that he didn't want to go to school, his father would reply that he didn't have to want to go to school, only realize that he needed to go. Mr. Gonzales shared with his son that this was how he felt about work every day.

You speak directly to Mr. Gonzales and congratulate him on getting to the core of the issue. You point out that it is more important that Pablo get to school, not that he want to go to school. You share that sometimes you don't feel like going to your job, but you do it because you like to be able to provide for your family. When Mrs. Gonzales asks you what they should do about Pablo's attitude toward school, you respond by asking him what he plans to do about his attitude about work. You go on to explain, "What is important is that he goes to work or school, not how he feels about it. You suggest that over time he will stop complaining less as he gets little or no attention for it.

You turn to Mrs. Gonzales and ask her and her husband to discuss among themselves and with their children how they are going to continue their success. You clarify that by success, you mean, how are they going to keep Pablo in school? Mr. Gonzales starts by telling you that he needs to go back to work tomorrow, so getting Pablo to school is his wife's problem after today. As you redirect him to talk to his wife, you state that it is the family's problem and you wonder how the family will continue to be successful. As you give this directive, you sit back in your chair as you slide it back slightly.

For a few moments the family says nothing as the parents look at each other. Mr. Gonzales turns to you and asks for help. You tell him that it might be best if he and his wife talk about their success in getting their son to school over the past couple of days. At this point, Pablo interrupts and makes a speech about how he will drop out of school as soon as he is 16. As Mrs. Gonzales turns to her son and starts to argue with him about his continued education, you address the parents directly. You remind that them that you asked them to talk about their success in keeping their son is school now, not in two years. You compliment Pablo on a good job distracting his parents but say that this is not the issue at hand. You ask Maria if Pablo is good at distracting the family.

She agrees that he is and goes on to complain that he often makes his parents mad by threatening to quit school. You ask her if this is keeping the family from doing anything else that she would rather do. She says they don't do much as a family because both of her parents are extremely busy. She also expresses anger because, when her parents aren't working, they're dealing with issues they have with Pablo. You thank her for her input and share with her that this observation might be important in the future but that right now you want the family to focus on continuing their success.

Turning back to the parents, you comment that you, like the rest of the family, get distracted by Pablo's talking about dropping out of school and again ask them to discuss their success. Mr. and Mrs. Gonzales talk to each other for a period about how having Mr. Gonzales in charge of getting Pablo to school over the past few days really helped. However, they are concerned that their success will come to an end because he needs to return to work. As the conversation trails off and the couple seem at a loss as to how to continue, you suggest that they talk with their children about what worked over the past few days.

Maria starts by saying that she enjoyed how the whole family got up at the same time and got ready for school. She goes on to say how she felt the family was spending more time talking and doing things together. Pablo talks about how he liked having his father around more. Mrs. Gonzales agrees with her children about how nice it's been to have the children's father around the past few days.

In response to this, Mr. Gonzales becomes angry and seems overwhelmed. He talks about how much pressure there is on him at work and how now he feels as if his family is saying he needs to take care of the children too. At this point, you ask the parents about how they divide the household tasks. Mrs. Gonzales states that since she does not work, she is in charge of the kids and the house. Mr. Gonzales goes on to state that he earns all of the money and manages the family's finances. He describes how he and his wife reached this agreement in response to feeling that each of their childhoods suffered because their mothers were absent working.

You ask the parents to discuss whether this arrangement is still working. In response, Mrs. Gonzales discusses how overwhelmed she is with the children and the house. She says that for several years before Pablo started to get into trouble, she needed the children more than they needed her. Since Pablo began getting into trouble, she has been feeling like a bad, ineffective mother. She states that often she wants the support of her husband, but seeing how tired and overworked he always is, she avoids talking about her concerns. Mr. Gonzales goes on to discuss how he is tired of work and burdened by making all of the family's financial decisions. While the family has enough money to meet their needs, they don't have much to spare. He describes how he feels like a wet blanket, often telling his wife and children they can't afford certain things.

Mrs. Gonzales gets defensive and starts to talk to you, but you redirect her to talk to her husband with a gentle hand motion. She tells him that he has to say no because she's in the dark about the financial picture most of the time. The children agree with her and gang up against their dad by agreeing with their mother that they're in the dark about the family's resources. At this point, you interrupt and warn Mr. and Mrs. Gonzales that their children are in their argument. You go on to point out that they would be best served by having this argument without their children involved. Mrs. Gonzales turns to her children and tells them that she can handle this with their father.

At this point, you mention that time has almost expired and ask the parents if they feel that their parenting contract is working for them. They both come to the idea that their contract is obsolete. You suggest that they come to the next session without their children to renegotiate the contract. You suggest that, between sessions, they continue to work with Pablo to extend the family's success in getting him to school. The parents agree that they will return alone for the next session. As they leave, you inform the children that they will be needed again for the session after next.

Session Three

Two days before the next session, Mrs. Gonzales calls you and states that she wants to talk about some concerns. Before she can speak further, you ask if her husband knows she is calling. She reports that if he knew about what she's going to tell you, he would hit the roof. As you empathize with her, you state that this puts you in a difficult position. You explain that if you know a secret, it makes it difficult for you to be a therapist for the family. You explain that if you become an ally for one member, the others will be distant from you. You encourage her to attend the session but to tell her husband her concerns for her son. She responds that she is afraid her husband will become angry.

You confront her by stating that you may be wrong, but it is your sense that her husband wants to be more connected to the family. You cite how willing he was to work with Pablo in getting him to school. You ask her to think about it but encourage her to attend the next session.

On the day of the appointment, Mr. and Mrs. Gonzales arrive promptly. As the session starts, you look at Mrs. Gonzales and ask her where she would like to start. She begins by disclosing that three days ago when looking for something in her son's backpack, she found a bag of marijuana and some powder that she thought was cocaine. Mr. Gonzales looks both angry and concerned at the same time. He asks her what she did with the drugs, and she states that she flushed them down the drain. He exclaims, "That explains why Pablo's been on such good behavior the past few days!"

At this point, you ask him if he is angry at his wife. He replies that he is angry at his son, not his wife. He then talks about how he is hurt that she didn't come to him sooner and is concerned that she was worried about his anger. He talks about how when they were first together, he had some anger and abuse problems. However, he is sad that while he feels he has overcome these issues, his wife has been slow to recognize the change. At this point, Mrs. Gonzales starts to cry, and her husband holds her and comforts her.

After holding hands tenderly for several minutes, they ask you what to do about their son. You tell them that substance abuse is beyond the scope of your expertise, but you state that you would like to work with a colleague who has substance abuse expertise. You make the call to your colleague to set up a substance abuse assessment with her for Pablo. At the same time, you start to renegotiate the therapeutic contract such that your colleague will work with Pablo on his substance abuse issues and you will work with the family on their associated issues. At your colleague's recommendation, you set a time to meet with her and Pablo's parents to discuss the case before she meets with Pablo.

Case Discussion

In the first session, the therapist quickly theorized that the family's structure was contributing to Pablo's refusal to go to school. Part of this assessment was based on where family members sat. The children appeared to be moving toward developing a cross-generational coalition with their mother. This was demonstrated by the father's distance from the others at the start of the session as well as the parents' long-standing rigid division of labor. The division of labor appeared to have been functional at one point, but clearly it no longer met the family's needs. As is often the case, the family did not seem to be aware of the coalition that they were starting to develop or the impact it was having on the children, particularly Pablo.

The school representative's attendance at the session helped the therapist join with the family. Having the school dictate what the family needed to accomplish motivated them to address their issues. This helped establish the implicit goal of having Pablo return to school. From here the therapist worked as a member of the family-plus-therapist treatment system to help the family get Pablo to go to school. This also allowed the therapist to join with the family and become a quasi-member of the executive system. This was accomplished through discussion of the problem as well as broader social issues of ethnicity.

When there is a sudden and dramatic shift in a student's personality, the therapist's default hypothesis is drug usage. Rather than hinting at his concern, the therapist simply asked the family about these issues. In this case, the family initially denied any drug involvement. However, the therapist's question made the issue part of the parents' concerns and helped lead to the mother's discovery later on. By bringing it up early, the therapist signaled to the family that they could handle addressing this issue.

Since the session ended with the family still concerned, the therapist set a quick return date. By giving the family a simple homework assignment that helped address the cross-generational coalition, the therapist hoped they would make some progress on the problem between sessions. If that did not happen, the therapist would have new data to work with in the follow-up session.

During the second session, the therapist sought to reinforce the success the parents had made in getting their son to attend school. This occurred when Mr. Gonzales got his son off to school successfully. From the position of an additional member of the executive system, the therapist helped the parents learn not to be distracted by their son. Many parents lose track of an immediate issue when their child talks about a broader issue. This occurred in this case when the parents were working on getting Pablo to school and he tried to distract them by talking about not liking school and dropping out.

In this case, the issue is getting Pablo to school, not whether or not he will drop out in two years or whether he likes school. It is common for parents to get lost in trying to address their child's attitude toward school or homework rather then getting her or him to simply comply. When

Mr. Gonzales told his son that he didn't want to go to work every day but went anyway, he went a long way toward resolving the motivational issues.

In the enactment during this session, the family made a lot of progress toward getting Pablo to attend school. In addition, the parents began to function as a more enabled subsystem. The parents came to see a need to renegotiate their parental contract, and the therapist agreed to arrange a follow-up session to help them with these issues.

In the third session, the disclosure of Pablo's drug usage quickly changes the focus and direction of the interview. Rather than following the initial plan of working on the parents' contract, the therapist makes a referral to assist the family in addressing Pablo's substance abuse. This is a typical response when the course of therapy changes dramatically. Here the therapist renegotiates the therapeutic contract. Typically the therapist would work with the substance abuse counselor as part of a treatment team. The family therapist could continue to work with the family on improving the family's functioning while the substance abuse counselor works with Pablo on his substance abuse issues.

Evaluating Structural Family Therapy

On a basic level, one way to evaluate a theory of family therapy is to judge its impact on the practice of family therapy. Structural family therapy has influenced the thinking of many therapists as they practice with families. The concept of joining has become a universal explanation of how therapists seek to establish a practical working relationship with the family system. Likewise, enactment, where the family brings their problematic pattern of interaction directly into the therapy room, has become commonplace in many approaches to psychotherapy.

Structural family therapy was founded as an empirically supported approach early in Minuchin's career at the Wiltwyck school. An uncontrolled study compared clients receiving structural family therapy with other clients at the Wiltwyck school (Minuchin, Montalvo, Guerney, Rosman, & Schumer, 1967). While the sample was small, seven out of 11 families demonstrated improvement in the parents' ability to parent, as well as clinical success. Since then this theory has continued to be empirically validated and refined. As early as 1981, Aponte and VanDeusen concluded, "Structural family therapy appears to be at least as successful as any of the current schools" (p. 358). It was also established as a treatment of choice for a variety of presenting problems for which it was shown empirically to be effective. Later studies found structural family therapy to be an effective approach to treating conduct disorders (Chamberlain & Rosicky, 1995; Szapocznik, et al., 1989).

After working with delinquent boys, Minuchin tested his theory as a treatment for psychosomatic illness in children. Empirical support for the acceptance of structural family therapy and family therapy as a whole came out of these studies, which demonstrated the theory's clinical utility. Minuchin and colleagues (1978) reported a success rate of 90% in treating 53 cases of anorexia nervosa with structural family therapy. While again, this was an uncontrolled study, the degree of success provides very strong support for this approach. In studies of psychosomatic families, structural family therapy was found to be an effective approach to increasing diabetes treatment compliance and reducing the severity of symptoms in people with asthma (Minuchin et al., 1975).

More recently, Campbell and Patterson (1995) found structural family therapy to be successful in treating anorexia nervosa.

Stanton and Todd (1979) found structural family therapy to be an effective approach to addressing issues of substance abuse. In their comparison study, structural family therapy showed more than double the amount of positive change when compared to a family placebo and an individual therapy approach. This further established this approach as a useful therapy for dealing with the structural issues that families face when addressing the impact of substance abuse.

Given the several threads of research that have established structural family therapy as an empirically validated approach to family therapy, we can have confidence in its ability to produce change in families. In addition to the empirical evidence, we have over a generation of family therapists who can attest to the effectiveness of this approach. Its ability to give the family therapist a sense of the family's structure as well as its provision of an effective mapping technique are yet more evidence of its importance.

Learning Exercises

1. In formal organizations, a detailed job description delineates the roles and rules for each position. Think back to when you were a teen and write a job description for your position as a teenager in your family. What role were you expected to perform? What rules were you required to follow?

2. Partway through the class, rearrange the seating of students in your classroom. After a period of time, discuss how the change in class structure changed your experience in the class.

3. Draw a map of the structure of your family during your teen years. In what way did the structure of your family influence your decision to study family therapy? What aspects of family's structure will help you in your career and what aspects will hinder you in your career as a family therapist?

Discussion Questions

1. Share with your peers your job description as a teen (developed in the first learning exercise). Discuss the differences among the job descriptions. How did these differences affect the functioning of each family?

2. What is the structure of the training program you are currently enrolled in? How does that structure affect the experience of the students who participate in that system?

3. In the case of the Gonzalez family do you think the therapist paid enough attention to issues of race and social economic status? How could you have approached these issues differently?

Suggested Readings

Minuchin, S. (1974). *Families and family therapy.* Cambridge, MA: Harvard University Press.

Minuchin, S., & Fishman, H. C. (1981). *Family therapy techniques.* Cambridge, MA: Harvard University Press.

Nichols, M. P., & Fellenberg, S. (2000). The effective use of enactments in family therapy: A discovery-oriented process study. *Journal of Marital and Family Therapy, 26,* 143–152.

Web Resources

The Philadelphia Child and Family Therapy Training Center

http://philafamily.com/

The Minuchin Center for the Family Homepage

http://www.minuchincenter.org/home

Wikipedia's Information on Structural Family Therapy

https://en.wikipedia.org/wiki/Structural_family_therapy

Flashcards from Quizlet Structural Family Therapy

https://quizlet.com/8791229/minuchinstructural-family-therapy-flash-cards/

CHAPTER

10

STRATEGIC FAMILY THERAPY

Thinking About This Approach

The strategic approach was largely developed by Jay Haley, an early member of the Mental Research Institute (MRI; see Chapter 8) who helped start the family therapy movement. Starting in 1953, Haley was one of the researchers in the Bateson research project on communication in families of people with schizophrenia. As part of the project, he and John Weakland traveled from Palo Alto, California, to Phoenix, Arizona, to consult with Milton Erickson about his hypnotherapy approach. Haley left the MRI group in 1967 and went to the Philadelphia Child Guidance Center, where he joined Minuchin and continued to develop his theoretical orientation until 1976. From there he went with Cloé Madanes to direct the Family Therapy Institute of Washington, D.C., where he continued to develop and refine his model of family therapy (Zeig, Ritterman, & Welter-Enderman, n.d.). Haley continued to be an active speaker until his death in 2007.

Strategic family therapy was a popular and influential model during the 1970s and 1980s. Its development paralleled that of structural family therapy. In fact, Haley and Minuchin worked together for a number of years. Given this close working relationship, the structural and strategic approaches are frequently integrated into a structural strategic approach that itself has some empirical validation.

Haley's early emphasis on overcoming resistance was from a modern or first-order cybernetics perspective, but his later work evolved with the thinking in the field into a cybernetics of cybernetics perspective. Describing creative ways of dealing with resistance to change was central to this approach. Clients would often present for therapy asking to change something that they were resistant to changing. Strategic therapeutic techniques were developed to overcome the client's resistance. However, seeing the client system as separate from the therapist system and thinking in terms of overcoming resistance is one way this theory was stuck in a first-order view of therapy. Later, this approach focused less on resistance and more on developing a collaborative therapeutic approach. When the client and therapist are in a collaborative relationship, resistance simply is not an issue.

The strategic approach uses general systems theory to understand the family and how the family relates to its social environment. As Haley (1987) asserts when describing the foundations of his approach, "The therapist not only must think in different ways about human dilemmas but also must consider himself or herself as a member of the social unit that contains the problem" (p. 2). Thus, this theory is clearly a postmodern or cybernetics of cybernetics approach where the therapist-plus-client is the system that is changed during therapy. In addition, this treatment system is itself part of the larger context of the mental health system.

Like other approaches in the first generation of family therapy theories, the strategic approach is both brief and directive. Like the hypnotherapy of Milton Erickson, the therapist takes direct responsibility for assisting clients in resolving their problems by means of a unique strategy. Clear goals are negotiated between the client's family and the therapist, and a therapeutic contract is established. In strategic family therapy the therapist and client then work together to generate a solution to the client's problem.

In the strategic approach, the emphasis is not on developing techniques that can be universally applied but rather on looking at how the social context contributes to maintaining the problem. From here an attempt is made to solve the client's dilemma with an intervention that is unique to the problem. As Madanes (1991) states, "The emphasis is not on a method to be applied to all cases, but on designing a strategy for each specific problem" (p. 396). Through understanding the family, the therapist develops a unique intervention for each presenting problem. As Haley (1987) states in his classic work *Problem Solving Therapy*, "The emphasis is not on a method but on approaching each problem with special techniques for the specific situation" (p. 1). Thus, this approach is about developing skills at problem solving that assist the family in addressing its presenting problem.

Personality is of interest to a strategic therapist as a vehicle that can be used to drive the individual to change. Personality is not seen as an explanation of how a problem developed but is simply accepted. Thus, strategic therapy is one of the early models that shifts psychology out of the past and into the present in the form of action. In a similar fashion, diagnosis is of interest only as part of a description of what is currently going on with the client.

In his book *Uncommon Therapy* (1973), a tribute to Erickson's approach to therapy, Haley provides a straightforward definition of his work: "Therapy can be called strategic if the clinician initiates what happens during therapy and designs a particular approach to each problem" (p. 17). This approach, where the therapist pays attention to the client's social context and is directive in the therapy, is in direct opposition to the nondirective nature of psychoanalysis. As a goal is clearly defined by the therapist and client, the therapist takes responsibility for orchestrating change using direct or indirect interventions. On a superficial level one could criticize this approach as being manipulative. However, giving clients what they request— specifically, the change set forth in the therapeutic goal—is a very caring approach to psychotherapy. Strategic therapy is further defined by Haley as "not a particular approach or theory but a name for those types of therapy where the therapist takes responsibility for directly influencing people" (p. 17). Given this definition, we see the connection of this theory to several others discussed in this text, specifically that of the Mental Research Institute (see Chapter 8), where Haley started his career as a therapist, and brief solution-focused family therapy (see Chapter 11).

Haley's interest in paradoxical directives followed him from his early work with Bateson and the double bind studies of schizophrenia (Bateson, 1972). As part of this project, Haley consulted with Milton Erickson, a well-known hypnotherapist. Erickson developed a paradoxical induction to put resistant clients in a trance. In paradoxical induction, a client is given the suggestion to continue to resist the hypnosis. This situation forces the client to do something different. He or she must comply with the therapist or go into a trance. In strategic therapy, if a client is resistant, the therapist frequently selects something and encourages that resistance until the client is able to comply with treatment.

Our society is full of paradoxical situations. For example, people may suggest that a couple "become spontaneous" in an attempt to spice up a marriage. However, by being given a suggestion to be spontaneous, the couple is denied any chance of succeeding because, by definition, spontaneous behavior is done without preplanning. In fact, therapy itself can be considered a paradoxical activity. Clients seek the assistance of a therapist to accomplish things they want to be able to do on their own. Haley became a master in using paradox in a manner that forces the client to give up the symptom.

In his early work with Bateson and others at MRI, Haley became interested in the study of communication. Haley started to see that the problems presented in therapy are metaphoric communications (Haley, 1987). These communications are statements about the context the identified patient experiences. In other words, this model views a symptom as an adaption to the person's experiences, thus changing the notion of pathology radically. A symptom is the outcome of a system's struggle to adapt to its environment.

Frequently the client's problem is shaped by prior treatment the client has received. Likewise, the setting has bearing on the client's situation. For example, in an inpatient facility the medical staff often make decisions that impact the therapy in a way the therapist cannot control. Given this, Haley (1987) concluded, "The social unit for the therapist is thus not merely the family but also the professional colleagues" (p. 4). Thus it is important for therapists to be strategic in how they approach other helpers in their workplace as well as anyone else involved with their clients.

Innovations in Practice

Like some of its contemporary theories, strategic family therapy is a nonhistorical approach. Since the emphasis is on changing the problem in the room rather than resolving an intrapsychic conflict, there is little interest in the history of the development of the problem. This perspective helps move family therapy from an insight-oriented, historically focused enterprise to an action-oriented, present-focused one. Insight is no longer seen as necessary or sufficient to produce therapeutic change. Rather, it is action—doing something different in therapy—that produces change. This change could occur in the therapy room itself, or it could be in the form of assigned homework.

Homework is a task that the therapist assigns clients between sessions. In prior insight-based approaches, all therapeutic work occurred during the sessions, which were often held several times a week. Homework is designed to help the client address problems that have been defined during therapy. This illustrates the emphasis on action rather than insight. By assigning homework the therapist increases the families autonomy by encouraging the family to continue to address their problems between sessions and in their home.

Part of the success of this theoretical approach is that the rich descriptions of cases reported in the literature provided inspiration for a generation of family therapists. Not only that, but a whole series of techniques, such as the use of metaphoric communication, ordeals, and paradoxical prescription, provided guidance in working with families.

The Family Life Cycle

An important innovation of this approach is its shift in the context of how symptoms are viewed. Historically, symptoms were seen as the result of intrapsychic processes. For example, depression was seen as the result of a sick mind. However, as Haley explored Erickson's perspective in *Uncommon Therapy* (1973), the view of symptoms changed and symptoms began to be regarded as a by-product of family development. As Haley (1973) asserts, "Symptoms appear when there is a dislocation or interruption in the unfolding life cycle of a family or other natural group" (p. 42). Thus we see symptoms arise as a family is stuck between stages in its life cycle.

Haley divided the family life cycle into six stages in *Uncommon Therapy* (1973). The first life stage involves a courtship period where the primary task is to select and court a mate, thereby forming a relationship. Courtship, if successful, leads to the next identified stage, marriage and its consequences. The issues in this stage frequently revolve around the couple's sexual response to each other and are treated using a conjoint therapeutic approach. The next stage includes childbirth and dealing with the young and involves issues around the increased level of commitment required to rear a child. The middle stage of the family's development involves marriage and family dilemmas. Here the pattern has become fixed and children can be drawn into the struggle for dominance by the parents. Next, families are challenged by what Haley called weaning parents from children. This stage involves helping children gain the independence they require to start their own family life cycle as adults. Haley's subsequent book, *Leaving Home* (1980), dealt with this stage in much greater detail. Finally, the last stage, the pain of old age, is about aging and dying with dignity.

Video Call Out 10.1: Strategic/Medical Family Therapy

In the video Pamela Richey, M.S. supports the couple processing their grief and emotional pain that is a result of the couple being stuck in the childbearing phase. This couple has struggled with getting pregnant for a considerable time. Pam supports the couple as they share their feelings around their attempts to get pregnant. The couple discusses how the relationship has become work as they struggle with this issue.

This view of the family life cycle provides a context other than intrapsychic pathology for conceptualizing emotional problems. This has the practical advantage of normalizing a client's difficulty and leads the therapist to the goal of helping the family through the developmental stage in which they have become stuck. As the therapist helps clients address their symptoms, he or she also helps them deal with the challenges involved in the next life stage. This provides a conceptual map for the therapist's work with the family.

Metaphoric Communication

One of the innovations of this approach is its emphasis on the use of metaphoric communication as a way of overcoming resistance. Clients who are resistant to a direct literal directive are often responsive to a metaphoric directive. For example, Haley (1973) describes how Erickson uses the metaphor of enjoying a meal to talk with a couple who are resistant to talking about their sexual relationship. He describes how each one has a different style of eating. Finally, after engaging the couple in this conversation, he gives them the directive of planning a meal that they both enjoy.

When using a metaphor with a client, it is important to keep the communication metaphoric. Clients either respond to your metaphor or they do not. If they do not respond in kind, it is not useful to try to explain it. If your metaphor does not resonate with your clients, they may offer a countermetaphor. Once this occurs, you can respond by joining with them in their metaphor. Then you can make a metaphoric suggestion that could allow the clients to accomplish their desired change.

Directives

As previously stated, this theory actively shifts the focus of therapy from an emphasis on understanding to an emphasis on taking action. The most used call to action in the strategic approach is the directive. A directive is simply a call for the client to take a specific action and is parallel to the hypnotic suggestion. Directives can take a wide variety of forms, can be targeted at both in-session and post-session behaviors, and can involve one person or the whole family. Directives are simply requests that the client do something different that will change the way the family members relate to each other (Madanes, 1991).

Ordeal Therapy

One of the techniques developed by Haley is called ordeal therapy. In *Uncommon Therapy* (1973), he referenced Erickson's technique of providing a worse alternative to the presenting problem. Later he fully developed this technique of ordeal therapy into a book by that title, published in 1984.

An ordeal is a task the client performs in place of the symptom. It is necessary for the ordeal to cause greater distress or discomfort than the original symptom. In addition, the ordeal that is prescribed should be something clients can do that is possibly good for them. For example, a client might be instructed to balance his checkbook as an ordeal to overcome insomnia.

Paradoxical Intervention

A paradoxical intervention is a complex and sophisticated intervention based on a deep understanding of the client's frame of reference. On a superficial level, a paradoxical intervention often involves the therapist's prescribing the symptom. On a deeper level, this intervention forces a shift in the client's frame of reference or symptom as the client becomes able to control what he or she once considered uncontrollable. For example, a client who is experiencing fits of uncontrollable crying might be instructed to cry for an hour every morning. The instructions usually come without explanation. However, if asked the therapist would offer a simple explanation such as; if you get through your sadness early in the morning you will have more time for joy the rest of the day.

Clients typically present with problems that are viewed as involuntary. Likewise, they present as helpless to control the involuntary behavior (Madanes, 1991). The paradoxical intervention changes both of these aspects of the client's frame. For example, a child who has frequent temper tantrums might be instructed to have a temper tantrum at 9 a.m. every day for a week. If the client is able to follow through with the directive, she is no longer powerless to control the tantrum (she produced it at will), nor is it involuntary. Often this intervention leads to a spontaneous remission of the symptom. By changing when the symptom is performed, it comes more under the client's control and becomes less powerful to the client as a symptom.

Often it is not necessary for a client to enact a symptom fully. Sometimes it is more desirable and safer for the therapist to prescribe a symbolic act that is similar to the symptom. For example, a client who cuts himself may be encouraged to soak his hand in ice water to symbolize the numbness that cutting makes him feel. Pretending to have a symptom can sometimes serve as a useful approximation of the symptom. This is most useful where others play a significant role in maintaining the symptom. For example, a husband who is having headaches and receiving attention from his wife because of them may be encouraged to pretend to have a headache so that he may be comforted by his wife.

Questioning

The therapeutic interview in strategic family therapy focuses on developing a contextual understanding of the problem. The therapist seeks to understand how the problem is a communication about the functioning of the family system. With the assumption that communication is a metaphoric statement of how the identified patient is functioning within the family system, the therapist seeks to develop an understanding of how homeostasis is maintained in the system via the symptom. For example, a child who presents with an anger problem in school might be expressing her feelings concerning her parents' passive-aggressive arguments and cold war.

When a systemic understanding of the nature and context of the problem has been delineated, the strategic family therapist also seeks to establish a therapeutic contract. The contract involves agreement on what the problem is and how to best address that problem. It can focus on behavior, cognitions, or emotions. Questions focus on reaching an understanding of the resources available to the client that can be used in developing an intervention to address the stated problem.

Structuring

Strategic family therapy tends to be brief (fewer than 12 sessions) and focused around problem solving. Therapy is frequently structured around the standard therapy hour. However, therapy can be longer when couples and families are involved. Weekly sessions are not required in strategic therapy. Sometimes increasing the time between sessions can give the family time to work on the directives made by the therapist. Once the client reports that the presenting problem is resolved, the contract is seen as fulfilled and the therapy is terminated. However, if the client presents with another problem, the therapist can agree to provide another course of treatment to address it.

Strategic therapists are often flexible about the structure of the interview. While they prefer to work with whole families, they often see subgroups of family members. Some cases involve working with an individual, but with the perspective of understanding the context of the client's problem.

In *Ordeal Therapy* (1984), Haley clearly lays out six stages of therapy. These are straightforward and provide the structure for the entire course of therapy. They are as follows: (1) clearly define the problem, (2) obtain the client's commitment, (3) select an appropriate ordeal, (4), give a directive with a rationale, (5) continue the ordeal until the problem resolves, and (6) address changes in the social context that result from the ordeal.

Later, in *Problem Solving Therapy* (1987), Haley indicates that these stages are unique to each case. However, he places a good deal of emphasis on the need to address the presenting problem. The family's definition of the problem is more important than how the therapist conceptualizes the problem. Haley (1987) specifically cautions the therapist against trying to convince the family members of the family's "true problem" or educate them in systems thinking. The family's conceptualization is always taken as the starting point for the therapeutic intervention. For example, if a family views a child as the problem, this view is accepted. The family is recruited into participation in therapy to assist the child in overcoming his problem. This approach avoids resistance in the form of a power struggle over who has the correct view of the problem.

Responding

On the basic level, therapists' responses to their clients are direct and open. Strategic therapists hold themselves out as experts in the art of solving problems. The therapy process is based on an acceptance of the client's view of the problem and a focus on resolving that problem. Thus, the therapist's response avoids much of the client's resistance. In addition, the therapist is very deliberate in getting the client to buy into therapy before making a paradoxical directive or prescribing an ordeal. However, on occasion, clients come to treatment with a history of frustration with professional helpers. These clients often become resistant to the therapy process and the therapist must develop a strategy to avoid the client's resistance. Theoretically, holding therapists responsible for the change motivates them to be proactive in resolving clients' resistance to treatment.

Since the strategic therapist views symptoms as a form of metaphoric communication, careful attention is paid to communication. For example Young, Negash & Long 2009 explore how couple with low sexual desire may discuss their difficulty with the metaphor of a problem child. By understanding the nature of the communication, the therapist has insight into the client's context. It should be noted that the content of what is said is not as important as the process of communication. When therapists attempt to understand the communication a client is presenting via the symptom, they often respond by continuing to communicate about the problem. Strategic therapists will often counter the client's metaphor by introducing another metaphor that is similar to the client's. In this way, a therapist can talk indirectly about an issue that the client is unable to discuss directly. Murry (2014) provides an interesting example of the importance of viewing symptom in context in a case study with a couple that struggled with Anorexia Nervosa. In this case viewing the eating disorder as part of the couples triangulation process allowed the therapist to utilize a paradoxical intervention which disrupted the homeostasis in the couple's relationship.

Applications

Strategic family therapy was widely practiced in the 1970s and 1980s. Since then it has not been as widely practiced. Because strategic therapy is brief and effective in nature, it has been applied to a variety of settings. Casey and Buchan (1997) have applied strategic interventions to school psychology. In their case study, they describe the use of a variety of strategic interventions, including paradox and ordeal therapy, to address severely problematic behavior in a school-age boy.

Madanes (1990) developed a 16-step strategic approach to working with both the victim and victimizer of sexual assault in families. She argues that it is the morally correct thing to do to work with both parties to repair the injury. A guiding principle in this work is the notion that, in families where incest has occurred, there can be no secrets (Madanes, 1990).

Recognizing the power of strategic therapy in work with clients who are highly resistant, Scott (1994) has used strategic interventions in group therapy with male sex offenders. Scott argues that strategic interventions "enable a group therapist to create an environment that is supportive at the same time it allows for confrontation of denial" (p. 4). Sex offenders tend to be in denial about the impact of their offenses and to resist taking responsibility for their actions. This larger treatment program uses a combination of group, individual, and family therapy to assist this highly resistant population.

Many of the ideas and techniques from strategic family therapy have been used in the development of hybrid models, such as the brief strategic model (Scopetta et al., 1977). Combining strategic ideas with a structural framework, this model is one of the most influential in the treatment of substance abuse and adolescent behavior problems (Liddle & Dakof, 1995; Szapocznik & Kurtines, 1989; Szapocznik & Williams, 2000). At the University of Miami, this model is well researched in its use with adolescents who use substances. Recently Jones Lettenberger and Wickel (2011) developed a structural strategic approach to working with children with obesity. This approach recognizes the family impact on this health concern and offers some interesting treatment options that merit further exploration.

Acting as a Strategic Family Therapist

The strategic family therapist starts by getting to know the client on a personal level. Acting as a curious support, the therapist assesses the client's situation through conversation that seeks to understand the client's perspective about the problem. As the therapist starts to develop an understanding, he or she negotiates a therapeutic contract. Having a close relationship with the client reduces resistance to the therapist's suggestions.

In situations where clients are resistant, the strategic therapist uses a variety of techniques to address the resistance. These interventions include paradoxical directives and ordeals. In situations where direct conversation about problems is difficult for the client, the therapist often uses metaphoric conversation. Metaphoric communication allows clients to address their issues without becoming defensive. It is important to note that these techniques are used only in the context of a strong therapeutic alliance.

Working from a development framework, the strategic therapist works with the family to develop and execute a plan to address the problem. As part of the planning, the therapist assesses the context that maintains the problem as well as resources available to assist the family. From this model the goal is not only to help the family resolve the underlying issue but to also help the family back on track developmentally. Often time the strategic family will seek to help the family engage in developmentalyy appropriate tasks before fully addressing the presenting issue.

As the problem and the context supporting the problem are changed, the therapist focuses on supporting and maintaining the new system. This is done partly by attributing the success of therapy to the client.

Case Example: The Case of Roger's Dress

You receive a referral from the local domestic violence center for a bisexual male who presented at the shelter after being beaten up. Since the shelter does not accept male clients and since he was beaten by a stranger, he does not qualify for services through the shelter. You agree to the referral and make an appointment to see the client the next day.

Session One

Promptly on time, Roger, a young black man who looks his stated age of 25, shows up at your office for his intake appointment. He is well groomed and wearing stylish professional attire. After you ask about his accent, he reports that he was born in Jamaica to a Jamaican mother and a British father. He grew up in London, first with both his parents but later just his mother. His father was a musician and his mother was a dancer and later an actress. He has a rather thin build, and he has several bruises on his face along with the outline of a black eye. As you escort him in, you ask how he is recovering from his injuries. He tells you that he is recovering well, details the extent of his injuries, and describes in detail the attention he received at the emergency room as well as the domestic violence shelter.

You read from notes that you took during your conversation with the referral source and tell Roger what little you know about him. Roger states that he is bisexual and that he occasionally cross-dresses. He goes on to describe how over time he has developed a compulsion to cross-dress. On occasion he cross-dresses, goes out, and tries to pick someone up at a bar. He is attracted to a "macho-type" man. After Roger and the person he picks up at the bar leave together, the man often finds out that Roger is not a woman. On the most recent occasion, Roger's companion became enraged at this discovery and started to beat him. When you ask Roger if he is planning to press charges against his assailant, he states that he isn't planning to do that. When asked why not, he states that he doesn't even know the man's last name, had never seen him before the incident, and has not seen him since. Roger reports that he picks someone up like this every couple of months, and over the past two years since he has started to cross-dress he has been beaten five times.

Roger shares that this compulsion to cross-dress is a function of his poor self-esteem. He relates his poor self-esteem to his history of abuse by his father. He shares how in his prior therapy he worked on improving his self-esteem. He reports that he and his therapist had hoped that by building his self-esteem, he would overcome his compulsion to cross-dress.

Roger reports that for the most part he has a good life. However, he is concerned about his self-esteem. While he recognizes that he does have a good life, he feels as if he does not deserve this life. The only thing he really wants to change is his occasional compulsion to cross-dress. As he states his goals, you probe deeper into the nature of his goal. You ask if he wants to stop occasionally cross-dressing or if he wants to stop being beaten up while cross-dressing. Surprised by your question, Roger thinks for a few minutes and then responds that he desires to stop being beaten up while cross-dressing.

As you take a brief family history, Roger shares that his father has been estranged from him since he was six. He witnessed his mother being beaten by his father on several occasions and reports that he has posttraumatic stress disorder as a result of that as well as being physically abused himself. His mother lives across the country, and he reports that he talks to her every few weeks. He has no siblings.

Roger goes on to say that as a teen he was an outsider and struggled to fit in. He got into a very dark music scene and became a cutter. Roger states that he got over that compulsion years ago. When asked how, he states that he talked to a counselor at his university. In school, Roger found that he had a gift for talking to people and became interested in international business.

Roger also reports that he is in a yearlong relationship with the same man and that they are living together. You discover that Roger met Frank at Roger's place of employment, and they started living together after dating for just a few weeks. Both Roger and Frank work as successful junior executives, and Roger states that he really enjoys his work. Roger describes his relationship with Frank as that of two soulmates who have managed to find each other. He goes on to state that his poor self-esteem keeps him from having an egalitarian relationship with Frank. When they fight, Roger often gives in to Frank because he doesn't feel like his equal. When you ask Roger if Frank would like him to be his equal, he answers yes without hesitation. Roger goes on to say that Frank knows about his cross-dressing but accepts it as part of him. He reports that Frank is more upset that Roger is sometimes beaten than he is about the cross-dressing. Shyly Roger admits that sometimes he cross-dresses for Frank as part of their sexual relationship.

At this point, you discuss your heterosexual orientation in your personal life and explain that you are open to working with people with other life choices and styles. You ask Roger if he would be comfortable working with you. He states that you did come highly recommended and that you seem open to him. You ask him to agree to talk to you as soon as possible any time he feels judged or misunderstood. He agrees and states that this would be good for his self-esteem. He explains that Frank often asks him for similar feedback. You say, "I assume that you're also open to working with a white therapist as long as we agree to give each other respect and feedback." Roger laughs and in an exaggerated accent says, "Right. Try not to call your people 'crackers,' mate!"

After a good laugh, you note that time is coming to an end and inquire about bringing Frank in for the next session. Roger is surprised but open to the idea. He states that his other therapist was not interested in meeting Frank. You state that you think working with him in his relationship might help with the problem. He agrees and calls Frank on his cell phone to set a time next week for the three of you to meet. You ask Roger to call you if anything changes between sessions.

Session Two

Two days before the next session, Roger calls to tell you that he and Frank have broken up. He reports that this occurred over the weekend after they had a bad argument. They fought about Roger's need to cross-dress as well as "roommate issues." Roger states that his friends have come together to support him and that while he is very sad and lonely, he thinks that the breakup may be for the best. You thank him for calling and suggest that he keep his appointment.

Roger arrives at his appointment well dressed with just a hint of makeup covering his fading black eye. You comment that he is healing well and that if you didn't know his black eye was there, you wouldn't have guessed. He reports that he has been tearful every day since he broke up with Frank. However, despite his sadness, he has come to see the breakup as in his best interest. As you listen, he talks about how his relationship with Frank was holding him back.

As he describes his relationship with Frank, you ask him if, in hindsight, he sees the relationship as emotionally abusive. He describes how his friends have been telling him that for a while, but that he had a hard time accepting this view of Frank. You point out that you can still love someone who is abusive. He is tearful for much of the session, and you listen as he tells you how Frank made him feel bad about himself.

Without being asked, Roger starts to discuss how he has had a significant increase in his desire to cross-dress since his breakup with Frank. He describes how he has gone to thrift shops and flea markets and bought "new outfits." You respond to this disclosure with surprise, and before Roger can respond to your surprise, you clarify that you are surprised not about the increase in his cross-dressing—because people's "compulsions" tend to increase during times of stress—but are taken aback by his going to thrift shops and flea markets.

He becomes slightly defensive and tells of how, as an 18-year-old, he bought his first woman's dress at a secondhand store outside the town he grew up in. Since he was afraid of being seen by someone he knew, he went 50 miles out of the city to the country. He reports that he shops at flea markets so that he is not likely to run into someone he knows. You nod your head and say, "That makes sense, but a flea market doesn't seem to fit your sense of style."

You go on to describe how you've noticed that he pays attention to style in his manner of dress. You note that each time you've seen him he's had clothes that were professionally laundered and that the creases have always been sharp. You also note that his shoes are of good-quality leather with a bright shine. Roger laughs, states that you are pretty observant for a straight man, and asks, "Are you sure you're not gay?" You laugh with him and reply, "No, but that doesn't mean I'm not willing to learn about good fashion."

After a good laugh, you continue, "Seriously, that really seems out of character for you. How is that good for your self-esteem?" Roger states that he's never thought of it that way. You state that in your experience, flea markets are usually not very pleasing places to shop. They are about finding bargains or making purchases for the lowest price. You ask Roger if he is financially secure. He goes on to describe how his success in his work far exceeds anything he expected. He goes on to say that sometimes he feels a little guilty over his financial success. You state that that makes sense; you wouldn't expect him to have been taught how to enjoy his success and achievement, growing up in the family he did. You explain that abusive parents blame children as a rationalization for their abuse. Roger nods his head in agreement and seems to be deep in thought for a time. You simply let him sit with his thoughts.

As Roger comes out of his deep thoughts, he starts to talk about his compulsion to cross-dress. He goes on to describe how it's almost like a hypnotic trance. He states that often he doesn't plan to go to the flea markets; rather, he just kind of wakes up and finds himself already there. While he doesn't feel good about the activity, he continues to do it.

You again inquire about his goal, asking if he wants to stop cross-dressing or just to stop feeling bad about it. He is clear that he wants to stop the self-loathing that goes with it, not the act itself. You tell him that you have a series of steps he can take that are guaranteed to stop the bad feeling, but he will have to agree to follow your directions exactly. You ask that he go home and spend a week considering if he really wants to change how he feels about himself.

Session Three

Roger presents for the session in good spirits and with a bright affect. He reports that between sessions he did not engage in any self-destructive behavior. When asked how he did that, he reports that he spent a good deal of time with his circle of friends. They recognized that he was sad, and in order to take care of himself, he spent the week staying with a friend. He is concerned that if it hadn't been for this support, he would have given in to his compulsion to cross-dress. Recognizing that he can't rely on the support of friends indefinitely, he is concerned about the future.

He reports that he has been thinking about the challenge you gave at the end of the last session. He states that he is up to the challenge and willing to do just about anything to stop his compulsion to cross-dress and get beaten up. However, he clearly states that he doesn't want to give up cross-dressing completely. He only wants to stop doing it in a way that is bad for his self-esteem. You agree that he shouldn't have to give it up but simply should only do it in ways that aren't bad for his self-esteem. He agrees to your challenge from last week and states that he will follow your directive exactly in order to get over his issues.

You tell him that the only problem with his cross-dressing is that he is doing it in ways that are bad for his self-esteem. He agrees and asks how you build self-esteem when your low self-esteem is a result of your childhood and you can't go back there. You agree that he can't go back, stating, "That's why we need to move forward."

He again agrees and asks, "How do we move forward?" You ask him to take notes as you give him instructions so that he can follow them exactly. You further instruct him that it will take him several days to complete the assignment, but he should move slowly and reflect on how he deserves a good life as he completes each of the tasks. You ask him if he's ready for you to lay out the day-by-day plan. He says he is.

Speaking to Roger, you begin to lay out the plan: "On day one, you are to go to your favorite department store and buy the best-looking undergarments you can find. You are not to look at the price. You are to simply pick out what you are most pleased by." Roger interrupts and saying that he never shops without looking at the price and that he always looks for a bargain. You interrupt him and remind him that he agreed to follow your instructions exactly. You go on to emphasize that he deserves the best and tell him that he can bargain shop for his work clothes. Finishing day one, you continue, "When you return home with your purchase, you are to place it in a special drawer that you have cleaned out for just this purpose.

"On day two, you are to return to your favorite shoe store and purchase a beautiful pair of shoes, again not paying attention to the price, because you deserve it. This purchase is to be placed in the same drawer with the prior purchase. On day three, you are to get a handbag that matches the shoes you bought the day before, again with no concern for the price, focusing on how you deserve this. The handbag is to go in the special drawer too. On day four, you are to purchase an outfit that goes well with the prior purchases. This purchase also is to be made with no reference to the price, and placed in the drawer designated for your cross-dressing attire."

You emphasize that the key to this project is that he focus on how he deserves to be happy while he is fulfilling each task. During this time, he is to avoid going to a flea market. At no time is he allowed to shop there, simply because he deserves better and has earned the privilege through his hard work. If he feels a need to go to the flea market, he is to go to a department store immediately. There he can buy anything he needs to satisfy his impulse, but when he is there, he is to focus his thinking on how he deserves to feel good about himself.

Roger smiles while the instructions are given and asks, "Why can't I just make one trip?" You remind him that he agreed to follow directions exactly. You again place emphasis on Roger's need to focus on positive thoughts while he is following the directive. Roger asks what he is to do with the clothes after they are in the drawer. You simply respond, "Whatever you want." However, you emphasize that when he is done with them, he is to fold them neatly and return them to their place of honor. With that statement, you set a follow-up appointment in one week.

Session Four

Roger arrives for the session in a very good mood and starts to talk about how he has had a difficult week but that he has handled it well. He describes an incident a few days ago where Frank called him and asked him to get back together. He states that he recognized how he was being used and how Frank was trying to trigger him. He reports that he declined Frank's advances to get back to together because he "deserves better."

Roger describes in detail how after he got off the phone with Frank he felt a compulsion to go to a flea market and cross-dress. However, rather than do that, as he would have in the past, he visited his drawer and reflected on how he deserves to feel good and how he deserves nice things. He describes how he put on what he had bought up until that point, and rather than do the shopping for that day alone, he invited a friend to go with him. He reports that when he was shopping with his friend, he started to talk about his history of abuse by his father. His friend was very supportive and described how he was also abused. This brought their friendship to a deeper level rather than creating distance between them.

Roger becomes tearful and talks about how he had felt he was the only one who had issues from his childhood. Thus, when he made disclosures to his friend, he was surprised that he was not rejected. In fact, being able to share details about himself brought him closer to his friend. You talk with Roger about the importance of talking about his feelings. You make the distinction that as a child he needed to keep his feelings private to avoid further abuse. However, as an adult, privacy does not offer any new protection; in fact, it creates distance between him and others. Only people who have emotional problems themselves use information against another person.

You ask Roger to discuss how his improved self-esteem is a result of following the directive you gave him during the prior session. He describes how the act of reflecting on how he deserves to dress well and how he deserves to feel good was powerful in developing his self-esteem. He continues, stating that he carries the idea from his childhood that he deserves to be hit and to feel bad. However, over the past week he has been able to think about himself as a good person who deserves to feel good.

You ask Roger what will help this idea that he is a good person who deserves to feel good stick. He states that he needs to practice thinking about this and reflecting on his good qualities rather than his defects. You agree with him and encourage him to celebrate his new level of self-esteem. He states that he plans to celebrate by reflecting on the good that he brings to his friends. You agree that this is an appropriate way to celebrate.

As the session closes, you ask him if there are other issues he would like to address or if he is comfortable stopping treatment here. Roger states that he wants to continue treatment every few weeks just to make sure that he does not regress. You agree to this contract and set up a follow-up in three weeks.

Sessions Five, Six, and Seven

Roger continues treatment for three more sessions. During each of these sessions, he continues to talk about improvement in his self-esteem. He reports that he no longer has a compulsion to visit flea markets and cross-dress. He has put two outfits in his "special drawer" and hopes someday to meet someone special to share them with. At the final session, Roger reports starting a new relationship with a female coworker. He says that she makes him feel special for who he is and that he will take this relationship slowly and "see where it goes." You offer to see them as a couple should this become appropriate in the future. Roger thanks you for your help and support and decides to terminate treatment at this point.

Case Discussion

In the first session, the therapist seeks to develop a positive therapeutic relationship with the client. To do that, he starts with a discussion of Roger's injuries and how well he is healing, because these are the most obvious presenting issues. The therapist is also careful to pay attention to Roger as he discusses how he sees himself.

The therapist is struck by how unique Roger is. Noting that typical labels and categories of culture and sexual orientation would not apply here, the therapist is intrigued by Roger. By looking at the patterns of the problem, he develops the idea that the occasional beatings are a similar process to the client's prior compulsion to cut.

Careful attention is paid to how Roger describes the incident around his compulsion to cross-dress. The therapist does not assume cross-dressing is the problem and is careful to ask Roger in great detail what he wants to change. Thus, it is discovered that Roger does not want to stop cross-dressing, but he does want to stop being beaten up. He is also interested in improving his self-esteem so that he will feel better about himself.

Mostly, this session is spent developing a relationship with the client and seeking to understand the context of the problem. The problem is constructed as the client's habit of cross-dressing, cruising bars, and meeting men who beat him up after discovering in an intimate moment that he is not a woman. In addition, the therapist is careful to negotiate a safe relationship where the client is not judged. Because of concerns for the client's safety, the therapist wants to include Frank so that he can assess the volatility in the relationship.

The second session takes a different direction after Roger's relationship with Frank ends. Much of this session is spent helping Roger process the relationship. The focus is on exploring how the relationship with Frank impacted the client's self-esteem. By exploring the emotionally abusive aspect of the relationship, Roger is presented with an opportunity to build his self-esteem.

The majority of this session is spent developing a therapeutic goal. Roger is clear that his compulsion to cross-dress in flea market attire is detrimental to his self-esteem. Here the therapist sets the client up for a paradoxical intervention but first lays the groundwork by asking him to think about his commitment to change during the week between sessions. It is important to note that the therapist accepts the problem as defined by the client.

In the third session, Roger is given a paradoxical ordeal. The structure of the ordeal is to do the same thing (buy women's clothes to cross-dress), but to do it differently (at a nice shop while thinking positive thoughts). It is an ordeal in the sense that it is something the client has agreed to engage in. The therapist is careful to make sure the client has committed to the task before providing the instruction. In this session, Roger quickly agrees to the task. If a client does not agree to the task, it means that the therapist has not spent enough time preparing the client for the task.

The fourth session involves reinforcing the change that was made as a result of the directive. The client is supported as he reflects on the change that has occurred. Since change has been made, the therapist renegotiates the therapeutic contract. The client has reservations about stopping treatment, so the therapist agrees to continue to meet with him to ensure that the change is permanent.

Treatment continues over three more sessions while the client gets comfortable with the change that has been accomplished. Time is spent reinforcing the client's new self-esteem, and he is supported in his decision to start a new relationship with a woman. At this point, since the client has not introduced new problems, the treatment is terminated. While the therapist notes that the client is now in a relationship with a female, he sees this as consistent with Roger's bisexual orientation and does not question Roger about this issue.

Evaluating Strategic Family Therapy

After Haley left the double bind project in Palo Alto, he became more interested in developing his theoretical model than in empirically validating his approach. Therefore, there is little empirical research on strategic family therapy.

There is, however, some validation worthy of mention. A now-classic study by Szykula, Morris, Sayger, and Sudweeks (1987) sought to compare child-focused behavioral therapy with strategic therapy. In the design, clients presenting at a community-based outpatient child psychiatry clinic were randomly assigned to strategic or behavioral family therapy. Szykula and colleagues found both approaches to be effective and nearly equivalent in terms of measured outcomes.

An interesting paper by Richeport-Haley (1998) looks at strategic therapy as a method of approaching madness or schizophrenia. She notes that in underdeveloped countries where informal healers treat schizophrenia in the context of the family, the cure rates are much higher than in countries where the patient is treated outside the context of the family. As Richeport-Haley concludes, "the cross cultural literature supports an approach which relies on human support systems, skill-building, and a directive, strategic approach" (p. 74). This provides an interesting anthropological validation of the strategic approach.

Haley's approach has been combined with structural family therapy to produce a hybrid model referred to as brief systemic therapy. This model has been shown to be particularly effective in substance abuse treatment (see Chapter 14).

While there has been limited empirical validation of strategic family therapy, its impact on the field should not be underestimated. It was a very dynamic and popular approach to the field in the 1970s and 1980s, and many of the ideas generated in this school have been important in transforming the field into what it has become today. In addition, many of the initial ideas generated by this approach have been incorporated into other therapy approaches, such as brief solution-focused therapy, which has been well validated. This approach will likely remain an important influence on family therapy.

Learning Exercises

1. Part of helping people solve problems is understanding how they approach the world in which they live and respecting how they make decisions. Pair off and interview your partner for about 10 minutes. During this time, ask him questions about how he decided to come to school and how he chose his current program of study. After this, switch and let your partner interview you. Notice how the same decision was reached by different paths. Also notice how each path works for each individual. What problem was each person's decision to attend school an attempt to solve?

2. Divide up in pairs and talk about a behavior that you would like to change in your own life. After you describe the behavior, design your own ordeal intervention designed to help you break this negative behavior. After one week, report back to your partner on your progress.

3. As a class, break up into groups and assign each group a different stage of development. After each group has an opportunity to talk among itself, have each group report to the whole class the challenges and rewards involved in each developmental stage. Be sure to describe how each developmental phase can be successfully transitioned to the next phase.

Discussion Questions

1. Some question the ethics of encouraging a client to engage in a negative behavior as part of a paradoxical directive. Discuss the ethical issues involved in paradoxical intervention and describe situations where you think this intervention can be used ethically.

2. How does a paradoxical directive help a client overcome his or her natural resistance to change?

3. How can strategic family therapy be a useful approach for understanding and treating the individual in the context of his or her family?

4. What metaphors could you utilize to describe your learning style? What metaphor can be utilized to describe the teaching style of your favorite professors?

5. In what ways is strategic family therapy focused on cybernetics of cybernetics?

Suggested Readings

Haley, J. (1973). *Uncommon therapy: The psychiatric techniques of Milton H. Erickson, M.D.* New York, NY: Norton.

Haley, J. (1984). *Ordeal therapy: Unusual ways to change behavior.* San Francisco, CA: Jossey-Bass.

Haley, J. (1987). *Problem solving therapy.* San Francisco, CA: Jossey-Bass.

Madanes, C. (1990). *Sex, love, and violence.* New York, NY: Norton.

Web Resources

Wikipedia's Information on Strategic Family Therapy

https://en.wikipedia.org/wiki/Strategic_Family_Therapy

National Institute of Drug Abuse: Brief Strategic Therapy with Adolescent Drug Use http://archives.drugabuse.gov/TXManuals/BSFT/BSFT2.html

Flashcards from quizlet on Strategic Family Therapy

https://quizlet.com/2590778/mft-terms-strategic-family-therapy-flash-cards/

Milton Erikson:

The Milton H. Erickson Foundation Homepage

http://erickson-foundation.org/

CHAPTER

11

MILAN FAMILY THERAPY

Thinking About This Approach

Milan family therapy is an important inclusion in our overall understanding of family therapy. In Milan, Italy during the 1960's, this approach was coming into development through the dedication of Mara Selvini Palazzoli, Luigi Boscolo, Gianfranco Cecchin, and Giuliana Prata. The four practiced individually and came together to discuss their work (Campbell, Draper, & Crutchley, 1991). Karl Tomm (1984) introduced this approach to the United States with a two-part article published in the Journal of Marital and Family Therapy. As the principal players in the Milan school started traveling to the US, Tomm was inviting other brilliant minds to travel to Italy with him in hopes of collaboration. Ultimately, this alliance provided family therapy with an innovative international component.

Milan family therapy is based on second-order cybernetics, as articulated by Bateson and the MRI team. This influenced the group to be strategic in their early conceptualizations of family therapy. As this approach developed further, more emphasis was placed on the importance of the interview, until it eventually became an intervention in and of itself. This shift occurred as the field of family therapy was developing a cybernetic of cybernetic, or postmodern, approach. With its emphasis on cybernetics of cybernetics, Milan family therapy is clearly a second-generation model of family therapy. Because of its team approach, it was rarely practiced outside of training clinics. However, because of its contributions to interviewing from a postmodern perspective, it remains an influential model and will likely continue to shape thinking in the future.

The Milan team worked for several decades, undergoing multiple phases of development. Throughout the model's growth, its changing ideas contributed to the field of family therapy. The ideas presented helped the field evolve into the postmodern paradigm. One of the more interesting things about Milan family therapy is the number of changes that took place in regards to thinking in systems theory. In particular, if we pay attention to the shifts made in conceptualizing homeostasis, we are able to see the transition of the model from modern theory to postmodern theory. As this shift occurred, the emphasis of the team's work and writing advanced from technique driven to interview driven. The interview driven model stresses the significance of questions presented to clients in session as having a place in shaping their reality.

Innovations in Practice

There is a long held tradition in systems theory of looking at the relationship between stability and change, or homeostasis and morphogenesis in systems. According to Tomm (1984a), the Milan group's early phase focused on identifying the homeostatic mechanism. As Tomm describes, "There was a search for a 'pathological' homeostatic pattern which could be considered a nodal point and which, if changed, would enable the family to transform itself" (p. 115). This particular point was the target of the team's intervention. In *Paradox and Counterparadox*, written in 1978 by Selvini Palazzoli, Boscolo, Cecchin, & Prata, the idea of counterparadox was developed to cancel or nullify the paradox that exists in the family. This concept was in line with the strategic approaches of both the MRI team and Jay Haley.

Positive Connotation

In their analysis of the homeostasis of a system, the team developed a technique they would routinely apply in the early stages of treating a family. They were clear that this came out of their systemic perspective, which they recognized as transcending the "causal-moralistic bonds of traditional psychiatry" (Selvini Palazzoli, Boscolo, Cecchin & Prata, 1974, p. 433). In this situation they restate the presenting problem from an alternative perspective. Specifically, the identified patient or presenting problem is described as helping the family avoid an even worse situation or difficult problem.

It is vital to call attention to how the symptom might be saving the family from something even worse. Further, it may be helpful to ask the "sick person" how they were chosen and/or how they volunteered for this position. This intervention is paradoxical in nature. By giving the patient credit for their sacrifice, the family may face the underlying problem with renewed success. When this occurs, change occurs at a rapid rate, and there may be a tendency for families to celebrate the success and terminate therapy. At this point in the therapeutic process, the team must elect to pursue additional therapy sessions in order to prevent further selection of one individual family member as "sick." If the family is motivated enough to continue therapy, they continue exploring how they may be able to reach improved function.

Focus on interviewing

Tomm (1984a) describes the Milan team's focus regarding the importance of language and differences in the creation of therapeutic change. Again, following Bateson's line of thinking, the epistemology that clients most often utilize is linear. Differences or distinctions are ultimately generated through their use of language. These differences or distinctions often take the form of negative labels, such as bad, sick, or disturbed. For example, a family seeking treatment for their depressed child is likely to describe the identified patient (depressed child) through the use of distinctions between that child and his siblings or other children. Typically, parents may voice their concerns regarding the child's increased sleep habits, increased sensitivity, weight gain, increased amounts of crying, recent inability to take jokes, increased aggression, etc.

According to Tomm (1984a), it is possible to change a family's thinking about a client and their relationship with the simple linguistic trick of switching "to be" verbs with "to show" verbs. Referring to the example above, you may ask family members to describe how the depressed child, Ryan, displays his depression. When the father says, "Ryan is depressed," the follow up question is "How does Ryan show his depression?" Other questions incorporating action verbs can be helpful as well.

For example:
    How does Ryan do depression?
    How does Ryan express depression?
    How does Ryan use depression?
    How does Ryan practice depression?
    How does Ryan execute his depression?
    How does Ryan show his depression?

This simple linguistic change has profound implications, as it forces a shift from linear to circular thinking. Let me describe this concept by using the example from above. Notice the subtle, but profound difference, between the questions: "What shows Ryan is depressed?" and "How does Ryan show depression?" The answer to the first question is likely going to be a description of what lead up to the belief that Ryan is depressed and needs treatment. The answer to the second question is likely going to evoke descriptions of how Ryan acts towards others. When you begin to examine and consider the social component involved in the previous interactions, you have entered the world of circular causation. Circular causation is a cybernetics of cybernetics approach. This moves the view of depression from passive to active, thus allowing for a call to action, motivation to try something new, or ability to create a new possibility. All of which have the ability to ultimately generate change.

With a circular perspective, the importance of the client's context becomes a major focus in therapy. In addition, the focus is further refined by the family's relationships. The Milan team goes further to point out that relationships are always defined by descriptions of differences. This emphasis on differences shifts therapy to a more postmodern perspective, where the focus of therapy becomes engaging clients in conversations in which differences can help the family evoke change in the system.

The Milan team gradually moved into believing that families evolve and produce change as a part of their natural developmental process. Families develop patterns over time through a series of trial and error experiences. Successful or desirable patterns of interaction tend to be repeated. As clients have conversations about the meaning of the patterns, interaction maps are developed. Maps, showing how relationships are thought about, over time lead to more healthy interactions. The reflexive relationship between behavior and meaning are fundamental in our understanding of families. Later, we see this focus as central to Michael White's development of narrative therapy (see chapter 14).

One of the major contributions of Milan family therapy was the emphasis on the cybernetics of cybernetics, in the form of focusing on how the treatment system (client+family +therapist+treatment team) impacts the therapy. The Milan team was among the first to recognize how the therapist's views, perspectives, positions, and attitudes influence the family.

Questioning

A new approach to interviewing was described in the team's 1980 landmark paper "Hypothesizing-Circularity-Neutrality: Three Guidelines for the Conductor of the Session" (Palazzoli Selvini, Boscolo, Cecchin, & Prata). These principles represent one of the most significant contributions of this approach, for they provide clear directions on the line(s) of questions the therapist follows.

A preliminary hypothesis is quickly generated with only the first fragments of information about the family. Like an epistemologist who seeks to find the answer to the question "What sort of world is this?" the family therapist asks, "What sort of family is this?" The focus of questions asked by the therapist is based on their attempt to validate their hypothesis about the family. Palazzoli Selvini et al. (1980) describe the hypothesis's functional value: "The hypothesis, as such, is neither true or false, but rather, more or less useful" (p. 2). Here one sees the pragmatics of the model. Without hypothetical guidance, the therapeutic interview risks losing direction and focus. A lack of focus in an interview can become what Bateson called "Muddled," meaning what is important gets mixed in with the details.

To be useful, the hypothesis must be systemic, meaning it includes all members of the family. Focusing on the identified patient is often a starting point, but every member of the family is to be included in the hypothesis. To generate a hypothesis, you might begin by working back from the symptom. First you imagine the family as normal, and then you ask what each family member would have to do to produce the problem. When you can describe what each member does to support the problem, you have a systemic hypothesis.

Palazzoli Selvini et al. (1980) stated "By circularity we mean the capacity of the therapist to conduct his investigation on the basis of feedback from the family, in response to the information he solicits about relationships and, therefore, about difference and change" (p. 4). The process of circularity is grounded in two essentials: "1. Information is a difference. 2. Difference is a relationship or a change in relationship" (p. 4). In practice, circularity involves the use of triangles in order to uncover information about relationships. To accomplish this, family members are asked to describe the relationships between other family members. In doing so, a series of triangles is created, which allows news of difference to emerge.

If you wanted to find out what the relationship is between a father and his daughter in session, you might ask both the mother and son to describe the relationship between father and daughter. This may feel strange at first because you are asking people to talk about the relationship between others, however, people are often curious to hear what others think about their relationships. Most families will want to focus on the symptom, which often surfaces in the form of descriptions about what the identified patient does. For example, a mother might complain that her son, Billy, is oppositional defiant and "does whatever he wants." In order to be circular, the therapist might ask her "How does dad respond when Billy 'does whatever he wants'?" Then, the therapist could inquire into how Billy's sister responds to Billy. A circular therapist might then ask the father and sister to describe the mother's reaction to their reaction to Billy's problematic behavior.

The principle of neutrality refers to the perception the therapist strives to leave the family with, specifically that they were neutral. The therapist does not want to be perceived as allied with any one family member. Palazzoli Selvini et al. (1980) points out "... as long as the therapist invites one family member to comment upon the relationship of two other members, he appears at that time to be allied to that person" (p. 6). However, this appearance of an alliance disappears as the therapist asks other family members to describe the relationships they participate in. In session, the therapist becomes allied for a brief period of time with each member in a roughly equal manner. Palazzoli Selvini et al. (1980) proclaim "The end result of the successive alliances is that the therapist is allied with everyone and no one at the same time" (p. 6).

In family interviews there is a tendency for family members and/or subsystems to attempt to enter into a privileged relationship or coalition with the therapist. The therapist who is quick to effectively neutralize these attempts is able to maintain neutrality. In clinics where therapists collect fees and perform other administrative tasks, such as scheduling, this is slightly harder to avoid. In these instances, the impact may be reduced if the therapist is efficient as possible in their execution of neutralization.

Structuring

A considerable amount of the structure of the Milan team's approach is driven by the fact that they practiced and conducted their research in a clinic. Clients would travel by train from all over Italy to receive services. Because it wasn't practical for the families to travel weekly, the team experimented with greater spacing between sessions. They found that the longer the period of time between sessions, the more conductive to therapeutic change. They limited therapy to 10 sessions, much like brief therapy. However, the 10 sessions would commonly span a number of years. So this approach is "brief" in terms of number of sessions, but "long" in terms of overall duration of treatment.

The Milan team would work as a unit treating the case from intake to discharge. The team would designate one member as the therapist, and the remaining members served as the observing team, viewing the case from behind a one-way mirror. The observing team would phone in questions and consultations to the therapist as the treatment was occurring. In addition, the therapist would consult with the team at designated times, and as needed throughout the session.

Tomm (1984b) describes the Milan team's five-part ritualized structure for working with families in the clinic. Table 11.1 describes the amount of time typically allotted for the Presession, Interview, Intersession, Intervention and Postsession, along with the key task for the therapist/ team members. To more fully appreciate this approach, we will look at each part of the session in greater detail.

TABLE 11.1	Milan Team's Structure for Psychotherapy	
Part	Time in Min	Therapist/Team's task
Presession	5–20	Team generates hypotheses of family based on intake data or between session contacts.
Interview	50–90	Family interview utilizing hypothesizing circularity and neutrality principles.
Intersession	15–40	Refine systemic hypotheses and develop intervention.
Intervention	5–15	Provide family with systemic opinion. Possibility of a directive for change.
Postsession	5–15	Team evaluates hypotheses based o family's inital response to intervention.

Presession

The Presession begins once clients initiate contact with the team in hopes of receiving treatment. Prior to each session, the team briefly meets to discuss and potentially modify their circular hypothesis about the family.

The Milan team has a structured intake process. In this approach, treatment initially begins during the intake. Instead of support staff gathering information from the referral source, they instruct the contact to call the treatment team during specific hours, in which they are all available to be a part of the conversation. When the therapist talks to the referral with the team present in the room, they are hypothesizing about the nature of the family and their problem. By paying close attention during the conversation, the therapist may begin formulating their map of the family. The process of developing interventions for the clients also begins during the Presession.

From the beginning of treatment, the therapist applies neutrality in an effort to avoid taking sides with family members. Due to this neutrality stance, the therapists keeps the intake as brief as possible, as an implicated alliance with the treatment team may be formed the longer spent on the phone with the caller. Again, while paying attention to the conversation, specifically the phrasing of questions, the team begins to construct a neutral stance. Tomm (1984a) provides an example of maintaining neutrality when asking questions: "Thus, if a mother calls to say her daughter is seriously disturbed, rather than ask, 'When did your daughter start having problems?' the therapist could ask, 'When did you start having problems with your daughter?'"(p.122). With this simple shift, the location of the problem has changed. The locus of the problem moves from focusing solely on the daughter to the relationship between mother and daughter.

FIGURE 11.1   **Possible Loci of a Problem**

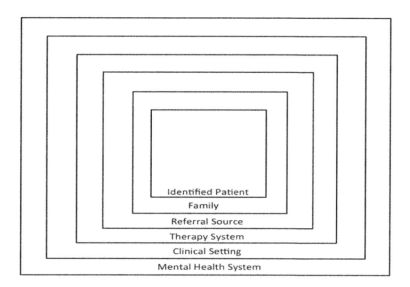

The Milan team has published on their view of "The problem of the referring person" (Selvini Palazzoli, Boscolo, Cecchin, Prata 1980). They believe that an understanding of the role of the referral person is important. The team suggests that the first question asked of a new client should be "Who referred you?" Once again, we are able to see the how the Milan school takes a cybernetic of cybernetic view in concerning itself with the system of family + referring person.

If you recall the illustration, 1.1, from chapter one, we can view family therapy as involving a system that is hierarchal in nature. Each lower level system is nestled within a higher level system. At each level, a system can be seen as either in a state of homeostasis or change. This type of view is helpful for a therapist developing a systemic view of treatment. Chapter 15 explores some of the clinical settings family therapists may practice in. I frequently tell students that they need to have a deep systemic understanding of the setting they practice in, as well as a systemic understanding of their clients. It is important to pay attention to the context that treatment occurs in. Figure 11.1 illustrates where the loci of a problem might be seen from by a Milan family therapist.

Interview

In the Interview, the therapist practices circular questioning, focusing from the general complaint to details about the families. A Milan family therapist generally does not interrupt problematic family patterns. If family members display distressed behavior that becomes disruptive, it is indirectly addressed. In practice, the therapist may ask questions about the process of the family in relation to the distressed behavior. For example, in the case of a young boy throwing a temper tantrum, the therapist will make inquiries into the other family member's responses to such behavior. In this situation, the therapist might ask, "Does your son act out more in front of small or large audiences?" This style of questioning is similar to what postmodern therapists would call "deconstructing his actions."

Intersession

The Intersession occurs after the therapist informs the family that they are going to take a break while they meet with the team. The team then engages in an in-depth analysis of treatment thus far. Tomm (1984b) summarizes "Team members are encouraged to articulate any intuitive impressions, even to 'discharge' their linear hypothesis (e.g., "He's a real bastard!"), and then move on to build a more circular and systemic understanding ("Why is he showing us this annoying behavior?" What effect is it having on whom?" etc.)" (p. 255).

The team takes the time necessary to develop an intervention that can be shared with the family. If at first the team is unsuccessful, the family will leave and be invited to return in a couple of days once an intervention has been developed. They may also be sent a letter providing a description of the intervention once the team has made a decision. In the event the intervention is not easily developed, or the team is divided regarding what intervention to employ, they will continue to collaborate and engage in dialogue to further understand the treatment system. This will help them as they work to develop a more useful intervention. After the Intersession, the therapist returns to the interview room and delivers the intervention to the family.

Intervention

The Intervention is often an abrupt end to the session for the family. While the brevity of the Intervention stage may seem abrupt to observers, it is done for strategic purposes. The team had come to recognize that if the family spent too much time with the therapist after hearing the Intervention, the family was less likely to change. However, the families that left with some confusion about the reason for the chosen Intervention or its execution were observed as more likely to change. When the family leaves somewhat unsettled, it is assumed that the family might develop a new and healthier homeostasis over time.

Family Ritual is an Intervention designed to address and disturb the homeostatic mechanism. Selvina Palazzoli, Boscolo, Cecchin & Prata (1977) describe families that are powerful systems with strong myths. Prescribing a family ritual that paradoxically supports and disrupts the family myth is a useful way to disrupt that pattern. A ritual is symbolic, and on the surface, supportive of the myth. However, the family can break out of the paradox by changing the myth. For example, a rigidly closed system might be given the ritual of locking the doors and windows, and then each family member give an uninterrupted 15 minute speech about how special and ideal the family is. In order to escape the ordeal of having to talk for 15 minutes, family members can break out of their myth.

A related paradoxical Intervention is to positively connote the presenting problem and/or the identified patient. In this situation, the symptom, or symptom barrier, is seen as a "savior" for the family. It is important to encourage family members to see the sacrifice of this person, and understand the "savior" is saving them from a more dangerous situation. This shifts the context of the symptom and challenges the frame that the symptom exists in. For example, a young adult who has failed to launch can be given credit for protecting his parents from facing the changes and dangers of having an empty nest. In addition to reframing the contribution of the identified patient, all family members are given credit for their role.

The invariant prescription intervention is the last of the Milan team's approaches. In families with children as the identified patient, parents are instructed to spend time away from their children. They are asked to do this without warning the kids, and without offering information about where they went or why they left. This intervention breaks the "games" played between parents and children. It also helps reestablish appropriate intergenerational boundaries.

Postsession

The Postsession starts immediately after the Intervention with a discussion regarding the impact of the Intervention. The team then begins the process of refining their hypothesis. Again, they are working on describing in systemic terms both the cybernetic system of the family and the cybernetic of cybernetic system of the family + team. When the family returns, the hypothesis developed in the Postsession is the starting point for the next Presession discussion.

Responding

In order to avoid therapeutic alliances with family members, the team tries to minimize contact with clients between sessions. However, when therapeutic involvement is necessitated by concerns for client safety, the therapist must abandon their therapeutic stance of neutrality and take action. After the crisis has been resolved, the therapist explains to the family the necessity of actions taken. Tomm (1984a) explains, "To examine this process from a neutral position reestablishes the therapist-family relationship as facilitative and therapeutic rather than directive and controlling" (p. 123). If neutrality can't be reestablished, the treatment system will stall and homeostasis will develop, ultimately leading to a pause in therapeutic progress.

Tomm (1984 a) describes the two responses made by the Milan team in situations where there is a lack of therapeutic progress. One possible response speaks to their protocol, which states the need to expand the current understanding of the system by increasing its size in treatment. The team assumes that the system they are working in is incomplete, and that a major piece of the system has not been included in treatment. The second response is to assume that a homeostatic relationship has developed between the therapist and the family system. In cases where there is a team working, they would explore this possibility through self-examination. In situations where the therapist is working alone, they may decide to invite a colleague to serve as a co-therapist, or they may seek consultation and supervision.

Applications

Milan family therapy is most easily applied to those training in clinic settings. It is typical to see the Milan approach in clinics with a pool of interns, as they are readily available to work on the teams. When interns are included, they are able to integrate what they learn from the experience into their knowledge bank of systemic based therapy.

The Milan team's approach was primarily active during the time when residential mental hospitals were closing because of the move to outpatient centers. With a cybernetic of cybernetic approach to thinking, this model influenced treatment being delivered in residential and outpatient programs. The model provided insight into how multiple systems influence the identified patient's well-being.

Selvini Palazzoli (1985) explored how systems, or cybernetic thinking, impacted outpatient care. In Massachusetts, Alexander Blount changed the context of the mental health center by focusing on relationships. He introduced the question: "In which ways do identified problems impair day-to day functioning of those people affected?" (Campbell, Draper, & Crutchley, 1991, p. 335). As a result, that mental health system shifted to a cybernetic of cybernetic perspective.

A classic paper written by Mara Selvina Palazzolia (1984), describes how consultants may employ systems theory when working in schools, treatment clinics, and other organizations. This describes the value of systemic thinking to promote healthier functioning in a variety of systems. Systems theory can be a powerful tool for understanding how social systems are connected in a hierarchical manner.

Benson, Schnindler-Zimmerman & Martin (1991) utilized a modified circular questioning technique to increase the participation of children in family therapy. By incorporating developmental appropriateness of questions and utilizing expressive art, play, and drama, the participation of children was increased in family therapy sessions.

Acting as a Milan Family Therapist

The Milan team posits: "The trend [is] away from the disturbed individual seen as an artificial isolated monad toward the study and treatment of dyads, triads, the entire family, and, finally, of the complex networks of networks of relationships in which every family is embedded" (Selvini Palazzoli et al., 1974, p. 429). Given this, they required meeting with the whole family for sessions, unless they had "special circumstances" preventing all members being present.

In circumstances where the entire family cannot be seen, the team is more likely to see a subsystem rather than an individual. It may seem to an outsider that the Milan team does not recognize individuals. However, to them an individual is a fragment of a family.

Case Example:

In this case, the therapist is working in a solo private practice and does not have access to a treatment team to work with. However, they continue to practice from the Milan perspective by engaging in circular questioning throughout the course of treatment. Despite the lack of a treatment team presence, the therapist still employs the multi-phase structure of treatment. In the phases of treatment when the therapist would typically consult with the team, they excuse themselves from the interview and reflect on the case in private. It is here that they refine their hypothesis and assess the degree that they maintained neutrality.

You receive a phone call from a friend working as a family practice physician. You are surprised that the call came straight from the doctor, since she typically has her nurse call with information about referrals to your practice. Your friend starts the conversation, stating, "I have a 15-year-old boy I am very concerned about." She expresses her concern regarding the young man's anorexia and its influence on his type 1 diabetes. The doctor claims the anorexia is making his diabetes "a nightmare to manage."

She goes on to state that this does not seem to be a "typical" course of anorexia, as he is completely food phobic. She has referred him to the psychology clinic at a local university for a course of systematic desensitization to address his food phobia. The doctor describes the young man's post-traumatic stress response. His trauma is related to the time he choked on a tortilla chip while on a youth mission trip with his local church. His pastor had to perform the Heimlich maneuver in front of his peers, which caused him embarrassment. Since then, he has become so fearful of choking again that he only eats broths, soups, and smoothies. This is further complicated by the fact that he is a type 1 diabetic, who at age 12 went into shock and a coma for 12 hours. Since this event, the young man has been having a difficult time managing his diabetes, and is often in power struggles with his parents over checking his blood levels.

You respond to the doctor by validating that there is a lot going on for the child and his family. Your friend goes on to describe that the young man, Alex, has "issues with food." You interrupt and ask if those are the family's terms, to which the doctor replies, "Yes they all call it Alex's food issue." She describes how the family had reorganized their schedules in order to spend large amounts of time preparing meals for him. Despite the parents' efforts, he has lost twenty pounds and continues to eat very little. The doctor concludes by expressing that if the client loses five more pounds, she will have to recommend him for inpatient therapy. You convey to the doctor that you understand the seriousness of her concern, and then request to know who will be monitoring his weight. She reports that his parents are currently weighing him at home every day. You suggest that they stop weighing at home him and instead that he go to her office Mondays, Wednesdays, and Fridays to be weighed. The doctor agrees that this might help with some of the conflict between the child and his parents and agrees to set up such an arrangement. She concludes by informing you that she will have the mom contact your office to set up an appointment, to which you thank her for the referral. As the doctor is hanging up, she asks you to call if she can further help you in any way.

A few hours later you receive a phone call from the mother. You quickly explain that you spoke with the doctor and have agreed to take their case. As mom starts to tell you her concerns about her son's "diabetes with complications from anorexia" you cut her off politely, stating that you would prefer to hear the history of the problem when all family members are present. Hearing a good deal of anxiety on the behalf of the mother, you agree to an appointment first thing the next morning. She agrees to bring everyone in for the appointment, and thanks you for getting her family in so quickly.

Session 1:

Presession

You start thinking about the organizing principles of hypothesizing, circularity, and neutrality. Since these concepts are circular and connected to each other, you begin by taking a look at the empathy you feel for the clients. As you imagine how scary being a young man with diabetes must be, or how awful it must be to be a parent of a child who has diabetes, you reflect on your own life experiences. You reminisce about how difficult it was to feed your child who was a picky eater. This empathy allows you to be neutral and nonjudgmental towards the members of the family.

This leads you to focus even more on circularity, as you ponder how important the diabetes is to this family. In fact, you begin to consider diabetes as the fourth member of the family, and you think about the relationship each family member has with it. You contemplate how the illness may be altering the system's normal developmental path.

It is here that you start to think about your hypothesis. Noting that the identified patient is an only child and that he is a teenager, you wonder about how the system has become stuck. A fan of the obvious, you imagine what a healthier response to diabetes might look like. You then muse the more important question: what would a healthy system look like?

Session

The family arrives to the session right on time, and they appear neat, well groomed, and seem in a somewhat somber mood. Mr. Costa is dressed in jeans, a work shirt, and boots. His wife, Mrs. Costa, has on nursing scrubs and is wearing an ID badge from the local hospital. They both explain that they are going to work after the session, hence their dress. He works as a contractor and she as a scrub nurse. Their son is tall and slender, and arrived dressed in a casual manner.

After the family settles in, you look at mom and say, "Well, since I know very little about you and your family, it would be best to start by asking 'What are we trying to address today?'" At this, dad looks at his son and says "Tell the doctor about your struggles with anorexia and diabetes." Alex looks at the floor and starts shaking his head. He then complains that this is all that the family talks about, "diabetes this and anorexia that." You ask Alex what else he would rather talk about. He pauses, and then says, "I don't know, anything."

His mother then starts to tell the history of his illness. She describes the incident of Alex going into a coma. When he was 12 years old, he was playing at recess and suddenly collapsed on the playground. Alex was rushed to the hospital, where they quickly determined his blood sugar level was 8x higher than normal. After about 12 hours he came out of the coma, but he was kept in the hospital for the next week. After a few minutes of mom describing this distressing event, there was a long enough gap in her speech for you to interrupt.

You ask mom to describe how Alex "does" diabetes. She pauses for a moment as she thinks about your question. She then goes on to describe how after his initial hospitalization he was resistant to monitoring his insulin levels. Mom then discloses that she would have to prompt him several times before he would comply. She describes how frustrated he would get as he vocalized how much his finger hurt from the constant pricks needed to draw his blood. The dialogue between the two would lead to a struggle that eventually resulted in both crying in their respective rooms. As mom pauses in her description of how Alex "does" diabetes, you comment that she has shifted to talking about her and her son's relationship.

You then turn to Alex's dad and ask him how his son "does" diabetes. He mostly dodges the question by saying that his son is now doing much better controlling his diabetes. However, dad eventually goes on to talk about how Alex is currently a candidate for an insulin pump, but the endocrinologist wants him to resolve his anorexia before he can get it.

You continue to engage the family in circular questioning. Your next question pertains to Alex's relationship with his mother. In asking about their relationship, you find out that other than struggling with Alex's self-motivation in maintaining his diabetes, the family has good relationships. You learn that both of Alex's grandfathers had diabetes. You also discover that both parents are only children, and they lost their parents when Alex was very young. As a result, the Costa's have little extended family contact. The family identifies their church as being at the center of their social lives. Both parents serve as lay ministers and they attend events several times a week.

Intersession

At this point in the session, you ask the family to take a 10-minute break so you can reflect on their situation and what you have learned thus far. They agree and return to the waiting room. As you reflect on the interaction, you are struck by the tension between the parents and the appearance of discomfort in each other's presence. You also consider how Alex appears to divert the interaction when his parents begin to converse. At this point, you ponder the hypothesis that the assumed problem in the Costa family is focused on Alex's diabetes and his managing of it. You further assume that this fixation distracts the family from dealing with something even worse than his illness. As you have decided to present a positive connotation of Alex's symptoms, you invite the family back in.

Intervention

After the family is settled back in the therapy room, you voice the idea that Alex's consistent difficulties with his diabetes might be the effect of his perceived need to protect his family from something more problematic. You bring attention to the fact that he is competent in all other aspects of his life, speaking particularly to his successes in academics and sports. As you describe the sacrifices Alex makes in struggling with these issues, you notice his eyes are increasingly widening. You also notice that the parents briefly make eye contact and then both look at the floor. With this silent interaction, you suggest that during the next session you only meet with mom and dad. Mr. Costa quickly jumps at this idea, while Mrs. Costa expresses some reservations. You press her slightly and say "Let's just try this once," while also considering if they both agree, you will have an opportunity to talk with them about ways they can further support their son. When you disclose this thought to the family, the mother agrees to a couples therapy session the following week, as long as a portion of the time is spent focusing on ways that they can support Alex.

Postsession

Before the start of the second session, you receive a phone call from the father. He states that he is reluctant to have a couples session because "We had talked about divorcing prior to Alex becoming ill, but we both agreed that we would stay together to help our son." You express that you understand his concern, but this is exactly why they should meet as a couple. You reassure him that you do not want to influence them to get divorced or remain married; you simply want to understand their marriage, so that they can help you provide the help their son needs.

This interaction confirms your hypothesis that Alex's medical concerns are a distraction to the family. You are concerned that he is sacrificing his well being for the sake of his parent's marriage. This leads you to deciding to further explore your hypothesis during the next session. By focusing your inquiry on the parent's marriage, hopefully the system will move past its stationary point. You are hopeful this will allow Alex the emotional space he needs to address his medical concerns.

Session 2:

Presession

Prior to the arrival of the clients, you reflect upon your hypothesis regarding the Costa family. You briefly review your notes and collect your thoughts. While there is no shift in your hypothesis, you are grateful for the quiet time to focus on your empathetic feelings concerning the family. Spending quiet time reflecting on your emotions will help you maintain neutrality if the couple tries to recruit you to take sides in their marital distress.

Session

You begin the session by thanking them for coming, and then ask Mr. Costa what his wife knew about the phone call he made. He reported that she had prompted him to call. Both begin to describe the difficulties in their marriage. They explain that about five years into their marriage, they started to drift apart. Mrs. Costa had difficulty getting pregnant, and when she was finally able to, had difficulty carrying a baby to full term. They report that prior to Alex, they had one miscarriage. After Alex was born, they experienced a second miscarriage, and then a third, in the course of just three years. Since Alex had been diagnosed with type 1 diabetes, they had grown even more distant.

Mr. Costa is mournful about the loss of intimacy in the marriage. Further, he is saddened by the resolved loss that "God did not want them to have more children." This statement appears to threaten Mrs. Costa, and they begin to argue about the importance of God in their marriage. You ask the couple to collect themselves, and then lead the session into a more structured dialogue by engaging them in circular questioning around their individual relationships with God and religion. As the session progresses, you begin to recognize opposing patterns between the two. Mr. Costa has become more distant in his faith, and has started to withdraw from activities in the church. On the other hand, Mrs. Costa has become more involved in their church, and she has started to engage in more prayer. As you continue to engage the couple with neutrality you notice they both appear to be less anxious about what the other is sharing. As they both express their perspectives, the other progressively listens more intently. You also notice that about three-quarters of the way into the session, Mr. Costa is starting to lean towards his wife. Shortly after this, she wraps her foot around his ankle and they remain intertwined for the remainder of the session.

As the session is coming to a close, Mrs. Costa asks what she should do to support her son. You validate her in asking a great question, and then ask for a brief update. Both agree he has made some progress, as he is eating some solid foods, and has gained a few pounds. Mr. Costa enthusiastically talks about how he and Alex made a late night food run the other night after Alex said he was craving a hamburger. Mrs. Costa says that she has noticed Alex is checking his blood sugar on his own more, and that she has rarely had to remind him. You voice to the clients that what you are hearing is great news. You then take a brief break to reflect and consider what they should do next.

Intersession

As you reflect on the session, you are struck that the couple has already made progress in moving closer to one another. You are optimistic that this has broken the homeostasis. If this turn out to be correct, you think they may drop their hyper-focus on their son's wellbeing. As a result, Alex may step up and take more responsibility in managing his own wellbeing. You also recognize the importance of church in this family, deciding to invite their pastor to the next session. This expands the size of the family's therapy system.

Intervention

You thank the parents for their sacrifice to save their son, and briefly recognize their accomplishments in all aspects of their parenting. After some praise, you point out the only exception to their total success as parents is in getting Alex to manage his own health. You suggest they accept being mostly successful parents and take a break on parenting Alex to focus on being a couple, sharing that the single best thing for a couple is to date again. Mr. and Mrs. Costa are asked to take a step back and observe the new trend their son is moving towards, and try to enjoy that he has started taking more responsibility for his well-being Mr. Costa seems interested in this idea, but Mrs. Costa experiences feelings of anxiety when thinking about not focusing on their son.

Recognizing the strong relationship she has with her church, you ask Mrs. Costa if she would bring her pastor to the next session to help get God's perspective, to which she agrees. In relation to the suggested date, you share that the purpose is for the couple to simply enjoy each other's company. As they are leaving, you inform them that you will get in contact once you have talked to their pastor to provide them with possible times and dates for the next session. Mrs. Costa says that they should be able to work with whatever day and time is set up for their pastor to attend.

Postsession

You are pleased that the couple was responsive to including their pastor in the next session. You are also moved by the shift that occurred between the couple as they began to orient back towards each other. The energy seems much more productive than the inward energy that was present in the couple prior to this session.

Session Three:

Presession

Prior to the session, Alex's doctor contacts you to report that Alex has been doing significantly better. He has been stepping up in terms of managing his diabetes, and has started to make better food choices. Additionally, he has started becoming much more aware of nutrition and what he is putting into his body. You also speak to the family's pastor on the phone. He seemed very happy to be hearing from you. He said that the Costa's are very involved in the life of the church, and as such, they are very dear to him. In light of the report from Alex's doctor, you decide that the family does not need to meet for about three weeks, just after the end of the holiday season. When discussing the schedule with the pastor, you share this with him and he says that he will make himself available whenever the family does come in for their next session.

Just days before the next session, you wonder if Alex is still improving in taking more personal responsibility for his well being, with the support of his parents. However, without any new data, you cannot think of an alternative hypothesis for the Costa's. You remind yourself to be open to alternatives should the clinical data present differently.

Session

As the family and their pastor enter the room, you notice the bond they all share. Their body language and casual conversation show evidence that they are very familiar and comfortable with one another. Mr. Costa begins the session by revealing that he and Alex are planning a road trip together in the spring. They have plans to spend the month of May hiking the Appalachian Trail.

After a bit of discussion about the trip, you look at Mrs. Costa and ask her what has happened in the past few months that she now feels comfortable with Alex being in the wilderness for so long? She responds, "Comfortable would be an understatement." She and Mr. Costa begin to engage in discussion regarding their son's recent improvements. They report that he has been making much better meal choices. While he is avoiding meat in his diet, he is eating a healthier and wider variety of foods. He is also managing his blood sugar level more habitually. His mother has largely stopped reminding him to take and or record his levels. They go on to share how that change has put him in line to finally receive an insulin pump. He should be able to get it just in time for the big trip.

At this point in the session, the pastor, "Pastor Tim" as they call him, joins in on the conversation regarding Alex's progress. You ask him to describe his observation of the Costa family's relationship with diabetes. He pauses and starts to describe how he can recall Alex first getting sick "like it was yesterday." Pastor Tim had only been at the church a few weeks when he got a call during dinner to visit the family at the hospital. He reminisces about his visit with the family, and states that he could immediately tell by the look on the doctor's face that Alex was in serious trouble.

Pastor Tim describes that while in seminary, he was educated in giving last rights to those sick and dying. At one point he had participated in an internship at hospice helping older adults "pass." However, he described the situation with Alex as very different, as he did not know how he would cope if he were to die. Pastor Tim continued to talk about how badly he wanted to leave the hospital, just walk out and keep going. But somehow, he stayed with the family and prayed for their son. Mr. Costa points out that he spent the night with the family, not leaving until Alex came out of his coma. Pastor Tim discloses that the Costa's relationship with diabetes has been difficult from the start and has remained so for years. When Alex was released from the hospital, he felt like his prayers had been answered, but he soon realized that Alex's struggle had just begun.

At this point everyone has tears in their eyes. Pastor Tim goes on to describe how he has watched diabetes make "normal" conflict between parents and children more intense. At one point, he looks at Alex and says, "It's easy for you to forget that your parents and I thought you were going to die. While it is not fair to you that every time you make a not so ideal choice we flashback, it happens." Alex looks up at Pastor Tim, and then scans the room to see everyone in tears. Alex proceeds to get up from his seat and walk over to his mom. He attempts to comfort her and says, "I got this. You can let go. I will not be perfect, but I will keep working and getting better." His mother holds her son. The father joins them, and now the entire family is embracing one another. You simply let them embrace in silence for a few minutes.

Alex builds on this moment and says that he realizes that this can only be his fight, a lifelong fight, but one that is solely his. He tells his parents that they cannot fight it for him, but they can support him in it. His father talks about how upset it makes him that Alex had to grow up so quickly because of his diabetes. Alex reassures him that it is OK, and that he would rather "Grow up too soon to have a chance of growing old someday." Noticing the session is coming to a close, you state that you would like to spend a few minutes with Pastor Tim planning the intervention. You excuse yourself and the Pastor, and the two of you go off to process the case.

Intersession

During the intersession, you thank Pastor Tim for his support and insight into the family. You also thank him for his courage to speak from the heart about the family's struggle against a potentially fatal disease. He reflects on what good people the Costa's are and how central they are to his church family. You recognize that, and then ask him if he thinks there is anything the family should now be directed to do. The pastor says that he can't think of anything, and you tell him that you think they are doing very well. With that, you suggest that the intervention should be for the family to just continue doing what they're doing. You decide to check back in six months.

Intervention

Once back in session, you tell the family that you and Pastor Tim admire how well they are doing. You additionally share that you both truly respect the family in taking a stand against diabetes. You voice to the entire family that should they continue to remain in therapy, you have little to offer them because they are making incredible progress on their own. You suggest that they come in for a "check up" in six months. Mr. Costa is very happy with the feedback, but Mrs. Costa looks slightly apprehensive. Pastor Tim notices her apprehension and asks her if she is uncomfortable with what has been proposed. She begins to question what will happen if they begin to regress in their progress, but you quickly interrupt her and say that if she begins to suspect regression, she can talk to Pastor Tim, or they should feel free to call you. You inform the family that in that event, you would work them in quickly.

Post session

As you write your notes from the session, you are still moved by the emotional intensity you witnessed between the family and Pastor Tim. You reflect on how helpful Pastor Tim was in confronting the family's situation.

About three weeks before the next scheduled session, Mrs. Costa calls to cancel. While she is grateful for your willingness to follow up, she does not think a follow up is necessary for the family.

About a year after the last session, you run into Alex at a basketball game at your local high school. You notice he has grown almost 6 inches and when he approaches you, you comment on his height. Alex shares that his family is doing very well. You respond by telling him that is fantastic news, and you then ask that he say hello to his parents for you.

Case Discussion

In this case, the therapist quickly hypothesizes that a family dynamic is involved in Alex's symptoms. This hypothesis leads to the creation of an intervention prior to seeing the family. Asking the physician to take on the role of monitoring the client's weight changes the dynamic within the family. This intervention moves the Costa's out of the role of managing Alex's symptoms. In situations where medical issues are closely related to family issues, it is best to get the medical provider to remain responsible for monitoring the physical symptom.

In the first session, the relationship between the family and Alex's diabetes is explored via circular questioning. The intervention utilized in the session was providing the family with a positive connotation of the symptom. In addition, part of the intervention for the session was to schedule a follow up session with just Mr. and Mrs. Costa.

In the second session with Mr. and Mrs. Costa, you were able to listen to the story of their struggles. Since religion is central to this family, you explored each of their relationships with God through the use of circular questioning. Noticing that the emotional tone of the relationship shifts during the session, you try to capitalize on that by suggesting dating as an intervention. If the couple can focus more on their relationship, it might reset the homeostatic mechanism in the entire family. Recognizing the importance of their spiritual life, you invite their Pastor to the next session.

Evaluating

The Milan approach was developed in a clinic setting where the team was free to experiment with new approaches in working with families. Given this, many of the techniques were developed in response to clinical experience. Most evaluations of this approach come from the reporting of anecdotal successes with schizophrenia (Selvini-Palazzoli, et al., 1978) and anorexia nervosa (Selvini-Palazzoli, 1978). When you think about the reported successes in the context of how difficult these two disorders are to treat, the results seem too good to be true. According to Mashal, Feldman, & Siegal (1989), there has been only one attempt to replicate the "astonishing" outcomes of the Milan approach. They explored the reported treatment outcomes and described satisfaction from 14 families, 5 couples, and 76 individuals, and found mixed support of the approach. However, the impact of the Milan approach can be evaluated by observing its influences on other theories.

Learning Exercise

1. Pick four students to go into the hall and create a presenting problem. Assign two students to play parents and two students to play children. After the "family" has a rough outline of a presenting problem, engage the family in 10 minutes of circular questioning. After 10 minutes, have the rest of the class work on developing hypotheses about the family and the problem. Repeat for several cycles so students can develop a feel of how hypotheses develop out of questioning, and how important neutrality is in the process.

2. Apply the principles of circularity, hypothesizing and neutrality to a situation in your life that you have found stressful.

Discussion Questions

1. How did this approach help shift family therapy from a modern to post-modern view of change?

2. What differences may there be between a therapist practicing from neutrality and a therapist practicing from objectivity when conducting an interview?

3. Describe ways you might approach a variety of referral sources (clergy, attorneys, doctors, probation, etc.) so that they would be willing to attend a therapy session. How could they be most useful to you in helping the family?

Suggested Readings

Campbell, D., Draper, R., & Crutchley, E. (1991). The Milan systemic approach to family therapy. In A.S. Gurman & D.P Kniskern (Eds.), *Handbook of family therapy* (Vol. II). New York: Brunner/Mazel.

Selvini Palazzoli, M. (1984) Behind the scenes of the organization: Some guidelines for the expert in human relations. *Journal of Marital and Family Therapy, 6*(2), 299–307.

Selvini Palazzoli, M., Boscolo, L., Cecchin, G., & Prata, G. (1978) *Paradox and Counterparadox*. New York: Jason Aaronson.

Selvini Palazzoli, M., Boscolo, L., Cecchin, G., & Prata, G. (1980). Hypothesizing-circularity-neutrality: Three guidelines for the conductor of the session. *Family Process, 19,* 3–12.

Tomm, K. (1984a) One perspective on the Milan systemic approach: Part I. Overview of development, theory and practice. *Journal of Marital and Family Therapy,10*(2), 113–125.

Tomm, K. (1984b) One perspective on the Milan systemic approach: Part II. Description of session format, interviewing style and interventions. *Journal of Marital and Family Therapy, 10*(3), 253–271.

Web Based Resources

Breakdown of Milan Systemic Family Therapy

https://postmoderntherapies.wikispaces.com/Milan+Family+Therapy

A Critique of Milan Systemic Family Therapy

http://www.priory.com/psych/milan.htm

Flashcards for Milan System Family Therapy

https://quizlet.com/21238910/milan-systemic-family-therapy-flash-cards/

SECTION 4

Postmodern Models of Marriage and Family Therapy

The models discussed in this section are the third and most recent generation of theories of family therapy. They were developed from a postmodern paradigm. These groups of theories stand out as examples of theories that regard reality as the product of social construction. This shift in paradigm has fostered an increased emphasis on therapeutic conservations. Postmodern therapists pay particular attention to how conservation that occur during a psychotherapy interview impact the client both in the session and between sessions.

The first postmodern model of family therapy to be discussed is the solution-focused brief model. Chapter 12 explores how this approach produces change in clients. Based on the idea that problems are maintained by belief systems, solution-focused brief therapy focuses on exploring possibilities of change in the present and future.

In Chapter 13, we concentrate on constructivist family therapy. This approach explores how the use of language gives rise to and maintains problems. The therapist engages the client in conversations that externalize the problem through a process of deconstruction.

Chapter 14 introduces the final model explored in this section, narrative family therapy. This approach is a specialized application of the constructivist model based on the idea that clients make sense of experiences in their lives through the telling and retelling of self-referencing stories. These stories or narratives are central to issues of self and personal agency. By acting as a coeditor, the narrative family therapist helps the client develop new stories that are problem free.

CHAPTER

12

SOLUTION-FOCUSED BRIEF FAMILY THERAPY

Thinking About This Approach

In recent years, solution-focused brief family therapy has been receiving an increasing amount of attention. In part, this may be the result of economic forces rather than the intellectual interest of practitioners. In the mid 1990s, health insurance companies began to move toward a managed care system with a preset limit on the amount of client contact. This trend in insurance led to a movement toward briefer courses of therapy.

At the center of this movement is the Brief Family Therapy Center, founded in Milwaukee, Wisconsin, in 1978. It was here that solution-focused brief family therapy originated. Steve de Shazer codirected the center with his wife and partner Insoo Kim Berg until he passed away in 2005 and she passed in 2007. They were the major voices of this school and developed what has become known as a solution-focused approach. Therapy at the Brief Family Therapy Center was conducted with the assistance of a treatment team that watches therapy from behind a one-way mirror. As a result, the development of this model has been closely linked to training, which makes this approach rich in the description of therapeutic process.

The solution-focused brief family therapy movement is a direct offshoot of the Mental Research Institute (see Chapter 8), with a similar emphasis on problem resolution. Also, like Haley's strategic therapy (see Chapter 10), this approach is heavily influenced by the work of Milton Erickson. Like other models of family therapy mentioned thus far, brief therapy focuses on the present rather than the past. A major contribution of this approach is its emphasis on solutions rather than problems as they exist in the here and now of the interview (de Shazer, 1982, 1988). The approach is often called "solution focused" simply for this reason. There is an assumption that people are addressing the problem on their own, that clients have the resources to solve their problems, and that clients have already taken steps to address the problems. The therapist often plays the role of a detective trying to see clues that suggest the ever-present solution to the problem.

From this perspective, therapy is a blend of art and science, making it a craft (de Shazer, 1988). Clients provide the creativity in terms of how they find answers or solutions to their problems. The therapist takes the role of a scientist who supplies the clients with useful questions. Thus, the responsibility of constructing solutions to problems is found in the resources of the client. In solution-focused brief therapy, the reality of a problem is seen as generated out of conversation about the problem. In fact, de Shazer (1985) argues that the postmodern or second-order perspective sets the stage for treatment: "From this perspective, clients can be seen as initiating the change process by the very act of bringing their problem to a therapist, thus making it public. This makes the definition of the problem subject to change" (p. 66).

De Shazer is clear that his theory is not a theory of family systems. His work is on the level of cybernetics of cybernetics and is an analysis of the therapy system. His theoretical interest lies in the system that is made up of the family plus the therapist, and he chooses not to theorize about how clients or their families function outside of this social setting (de Shazer, 1982, 1988). He limits the scope of his work to the therapeutic setting. In line with this, he adopts the constructionist stance that a complaint in the context of therapy is a result of someone's seeking help. The complaint is accepted as the starting point, and little time is spent hypothesizing about how the complaint was generated in the family system. Rather, the focus of therapy is on a solution to the problem.

The theoretical thrust of this approach is developing a systemic theory of change. De Shazer (1982, 1984) points out that the concept of homeostasis, central to systemic family theory, is stability or morphostasis. In de Shazer's description of the therapy system (family system plus therapist system), his focus is on change, or morphogenesis. In this approach promoting change takes center stage to understanding how families function. This is clearly a legacy of the MRI group's emphasis on analyzing the process of change.

Central to this theory of change are basic assumptions about the nature of the clients who present for therapy. De Shazer (1984) is critical of the view of the family as a homeostatic, closed system. Traditional psychotherapy and early family therapy relied heavily on the concept of resistance to describe stability in the therapy system. As de Shazer (1984) points out, "The concept of resistance locks many family-systems-based therapies into the prevailing epistemology of linear causation, 'force,' or 'power,' because it implies a separation between the therapist and the family system" (p. 13). This pits the family members in a battle against each other where each is fighting for the advantage. De Shazer's model tries to concern itself with the opposite of resistance: cooperation. Cooperation is seen as a process naturally occurring in all clients. As de Shazer (1982) states,

> each family (individual or a couple) shows a unique way of attempting to cooperate, and the therapist's job becomes, first to describe that particular manner to himself that the family shows and, then, to cooperate with the families and, thus, to promote change. (p. 10)

This idea is an extension of the idea of positive connotation, developed by a group of strategic therapists working in Milan, Italy, and referred to as the Milan approach see chapter 11. It is in going to the past or root of the problem that the client anchors her or his resistance. The goal of brief family therapy is to circumvent the resistance simply by developing a cooperative relationship. If the client is fully engaged in corporation resistance simply doesn't exist. De Shazer (1985) describes this further:

> First we connect the present to the future (ignoring the past), then we compliment the clients on what they are already doing that is useful and/or good for them, and then—once they know we are on their side—we can make a suggestion for something new that they might do which is, or at least might be, good for them. (p. 15)

Video Call Out 12.1: Brief Family Therapy

Dr. Jordan begins the therapy by getting a picture of the client's world by paying careful attention to the client's own language. He asks questions detailing her symptoms regarding how long she has felt this particular way. He is quick to pay her compliments about how she gets up in the morning despite the way she is feeling. This gives her credit for the change she has already accomplished. Furthermore, throughout this session Dr. Jordan utilizes the client's words in formulating his questions, as well as summarizing important aspects of what she says. This builds a collaborative relationship with her where the therapist plus the client become a team working on solving her problems.

Innovations in Practice

This approach emphasizes the solution to problems rather than understanding how problems develop. As a result, brief therapy has made relatively few contributions to the advancement of family therapy theory. In fact, only in the past few years have there been attempts to develop a theoretical explanation of solution-focused brief therapy. Rather, its contribution to the field has been to advance the theoretical understanding of change. Theoretical understanding is not necessary for conducting solution-focused brief family therapy. In fact, Berg and Miller (1992) claim that "those students least burdened with abstract theoretical notions are usually the most capable of learning solution-focused therapy and, for that matter, therapy skills in general" (p. 1).

The major innovation of solution-focused brief family therapy has been the development of new techniques. Many of these techniques have a theoretical origin in hypnotic suggestion, used in clinical hypnosis. However, a trance is not necessary for the interventions to produce change. A common theme in the interventions is the reframing of an unsolvable problem as solvable. This changing of how something is framed is seen as having an effect very similar to that of a hypnotic suggestion. Often, once a new frame is established, the problem quickly resolves.

The Miracle Question

One of the most popular and interesting interventions to come out of this approach is the miracle question de Shazer & Dolan (2007). This question is asked early in therapy, usually about halfway through the first session. The client is asked to speculate on what it would be like to live her or his life without the presenting problem. For example, in working with a client, de Shazer (1988) asked a series of questions such as, "Suppose that one night while you were asleep there was a miracle and this problem was solved. How would you know? What would be different?" (p. 5). This questioning style forces the client to focus on the future and does not provide an opportunity for the client to get defensive or call up resistance. This creates a collaborative between the therapist and clients. The word *suppose* tells the client that this is not real, so the client is invited to imagine having the ability to solve the problem. The idea of a miracle tells the client that anything can happen. The question "How would you know?" invites clients to make comparisons between their lives now and their lives without the problem. The purpose of the miracle question is to further focus the interview into the future. It encourages the client to think about specific goals. Given this, the goals are shifted from internal ("I want to feel better") to external ("My partner would notice that I am in better spirits").

Video Call Out 12.2: Brief Family Therapy

Dr. Jordan employs the miracle question intervention to help the client imagine her 'miracle' or 'perfect' day. He does so in hopes that it will assist her in rediscovering that 'go-getter' energy she has inside herself, so she can draw upon that once again to get her back to the self she desires. This miracle question allows the client to focus on the future without any resistance. This further creates a collaborative relationship between client and therapist.

Small Changes

The emphasis of the brief family therapy approach is that of "minimal elegance" (de Shazer, 1987). The goal is to reduce therapy to the simplest possible techniques. According to de Shazer and Berg (1985),

> a problem should be approached in the most simple manner first. If that does not work, then collect some more information and then try the next most simple solution, as long as it is different from the first one. Simply stated, the rule is: If all you need is a screwdriver, do not use dynamite. (p. 98)

The basis for this belief is the observation that a small change produces larger changes. Attempting radical change is seen as a waste of time and energy. From this perspective, it is far better to simply produce a small change and allow the ripple effect to produce the large or radical change. The goal is to solve the problem by making small changes.

Video Call Out 12.3: Brief Family Therapy

Shortly after asking the miracle question, Dr. Jordan asks the client to rate this particular day, as she did before, and asks whether the client has experienced these kinds of days in the pastbefore. He then asks about a small change for the client by asking her to consider what may bring her up from a rating of 4 to a 4.5 on her rating of the day. By looking at a small change in detail we see the client become motivated to consider further change. This is followed up by asking her to reflect upon what she can do and control to help raise this number.

Locked-Away Solutions

In *Keys to Solutions in Brief Therapy,* de Shazer (1985) develops a metaphoric view of therapy that sees problems as a result of locked-away solutions. The goal of therapy is therefore to unlock what is inhibiting clients from solving their problem. De Shazer further develops this metaphor and encourages the use of "skeleton keys" when working with families. Skeleton keys have the advantage of fitting a variety of locks: that is, they are more general. This is very similar to Haley's view of strategic therapy (discussed in Chapter 9) and fits Haley's definition of a strategic approach.

Within this approach, there is also rich description of the way the therapist relates to clients. De Shazer (1988, 1994) likens the therapist to a detective in the tradition of Sherlock Holmes, who had an uncanny ability to notice details that were so obvious others missed them. The therapist looks for the elusive clue that, once discovered, allows the family to solve their problems. Like Holmes, the therapist does not have to dig deep to find these clues. They are seen as hiding in plain view. Often these clues are competencies that clients do not perceive. In other words, as clients tell their story about their inability to solve their problem, they gloss over instances when they were competent. This overtime leads clients to be perceived as incompetent. Asking questions from the perspective that the client can solve their problems gives the client an opportunity to see themselves as competent.

Questioning

In brief family therapy, questions are phrased to discover exceptions to the client's implicit rule that the problem is always occurring. De Shazer (1988) describes this focus in therapy by discussing exceptions to standard practices in psychotherapy:

> Most initial therapy sessions begin with the client describing the complaint or problem that led her or him to seek therapy. Frequently, the therapist will then explore the complaint in great detail, although what the therapist considers being important varies from model to model. As a solution focused model has become more developed, this phase has become shorter and shorter, and has taken on less and less importance. Within a very short period of time the

therapist begins constructing a solution by initiating a search for exceptions, i.e., the therapist explores with as much detail as possible times when the complaint did not happen. (p. 51)

If, in future sessions, the client does not report any change, the therapist focuses on *when* change will occur, not *if* change will occur (de Shazer, 1984).

Scaling Questions

To assist with the discovery of exceptions, the therapist can ask scaling questions de Shazer & Dolan (2007). To do this, the therapist asks the client to rate the presenting problem on a 10-point scale. Typically 0 is the complete absence of the problem and 10 is the worst the problem has ever been. Once a client has placed the problem on the scale, the therapist can interview the client on what would represent a small change. For example, when parents are asked to scale a "problem" child's behavior, they might assign an 8. The therapist can then inquire what would be different in the child when the problem is a 7 or even a 7.5. This gives the family an opportunity to notice even small differences in the child's behavior.

Solution-focused therapists believe that clients often make some improvement prior to starting treatment (i.e., between calling for an appointment and the first therapy session). The therapist utilizes this phenomenon via the scaling question. The therapist simply asks the client to scale the problem in terms of its severity last week and then to compare that to its rating on the scale today. This often demonstrates progress that the therapist can use as motivation to create further progress.

Video Call Out 12.4: Brief Family Therapy

Throughout the session Dr. Jordan asks the client to share what her life was like before she began to feel the way she does now. He utilizes the scaling question intervention as a means of identifying changes in her life. He asks her to scale herself at a variety of points. Where she currently is, where she was yesterday, and where she was in the prior two weeks. This provides for a variety of data points to call attention to the natural changes in the client's well-being. In addition, Dr. Jordan seeks to discover any exceptions to the client's current feeling state and asks for further detail regarding this to get a more vivid picture.

Structuring

Usually therapy is structured within a 50-minute session. In working with a family or couple, sessions are often extended to two hours. In each session, about 20 minutes before the end, a break is taken so that the therapist can consult with the treatment team. If there is no treatment team, the therapist reflects in private during the break, acting as her or his own treatment team. After this break, the therapist returns with a compliment for the client and an intervention in the form of homework.

Unlike more traditional approaches, solution-focused brief family therapy does not necessitate seeing clients every week. Therapists often ask clients how long they would like to wait between sessions. An interval of two to three weeks is common. It is assumed that the client has all of the resources necessary to solve the problem, and spacing the sessions gives the client an opportunity to address the problem. The extended period between sessions also allows clients time to engage in finding solutions on their own. Thus, there is a "try this at home" attitude in this work.

Unlike therapists in other schools of family therapy, brief family therapists do not insist that all family members attend sessions. They are willing to work with whoever is available to come. In fact, brief family therapists will conduct "couple" therapy with one person. This is consistent with their assumption that a small change in one will lead to a larger change in the entire system.

Responding

In a solution-focused brief therapy interview, the goal of the therapist is to be compassionate and responsive to clients' needs. Such an interview is designed to be supportive and to focus on the solution to the problem rather than on an understanding of the history of the problem. Given this, there is little interest in discussing the past. The emphasis is on the near past (ideally, the time between sessions), the present, and most important, the future. However, the past is not ignored if it is important to the client. The therapist will listen to the client's history of the problem until the client feels the therapist is up to date and will then shift the focus of the interview to the present and future.

In this approach, there is little confrontation of a client's maladaptive patterns of relating. The idea of providing clients with insight into their difficulty is also discarded. The goal is not to find out what is dysfunctional but to discover the aspects of the client's life that are working and expand these adaptive patterns to new areas. This provides a positive focus in the interview process. For example, a therapist might ask a client at the beginning of a second interview, "What has gotten better since we last met?" This is followed by many queries to ask what else could be better. During an intake session, the therapist might ask what has improved since the appointment was made.

Applications

Solution-focused brief family therapy has been applied to several treatment modalities. It has been used extensively to treat individuals, couples, and families in a variety of settings. Solution-focused brief family therapy with individuals can be distinguished from brief individual therapy based on the theoretical orientation of the therapist. By taking a systemic theoretical stance, the therapist can conceptualize absent family members during the interview. Questioning the client about those family members allows family issues to be addressed during an individual session. Brief family therapy is further distinguished from individual therapy practiced on a time-limited basis by its focus on the client plus the therapist. This is a second-order cybernetics stance that includes appreciation not only of the client's system, but also of the treatment team of client and therapist.

De Shazer (1978, 1979) also developed a model for applying the concepts of solution-focused brief family therapy to marital therapy. His work is an extension of Heider's (1946) balance theory, which is used to predict the stability of a relationship. It is possible for a relationship to be stable and yet not rewarding for the couple. If the relationship is stable and not rewarding, the first task of therapy becomes making the relationship unstable. Once unstable, the relationship can be changed for the better. However, more recent discussions of marital therapy have adopted an even more simplistic orientation. De Shazer and Berg (1985) published an interesting case report of solution-focused brief family therapy with a couple. Here, they reject the idea that there is a difference among individual, couple, and even family therapy in terms of how a case is approached. Their theoretical discourse is reduced to discussing simplicity and cooperation.

The solution-focused brief approach has been successfully applied to work with people with addictions and their families (Berg & Gallagher, 1991; Berg & Miller, 1992; Berg & Reuss, 1997; Juhnke & Coker, 1997; Mason, Chandler, & Grasso, 1995; McCollum & Trepper, 2001; Miller & Berg, 1995 Smock, Trepper, Wetchler, McCollum, Ray, Kent 2008). This approach outright rejects traditional assumptions of working with people with addictions. It discards the disease model of addictions, the concept of an addictive personality, and abstinence as the only realistic goal for treatment. The drinking problem is treated as any other problem for which the client is requesting help.

Since a solution-focused brief family therapist does not insist on seeing the entire family in the therapy session, this approach has a great deal of flexibility in terms of who can be treated and in what settings it can be practiced. For example, it has been used in inpatient settings (Vaughn, Young, Webster, & Thomas, 1996; Webster, 1990; Webster, Vaughn, & Martinez, 1994), in schools (Metcalf, 1995; Murphy, 1996) and in the foster care setting (Flemons, Liscio, Gordon, Hibel, Gutierrez-Hersh & Rebholz 2010). Solution-focused brief family therapy is also being used with clients who have a wide variety of difficulties, such as encopresis (Shapiro & Henderson, 1992), and with families dealing with issues of sexual and spousal abuse (Dolan, 1991; Sirles, Lipchik, & Kowalski, 1993; Tambling 2012). This adaptability may be a result of the therapist's ability to be supportive of a client's struggles while having respect and appreciation for the client's uniqueness. Solution-focused supervision (Marek, Sandifer, Beach, Coward, & Protinsky, 1994; Wetchler, 1990) is also increasing in popularity and becoming a common method of supervision. In this approach, the supervisor lets the supervisee set the goals for supervision.

Solution-focused brief family therapy has also been applied to situations where the presenting problem is more emotional than pragmatic. Authors such as Lipchik, Kiser, and Piercy (Kiser, Piercy, & Lipchik, 1993; Lipchik, 2002; Piercy, Lipchik, & Kiser, 2000) describe how it is important not to confuse this model's minimalist eloquence with a noncaring stance. Piercy and colleagues (2000) clearly state, "We believe it can be helpful to reframe emotions as strengths" (p. 26). This ability to assist clients in dealing with their emotions has led to applications in bereavement therapy (Butler & Powers, 1996; Davey, 1999) as well as in assisting families coping with suicide (de Castro & Guterman, 2008).

Acting as a Solution-Focused Brief Family Therapist

In this approach, two stages are involved in the beginning of treatment: the pre-session planning and the prelude. The pre-session planning is a meeting of the treatment team before contact is made with the clients to discuss relevant experiences team members have had with similar presenting problems. The purpose is not to develop a single view of the family but a multiplicity of views. As de Shazer (1982) states, "the presence of more than one systemic or ecosystemic thinker behind the mirror often provides the team with different maps of the family and therapy system. This increases the team's ability to achieve an isomorphic map" (p. 32). As previously stated, isomorphism refers to the tendency of structures and processes to be reproduced on different levels. When the treatment team develops an isomorphic map, the therapy is more likely to produce significant change.

The second beginning stage is called the prelude. This is a purely social portion of the initial interview in which the person conducting the interview avoids a direct discussion of the presenting problem. The goal of this stage is to "build a nonthreatening, helpful relationship with the whole family and to learn something about how the family sees its world" (de Shazer, 1982, p. 33). Behind the mirror, the team develops a description of the family and an idea of how the members interact around nonproblematic issues.

After the prelude of the interview, the therapist engages the family in a data collection phase that is the main portion of the intake interview (de Shazer, 1982). This is initiated with the question, "Well, what problem can we help you with?" (de Shazer, 1982, p. 32). Each family member is encouraged to give her or his view of the problem, giving as much detail as possible. If the family brings several complaints, it is important to agree on which complaint should be addressed first. The focus of this portion of treatment is to establish therapeutic goals. Behind the mirror, the treatment team further defines its map of the family system.

Since the scope of this model is limited to descriptions of family–therapist interactions, there is no formal diagnostic or assessment procedure. The idea of pathology is counterintuitive to this approach. However, de Shazer is very interested in the relationship between client and therapist. His descriptions of the styles of client relationships are discussed here because, like the diagnostic procedures used in other perspectives, they help determine how the therapist conceptually frames the therapy. These styles are labeled "visitor," "complainant," and "customer." These styles are not fixed and, in a family, different members can present with different styles.

The first style of client–therapist relationship is called a visitor relationship. Visitors do not have a complaint of their own and are usually sent by a family member, such as a parent, or an official, such as a teacher or judge. De Shazer (1988) cautions against trying to intervene with a visitor:

> Since there is no complaint to work on, therapy cannot begin (this situation is outside the theory's scope of conditions) and therefore it is a mistake for the therapist to try to intervene no matter how obvious the problem may be to an observer. With "visitors" like this, any intervention is likely to be rejected and, thus, the therapist's error in not recognizing these people as visitors sets up a classic "resistance relationship" between him and the other people in the office. (p. 87)

In this situation the goal is to change the visitor into a customer. De Shazer (1988) suggests that the therapist be nice, take the client's side, and call attention to what works. He further suggests simply ending the first session with a compliment rather than a complaint or task. This allows the client to return to the next session with a complaint of her or his own or an issue to address.

Complainants are clients who come to therapy ready to get down to business and with the expectation that the interview is a means to an end. The complaint may be vague or unfocused but is seen as a starting point for therapy. It takes the form of "something is wrong; please fix it" and can be implicit or explicit. By focusing on what the client is doing, complaints can be changed to motivation.

A customer is a complainant willing to do something about the complaint. Thus, a customer has started to formulate goals for therapy and ways to resolve the complaint. Customers are ready to work or have even started to work on their own. Here the intervention phase of treatment can begin.

In early work at the Brief Family Therapy Center, the intervention phase of treatment was broken into two steps, called the compliment and the clue (de Shazer, 1982). The compliment seeks to acknowledge the family's experience both in the therapy room and at home. This puts them in a positive frame for receiving the clue. The clue involves having the family observe for situational cues surrounding the defined problem. For example, the family is asked to observe what happens before Megan throws a temper tantrum and what time of day the tantrum happens.

Later sessions involve interventions consistent with the family's compliance with prior homework. For example, if the family modified the last assigned task, the team will give the family a similar task that the family can also modify. If the family had a vague response to the task, future tasks will be presented in a vague manner. This allows the family-plus-therapist system to engage in hunting behavior. This pattern continues until a solution is discovered. From here, therapy follows a simple rule: "Once you know what works, do more of it" (de Shazer, 1988, p. 55).

In the brief approach, treatment is ended as quickly as possible. When clients report that the problem has been solved, the therapist simply congratulates them. If the family is hesitant to end treatment, a follow-up session might be set for a month or two later. Usually, the therapist highlights the changes and says good-bye to the family members.

Case Example: The Case of Josh's Soiled Pants

Mrs. Jackson calls requesting therapy for a problem she and her husband are having with their five-year-old son, Josh. Dr. Horn, Josh's pediatrician, gave Mrs. Jackson the clinic's phone number after she took her son in for an examination regarding the problem. Josh has been soiling his pants for about six months now, and Mrs. Jackson is very frustrated by this. Before, Josh had been doing fine with bowel control. Mrs. Jackson states that Josh is a nervous child and has had asthma since he was three. His asthma is well controlled with treatment.

On the phone, Mrs. Jackson is very hurried and asks about the therapist's training and experience. The therapist simply replies that she has a master's in marriage and family therapy from Appalachian State University and 10 years' experience treating families. She also shares descriptions of children she has helped with a similar problem. Mrs. Jackson asks the therapist about her experiences working with African American families. The therapist discloses that while she is Caucasian, she has worked with many African American families. The therapist takes this opportunity to discuss how the team approach is used as well as how this approach combines experience and wisdom.

The therapist points out that the team has two members who are African American. She goes on to state that she would be willing to make a referral to an African American family therapist if Mrs. Jackson would like her to. Mrs. Jackson states that she thinks she should be comfortable working with the therapist. The therapist invites her to bring up issues of race if and when they come up in therapy, and Mrs. Jackson agrees to this contract.

The therapist then sets an appointment for three days later and asks if Mr. Jackson would also be able to come. Mrs. Jackson says, "Yes, of course," as if she is surprised by the question. The therapist asks if there is any other family living in the home or in the area, and Mrs. Jackson responds that Josh is an only child and that their families live in another state. The therapist ends the call by giving Mrs. Jackson directions to the clinic.

In pre-session, the team discusses cases they have worked on where a child has had encopresis. The therapist shares her surprise at Mrs. Jackson's inquisitive manner about her credentials. The team hypothesizes that Mrs. Jackson may be a perfectionist. The therapist agrees that this is the sense she got on the phone. The therapist also wonders about Mrs. Jackson's response to her question about Mr. Jackson's attending the session. One team member hypothesizes that, having no family in the state, the Jacksons are isolated. The team is also curious about what has been different these past six months that Josh has been soiling his pants. One team member notes that Josh most likely started school at about the same time he dirtied his pants.

Session One

The Jackson family arrives at the session five minutes late, in a rushed state. They explain that they had problems finding a place to park at the clinic. Josh is small for his age and looks disheveled. His parents are dressed impeccably. His father is wearing a suit and tie and his mother is wearing a business suit. The family are out of breath when they arrive, and it takes a few minutes for them to get settled.

The therapist greets the family and explains that she works with a treatment team. She asks the family if they would like to go behind the mirror to meet the team. The family is comfortable with not meeting the team, so the therapist begins the session.

The therapist begins by asking the standard question, "How can we help you?" After a rather vocal exhale, Mrs. Jackson admits being at wit's end with Josh and his dirty pants. She states that she is so frustrated with the behavior and is at a loss to understand it. Mr. Jackson rolls his eyes in agreement and asks what makes a five-year-old do such a thing. The therapist responds that she doesn't know. She explains that each child has her or his own reasons. The therapist asks Mr. Jackson what Josh says when his dad asks him about his pants. In response to this, Mr. Jackson turns to his son and asks with contempt, "What is wrong with you, boy?" His son shrinks in his seat and shakes his head.

To stop this negative discussion, the therapist attempts to redirect the conversation by asking Mrs. Jackson to talk about what Josh does well. Mrs. Jackson looks proud as she tells the therapist about Josh's good grades. She also states that he is easy to get along with and has good manners. The therapist agrees with her praise of Josh's manners and points out his good behavior in the session. She notes that Josh takes his chair and speaks when asked, and he follows general rules on how to behave in public. Mr. Jackson joins this conversation by pointing out his son's athletic potential. He states that he plays catch with his son and that Josh has a great throwing arm for a five-year-old. The therapist engages Josh by asking him if he likes to play ball. Josh responds positively, and the therapist spends several minutes engaging him in conversation about his enjoyment of playing ball with his dad. The therapist then turns to Mr. Jackson and compliments him on being involved in rearing his son.

Mr. Jackson responds that he spends as much time with his son as he can. However, work has been crazy since his company was "taken over by a barbaric competitor." Mrs. Jackson interrupts and explains that, since Big Josh is so busy at work, she has taken more of a role in Little Josh's life. Prior to all of the stress at work, Mr. Jackson took Josh to and from day care. Now, Mrs. Jackson is the one who takes Josh to school and picks him up.

Mr. Jackson interrupts and states that he is afraid that Josh will be thrown out of school for "dirty pants." As he looks with anger at his son, he explains that the school will not allow children who poop their pants in school. The therapist asks Mr. Jackson if the school has complained about Josh, and Mr. Jackson replies, "No, not yet." The therapist asks if this is a relief to him. Mr. Jackson states that it is, but that he is getting sick of this problem.

The therapist asks Mr. Jackson if the dirty pants are the only problem that he wants to work on for now, and Mr. Jackson says this is the only thing that is wrong. The therapist compliments both parents on the good job they have been doing rearing their son and then asks Mr. Jackson when Josh is likely to dirty his pants. Mr. Jackson states that it happens mostly on the weekends when he is at home and one or two nights during the week. He explains that so far there have been no problems at school. The therapist states that it is a good sign that Josh has this problem only a few times a week rather than every day. "Pants that are dirty a few days a week are a much easier problem to solve than pants that are always dirty," the therapist reassures the parents. Noticing that there is only 20 minutes before the session ends, the therapist excuses herself to talk to the team behind the one-way mirror.

The team has compliments for the parents regarding their level of concern. They also think that it is good that Josh is able to keep his pants clean at school. They wonder if the parents can predict when Josh is going to have clean pants and suggest this as a homework assignment.

The therapist takes the compliments back to the family, who receive them well and seem relieved. The therapist asks the parents to see if they can observe their son and figure out a way to predict when he will not dirty his pants. They are to do nothing differently except try to learn how to predict their son's clean pants. The therapist thanks everyone for coming and, after setting a follow-up appointment for one week, walks them out.

Session Two

In pre-session, the team discusses how the family is preoccupied with Josh's problem. They point out that if it weren't for this problem, the family would be satisfied with their life. They are also struck by how this problem originated at about the same time Dad began having problems. They think that involving Dad more with his son may help solve the problem.

The Jacksons arrive at the session on time and in good spirits. The parents look much the same as they did last session, but Josh is neat and much better groomed. The therapist quickly notices the difference and joins the family in their positive mindset. She asks how things went last week, and the family states that Josh had only one accident. The therapist turns to Josh, congratulates him for a job well done, and puts her hand up for a high five. Josh becomes shy, grins as the therapist compliments him, and gives her a high five.

Therapist: How were you able to achieve this success?
Josh: I don't know.
Therapist: Is that an "I don't know" or is it that you don't want to tell?
Josh: I just don't know.

At this point, Mr. Jackson interrupts to say that, while this is a step in the right direction, he still does not have faith in his son. The therapist asks Mr. Jackson if Josh was able to complete his homework. Mr. Jackson responds that he didn't notice much of a difference and describes how they all had a great week. They took the week off work and kept Josh out of school and went around town doing the things that they enjoy but never get around to doing. The therapist points out that it was a good week for everyone. Mr. Jackson nods in agreement.

The therapist engages Mrs. Jackson by asking her how the week was for her. She states that it was great. She also took the week off work and says that it "felt like they were a family." The therapist asks if she could notice the difference in her son on days he did not dirty his pants. She states that she did notice the difference. She goes on to describe how much more enjoyable her time with her son has been.

At this point, the therapist asks Josh the miracle question: "If one night while you are asleep a miracle happens and the problem is solved, what will be different?" At first Josh shrugs his shoulders and replies, "I don't know." The therapist tells him to make up an answer since it was a miracle that happened overnight, so anything can be different. Josh pauses and describes how he would wake up less troubled. He would have a good day and not worry about pooping his pants. After a pause he adds that since he wouldn't have to worry about pooping his pants, his family wouldn't have to worry either.

The therapist then asks Mr. Jackson the same question. His response is similar to Josh's, but he is quick to note that it would take a couple of days to be sure that the miracle had occurred. The therapist agrees and asks Mr. Jackson what would first lead him to suspect something was different. Mr. Jackson says, "Nothing big, just a lot of little things." Both Josh and he would be less anxious.

When Mrs. Jackson is asked the same question, she is quick to point out that she would first notice the change in her husband. She states that Big Josh gets so worked up when Little Josh has problems. At this point, Mr. Jackson starts to interrupt, but the therapist gently cuts him off by saying that she wants to hear the rest of Mrs. Jackson's answer. Mrs. Jackson goes on to describe how much less tension there would be in the house and how everyone would have more patience with each other. The therapist asks her how she is able to notice when people are more patient with her. She states that the big difference she notices is that they make time to do things together, like eat at the kitchen table.

At this point the therapist breaks to consult with the treatment team and excuses herself from the family's presence. The team is quick to point out the improvement in all of the family members.

Of particular note is the improvement in both Big Josh's and Little Josh's moods. The team further offers the observation that the family does better when they have time for each other.

The therapist relays the team's compliment to the family, and they receive it warmly. When the therapist offers the observation that things go better when they have time together, the parents start to become defensive. They are quick to point out that they had last week off. The therapist responds that of course that would be different and that not every week can be like that, but suggests that perhaps they could find a little more time together between sessions. She adds that often just a tiny bit more time can have a large effect.

Session Three

The family arrives at this session in bright spirits with news of no accidents in the week between sessions. The therapist gives the family a hearty congratulations and asks them how things are different now that they have solved the problem. Mrs. Jackson is first to respond as she points out that the family had a "wonderful" week together. When asked what made it wonderful, she says that they were able to get along.

Mr. Jackson echoes his wife's view that it was a wonderful week. He states that between sessions he had a change in perspective and decided that he was taking his job too seriously and neglecting his family. He decided that his new job was his family and that work should come second. He states, "I have my job so I can take care of my family. It's not that I have my family so I can do my job." He reports that he was even able to sneak out of work early once last week to pick up Josh. To his surprise, no one at work found out, and he began to doubt if they cared. He reports that this shift in perspective has been a relief to him. The therapist agrees and states that Mr. Jackson looks like a new man. The therapist goes on to point out that Mr. Jackson now smiles with his whole face, not just his mouth.

When the therapist checks in with Josh, the little boy is not sure what is different. Josh states that he is now a big boy and does not poop in his pants anymore. The therapist congratulates him and asks him if he enjoys being a big boy. Josh agrees that there are benefits to being a big boy, but can give no specifics. When the therapist asks if he notices anything different in his family, Josh reports that everyone has been getting along well. At this point the therapist consults with the team.

After breaking with the team, the therapist returns with their congratulations to the Jacksons on solving the problem and suggests that the family may want to stop treatment now that the problem is solved. At this suggestion, Mr. Jackson is cautious and asks if the therapist expects there to be any further problems with Josh. The therapist responds by stating that she doesn't know what will happen but suggests that they schedule a follow-up session in one month.

Follow-Up

The family calls to cancel a few days prior to the session. They thank the therapist for working with them and state that everything is going well. Mr. Jackson has taken a new position that results in only a small cut in pay but a large decrease in responsibility. He hints on the phone that he and his wife are thinking about having another child.

Case Discussion

In the first session, the Jackson family was very frustrated by Josh's difficulty in keeping his pants clean. The therapist struggled to get past the family's negative perspective of the problem, but, over time, the therapist's positive perspective began to take hold. While it was tempting to criticize the parents for their negative attitude, to do so would have resulted in a negative isomorphic pattern. Criticizing people for being critical is not productive in getting them to stop. Instead of being critical, the therapist adopted the strategy of focusing on the positive. The therapist also did not seek to diagnosis either the parents' anxiety about their son's difficulty or the child's difficulty. She viewed the difficulty simply as a problem the family was seeking help in solving.

The team joined the therapist in her positive perspective and sent several compliments to the family. They also viewed the dirty pants as merely a problem and began with the simple assignment of having the parents observe the behavior by making predictions. If the parents were successful in making the predictions, this would make the problem seem less overwhelming and out of control.

In session two, the therapist built on the family's success. Ignoring the fact that the parents did not fully complete the assignment, she emphasized the family's success. Most of the session was spent exploring the miracle question. While it is interesting that each member emphasized being less anxious, the therapist simply accepted each member's view. The team focused on the positive improvement and noted the difference that occurred when the family had time for each other. After conveying the team's observation to the family, the therapist sought to alleviate Mr. Jackson's defensiveness without backing off on her suggestion that they spend a little more time together.

The third and final session was focused on making the change the family had accomplished between sessions stick. This was done by encouraging them to maintain their positive attitude. It is interesting to note that the insight about the father's need to spend more time with the family was first mentioned by the father. The therapist had shown restraint in prior sessions by not making that suggestion. Because Mr. Jackson came up with the idea on his own, it had a more profound impact on him. The session and course of treatment ended in an open manner, allowing the family to return should their situation change.

Evaluating Solution Focused Family Therapy

For the most part, the theoretical critique of brief therapy is on the level of questioning the basic assumptions of the approach. This critique focuses on the simplification of the client's view of the problem. There is a concern that clients might respond by simply not disclosing their problems to the therapist: that is, clients will avoid talking about deep-seated problems to avoid burdening the therapist.

Likewise, several solution-focused therapists have raised concerns over this approach's mandate to remain positive (Efron & Veenendaal, 1993; Lipchik, 1992, 1993; Storm, 1991). In some instances, clients can experience this as the therapist's taking a cheerleading stance with them. This can be interpreted as patronizing. Since discussion of feelings is typically avoided in brief therapy, this stance can be seen as emotionally distancing and, as a result, distance the therapist from the client. Because of this, some solution-focused therapists are including a discussion of feeling in their work.

Lipchik (1993) states that she includes a discussion of feelings because "[she senses] within all [her] clients... the desire to be loved and affirmed by a significant other or others" (p. 27). This is an important point, because not all clients are interested in solving their problems. Some may simply be seeking affirmation. A reasonable approach with such a client is to be affirming until the client can develop the skills that would enable her or him to seek affirmation from others.

These critiques can be resolved by taking a both/and stance in applying the solution-focused approach, rather than strictly adhering to the techniques. When clients are hesitant to discuss the solution to the problem, it may be helpful to discuss how the problem makes them feel. Clients may be open to addressing their problems themselves only after first discussing the feelings that have resulted from the problem.

Another difficulty with this approach may be the speed at which it encourages clients to resolve their problems. If clients have experienced a problem for a long time or if they have incorporated the problem into their self-concept, giving up the problem may result in a profound loss of identity. It may be appropriate to encourage change at a slower rate or to continue to support the client after the change has been made. In many instances, a new "problem-free" identity may take a while to stabilize.

Literature on the effectiveness of brief therapy in general is very well developed and widely available. It has been established that there is no clear association between therapist orientation or treatment modality and the number of sessions in which clients participate. In a comprehensive review of the literature, Bergin and Garfield (1994) concluded that "almost all psychotherapy is brief" (p. 826).

The effectiveness of brief family therapy is less established empirically. There are only a few published studies on this approach. In a brief description of an outcome study conducted using a random sample of clients at the Brief Family Therapy Center from 1978 to 1983, de Shazer (1985) claimed a 72% success rate. On average these clients were seen for six sessions. However, very few details of this study were provided, and an evaluation of the methodology of the study has not been possible.

De Jong and Hopwood (1996) provide a complete report of a comprehensive study of outcome of 275 clients seen at the Brief Family Therapy Center from November 1992 through August 1993. Their conclusions were supportive of brief family therapy, and they found that over 75% of clients made progress toward a treatment goal. They also found that, during the final session, clients who described the treatment as successful also reported higher satisfaction with therapy at follow-up seven to nine months later.

Gingerich and Eisengart (2000) provide a comprehensive review of solution-focused brief therapy outcome studies. These authors reviewed 15 studies that used control groups and made the tentative conclusion that this approach may be helpful with a broad range of clients. Since studies are becoming more methodologically rigorous, Gingerich and Eisengart conclude that solution-focused brief therapy "is moving from an 'open trail' phase of investigation to an 'efficacy' phase" (p. 495).

Recently, Smock and colleagues (2008) conducted a research project validating the use of solution-focused group therapy for people who abuse substances. Solution-focused group therapy simply involves applying the principles of solution-focused brief family therapy to the group setting. An important finding of Smock and colleagues' study is that "not only is SFGT cost effective, but also its effects can have a lasting impact" (p. 117). This single study's exciting findings are not conclusive. However, given the cost effectiveness of solution-focused group therapy, we can expect an increase in the popularity of this approach for substance abuse. This should in turn lead to additional empirical evaluation.

The most recent evaluation was less enthusiastic about the effectiveness of solution focused brief family therapy. In a 2011 the English Department of Education commissioned a meta-analysis of 83 studies was conducted. Applying rigorous standards they were disappointed to find only 5 studies were considered of high quality. Despite the methodological limitations of this approach Bond, Woods Humphrey, Symes & Green (2013) conclude this study with acknowledging the majority of the reviewed studies support solution focused brief therapy.

Learning Exercises

1. Practice asking yourself the miracle question. For a couple of nights, reflect on the miracle question before you go to bed. Practice articulating what your particular miracle would be like, and try to develop a detailed description. Each night, reflect on the day and notice what parts of your miracle you brought into existence. Without asking how or why you were able to do this, think of ways to do more of it. Discuss this exercise with your peers in small groups. Does the discussion itself change anything?

2. This exercise is designed to help you get familiar with finding exceptions and focusing on success. In small groups, discuss your study habits. Do not focus on your need to study more or harder. Simply describe to your peers the ideal situation under which you learn. For example, do you cram for an exam, or do you do best with a review every day between exams? After you describe your ideal study situation, describe what you consider to be your most successful class. How does this focus on success make you feel? How does it make you feel about the others in your group?

Discussion Question

1. To maintain the positive stance that is central to this approach, what assumptions does one need to have about the nature of individuals and families?

2. What time frames (past, present, and future) do the various interventions in solution-focused brief family therapy focus on?

3. Had the clients in this chapter's case example become more concerned about issues of race during the session, how could the therapist have responded to their concern?

Suggested Readings

Berg, I. K., & Miller, S. (1992). Working with the problem drinker: A solution-focused approach. New York: Norton.

de Shazer, S. (1984). The death of resistance. *Family Process, 23,* 11–17.

de Shazer, S. & Dolan, Y. (2007) *More than Miracles: The State of the Art if Solution-Focused Therapy.* London & New York: Routledge.

de Shazer, S. (1994). *Words were originally magic.* New York: Norton.

Web Resources

Wikipedia for SFBT

https://en.m.wikipedia.org/wiki/Solution_focused_brief_therapy

Solution-focused Group Therapy

http://www.nrepp.samhsa.gov/ViewIntervention.aspx?id=281

Institute for SFBT

http://www.solutionfocused.net/

Psychpage on SFBT

http://www.psychpage.com/family/library/sft.htm

CHAPTER

13

CONSTRUCTIVIST FAMILY THERAPY

Thinking About This Approach

In the late 1980s and early 1990s, the postmodern movement, which adopted the position that reality is socially constructed, occurred in family therapy as well as philosophy and the other social sciences. The boundaries of this school of thought, like those of the paradigm itself, were rather diffuse, and theorists working separately in a variety of locations throughout the world were involved in its development. Given this decentralization, it is impossible to identify a single contributor or institute that initiated the constructivist approach. Important influential figures include Karl Tomm of Canada, Tom Andersen of Norway, Victoria Dickerson and Jeffrey Zimmerman of San Francisco, Harold Goolishian and Harlene Anderson of Galveston, Michael White of Australia, and David Epston of New Zealand (Chapter 12 focuses on the work of White and Epston). Although the constructivist approach is like the solution-focused brief model in that it is grounded in a postmodern worldview (see Chapter 10), solution-focused brief family therapy places much more emphasis on the development and use of interventions.

The emphasis on reality construction is a hallmark of the third generation of family therapy theories, making constructivism clearly a second-order systemic approach. Not only does it emphasize the construction of reality, but it views therapy as a process of co-constructing an alternative reality. Ideally, the new reality does not include the problem. Since constructivist theory assumes that we socially construct our sense of self, the social process of therapy is used to co-construct a new self that is free of the presenting complaint.

PHOTO 13.1   **Harlene Anderson & Harold Goolishian**

In contrast to the structural functional view of social interaction, the constructivist perspective conceptualizes society as an idea that is shared by others in conversation. Therapeutic change is the result of change in dominant discourses in individuals and communities of individuals. Thus, this position rejects the mechanical cybernetics systems view. The constructivist therapist spends little time on diagnosis, problem formulation, or seeking to describe the client's homeostatic mechanisms. In fact, from this perspective, to describe stability would be to encourage it.

There are two distinct but overlapping views on how the co-construction process in therapy unfolds. One view emphasizes language as the central tool in the construction of reality. Paying attention to how clients speak about their problems is a central feature. This approach recognizes that we are first shaped by the language others use to label us and later participate in shaping the language we use to describe ourselves and others. We will refer to this perspective as the constructivist approach.

The other view emphasizes the role of narratives in clients' lives. A narrative is simply any literary device that tells a story. It is important to note that clients come to therapy telling stories of their struggles with their problems. By intervening directly within the story, the therapist is able to co-construct an alternative reality with the client. For our purposes, we will refer to this view as the narrative approach, which is explored in detail in Chapter 12.

In the constructivist language-based approach, the most influential theory has been developed by Harold Goolishian and Harlene Anderson at the Houston Galveston Institute (formerly called the Galveston Family Institute). Since Harry Goolishian passed away in 1991, Harlene Anderson has led the institute, which provides training and workshops on what she calls the collaborative language systems approach (Anderson, 1995) and later the collaborative approach (Anderson, 1997) to treatment and clinical supervision. She explains, "These terms refer to my conceptualization of therapy: a language system and a linguistic event in which people are engaged in a collaborative relationship and conversation—a mutual endeavor towards possibilities" (Anderson 1997, p. 2). In this approach, the client and therapist form a partnership to address the client's problems (Anderson, 1995). This chapter will focus on the constructivist theory, paying particular attention to the collaborative language systems approach.

Innovation in Practice

The constructivist approach moves away from the use of techniques to change the client and instead fosters empathetic conversations that allow new meanings to emerge. This approach emphasizes the importance of the interviewing process. The major theme of the constructivist interview is moving the therapist out of the expert or "in charge" role. In its ideal form, the therapist is an egalitarian partner with the client families. The family is seen as a culture with its own set of values and norms. Given this "native" culture, the values and ideas of clients are highly respected. For this reason, this approach is particularly well suited for work with minority clients.

It should be noted that constructivist theory is different from a Rogerian, nondirective style. The constructivist therapist does not just reflect on the conversation but is an active participant in it. The therapist and client are viewed as equal, freeing the therapist to offer opinions, ideas, and feelings. The therapeutic interview consists largely of asking the client questions so that the therapist can better understand the client's conceptualization of reality. This process is often referred to as deconstructing the client's reality. For example, one therapist worked with a family referred because the dad was reported for abuse after using corporal punishment on his young son. The therapist noted that when the dad talked about his love for his son, he always talked about his responsibility to discipline him. The therapist asked the dad about the relationship between discipline and love in his reality in order to deconstruct these ideas. The father explained that when he was growing up his parents "beat some manners" into him and that he felt morally obligated to do the same for his son. As this reality emerged, the client was invited to join the therapist in constructing an alternative reality that would no longer support the problem. The client was invited to think of love and discipline as two related but separate issues. As they were separated, the father found that he could be free to love his son with less of an urgent need to discipline him harshly.

In describing the development of the collaborative language approach and its connection to strategic therapy as practiced at the Mental Research Institute in Palo Alto, California (see Chapter 8), Anderson (1995) describes how initially they focused on speaking the language of the client to gain access to leverage for promoting change in the family. However, as a result of this experience, the conceptualization of the process changed. Anderson (1995) says, "As we immersed ourselves in the client's language and meaning, our own agendas about such things as outcome, how families ought

Video Call Out 13.1: Constructivist Family Therapy Video

In the constructivist video what is missing is more striking than what is present. Throughout the interview Dr. Krepps offers no suggestions or interventions. The entire interview involves constructing the problem in ways that imply the solution. The closest he comes to an intervention is towards the end in calling attention to the fact that they have had the relationship they seek. This implies that they can once again co-create this relationship. This is empowering by implication where the "expert" has faith that they can solve their own problem.

to be, and in- or end-of-session interventions dissolved" (p. 28). Out of this shift came the notion of a co-construction of new realities. Anderson (1995) says, "The ideas and actions we now called interventions emerged from therapy conversations and were logical to the family and its members and coherent with the immediate or local conversations" (p. 28).

Anderson (1993) suggests that the therapist can access the client's construction of reality by adopting a "not knowing" stance. Such a stance allows the therapist to join with the client in the search for meaning and new options. As Anderson suggests, this stance results in a genuine con-

Video Call Out 13.2: Constructivist Family Therapy Video

In this Video Dr. Krepps is careful to avoid any preconceptions or assumptions about the couple. He is careful to ask the couple their perspective on their problem and their attempts to solve it. By asking the couple what is different in their therapeutic conversation the therapist is able to access how they are making meaning and constructing their situation.

versation in which "the therapist's pre-experiences and pre-knowledge do not lead. In this process both the therapist's and the client's expertise are engaged to dissolve the problem" (p. 325). This stance is critical because it allows the tone of therapy to be one of curiosity rather than judgment. This frees clients to respond in a nondefensive and open manner.

As we see in the above example where the therapist helped a father who used corporal punishment, deconstruction is a process of discovering meaning and power in structures of everyday conversation and practice. As White (1993) explains, "many of the methods of deconstruction render strange the familiar, taken-for-granted realities and practices by objectifying them. In this sense the method of deconstruction is a method that exoticizes the domestic" (p. 35). In practice, this is accomplished by viewing a person's problem as having an existence beyond the person. For example, a constructivist therapist might ask a client to draw a picture of his depression.

It is important to note how objectification affects our lives. This is even more critical for those who are affected by what would traditionally be called an illness. In people with emotional suffering, the process of objectification tends to become the dominant part of their identity. For example, it is not strange for someone to state that she is depressed. However, it would be strange for someone suffering with the flu to say that she is influenza. The tendency to identify with the diagnosis is the result of internalizing the diagnosis. By externalizing a diagnosis or problem, deconstruction occurs. In practice, this involves asking a series of questions designed to draw a distinction between the person and the problem. For example, a therapist might take a history of the influence of alcoholism on a person's life. Or, toward the same end, a therapist might help a person with an anxiety disorder describe how he was recruited to live the fearful lifestyle. Over time people can begin to see their identity as separate from their struggle with their so-called mental illness.

The Reflecting Team

A significant innovation in the marriage and family therapy field can be credited to the constructivist approach of Tom Andersen (1991) from Norway, a country that takes a socialized approach to medicine and treatment of mental illness. Dr. Andersen would travel to remote locations to assist local mental health workers with some of their most resistant cases. Andersen's technique evolved into an open and transparent process in which the client was invited to observe the treatment team, thus reducing the client's resistance. The reflecting team is an innovation that reduces the social distance between a treatment team and the clients. Andersen (1991) is clear that he was greatly influenced by the Milan group's use of positive connotation. Positive connotation is a technique where the family's problem is viewed as a positive attribute of the family. The conversation of the reflecting team provides a format for new information and new realities to be quickly and profoundly developed.

The therapy session is structured so that the therapist and client are observed through an observation window by the reflecting team. While the interview is happening, the treatment team listens in silence to the interview. At a point when there is a natural break, roles are reversed and the therapist and client observe the team engage in a conversation about the client's struggles. In this conversation, open-ended questions may be asked about both the problem and the client's strengths. The team works to understand the client in the context of his or her struggle without offering advice or making value judgments. When the conversation reaches another natural break, the client and therapist once again have a conversation. The therapist asks the client, "What about the conversation you just heard was helpful?" The therapist continues to listen to the client's view of the usefulness of the team's input without being defensive, drawing a conclusion, or making a value judgment.

In practice, this conversation often has a profound emotional impact on the clients, who see their problems in a different light. Perhaps this is because few people have developed skills for defending themselves against indirect information. Given this, it is important that the team be focused on clients' strengths and the positive aspects of their struggle. It is inappropriate and not helpful to talk about the client in a negative way.

Because of logistical difficulties in training and gathering a team, reflecting teams are most often used in training institutions and in cases where the therapist and client seem stuck at an impasse.

Metaphors

The central metaphor in constructivist therapy is that of reality as a co-constructive process. By rejecting the notion of an objective reality, this approach emphasizes subjective experience and subjective reality and thereby localizes problems. Thus, a constructivist therapist would be quick to adopt any metaphor clients use to describe their difficulties. After a period of speaking from the client's perspective, the therapist and client start to collaborate in creating a new reality.

Thus there is an emphasis on the relationship between emotions and meaning in this approach. The therapist monitors the client's emotional response to the use of language in the session. In particular, the therapist is concerned with how specific terms such as diagnostic categories can become prescriptive rather than descriptive. For example, if a client is diagnosed as depressed they can embrace this and interpret lapses in energy and/or mood as further evidence of the depression In therapy the goal is to free clients from the oppression of how they are defined and how they define themselves through the use of language.

Hermeneutics

An important element of constructivist theory is the study of hermeneutics, which originated in the methodological principles used to study religious texts. According to Anderson (1995), "hermeneutics concerns itself with understanding the meaning of the text or discourse and with understanding as a process that is influenced by the belief, assumptions and intentions of the interpreter" (p. 30). Here we see that a text or spoken discourse is open to interpretation. Each person has an interpretation of a social interaction that is a truth for them. While there is no definitive truth, truth exists in relationships. Thus, truth is limited by our language and our ability to communicate.

Building on these assumptions, we see that the ideas that people hold about themselves and others are the result of social interaction in the form of conversation. This is true even for ideas for which we take exclusive ownership. Ideas such as our identity and self-concept have multiple authors. Often when people are asked to describe their personal attributes, they simply repeat what they have heard others say.

Given this idea, we see that therapy itself is not a process of establishing a truthful view of clients and their problems. It is a fallacy to think that the therapist, client, or client and therapist can determine the true problem. A definition of the problem is open to interpretation, and for this reason Anderson (1995) places statements of a client's problem in quotation marks. While we can never construct an absolute truth, we can co-construct multiple truths that the client can use. As clients try these truths and accept them, they often shift their thoughts. This can produce new feelings or behaviors.

Freeing Self-Identities

From a constructivist perspective, the goal of therapy is to free clients from the restrictions self-imposed by their socially constructed self-identities. This can come about as a result of conversations in which the therapist pays close attention to how clients describe their life situation. Clients who are able to live relatively unrestricted lives are said to have self-agency or personal agency. Anderson (1995) summarizes the goal of therapy this way: "The business of therapy is to help people create and gain access to self-identities that are freeing—that allow them to develop understanding of their lives and its events, that permit self-agency or simply a sense of self-agency" (p. 31).

This postmodern view addresses issues that could be seen as occurring on the individual level. Perhaps this corrects for the criticism of theories such as the structural and strategic models that have been faulted for losing the individual. The constructivist acknowledges that both the individual and the family are socially constructed and of paramount importance to our theoretical understanding.

Constructivists bridge the gap between a focus on individuals and a focus on families by defining family as a series of relationships. As Anderson (1997) states, postmodern psychotherapy "suggests that the focus is neither the interior of the individual nor the family, but rather the person(s) in relationship" (p. 28). Thus, we can shift our focus away from the structure of an individual to the structure of families and can seek to understand how people in relationships give rise to families and how families in relationships give rise to broader social units. Here we are no longer striving to understand individuals, families, or societies. We are seeking to understand individuals in relationships that create families and even whole societies.

We see here a parallel to the experiential therapist's view of mental health as the ability to be emotionally responsive. By perturbing the system and having an emotional response in themselves, experiential therapists promote change. The constructivist therapist is similarly very personally involved in language with his or her clients to explore themes in their construction of their self-agency. Anderson (1995) concludes,

> From this perspective psychotherapy is a process of expanding and saying the unsaid—the development, through dialogue, of new themes and narratives—from which new meaning may arise and, in turn, new histories may be created that actually give rise to change. (p. 32)

Questioning

Two features distinguish the interviewing process conducted from a constructivist perspective. First, the interview is conducted using an active rather than passive voice. This helps with the deconstruction process discussed above. For example, if a client describes her relationship with drug addiction, she is not seen as a victim of the disease but rather as a participant. Or, if a client states that he is psychotic and hearing voices, the therapist might inquire how he relates to the voices in his head. Second, the constructivist therapist seeks to speak the client's native language. By using the client's phrasing, the social distance between the client and therapist is reduced, thereby reducing dependency and helplessness. This also sets up a collaborative relationship between client and therapist.

Anderson (1995) describes respectful listening and shared inquiry, key principles in the process of interviewing clients from a collaborative language approach. Respectful listening involves being an active listener who communicates to clients that they have something valuable to say. Shared inquiry is the free-flowing exchange of ideas and questions in a give-and-take manner adapted to the client's natural style and rhythm. It is a shared analysis of the client's experience without overemphasis on the client's problem.

One of the ways to follow these principles is to use questions that build on the client's statements. From here it can be useful to ask a question in the form of an unfinished sentence. As Anderson (1995) explains, "unfinished sentences and hanging words invite the client to finish the thought" (p. 39). For example, if a client states that she is angry, the therapist might respond, "Angry. Okay. About... ?"

Structuring

The structure of the constructivist session varies greatly. Sessions are held as needed. Family members are invited to participate when it is decided that their presence may be helpful. Invitation to a therapy session is based on whom the client is talking to about the problem. Social roles such as those of parent, significant other, or sibling are not considered in deciding whom to invite to the session. Other members of a system might be invited in for a session based on the idea that the client is talking with them outside the session. Therefore, therapy attendees may vary from session to session. For example, in work with an adolescent client, peers might be invited to therapy because the teen identifies those friends as people he talks with between sessions about his problem. Of course, proper consent would have to be obtained beforehand.

Constructivist therapists start treatment by making the client comfortable. It is typical for them to share with clients the information received about them from the referral source. This is done to level the social distance between therapist and client. The client is left to set the agenda for the session. The therapist may ask clients what they would like to discuss or even how they would like to spend the therapy session. Here the therapist takes what is sometimes called a "not knowing" stance. The therapist simply states that he or she is not in a position to know what is best for the client.

There is no formal assessment or diagnostic framework consistent with this approach. However, a constructivist therapist is interested in how clients conceptualize their problem and therefore asks deep, probing questions. This is done not to uncover unconscious material or to give insight, but to provide a basis for the therapist to understand clients' views of themselves. In this phase, the problem is deconstructed and its meaning is articulated.

Termination of therapy, like therapy itself, is co-constructed. The therapist and client discuss the need for future consultation. If they agree that there is such a need, the next appointment is set. If they cannot reach an agreement and the client does not see a need for another session, the therapist might simply recognize the client's reality and perception. After sharing his or her view with the client, the therapist allows the client's reality to prevail.

Responding

Constructivist therapists try to respond directly to their clients out of respect for them. They highly value honesty and directness. The most striking demonstration of this is the inclusion of a reflecting team in constructivist therapy. Members of this treatment team do not hold private discussion but rather open up their discussion of the client's struggles for direct observation.

The constructivist therapist rejects the notion of a deliberate intervention. Focusing on the emergent result of a co-constructed reality is more in line with a constructivist orientation. Thus, therapists are unlikely to give clients any type of direction. In response to an inquiry by the client about a course of action, the therapist is likely to continue to deconstruct and externalize the problem. From here, he or she is likely to wait patiently for the client to suggest a way to proceed. Once this occurs, the therapist is able to support what the client sees as a useful course of action. The client may be invited to experiment with that course of action and then report the results of the experiment in the next session.

Constructivist therapists are often interested in hearing from marginalized voices. As a result, they will not deconstruct or instruct marginalized people (Anderson, 1995), but simply seek to converse with them. Here the constructivist approach departs from the closely related narrative approach. Rather than helping clients edit their narrative, the collaborative therapist "is more like a coauthor, whose expertise is in a process" (Anderson, 1995, p. 41).

Applications

The collaborative aspects of this approach make it attractive for use with diverse clients. Winek and Carlin-Finch (1997) have developed a model for working with clients of a gender or race different from that of the therapist. This four-stage model is based on an anthropological metaphor where the therapist seeks to gain understanding of the client family's construction of race and gender. By acting like an anthropologist and talking with clients about these issues, the therapist can avoid making critical errors and develop a collaborative relationship with them.

The constructivist approach has been applied to career development (Hosking & Bass, 2001). In discussing what this perspective brings to career development, Brott (2004) claims, "This perspective reflects the shift from finding a job to finding one's self; from the psychometric self to the storied self; from getting information to generating experiences; from objectivity to subjectivity" (p. 190). More recently, Maxwell (2007) applied constructivist theory to counseling gifted female adolescents. She concludes that "a developmental, constructivist approach that encourages some reflectivity in students and compels them to continually construct, deconstruct, and reconstruct their life stories may hold promise for the gifted population" (p. 218).

In an interesting report from Portugal, Fernandes (2007) applied the constructivist approach to her work with a 29-year-old student who was experiencing anxiety over cognitive dilemmas regarding his sexual orientation. In this situation, his constructions of himself did not fit with his desires, and therefore he was assisted in developing new constructions of himself. This case illustrates the diversity of cases in which this approach can be used as well as the international interest in the constructivist approach.

Acting as a Constructivist Family Therapist

The constructivist family therapist approaches clients with curiosity about their situation. He or she is interested in deconstructing the meaning of the language clients use to describe their situations. The therapist seeks to help clients develop an understanding that increases their personal agency and to produce for them a more acute perception of the way they construct their world.

Producing an understanding for the client is not done for the purpose of making suggestions about what the client should change. In fact, constructivist therapists avoid giving advice or making suggestions. They see clients as the experts in their own lives and work to empower them to make decisions and to live a life that works for them.

Case Example: The Case of Alecia's Anorexia

The therapist is asked by a local psychiatrist to consult on a case involving a Caucasian family with a 15-year-old girl named Alecia, who has a two-year history of anorexia and depression. She presents with a distorted and negative body image and has a restricted diet and an aversion to healthy foods. Alecia is 5 feet 5 inches tall, has a body weight of 90 pounds, and has not had her menstrual period for seven months. She had been playing on the champion soccer team at her high school, but after she collapsed twice on the field due to exhaustion, her parents and doctor decided that she had to stop playing soccer. Alecia is also in individual treatment with a social worker and her depression has been responding well to treatment. However, her social worker thinks that her therapy could be advanced with some family sessions. The social worker does not feel comfortable conducting the family therapy himself, so he has made a referral in consultation with Alecia's psychiatrist. Alecia's father, Dr. Bob Richardson, is an emergency room physician, and her mother, Dr. Lynn Kowalski, teaches part time at the local community college. Her 23-year-old brother, Sam, is attending a university several hundred miles away, and her 11-year-old adopted sister, Sally, lives at home and is described by the parents as being without a problem or a care.

Since Alecia's psychiatrist is concerned that she will have to go into an inpatient program if her weight drops any more, the therapist schedules a two-hour session with the family.

Session One

The family arrives promptly for the session but does not bring Sally, the younger daughter, who is busy with after-school activities. Alecia is dressed in a trendy style, contrasting with her parents' more conservative dress. She looks too thin for her frame, and her skin is rather pale and seems to hang a bit off her arms. Alecia states that she doesn't want to see another psychologist about her problems. The therapist responds by saying that she isn't a psychologist but a family therapist. The therapist points out that she isn't interested in seeing Alecia more often than needed, and that her job is to help Alecia get over her problem. Alecia is somewhat relieved, and the therapist asks her, "What would you like to talk about today?"

Alecia responds by saying that she is depressed and anorexic. At this point, her father interrupts and discusses her medication for the depression. He points out that Alecia is responding well to the meds and that her depression has lessened. However, he is concerned about the lack of improvement in her ability to deal with her anorexia. Dr. Kowalski jumps in and discusses her daughter's eating habits. As the discussion progresses, the therapist observes Alecia as she sinks into the chair.

The therapist politely interrupts the parents and asks for permission to get the story from Alecia. They agree, and the therapist asks Alecia about her depression. Specifically, the therapist asks Alecia what kind of depression she "does." Not understanding the question, Alecia becomes puzzled and curious. The therapist asks her again what kind of depression she does, explaining that some depressed clients do "stay in bed" depression, others withdraw from friends, and still others stay up at night thinking about how miserable life is.

Alecia nods in understanding and states that she is an "I don't care" depressive. She goes on to elaborate that when she is most depressed, she just develops a "piss poor attitude." After she provides several examples of how she demonstrates this attitude, the therapist asks her parents if they agree with Alecia's description of how she does her depression.

Her mother agrees, then begins to elaborate on how her daughter can get into such a poor state so quickly. She begins to list a variety of things that trigger Alecia. As the discussion progresses, Dr. Richardson nods in agreement with his wife. The therapist informs the parents that she is getting a good idea of how Alecia gets into her depression and then asks for any observations of how Alecia comes out of her "piss poor mood." Alecia and her parents are at a loss to describe how she comes out of these moods. The therapist suggests that this would be a good thing for the family to keep track of.

Turning to Alecia, the therapist asks if depression has something to say about this meeting. Alecia responds that, on the way here, depression was telling her not to talk to the therapist and that she should be in a bad mood. The therapist points out that Alecia seems pretty "not depressed" right now. Alecia agrees and attributes this to the fact that the therapist is easy to talk to. The therapist thanks her and congratulates her for keeping depression from entering the room. Laughing, Alecia says, "You're right, but I don't know how I kept depression out of here." The therapist asks her to try to find out how she did that. Specifically, the therapist asks her to think between sessions about what she said to her depression to keep it out of the office.

At this point, Alecia's mother begins to discuss how she herself had to struggle with depression when she was a teen. She says that things are so different now that it is no wonder that Alecia's struggle is worse than hers was. The therapist asks Dr. Kowalski to tell Alecia how she beat her own depression. Alecia's mother responds that she got married and had children, so there was no time for depression. The therapist turns to Alecia and says, "There's the solution to your depression. Get married and have children." The family has a good laugh at this, and when things quiet down, Dr. Richardson shares that this is one of his fears. The parents agree that Alecia would be a good wife and mother. However, they are quick to clarify that they would not be ready for her to get married and have children before she graduates from college. Alecia points out that her parents don't have to worry about her being a mother anytime soon. Both of her parents agree that she "is a good girl," but her mother brings up how her anorexia has stopped her period.

At this point the therapist asks Alecia to tell about the relationship of her depression to her anorexia. The therapist asks, "If you had to describe who is more in charge in your mind, depression or anorexia, who would it be?" Alecia responds that the anorexia is mostly in charge and that the depression helps her out by taking her mind off the anorexia. The therapist then asks, "What does anorexia tell you that stops you from eating?" Alecia responds, "It tells me that I'm not hungry." The therapist asks, "Yes, but what does it say when you are really hungry and you start to feel the hunger pains?" Alecia looks at the floor and states, "It says, 'You will look so good when you're thinner and this will really get your parents.'" At this point, her parents looked shocked and the therapist states, "I can see that really works." Alecia nods her head in agreement.

The therapist tries to find unique instances when Alecia has resisted the voices of depression or anorexia. Alecia describes a time when her friends came over and took her out when she was feeling "blue." The therapist responds in support of this and asks Alecia, "Is 'blue' a better word for your depression?" She responds that it may be a better word since what she has is not like the depression of people in the mental hospitals. Continuing, Alicia says that the only time anorexia doesn't control her is after a soccer match. Then her anorexia is "too tired to talk," and Alecia is able to eat. The therapist encourages Alecia to use this to her advantage and even suggests that she get up 15 minutes earlier than her anorexia. Alecia laughs, but agrees that it might be a good idea.

Turning to Alicia's mother, the therapist asks what effect the anorexia has had on her relationship with her daughter. Tearfully, Dr. Kowalski explains that it gets in the way of her being close to her daughter. She describes being able to see a different look in her daughter when anorexia and depression are trying to get at her. The therapist asks how she responds to this. Dr. Kowalski replies that she gives her daughter advice and "pep talks." At this point, Alecia starts to roll her eyes. The therapist laughs and says, "I bet anorexia and depression love the pep talks." Alecia nods in agreement, but corrects the therapist by stating that anorexia and depression are bored with the pep talks.

The therapist asks Alecia's mother if she can think of a time when the pep talks worked. Her mother can't, so the therapist suggests that she do something different. When asked what, the therapist tells her to do something different and emotional, explaining that emotional problems need emotional solutions. The therapist explains, "It doesn't matter what you do, just as long as you don't let Alecia's depression and anorexia influence your life. Doing something different should make your daughter stronger and anorexia and blueness weaker."

At the end of the session, the therapist discusses the length of treatment and the logistics of collaboration with the psychiatrist. The family is concerned about the amount of treatment, so the therapist informs them of her plan to organize a meeting with the other professionals involved in the case to discuss treatment issues. The therapist offers an evening appointment in three weeks so Alecia will not have to miss school. In addition, the therapist asks that the younger daughter, Sally, come to the next session so the therapist can meet everyone. Dr. Richardson offers that his son Sam will be back from the university then and that he can come too. The therapist agrees that this is a good idea.

Between sessions, the therapist contacts both Alecia's social worker and the psychiatrist and informs them of the progress made during the family session. The social worker reports noticing some improvement in Alecia's mood during their last session. The therapist encourages him to continue to externalize Alecia's depression and also her anorexia. The psychiatrist agrees to continue to monitor Alecia's weight and is concerned that if it continues to drop she will have to be hospitalized. Alecia's doctor agrees that he will weigh her once a week and have his staff call the therapist to notify her of the results. The therapist encourages the doctor to negotiate a weight with Alecia and her parents that will allow her to start playing soccer again.

Session Two

As the second session starts, the therapist is introduced to Sam and Sally. She is struck by how much Sam is like his father, both in looks and in mannerisms. Sally is very shy and talks very little during the session. To keep Sally involved in therapy, the therapist asks her to draw a picture of the members of her family. Sam begins by offering that, while he is here to help his sister, he doesn't see his family as dysfunctional.

The therapist thanks him for his willingness to help his sister and questions him about his concern about his family's being dysfunctional. As the therapist traces his concern, she learns that Sam has made the assumption that, since she asked the whole family to the interview, she must see his family as dysfunctional. The therapist shares that her assumption is not that the family is dysfunctional but that they are concerned and could be helpful. She states that she assumes the family are the experts of their own lives. Her expertise lies in helping them have conversations that they will find useful. In other words, what she has to offer is her expert skill in providing conversations that can help people change and address old problems in new ways. The therapist states that she doesn't believe in dysfunction and shares with Sam the way she is constructing the family.

The therapist shares that she sees the family as stuck rather than dysfunctional. They seem stuck trying to find a way to launch Alecia as an adult. Since Sam is successfully on his way to being an adult and doing well at the university, the therapist suggests that he might be able to assist his sister with the process. At this point, Sam shares some of his anxiety about graduation from college next year and having to be further independent. The therapist listens to this and empathizes with his struggles.

When there is a natural break in the conversation, the therapist asks the family members to describe the roles they each take. During this discussion, it is quickly apparent that Alecia is seen as the "family rebel," "stubborn one," "most honest member," "most creative," and "most thrill seeking." Focusing on the label of rebel, the therapist asks Alecia to describe what this means to her. As Alecia describes her experience with rebellion, the therapist is struck by the idea that Alecia is enticed by the idea of being a rebel. In order to get a better sense of what this means, she spends a considerable portion of the session exploring what Alecia's identity as a rebel means for each family member.

During this exploration, Sam calls Alecia a "small-time rebel." When Alecia becomes curious about this, the therapist encourages Alecia to explore what he means. Sam explains that she is "small time" because she rebels against things that are small and insignificant on a grand scale. He goes on to elaborate that Alecia spends so much time on the small things that she misses the big things. The therapist states that she understands what he is driving at and points out that the great rebels in history rebelled against very select things rather than everything. They carefully chose what was essential to rebel against. For example, if Alecia wanted to hang out with some of her friends one Saturday, she could without really rebelling against her parents.

The therapist checks in with Sam and asks him if that's what he means by "small-time rebel." He agrees that the therapist understands. He goes on to point out that Alecia is so busy rebelling against everything else that she is unable to rebel against her anorexia— or anything else important, for that matter. Sam continues by explaining how in one of his classes they discussed how society gives women messages about beauty that "real women" can't live up to. Rather than reject or rebel against society's notion of beauty, women starve themselves. The therapist nods her head in agreement and adds, "Not some women. Your sister." In response, Sam nods his head too and states, "That's exactly what I'm talking about."

Alecia becomes tearful and describes how she has become more deliberate in her struggle with anorexia. The therapist simple asks out loud, "Deliberate . . . ?" Then Alecia's mother discloses that she herself has a history of struggling with her self-image and weight. Alecia's father points out that her maternal grandmother also struggled with her weight when she was younger. As a young woman, she was reported to be a 95-pound Southern belle. Hearing this, the therapist suggests that rebelling against anorexia may have been a struggle for three generations in this family. Alecia's father points out that it's three generations that they know about and that it may have been a longer struggle. The therapist agrees and suggests that this issue may be related to women's identities in this family. She suggests that a session with the three generations of women may be helpful. Alecia's mother blushes and states that it would be difficult to sit in a session with her mother. The therapist asks why and learns that it is due to different views of religion. Dr. Kowalski is afraid that her mother would blame Alecia's anorexia on their not going to church. The therapist responds that Alecia's mother is a rebel against her family of origin by not going to her mother's church. Alecia's mother goes on to say that while she rebels against the rigidity of her mother's view of religion, she is a God-fearing woman.

At this point, Sally shares the drawing of her family that she has been working on so diligently. In the picture, the family is a tight group, all holding hands. However, Alecia is outside the circle looking at the family. The therapist asks Sally about her drawing, and Sally explains that sometimes Alecia is not part of the family, so that's why she drew her that way. The therapist asks if Sally thinks Alecia wants to belong in the family, and Sally says yes. Turing to Alecia, the therapist asks, "How does this picture impact you?"

Alecia shares that sometimes she too doesn't feel like she belongs in the family. She looks to Sam and shares, "It's different for boys. They come and go and no one expects them to be connected." Dr. Kowalski is quick to agree and describes how her brothers had an easier time leaving home. She also shares that one of her brothers, who stopped going to church altogether, takes less flack from her mother than she does for changing church attendance. The therapist wonders aloud if this has something to do with why women are much more likely to develop anorexic eating patterns than men are. The mother agrees and states, "There are more expectations for women not to be apart from the family." The therapist notes that time is running short and agrees that this is an important issue for the women to continue to talk about. She invites them to continue the conversation after the session ends.

As they get ready to go, the parents report that Alecia has been making steady progress. She has been eating better, has been less depressed, and has been accepting more limits. The therapist supports the changes already made and further suggests that Alecia may have already started to rebel against her depression and anorexia. A follow-up is scheduled for four weeks' time. The therapist notes that the family can call and get an appointment sooner if things change between sessions.

Just before the family leaves the session, Alecia's father asks the therapist's opinion as to whether it would be a good idea to allow Alecia to travel to a university out of state for a four-week study course in civics over the summer. Alecia's mother is fearful that her daughter will not do well and need to come home. Alecia is defensive about the subject because she really wants to go and feels it is a good opportunity. Her parents agree that it is a good opportunity. The therapist shares that she thinks it would be good for the family to talk about the issue between sessions and suggests to the parents that they base their decision on how well Alecia does between now and when she is to leave. The father asks if writing down his expectations for the trip would be helpful. The therapist supports this idea and then goes on to suggest that he and Alecia's mother should collaborate on this project, and that perhaps they should discuss with her doctor and social worker how this trip could happen.

Session Three

Alecia and her mother and father arrive at the session in good spirits, joking with each other. Alecia reports that she has gained 5 pounds. She also reports that her grades have improved and that she has not received any suspensions at school. The therapist asks Alecia what has happened to her "piss poor attitude," and Alecia states that she has adjusted her attitude.

The therapist asks the family what they attribute Alecia's success to. Alecia's father immediately starts to talk about Alecia's antidepressant medication and how he is sure the dosage is right and really helping her a lot. The therapist asks him if there is anything that Alecia is doing differently that is helping. Dr. Richardson notes several changes in Alecia's behavior and says that her level of reasoning has increased. Alecia's mother recalls several instances where Alecia resisted peer pressure and didn't get into trouble with her friends. She also notes that Alecia has been less rebellious.

Alecia states that when her parents wrote down what it would take for her to take her trip, she got to work beating the depression and anorexia. When the therapist asks how she accomplished this, Alecia states that she started to rebel against the depression. She reports that if she thinks of her parents as on her side, she is stronger in her stand against the depression. When the therapist asks Alecia where she got the idea that her parents were not on her side, Alecia states that depression gave her that idea. When the therapist asks Alecia about her anorexia, she states, "Oh, that only hangs out with depression. If I beat the depression, I beat the eating disorder."

The majority of the session is spent helping the family plan for Alecia's forthcoming trip. Alecia's father is able to talk about how he felt anxious about his daughter's being away without family support. Given his concern, he made arrangements for her weight to be monitored by a colleague in the city where she will be staying. In addition, he has made the point that if she loses any weight, he and his wife will go and pick her up the next day. Alecia has agreed to the plan.

There is also a brief discussion on ways Alecia's mother can improve her relationship with her daughter. The therapist explores with both Alecia and her mother what a better relationship would be like. She encourages Dr. Kowalski to have the relationship she would like with her daughter. This makes her rather emotional, and she becomes tearful. Alecia states that if her mother got along better with her grandmother, she and her mother might have an easier time getting along. Dr. Kowalski agrees and states that she is now more open to talking with her mother about issues they have been avoiding, some of them for years. She asks the therapist if she would be willing to meet with her to discuss the issues she has with her mother, and the therapist responds that she would be happy to set that up.

The end of the session is spent saying good-bye. The therapist makes it clear that the family can return with Alecia should anorexia and depression again become more of an influence in the family's life. The family shares that the experience has been meaningful to them. The therapist invites them to write her at a future date to update her on the depression and anorexia. The family states that they might take her up on that.

Case Discussion

The therapist tries to establish a positive therapeutic relationship at the start of the first session by identifying with Alecia's desire to meet as little as possible. Almost immediately the therapist seeks to externalize and deconstruct the depression. While Alecia's parents, especially her father, take a medical view of her depression, the therapist moves the depression from a state of her being to an activity or attitude. This is done simply by changing the voice from passive to active—that is, by asking her how she does her depression. This move is in line with the therapist's belief that illness is a product of conversations, specifically conversations about illness that conclude that mental illness resides in the self of the client.

The therapist notes to herself that the family is diagnostically oriented in their style of talking about Alecia's problem. As a result of this view, she seeks to create a distinction between Alecia and her depression. Building on the foundation of the externalization, the therapist asks Alecia what gives voice to the depression. Asking her what the depression is saying to her makes her less objectified by the diagnosis.

After Alecia's mother brings up her own history of depression, the therapist continues to externalize Alecia's problems. She does this by asking about the relationship between anorexia and depression, again giving the diagnosis a voice. It is here that Alecia feels safe enough to make the important disclosure that her anorexia encourages her to not eat to upset her parents.

Toward the end of the session, the therapist is able to help the client redefine her depression as feeling blue. This description is useful because it does not have ominous medical associations. The therapist is also able to explore the impact of the client's problems on her relationships. The therapist encourages the mother to work toward improving her emotional connection with her daughter rather than giving her lectures.

Between sessions the therapist seeks to join with the other helpers and develop a unified approach. The other helpers are considered an extended part of the family system. Here, as with the family, the therapist is seeking to engage in conversations that will allow new realities and solutions to emerge.

In the second session the therapist works with the members of the family new to therapy to establish a positive working relationship. She welcomes them and engages them in age-appropriate ways. When the family talks about roles, it is quickly revealed that Alecia has the role of rebel in the family. Since this seems like an area that could produce some rich conversations, the therapist probes for detail and has the family deconstruct what it mean for Alecia to be a rebel.

It becomes apparent that there is a family history of women struggling with depression and anorexia. This occurs in the context of the women's rebelling against societal standards for weight as well as their fighting to be adults in the context of their extended families. The therapist explores with the family the role gender plays in their problem, traditionally called anorexia. Since time is short, the family is invited to continue the conversation between sessions.

The clients introduce the topic of out-of-town studies just as the session ends, and the therapist responds by listening briefly, then empowering them to have a conversation and reach their own decision. The guideline she suggests is basing the decision on Alecia's functioning and discussions with the other caregivers involved.

In the third and final session, the clients report a good deal of success. They have a discussion about expectations, focusing on how they have changed. It is important to Alecia's father that they negotiate a contract, and the therapist listens to the family's plans without making an evaluation.

The most important work in this session is the therapist's listening to Alecia as she tells her story of how she is beating depression and anorexia. By carefully listening, the therapist reinforces the change. The therapist also encourages the women to continue to work on the intergenerational aspects of the relationship.

At this point, the therapist and clients are comfortable stopping therapy. The therapist is clear that she would welcome Alecia back to therapy should the need arise. Since Alecia is going of town soon, there is no need to set a follow-up appointment with her. However, Alecia's mother has some issues to discuss, and the therapist is open to following up with her.

Evaluating Constructivist Family Therapy

Theoretically, it is clear that the constructivist approach has had and will continue to produce a lot of interest. This approach has the potential of replacing the cybernetic, homeostatic view of systems theory and moving toward a more language-based paradigm. While the notion of homeostasis provides a good explanation of stability and social construction of reality provides a good explanation of change, what is needed is a strong explanation of the relationship of stability to change in systems theory. Perhaps there is some promise of this occurring within the constructivist approach.

One of the strengths of this approach is its ability to deal with both individuals and families. By looking at how families share in the construction of reality, we are able to successfully link working with individuals and working with families within one theory. Both individuals and families can be viewed as wholes that participate in the construction of reality.

There has been little empirical validation of the approach. This is a function of the difficulty of applying modern logical, positive research methodology to postmodern theoretical models. A notable exception was Winek (1998), who applied a combination of qualitative and quantitative methods to explore the process of constructing therapy. This study used intensive post-termination interviews and behavior coding of the therapy session to describe the co- construction process that occurred during three complete therapy cases.

While this research did not test therapy conducted from a constructivist paradigm, it did examine how reality was co-constructed in each of four general stages of therapy. Winek (1998) concluded that each stage of treatment's progression to the next stage in the model was marked by successful co-construction of the critical issues of that stage. Furthermore, he concluded that stagnation in the process of therapy could be attributed to an impasse in the co-construction process. The most interesting finding in the research was that, if the success of an intervention is measured by the amount of time spent discussing it, in all three cases the interventions the client suggested were more successful. When a therapist suggested an intervention, the client spent far less time discussing it. Thus, this research provides preliminary validation of the notion that progress in therapy is marked by a co-construction of issues.

Learning Exercises

1. Get into small groups. Take turns describing the decisions you made concerning your undergraduate education. Describe how you decided such things as where to go to college, what your major would be, and what your minor would be. What do these decisions tell you about the person you are? As your peers describe their experiences, listen to how they describe them. Are there stylistic elements you can observe in how they describe their education? Discuss these stylistic elements. As you listen, notice the mood of the person providing the description. Discuss your observations after everyone has shared.

2. Write down three or four of your core beliefs. This is most easily done by finishing the sentence, "I believe . . ." Once you have developed this list, try to outline the history of each belief. When did you start believing this? Also consider which significant people in your life share your beliefs. Once you have done this, return to small groups and discuss your beliefs and their history.

3. Assign 6 class members to be a reflecting team. Have the remainder of the class engage in discussion of this theory. After 20–30 minutes have the reflecting team reflect upon the class process. When there is a natural break in the reflection have the class discuss the impact of what they hear in the reflection.

Discussion Questions

1. How can therapeutic conversations change lives without making interventions?

2. Provide an example of when you made a significant shift in your thinking. What behavioral and emotional changes went along with this shift?

3. Deconstruct your views on the underlying cause of mental illness. How could a condition such as borderline personality disorder be viewed as the result of a shared reality construction?

4. What types of conversations do you engage in that elevate how you think about yourself? What types of conversations do you find yourself in that lower how you think about yourself?

5. While the constructivist approach focuses on the social construction of thoughts and ideas, is it reasonable to assume that emotions undergo a similar social construction process? How are emotions co-constructed?

Suggested Readings

Andersen, T. (1991). The reflecting team: Dialogues and dialogues about the dialogues. New York: Norton.

Anderson, H. (1994). Rethinking family therapy: A delicate balance. *Journal of Marital and Family Therapy, 20,* 145–149.

Anderson, H. D. (1995). Collaborative language systems: Toward a post-modern therapy. In R. H. Mikesell, D. Lusterman, & S. H. McDaniel (Eds.), *Integrating family therapy: Handbook of family psychology and systems theory* (pp. 27–44). Washington, DC: American Psychological Association.

Anderson, H. (1997). Conversation, language, and possibilities: A postmodern approach to therapy. New York: Basic Books.

Winek, J. L., & Carlin-Finch, S. C. (1997). Constructions of therapy, race, ethnicity and gender: An anthropological metaphor. *Contemporary Family Therapy, 19,* 523–535.

Web Resources

Harlene Anderson Website

http://www.harleneanderson.org/iss.html

Houston Galveston Institute

http://www.talkhgi.org/

Internet Encyclopedia's Breakdown of Constructivist Psychotherapy

http://www.pcp-net.org/encyclopaedia/const-psther.html

Wikipedia page on social constructionism

https://en.wikipedia.org/wiki/Social_constructionism

Wikispaces on constructivist theories

https://postmoderntherapies.wikispaces.com/Constructivist+Theories

CHAPTER

14

NARRATIVE FAMILY THERAPY

Thinking About This Approach

Given that the narrative approach uses much of the same philosophical orientation as the constructivist approach, it can be classified as a subtheory of that broader theory. However, the narrative approach has a more developed interviewing procedure than that used by the general constructivist therapist. Narrative therapists are also somewhat directive, much like the strategic therapists of the prior generation of theories. While they do not use behavioral directives, narrative family therapists are deliberate in the type of reality they co-construct with their clients. Acting as a coeditor in the client's evolving life story, they engage the client in caring conversations that allow new realities to emerge. These conversations challenge or perturb the client's system in a way somewhat similar to how experiential therapists of the prior generation would perturb the client system to produce therapeutic change.

This approach was developed by Michael White in Australia during the 1980s. White was an active writer and presenter of his ideas until his untimely death in 2008. His colleague from New Zealand, David Epston, was a frequent collaborator with him and had a significant influence on this movement. White and Epston's work was informed by postmodern thought. In particular, they were influenced by philosophy and anthropology. Jill Freeman and Gene Combs who co-founded the Evanston Family Therapy Center helped to establish the narrative perspective in the United States. Their 1996 book *Narrative Therapy: The Social Construction of Preferred Realities* help clarify and expand on White's ideas.

PHOTO 14.1   Michael White & David Epston

"Michael White and David Epston." Copyright © 1980 by Michael White and David Epston. Reprinted with permission from Dulwich Centre Publications Pty Ltd and David Epston.

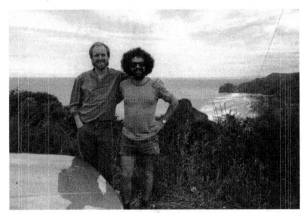

The goal of this approach is to engage clients in conversations that increase their experience of personal agency. According to White (2007), personal agency is the capacity for responsible action, and it is the therapist's responsibility to provide opportunities for this to develop. White asserts,

> We have a responsibility to avoid falling prey to conclusions that a person is "simply lacking motivation," is "hopelessly irresponsible," is "resistant," is "incapable of foreseeing the consequences of her or his actions," is "unable to reflect on her or his behavior," is "a concrete thinker," or is "incapable of abstract thought." (p. 281)

This is similar to the strategic stance, where the therapist is responsible to produce therapeutic change (see Chapter 9). This position also sets a positive and hopeful tone for the therapy and creates an environment conducive to increasing the client's personal agency.

Innovations in Practice

White and Epston (1990) claim that their narrative approach is based on a "text analogy" that can be used to describe the therapeutic process. In the text analogy, reality is understood to be the result of a process of social construction through shared stories. As White and Epston state, "in order to make sense of our lives and to express ourselves, experience must be 'storied' and it is this storying that determines the meaning ascribed to experience" (p. 10). Thus, listening to and telling a story helps us make sense of our subjective experience. For example, getting to know someone involves sharing personal stories. The simple process of sharing a story provides us with a way to conceptualize a new person in our lives. Another example of the importance of stories in our lives can be observed in marital relationships. Couples who are getting along well enjoy sharing stories with each other. However, couples with a troubled relationship tend to stop generating new positive stories to share with each other. In fact, distressed couples tend to create and tell stories that illustrate the faults in their relationship. This can continue into a separation or divorce, where the couple continue to develop stories that tell the story of the failed marriage.

In each person's life are stories that dominate others. These dominant stories have a great deal of influence on our identity and personal agency. A dominant story can take over a person's self-definition. If a political organization, institution, or medical practitioner is involved in the telling of a person's dominant story, it can be particularly influential on that person's narrative. For example, being labeled a felon, a graduate student, or a schizophrenic can have a tremendous impact on the rest of one's life. As we tell and then retell ourselves our dominant stories, our world takes shape. New stories are generated, told, and retold that in turn support our view.

Alternative Stories

Despite the prevalence of these dominant stories, alternative stories do exist. As White and Epston (1990) assert, there are "aspects of lived experience [that] fall outside of the dominant story and provide a rich and fertile source for the generation, or regeneration, of alternative stories" (p. 15). However, people tend to ignore the alternative stories unless they are supported in some way. It is this process of generating and regenerating alternative stories and supporting them that produces change in the client's personal agency and ultimately behavioral and emotional change.

Externalization

The narrative approach is based on two processes that White and Epston (1990) call externalization and reauthoring lives and relationships. While this is in essence a style of interviewing, it produces the opportunity for clients to experience shifts in their thoughts and feelings. The first step of the therapy process involves the deconstruction of the person's problem. This is accomplished by objectifying the problem. Once objectified, the problem becomes what White (1993) calls externalized: that is, the problem is separated from the identity of the person. This step is necessary to lessen the grip the current dominant story has on the person's self-concept. Once separated, the person is no longer able to use the problem as a core concept in her or his self-definition. This gives the client an increased sense of personal agency.

White and Epston (1990) conclude that externalization also:

1. Decreases unproductive conflict between persons, including those disputes over who is responsible for the problem;
2. Undermines the sense of failure that has developed for many persons in response to the continuing existence of the problem despite their attempts to resolve it;
3. Paves the way for persons to cooperate with each other, to unite in a struggle against the problem, and to escape its influence in their lives and relationships;
4. Opens up new possibilities for persons to take action to retrieve their lives and relationships from the problem and its influence;

5. Frees persons to take a lighter, more effective, and less stressed approach to "deadly serious" problems; and

6. Presents options for dialogue, rather than monologue, about the problem. (pp. 39–40)

It is most helpful if the terms use in the externalization are words clients themselves would use. These terms should be stated directly and flow naturally out of the conversation. The externalization is given in practical terms. For example, White is noted for externalizing encopresis in a young boy as "sneaky pooh." A manic episode may be externalized as "overenthusiasm." As White (2007) points out, externalizations "employ practices of objectification of the problem against cultural practices of objectification of people" (p. 12). As the problem moves outside of the identified patient, it is less supported by beliefs about identity or personality and is more likely to change. It is here that the influence of postmodern anthropology can be seen in narrative therapy theory.

Recently White (2007) identified four stages of externalization: (1) negotiating a particular, experience-near definition of the problem; (2) mapping the effects of the problem; (3) evaluating the effects of the problem's activities; and (4) justifying the evaluation. These four stages provide guidance as the therapist leads clients through the externalization process.

Negotiating a particular, experience-near definition of the problem involves a significant shift in how the problem is viewed. Often clients present with problems that they see as global, impacting all parts of their experience. For example, the mother of a teenager might describe the problem as a son who is lazy and unmotivated to work in school. In addition, she may tell how the trait of laziness manifested itself early in his development. The therapist's purpose here is to recognize how the problem impacts current events in the clients' lives. This might involve seeing the teen as a person who thinks before he acts and then exploring when this might be of benefit to him.

The second stage, mapping the effects of the problem, involves having a conversation focusing on how the problem has affected various domains of the clients' lives. White (2007) identifies a partial list of domains where complications can be identified:

- Home, workplace, school, peer contests
- Familial relationship, one's relationship with oneself, friendships
- Identity, including the effects of the problem on one's purposes, hopes, dreams, aspirations, and values
- One's future possibilities and life horizons (p. 43)

The function of this conversation is to stand in contrast to the natural tendency of clients to engage in internalized conversations where they become one with the problem, thus further ingraining the problem. For example, a person with alcoholism that is related to self-hatred might be asked about the consequences of her self-hatred. As she describes her activities, she might be interviewed about the consequences of these activities. By simply describing these consequences and not challenging them, the therapist has access to her internal dialogue without prompting a defensive or resistant response.

The therapist is interested in how the problem's activities affect the identified patient's life. For example, a child with soiling problems might be asked, "Is sneaky pooh okay with you?" He might also be asked, "What do you think about what sneaky pooh does to you?" As White (2007) explains, "for many this is a novel experience, for it is very often the case that this sort of evaluation has been mostly undertaken by others" (p. 44). The process of cataloging the effect of the problem is called editorial (White, 2007).

The final stage of the externalizing conversation is justifying the evaluation that has occurred in therapy. This stage explores the *why* of the prior evaluation. The therapist simply asks why the evaluation is or is not okay. Again, the therapist simply accepts the client's evaluation at face value.

Reauthoring

Once the problem is externalized, the narrative therapist turns her or his attention to helping the clients reauthor their lives and relationships. This reauthorship refers to the process of creating a new dominant story. The new dominant story is designed to be free of the problem, reducing the impact of the problem on clients' lives. White (2007) describes it this way:

> Reauthoring conversations invite people to continue to develop and tell stories about their lives, but they also help people to include some of the more neglected but significant events and experiences that are "out of phase" with their dominant storylines. (p. 61)

A key component of this process is the search for unique outcomes. A unique outcome is an experience where the client resisted the influence of the problem in her or his life. It is of little concern to the therapist when this outcome occurred; the past, present, and future are all fair game. From here the therapist probes for details regarding how the client achieved this outcome. This encourages the client to have more unique outcomes and to further resist the influence of the problem.

Implicit in this approach is the metaphor of the client's being oppressed by the problem. The client is encouraged to take the lessons she or he learns about having a successful rebellion and use them against the problem, thereby increasing resistance against the influence of the problem in the client's life.

Epston (1994) has developed a simple and eloquent technique for furthering the effect of the reality co-constructed in the therapy session. During the session, he takes careful notes focused on the new reality unfolding within the client. These notes are then used to produce a letter, which is sent to the client. The client receives the letter between sessions. A conversation removed from the context may fade or be altered by our memories. However, as Epston (1994) argues, "the words in a letter don't fade and disappear the way a conversation does. ... A client can hold a letter in hand, reading it days, months, and years after the session" (p. 31). Copies of these letters are placed in the client's file and serve as the progress notes for the session.

White (2007) describes two distinct types of questions, which he labels landscape of action and landscape of identity. Landscape of action questions help establish the plot and the underlying theme of the story the client is telling. Landscape of identity questions establish for each member of the family her or his thoughts and feelings about the action that occurs in the story. As White states,

> in therapeutic conversations that are oriented by reauthoring conversations, the concepts of landscape of action and landscape of identity assist the therapist in building a context in which it becomes possible for people to give meaning to, and draw together into a storyline, many of the overlooked but significant events in their lives. (pp. 82–83)

One of the types of conversations useful in helping clients reauthor their stories is what White (2007) calls remembering conversations. Here clients are encouraged to remember and talk about significant persons or characters whom they have associated with in a positive way. This is based on the assumption that identity is formed by those we associate with rather than a core self. Fostering remembering conversations goes beyond taking a history, as it involves encouraging clients to reengage with past associations that have impact on their current identities. Narrative therapy theory emphasizes how identity is a product of how we think and speak about important characters in our life stories. For example, a therapist might have a conversation with a teen about a person who is significant to her, or a child might be invited to discuss how his favorite superhero influences his identity.

Definitional Ceremonies

Another technique of narrative family is the use of definitional ceremonies, which White (2007) describes as rituals enacted to further the impact of externalizing conversations. An outsider is brought in to witness the client's story. As White explains,

> outsider witnesses engage one another in conversations about expressions of the telling they were drawn to, about the images that these expressions evoked, about the personal experiences that resonated with these expressions, and about their sense of how their lives have been touched by the expressions. (pp. 165–166)

A definitional ceremony is not a place for the witness to draw conclusions, make suggestions, or offer evaluations. The ceremony is structured around three overlapping stages: the telling of the significant life story, the retelling of the story by the witness, and finally the retelling of the outsider witness's retelling. In some ways, this resembles Tom Andersen's (1991) reflecting team approach (see Chapter 11).

Highlighting Unique Outcomes

White (2007) further describes conversations that highlight unique outcomes as part of the process of reauthoring a client's life story. Since many of the experiences in our lives are not given meaning, this phase of the treatment calls for the therapist to help the client give meaning to some of those ignored experiences, specifically those that are counter to the client's dominant story about her or his problem. In mapping this type of conversation, White uses four categories similar to those used in mapping the externalizing conversations. These phases are (1) negotiation of a particular, experience-near definition of the unique outcome, (2) mapping the effect of the unique outcome, (3) evaluation of the unique outcome and its effects, and (4) justifying the evaluation.

In the negotiation of a particular, experience-near definition of the unique outcome, the goal is to develop a rich description of the unique outcome. For example, a client who struggles with an eating disorder might be encouraged to describe an incident where he was able to eat a healthy meal without purging afterward. From here, the client is interviewed about the meaning of the unique outcome.

The next phase, mapping the effect of the unique outcome, involves tracing the effects of the unique outcome on the various domains of the client's life. The therapist explores with the client a variety of domains, which may include family relationships, work, school, friendships, peers, and so forth. Here the therapist explores the current effects of the unique outcome on the client. If the client is unable to describe the current effects, the therapist engages the client in a discussion about potential future effects.

Next the therapist invites the client to evaluate the unique outcome and its effects. This involves simply asking clients what this unique outcome means in their life story. White (2007) points out that many people find this a novel experience because they have often been judged by others. As a result of this history, clients may have a difficult time making the evaluation. If this happens, White suggests that the therapist summarize the evaluations of other unique outcomes the client has had or talk about evaluations other clients have made regarding similar outcomes.

Justifying the evaluation involves asking the client to evaluate the evaluation. The therapist simply asks the client why the evaluation is acceptable or not acceptable. If the client has a difficult time justifying her or his evaluation, the therapist can provide an editorial summary of the interview to assist the client in justifying the evaluation.

Questioning

Unlike other postmodern theories of family therapy, the narrative approach emphasizes the interview itself. This approach is designed to shift clients' thinking about their situation and ultimately their feelings. Given this, there is a good deal of emphasis on listening to how clients see their situation. Weingarten (1998) describes her shift from a modern to a narrative perspective as "shifting my attention from what I think about what my clients are telling me to trying to understand what my clients think about what they are telling me" (p. 5).

As shown above, White (1993) describes two forms of questioning that allow the client's alternative story and unique outcome to be discovered. These are called landscape of action and landscape of identity questions. Landscape of action questions ask the client about steps already taken to address the problem. For example, a therapist might ask a client how she was able to overcome her fear of starting treatment. Each line of questioning involves asking deep, probing questions that bring out more detail of the client's story.

Landscape of identity questions get at what clients' actions mean about their self-concept or consciousness. Thus, when the client describes overcoming her fear, the therapist could ask, "What does your success at facing your fear say about your ability to be successful in therapy?" This could be followed with, "What does your potential success in therapy say about your ability to be successful in life?"

Structuring

The narrative approach is structured to be flexible and responsive to the client's needs. While there are no hard rules on whom to include in therapy, the sessions tend to be rather inclusive. As the therapy session is scheduled, the therapist will ask the client who might be helpful to include in the process. Thus, the therapy can include not only members of the family but also other systems that support them, such as neighbors, coworkers, other therapists, medical personnel, school personnel, and parole officers.

In addition, narrative therapy often involves contact with the client between sessions. This can take the form of notes, cards, or e-mails of encouragement sent between sessions from the therapist to the client, allowing for a deeper connection between the client and her or his therapy. Often these are written during the session to be sent in a number of days. These notes frequently highlight parts of the therapy session that the therapist finds most moving.

Celebration of success is also included in the structure of therapy. This is especially true in work with children. Party supplies are kept in the office, and success is celebrated as often as possible. Likewise, certificates that mark success are developed and printed for clients to take home. These certificates serve to make abstract changes more real and hopefully more lasting.

Responding

White (2007) has developed a conversation style that he refers to as a scaffolding conversation. This conversation sets the tone of the therapist's response to the client, and as such, it is more of an attitude than a technique. White believes personal development is a process of bridging the gap between the current, familiar experience of the client and what might be possible. By asking clients questions with an attitude of opening up possibility and by moving from experience to abstraction in small steps, the therapist can help clients further develop their sense of personal agency.

Narrative family therapists focus on the client's story surrounding the problem and, as a result, offer little or no direct advice. However, the process of paying very close attention to the client's story allows strong relationships to develop. The narrative approach emphasizes a deep under-standing of how clients view their problems. This takes the form of what Weingarten (1998) calls radical listening, which she defines as "helping a voice to be heard" (p. 5). This process enables clients to shift their story through a collaborative process with the therapist. By hearing their subverted stories, clients are empowered to restory their lives. Once the new story is developed, behavior and feelings shift in line with the new narrative.

Once a unique outcome is discovered, the therapist becomes active in encouraging the client to discover and gain more influence over her or his problem. The therapist is very eager to share in celebrating the success of the client. Often therapists will provide certificates of success for the client to take home to make the change seem more real and permanent.

The definition ceremony is structured to protect clients in the retelling of their story. Prior to the meeting, the witness, often a former client who has resolved similar issues, meets with the therapist to ensure that she or he will not be judgmental or evaluative of the client. In interviewing the witness, White (2007) identifies four categories of inquiry. These focus on (1) expression, (2) image, (3) personal resonance, and (4) transport. Expression refers to the part of the story to which the witness is drawn. Image is about what the witness sees in response to the expression, and personal resonance refers to why the witness was drawn to the story. Finally, transport is a description of how the witness has been moved by the story retold by the client.

Applications

One of the strengths of narrative family therapy is the diversity of settings to which it has been applied. The theory's founder, Michael White (1989), provides case examples of applications of his narrative approach to work with clients diagnosed with diverse and difficult problems such as anorexia nervosa, schizophrenia, encopresis, and enuresis. Building on White's work, Dickerson and Zimmerman (1992) applied the narrative approach to work with families with adolescents identified as having problems. They provide examples of externalizing that are developmentally appropriate for this age group.

Several authors have followed White's early trend of applying narrative therapy to work with children. Larner (1996) describes how a child's play can be used to understand the family's presenting problem. Larner assumes that "the child's play and art is understood as a narrative on the symptom or problem that prompted a family's request for psychological help" (p. 423). Noting that children often get brought to a therapist with an identified problem, Turns & Kimmes (2014) explore externalization of children's problems as a way to prevent the child from self-identifying with the problem. They look at Erickson's developmental theory as a framework to target age appropriate externalizations of problems in order to support a child's development of healthy self-concept. Lambie and Milsom (2010) write an interesting article on how school counselors can utilize a narrative approach to working with student that have a learning disability.

Other interesting applications of narrative family therapy speak of how broadly this theory can be applied. First, Carlson (1997) has explored the use of art in narrative therapy and found it to be a useful way to further clients' ability to reauthor their lives. Second, by applying the theory of narrative family therapy to issues in business organization, Barry (1997) discusses how business owners can set about changing the way their company responds to the business environment. In 2002, Launer, a British primary care physician, developed narrative-based primary care. After receiving training in narrative family therapy during a sabbatical from his medical practice, he developed an approach to primary care medicine based on the principles of narrative family therapy. In a similar vein Fraenkel, Hameline & Shannon (2009) describe how applying narrative and collaborative practice can shape how a multiple family group program can provide support for homeless families. Building on the utility of Narrative principals being applied to larger systems, Freeman & Combs (2009) provide an interesting exploration of the use narrative principle in consulting with organizations.

In addition, an interesting project by Focht and Beardslee (1996) used narrative therapy as an intervention to prevent children whose parents have an affective disorder from developing an affective disorder. In a similar vein, McLuckie (2005) uses narrative family therapy for the treatment of pediatric obsessive-compulsive disorder. He helps the family externalize the obsessive-compulsive disorder as "fear of worry" and behaviors such as compulsive hand washing as "worry washing." Eppler and Carolan (2005) discuss helping children develop a biblionarrative of important events in their lives. A biblionarrative is a written story of the child's experience that assists with the treatment goals of "creating dialogue, building family assets, and teaching communication skills" (p. 41). In order to assist families with the transition to being a step family Gibson (2013) helps adolescents and their parents remember and reauthor their family experience.

Because of its deconstruction of cultural and social narratives as well as its use of a social justice perspective and metaphors of overcoming oppression, this approach can be applied in cases where diversity is an issue. Milan and Keiley (2000) have applied narrative family therapy to work with biracial youths and their families. Working with Latino families, Bermudez and Bermudez (2002) have developed an expressive art and narrative technique where clients create a family altar. As the family members create this altar, they develop a family narrative that incorporates issues of spirituality.

Since White was Australian and Epston is from New Zealand, narrative family therapy has been successfully applied to settings outside the United States. Vetere and Dowling (2005) published an edited volume exploring narrative therapy with children and the family based on work performed in the United Kingdom. Nwoye (2007) applied a narrative framework to their work with people affected by the HIV pandemic in Africa. Chen (2012) describes how Narrative therapy can be useful for Chinese adults who were raised as an only child as a result of China's 1979 limit to one child per family.

Given the wide variety of settings in which narrative therapy has been applied, we can conclude that this model will continue to be influential for some time to come.

Acting as a Narrative Family Therapist

In the interview, the narrative family therapist emphasizes the interpretation and meaning of the client's story. Like the constructivist family therapist, she or he has little concern for prescribing actions the client should take. The therapist believes that helping clients change their sense of self will produce changes in their behavior.

To separate clients from their problem, the narrative family therapist helps them externalize the problem. This is best accomplished by carefully listening to their story and finding a metaphor or statement that place the problem outside clients' internal experience of self. Frequently, the metaphor of being oppressed by the now externalized problem is developed with the client.

There is considerable emphasis on helping clients reauthor the stories they tell about themselves. Acting as coeditor in the client's ongoing life story, the narrative family therapist focuses on finding or creating exceptions to the dominant story. Once a unique outcome is discovered, the therapist deliberately pays increased attention to that narrative.

To further the process of reauthoring clients' stories, therapists regularly send letters to their clients to reinforce their new stories. The therapist also moves between landscape of action and landscape of identity questions to help the client internalize the new story. Likewise, remembering conversations and definition ceremonies can be used to further the reauthoring process.

Case Example: The Case of John's Anger

You receive a phone call from Ms. Sandra James regarding her son, John, age 7. She reports that since John's younger sibling, Mary, age 2, was born, he has been having difficulty with being angry and aggressive. She describes how John has temper tantrums when he notices that his sister is getting attention. She also describes an incident where John tried to push his sleeping baby sister off her bed. This problem with anger was getting worse slowly, but it has increased significantly over the past six months. Yesterday Sandra had to pick John up from after-school care because he hit one of his classmates. The child care staff have had several conversations with Sandra about her son's anger and temper. Since they have not seen any improvement, they have suggested that John see a therapist to address his issues with anger.

Sandra lives on the local military base with her mother, Mrs. Kesley. Her husband, Sgt. David James, is serving in the army overseas in a noncombat role, or as she says, "working on trucks." He was deployed seven months ago, and Sandra is disappointed that she hasn't been able to hold the family together in his absence. Her mother came to live with them to help with the children just after her husband left.

You ask to see the entire family, and Sandra is slightly taken aback by this. She was expecting to drop John off while you worked with him. You explain that while that is how some therapists work, you prefer to work with all who are affected by the problem and who might be able to help John. You tell Sandra that you want her mother to attend, since she helps care for the children. Sandra laughs nervously while she tells you about her mother's negative comments about therapy. She reports that her mother went to therapy shortly before she divorced and "got nothing out of it." You reassure her that you are comfortable working with grandparents, and you invite her to have her mother call should she be concerned about coming to therapy.

Session One

The clients arrive on time, well groomed and apparently in good spirits. You introduce yourself to Sandra first and welcome her to your office. She immediately introduces you to Mrs. Kesley, who is holding Mary asleep on her shoulder. As you get to know her, you ask her what the children call her. She replies that they call her Grandma. You ask her if she minds if you call her that. She smiles and states that of course you can call her Grandma when the children are around.

Next you greet John, who shakes your hand and says, "Pleased to meet you, sir," in a rehearsed manner. You show them to their seats and ask John if he could tell you the story of how they have come to your office today.

John shrugs his shoulders and states that he was told by his mother this morning that he was going to a doctor to talk about his anger. He says that he got out of school two hours early to make the appointment with you and that he is going to the store and out to eat with his family after the session is over. You are impressed by how verbal John is, and you share with the family how delighted you are that John speaks so well and is so bright. You ask Grandma if this comes from her side of the family. She smiles and agrees that it must come from her side of the family.

You continue talking with her and ask her what she thinks the problem is. She describes in detail John's difficulty with anger. While she talks, John and his mother nod their heads in agreement. Grandma goes on to say that John has become "just an angry boy." As you probe for details, she states that "it's like he's been hijacked by his anger." You respond to this by asking her, "Has anger hijacked John, or has anger kidnapped him?"

John's mother responds by looking at John and explaining the difference between *hijacked* and *kidnapped* to him. He dismisses her by saying he knows what they mean. Turning to John, you ask him if it's more of a hijacking or a kidnapping. He quickly responds, "Kidnapped, because I'm a kid." Everyone laughs, and John has a big smile on his face. You compliment him by saying what good insight he has and tell him that you will enjoy helping him deal with his kidnapping problem.

You turn to his mother and ask if "anger-kidnapped John" is a good description of the problem for which they are seeking therapy. She agrees and jokes that she would be willing to pay whatever ransom is demanded. She rethinks her answer and decides that she has paid a ransom several times, but anger still does not release John. You ask her, "When did you first notice that John had been kidnapped?" She becomes tearful and says, "I think anger came for John a few weeks after David got shipped back overseas." She describes how mad she was that her husband got called twice for duty overseas when some have yet to serve. Then she pulls herself together and states, "We're a military family, and that's what we do."

You ask John, "What does your anger do to you as you go about your day?" He describes how anger sneaks up on him when he doesn't expect it. He goes on to describe how, even when he is trying to do well, he sometimes finds himself getting angry. He describes how his anger goes from small to big in a matter of seconds.

John's mother and grandmother echo his concern about anger intruding in his life and making him have some rather uncomfortable times. They report that, as a result of his anger, John has been less able to play with peers. They are both concerned that, because of the fighting at school and with friends, he will soon find himself without friends. When you ask if John is a good friend when his anger doesn't sneak up on him, they both agree that he is. You summarize by stating that it's anger that's keeping John from having a better relationship with his peers. John, his mother, and his grandmother all agree.

Grandma starts to describe how John's anger is taking a toll on his mother and father. She describes how her daughter is stressed from being a single parent while her husband is overseas. John's anger is creating stress between Sandra and David when they talk over the Internet. John's mother shares how she is torn between wanting to talk to her husband about John because she feels she needs the support and not wanting to stress out her husband. You point out that John's anger is stressing out the other members of the family as well as John.

Then you ask the family if there are other areas of John's life where anger is intruding. His mother describes how she has started to limit his activities because of his anger. She decided that as a punishment for pitching a fit at the soccer tryouts, she wouldn't let him play this season. While John enjoys playing soccer, she states that she couldn't let him play when she's afraid he'll lose his temper during a game and embarrass himself and his family. Grandma describes how she is less willing to take John out in public because she's afraid he'll make a scene. As a result, they don't have as many outings as they did in the past. You summarize this portion of the discussion by stating that anger is keeping John from doing things he enjoys.

Near the end of the session, you ask the family if their evaluation of John's struggle with anger is fair. They all agree it is fair. John's mother's eyes moisten. However, before she starts to cry, Mary wakes up disoriented. You spend a few minutes talking to Mary and getting to know her a little.

You invite the family back in a week to continue to discuss John's difficulty with anger. You tell the family that in the next session, you and they will work on ways to reduce and possibly even eliminate the negative effects of anger in John's life. You reassure the adults by stating that while all anger is unique, you have had good success with several children in getting the problem of anger out of their lives. You thank them for coming and escort the family out of your office.

Session Two

When the family arrive for this session, they all seem to be in a good mood. Sandra explains that a neighbor volunteered to watch Mary and that they took her up on the offer. You support their decision to leave Mary at home and state that if she is needed, she can come to a future session. As the session starts, Sandra describes how John's anger was "terrible" at a birthday party he went to on Saturday. She describes how he got into an argument with the friend who was having the birthday. After she finishes the description, you ask her what the trend has been between sessions. Specifically, you ask, "Has anger been less successful in kidnapping John in the time between sessions?"

John's mother states that overall the trend has been positive. She can't think of another major anger kidnapping, and when pressed, she and her mother can think of only a few minor problems. John quickly adds that there were a few other times when anger kidnapped him but that there weren't many of them. You conclude with John that this is strong trend.

Continuing to interview John, you ask him, "Can you tell me a story about a time when anger tried to kidnap you and you were able to resist being kidnapped?" John responds, "Oh, yes, lots of times. I start to get angry and I stop myself."

"Great!" you respond, and you tell him that you would love to hear a story of an actual success in resisting anger. You say that what you really want is a story that is an example of how he has been able to do that. John says, "I'm not good at telling stories. Can my mom and grandma help?"

"Yes, yes, the more the better. You start, and they'll join in and give details as needed," you say, smiling at Sandra and Grandma.

After thinking a few minutes, John says he can't think of a story. You probe deeper and ask John if he is having problems thinking of a story or having problems thinking of a way to tell the story.

After thinking another few minutes, John concludes that he does have a story in his mind. He is just having a hard time telling it. You offer to start the story for him as you point out that stories are often hard to start.

You begin the story for John: "Once upon a time just a few days ago, John had a brush with anger. Like many times before, anger tried to kidnap John. However, this time was very different. This time John was able to get the better of anger." You motion to John and he jumps in from here. He tells about a time when he was at a store and his mother didn't let him get a drink from the snack bar. He recalls how he felt himself start to get angry but simply told anger to leave him alone. He discovered that when he started to feel mad he could simply tell his anger, "You're not going to get me."

He goes on to explain that at first he was surprised, but since then he has had several successes.

You tell him how other clients who have had problems with being kidnapped by anger also had success just by telling anger to go away. John exclaims, "People talk to anger?" You respond, "Sure. Some say the words out loud; some just think the words. Lots of people talk to their anger. Lots of people talk to their feelings."

Sandra starts to tell how she talks to her feelings in her head. She goes on to describe how she has been sad since John's father left to go overseas. She tells her son how she is able to feel better when she tells her sadness that everything will be OK, that John's dad will come back soon and that they'll be a family again. She states that she remembers the incident John talked about and believes that this might have been a turning point for him. She recalls that after she said no to the drink at the store, she realized that it might make John mad. She remembers feeling glad that he didn't get mad, and she reports that she was aware of his conversation with his anger.

Grandma tells how she remembers a time when John started to get mad over being told to stop watching television and come for dinner. She notes that he started to get mad, then turned around and complied with her request. John also recalls that event and says that he told anger to leave him alone then, too.

You state that this is good news and that perhaps John has anger on the run. Now that he is learning how to tell anger to leave him alone, he is starting to beat anger's attempts to kidnap him. He agrees, and so do his mother and grandmother, but they are all cautious about believing this change will stick.

In response to this concern, you start to ask questions about the meaning of the change. Specifically, you ask what such a change means concerning the type of person that John is becoming. The consensus is that such a change indicates that John is becoming a young man who is able to manage his feelings. In addition, it shows that he is a good boy who cares for his family and who, when needed, can put the needs of his family before his own needs.

As the session ends, you ask the family what their plan is to celebrate the change. John's grandmother suggests that they go to the snack bar for a drink. His mother states that she thinks that's not a big enough celebration. You agree with her. Then she suggests that they take John out to eat at his favorite restaurant. All agree that this is a fine idea. You invite them back to therapy in three weeks to tell more stories of success in overcoming John's anger.

Correspondence Between Sessions

Between sessions, you send John the following note.

Dear John:

> I was thinking today about your battle with anger and wanted to remind you
> that this is a heroic battle. Remember that you have made tremendous progress
> and I believe that you can keep it up.
>
> Regards,
> Rashad

Session Three

Three days before the next session, Sandra calls to cancel the last appointment. She states that John is doing much better with his anger issues and thinks that therapy is no longer needed. You congratulate her and ask if she could stop by with John anyway. You say that it is great that they have successfully completed therapy and that you would like to see her and John for just 15 minutes or so. She agrees to the brief appointment, but she requests a change in the time so that she will be better able to make it. You make the arrangements.

Three days later when John arrives, he walks into your office with a big smile, and you put your hand up to ask for a high five. When you ask John how it's been going in his struggle with anger, he states that he thinks he has the problem beat.

You give a cheer and go over to your desk, where you have a small bucket of confetti. You take a handful and give Sandra and John each a handful, and then you all throw the confetti up in the air and cheer. You and John start to dance around the room, chanting "John beat anger!" John has a big smile on his face and holds his head up with pride as he dances with you.

After a few minutes, all of you sit down, and you give John a certificate that you have had printed between sessions. It reads:

Certificate of Success

This Certificate is awarded to

John James,

who has displayed courage and bravery in confronting and beating anger's control over him.

Witnessed by
Rashad saeed

As you present it to him, he smiles even wider, and you point out that there is space for his mother, grandmother, and others to sign the certificate. You ask him who else should sign it, and he states that he thinks his dad should sign it. His mother says with a smile that they could send it to his dad, who could sign it and send it back to them. John says that would be great, and then he could hang it in his room.

You talk briefly with Sandra about the idea of her helping John make a book that describes his success. You tell her that children who have been successful often enjoy making such a book and find it helpful in keeping the success going. You show her and John some of the books on your shelf that other children have written. You tell them that, while they don't need to write a book because they were so successful so quickly, other children might benefit from reading John's story, and if they write one you would like a copy to share with others.

Both John and his mother leave the office smiling as you shake their hands and say good-bye. Sandra turns and thanks you, saying that the therapy was much different from what she thought it would be. She shares that she had been afraid you would make her feel like a bad mother and that she was reluctant to come to therapy. You joke with her, saying that you are sorry to disappoint her, and tell her that if she would like to come again she will be welcome.

Case Discussion

The therapist immediately starts to build a therapeutic relationship with the family. He seeks to understand the presenting problem in the context of the family. The therapist is also quick to work toward externalizing the problem. The grandmother starts the process by discussing how anger hijacks John. As the family tells the story, they decide that it is more accurate to say that anger kidnaps John.

Most of this session is spent mapping the influence of anger on John's life. As the map is detailed, the therapist engages the clients in therapy through their participation in telling the story of John's anger.

At the close of the session, the therapist feels they have made significant progress. The most important accomplishment is that the clients have developed a useful externalization of John's problem. With the therapist's assistance, they have externalized the anger as a kidnapper of John.

In the second session, the clients present with a failure, and the therapist continues to ask questions until there is space in the conversation to inquire about the possibility of unique outcomes. The clients describe a unique outcome in the form of an overall reduction in the frequency of anger kidnappings. Once this unique outcome is discovered, the therapist helps the clients recognize and celebrate the change.

With the therapist's guidance, the family has a good conversation about keeping anger away from John. Both his mother and grandmother participate in the conversation, offering him support. The therapist draws attention to the degree of John's success by asking both landscape of action and landscape of identity questions. He encourages the family to celebrate between sessions. The therapist also sends John a letter of encouragement between sessions.

The third and final session focuses on making the change stable. A certificate is given to document the change, and the therapist joins John and his mother in celebrating what they have accomplished.

The therapist is glad that the family is going to send the certificate to John's father for him to sign and return and hopes that this will help keep his father involved in his rearing.

The therapist hopes that John will make a book documenting his success. While this is not necessary, making a book means the change is more likely to be fixed. In addition, other clients might be inspired by John's book.

Evaluating Narrative Family Therapy

Theoretical Critiques

The narrative approach has been criticized as departing from the systems approach. However, in many ways this approach is very systemic. The narrative therapist sees the problem as located in the use of language. This is very similar to the notion that the problem lies in communication among family members. In the constructivist narrative approach, the emphasis on language brings back into consideration the content of the communication. By looking at the meaning of the language, the therapist focuses on both the process and content of the language and communication. Of particular interest in this approach are outcomes that are free of pathology and oppressive language, which is compatible with general systemic thinking.

The "not knowing" stance used in narrative therapy has also been criticized. This critique states that once one has understanding, it is impossible to not know, and thus it is not realistic for experienced therapists to act as if they do not know. A better description of this stance would be to describe the therapist as nonauthoritarian. This nonauthoritarian stance, combined with genuine curiosity, forms the basis of the client-therapist relationship from the constructivist perspective.

Minuchin (1998) provides a critique of postmodern family therapy in an essay titled "Where Is the Family in Narrative Family Therapy?" Minuchin argues that, in its mission to give voice to underprivileged people, this approach has emphasized contextual issues such as gender and culture. He warns that this emphasis has gone too far:

> In the process, theorists seem to have misplaced the family—that prominent, intermediate locus of context and culture within which people live—and practitioners have returned to an emphasis on individual human psychology that not only is traditional but does not fit the parts of postmodern theory that emphasize social relatedness. (p. 403)

While this critique has some merit, it is based more on practices associated with postmodern theory than on the theory itself. In many ways, the narrative family therapy model is a meta theory that allows for practices emphasizing both the family and underrepresented individuals.

Despite the critiques, this theoretical orientation is at the cutting edge of theoretical development. The postmodern stance and emphasis on language will play into the development of the next generation of theories of family therapy. Given the diversity of settings and populations to which this theory has been applied, we can expect that this approach will influence the next generation of therapists.

Empirical Evaluations

While White himself did not test this approach empirically, his work is rich with examples, case samples, and anecdotal reports. Recently the narrative approach has had some degree of empirical scrutiny. This is remarkable when one considers that postmodern research methods are not well developed and that the narrative approach is relatively new to the profession.

Narrative therapy has received some interesting empirical validation as an approach to working with families with children. A preliminary study of narrative family therapy by Besa (1994) looked at the effectiveness of narrative interventions in reducing parent–child conflict. While the study had a small sample (N = 6), it clearly demonstrates narrative family therapy to be effective in reducing parent–child conflict. Ramey, Tarulli, Frijters & Fisher (2009) conduct an interesting study on the process of narrative therapy. They studied video of session conducted by 3 narrative therapist treating 8 different childrene. By coding verbal statement the researchers were able to demonstrate how the children followed the therapist's externalization statements and progressed through therapy as the White's predicted. While the authors were clear on the limitations of such a small study the methodology utilized could provide an interesting area for further study.

Part of the lack of verification in research has been due to the differences in assumptions underlying this approach and those underlying scientific methodology. Most research methodology has been developed in the logical positivistic tradition. Postmodernists have been reluctant to apply linear objective methods to nonlinear subjective work. However, as Simon (1992) points out, the two approaches are not mutually exclusive. It is possible to have a second-order mindset while doing first-order research. A simple follow-up study with clients who have experienced a narrative-based approach to treatment would go a long way toward establishing the efficacy of this approach.

Learning Exercises

1. Pair off with a fellow student and tell each other the story of how you decided to apply to graduate school. As your partner tells her story, pay attention to the way she tells the story of her success and share some of your observations. Switch rolls and repeat the process.

2. Pair off and tell your partner stories that define and illustrate some of your positive qualities. As you listen to your partner tell his story, practice asking landscape of action and landscape of identity questions. After the story seems complete, take turns telling how you felt during the interview. Switch roles and repeat the process.

Discussion Questions

1. What are the similarities and differences between offering an interpretation and restorying?

2. In what ways is retelling a story similar to the concept of reframing as developed by the MRI approach?

3. During the externalization process as well as during the mapping of unique outcomes, narrative therapists ask *why* questions. This can be contrasted with the strategic therapist's avoidance of *why* questions. Describe how each position fits its respective model.

4. When, where and from who did you hear stories about your family from? What where the themes of the stories that were told in your family.

Suggested Readings

Dickerson, V. C., & Zimmerman, J. (1992). Families with adolescents: Escaping problem lifestyles. *Family Process, 31,* 341–353.

Freedman, J., & Combs, G. (1996). *Narrative Therapy: The Social Construction of Preferred Realities.* New York: Norton.

White, M. (2007). *Maps of narrative practice.* New York: Norton.

White, M., & Epston, D. (1990). *Narrative means to therapeutic ends.* New York: Norton.

Web Resources

The Dulwich Center Homepage

http://dulwichcentre.com.au/

Wikispaces Narrative Family Therapy

https://postmoderntherapies.wikispaces.com/Narrative+Therapy

Wikipedia page on Narrative Therapy

https://en.wikipedia.org/wiki/Narrative_therapy

Narrative Therapy Centre of Toronto Homepage

http://www.narrativetheycentre.com/index.html

SECTION 5

Processes and Outcomes in Marriage and Family Therapy

To fully understand theories of family therapy, it is important to understand contextual issues as they relate to its practice. Thus, it is essential to discuss issues in the practice of family therapy. Chapter 15 looks at processes that relate to the practice of family therapy. We begin with a discussion of family process, focusing on how understanding family process informs our practice. Next, we discuss professional processes. There we focus on the role of professional organizations in supporting the practice of family therapy. This is followed by a discussion of ethical issues unique to family therapy. We end with a discussion of integrative practices as they relate to theories of family therapy.

We conclude this text by discussing research outcomes in Chapter 16. Here we explore selected models that have been empirically developed and evaluated. We also explore areas where family therapy has been shown to be an effective approach. Finally, we explore factors common to all psychotherapy approaches that have been shown to predict success.

CHAPTER

15

FAMILY, PROFESSIONAL, TRAINING, AND INTEGRATIVE PROCESSES

Introduction

Since family therapy is a scientific art that is concerned with process and patterns in process, let us now turn our attention to four key types of processes important to the understanding of family therapy. If we think of process as second-by-second interactions, as well as longer lasting interactions and practices, we see that the patterns that occur are important in describing the social phenomenon we are interested in studying. We also see that over time, process becomes the social structures of that same phenomenon. So, to understand family therapy, we need a basic understanding of the processes that are important in families and in family therapy itself. In this chapter, we focus on four important concepts: family processes, professional processes, training processes, and integrative processes.

Family Processes

Family process is the interaction that occurs within each family. This is contrasted with the content of the family, which is what the family says in their communication. In other words, process is how the content is delivered. For example, the tone of communication often carries information about the family's process. Issues that are important to our discussion include relational space, which refers to a family's rules for interaction and the way they divide up their living space, and socialization, which has to do with how families assist new members in interacting with the family as well as with broader systems.

As described below, process is how family systems interact in their natural environment. Broderick (1993) published a classic book on this subject that is still very current in terms of its insight into how family process impacts our theoretical understanding of families. Family process can take several forms. In looking at family process, we can concern ourselves with the communication in a system. We can think of family process as who says what to whom, in what way, with what outcome. Looking at process can also involve focusing on how families use their relational space. That has to do with how they organize and use space in the family living environment and how that impacts their functioning. We can concern ourselves with how families socialize their children to become responsible members of the next generation of the family, as well as responsible members of society. Family processes have a good deal to do with how families are able to establish normal family development. Finally, family processes impact how families move through the family life cycle. Family members are born, develop, become socialized, mature, reproduce, age, and die, all within a coherent cycle.

As early pioneers began to invite family members into psychotherapy sessions to help solve mental health issues, they needed a new conceptual framework to understand how families interact both inside and outside the treatment room. The term *family process* (Jackson, 1965) was coined to describe the emerging framework. In 1961, the journal *Family Process* was founded, and it quickly became what Broderick (1993) has called the "house organ" of the new movement.

Process Versus Content

Since family process theory concerns itself with the difference between process and content, this was one of the first areas studied within the family process paradigm. One early and important study came from Kantor and Lehr's (1975), *Inside the Family: Toward a Theory of Family Process*. This study looked at moment-by-moment interactions of subject families. The study's data was collected by placing a voice-activated recorder in each room of the subject families' homes.

To understand the process that families undergo to regulate their functioning, early pioneers concerned themselves with understanding the system's capacity to self-regulate and to pursue a goal (Broderick, 1993). One of the key ways a family self-regulates is by managing its relational space in terms of both emotional space and physical space. Another key goal that families set for themselves is the socialization of the young.

Relational Space

Scholars have long been concerned with the dynamic balancing that families go through to regulate the space between members. Broderick (1993) summarizes this phenomenon as follows:

This process of regulation involves the ever-shifting balancing of two opposing forces: the centripetal forces that link each member to every other member, which we shall call *bonding processes*; and the centrifugal forces that separate each member from the other members, and which we shall can *buffering processes*. (p. 90)

Adopting the bonding–buffering dichotomy, we see that this is a major issue for couples. If we apply this notion over the life course of a couple's relationship, we see that relational space shifts from bonding to buffering over time, and especially as the children develop. We see that couples have differing needs for bonding and buffering. Being out of sync with these processes is a major issue seen in couple therapy. Couples who fail to resolve this difficulty can triangle in their children as a means of bonding with each other.

The process of bonding between young children and their parents is often referred to as *attachment*. This led to Bowlby's (1969, 1973) development of a whole class of theory, called attachment theory (see chapter 5). This theory focuses on how people's early ability to attach to a secure caregiver influences their style of relating throughout their lives. This theory is at the core of emotionally focused couple therapy (see Chapter 16). As children enter adolescence, their needs shift from that of bonding to that of buffering. This implies that families need to change their structure and process in response to the differing demands of different developmental stages.

Relationship space between families and wider systems must also be regulated. Families must regulate who is able to enter the family's physical space. They need to be able to let in desirable influences but exclude undesirable or even dangerous influences. For example, if the parents in the family use methamphetamine, they might allow undesirable associates into the house and even dangerous chemicals into the family's living space. Families must also make decisions about regulating the space between family life and the amount and type of work members engage in.

Additionally, families have to manage issues of hierarchy and the division of labor in the family. In terms of a power metaphor, which family members have the power to impose their will on other family members? Families must decide how to allocate resources within the family. For example, does a family support the elder girl's desire to take piano lessons at the expense of her younger sister's figure skating lessons? How does a family deal with a situation where the parents have been saving for their child's education and then the child is arrested? Do the parents have the child pay for their legal defense out of their college savings?

Socialization

The study of how children learn to become productive members of their families, and ultimately society, has a long history in the social sciences. Unfortunately, much of the initial research in socialization was written from a linear perspective. We see that socialization is a two-way process: children are influenced by their parents, but equally important and much less studied, are the fact that parents are changed by their children. However, marriage and family therapists can still extract much useful information from studies of socialization.

One of the most important factors influencing how children grow up is the emotional warmth of their parents (Broderick, 1993). Supportive behaviors on the part of the parents, such as praise, interest, positive attention, physical attention, and terms of endearment, go a long way toward impacting a child's development positively. The style of parenting is also important. The number of parents who emulate their own parents' approach to parenting, even when they feel their parents did not do a particularly good job of parenting, is remarkable.

A variety of factors influence socialization. These include the child's gender, talents, and temperament. We also need to think about the cohort effect when considering socialization. A cohort is a group of peers who provide socialization of the child, in addition to the socialization provided by the parents. A child's level of self-esteem also has an impact on his or her socialization.

For a family to understand what normative processes in healthy families look like, it is necessary for a family to have a basic understanding of family process. While no family is ideal in its function, we can identify degrees of functionality in a family. It is common for novice family therapists to simply point out the family's deficiencies. While it is important to take an assessment, simply talking about your observations does little to help the family improve their situation.

Professional Processes

Professional processes are processes that are important to understanding the profession of family therapy. First, we discuss the view that family therapy is a profession in its own right rather than simply a technique of counseling or psychology. I then present a description of professional organizations that support the practice of family therapy. Since much of the family therapy field sees the client as a family rather than as an individual, therapists must have an understanding of some unique issues in order to practice effectively and ethically. This turns our attention to issues of diagnosis and relational ethics in the practice of family therapy.

Beginning early in the development of marriage and family therapy (MFT), there was ongoing debate as to the nature of MFT as a profession. Some have taken the position that family therapy is simply a technique of counseling or social work that does not represent a unique approach. Others take the position that MFT is in fact a unique profession that merits its own professional identity and its own licensing body to regulate its practice. Tensions linger between professional organizations, particularly between the American Counseling Association (ACA) and the American Association for Marriage and Family Therapy (AAMFT). The ACA's policy statement maintains that MFT is not an independent discipline, but rather a subspecialty of counseling (Bowers, 2007). For the most part, however, marriage and family therapy is recognized as a unique profession.

As we saw in Chapters 1 and 2, the profession of marriage and family therapy developed out of a variety of professions. In 1963, California became the first state to license family therapists. Other states have since followed suit. As of 2009, all 50 states, the District of Columbia, and two provinces in Canada regulate the practice of marriage and family therapy (AAMFT, n.d.).

In most states, what is regulated is the legal right to call oneself a marriage and family therapist. Other mental health providers such as professional counselors, psychologists, pastoral counselors, social workers, psychiatrists, and nurse practitioners are not prohibited from seeing whole families in their practices. Family therapy, as a technique, is within the scope of practice of individuals from other mental health fields as long as they are competently trained. In the same manner, seeing individuals is within the scope of practice for family therapists as long as they are appropriately trained.

The American Association for Marriage and Family Therapy

In 1942, the American Association for Marriage Counselors was established. This organization later became the American Association for Marriage and Family Therapy. In the debate over whether family therapy is a profession that merits a distinct license or a practice that falls under the scope of other professional licenses, AAMFT has taken the position that family therapy is a unique profession. To further this goal, they established the quasi-independent Commission on Accreditation for Marriage and Family Therapy Education (COAMFTE). In 1978, the U.S. Department of Health and Education recognized COAMFTE and the focus shifted toward graduate degrees in marriage and family therapy as the primary entry path to the profession (Bowers, 2007). Currently, 127 programs are fully accredited by COAMFTE.

To further the AAMFT's assertion that marriage and family therapy is a profession in its own right, and to develop its professional legitimacy, marriage and family therapists have had to clearly define their unique contribution to the mental health landscape. The first two pieces of that task were to establish licensure of marriage and family therapists and to establish training guidelines for those who wish to identify themselves as marriage and family therapists. Next, to further the development of the profession, AAMFT published a definition of the scope of practice. This defines the profession to others and in many instances has become part of the legal landscape as lobbyists have campaigned for this definition to become part of the legal definition in licensure laws. AAMFT's definition of marriage and family therapy is "the diagnosis and treatment of mental and emotional disorders, whether affective, behavioral, or cognitive, within the context of family systems" (Bowers, 2007, p. 16).

Other Professional Organizations

In 1977, the American Family Therapy Academy (AFTA) was founded. AFTA was designed to be an advanced organization of leading researchers and clinicians. Membership requirements included a terminal degree (doctoral degree), five years' clinical experience, and experience in teaching or significant research performance. AFTA holds annual meetings and a biannual clinical research conference and publishes a yearly monograph. Originally the academy was rather exclusive in their membership by only allows members in by invitation only, however, they have moved to more inclusive membership in recent years. While AAMFT focuses more on professional advocacy, AFTA is more focused on advancing the understanding of family therapy and developing family therapy mastery.

During the same year, 1977, the United Kingdom's Association for Family Therapy and Systemic Practice (AFT) was founded. This organization focuses more on the practice of family therapy than advocacy for the profession. They provide a code of ethics for "main health and social welfare professionals" and seek to improve the standards of care for families. They publish a Journal, *The Family Journal,* as well as provide an annual conference in the United Kingdom that focus on aspects of family practice. Similarly, the Australian Association of Family Therapy (AAMF) was founded in 1979 and incorporated in 1989. They provide a code of ethics, annual conference, and publish a journal, *Australia & New Zealand Journal of Family Therapy.* In 2012, family therapists in Asia founded the Asia Academy of Family Therapy (AAFT). They offer professional development and support to family therapists in Asia.

In 1986, a group of counselors felt it was necessary to develop a division of the American Counseling Association to support counselors of couples, families, and systems. As a result, the International Association of Marriage and Family Counseling (IAMFC) was developed and chartered in 1989. This organization has over 2,000 members and publishes a journal titled *Family Journal.* IAMFC seeks to be the professional home of counselors who work with families and couples. Most of their members hold licensure as counselors. They have more of an international emphasis and hold an annual conference, usually in the United States, and an annual counseling institute internationally. In 2011, they published ethical standards providing a "framework for the ethical practice of by IANFC members and other professionals engaged in couple and family counseling" (Hendricks, Bradley, Southern, Oliver, & Birdsall, 2011, p. 217).

The Diagnostic and Statistical Manual of Mental Disorders

The *Diagnostic and Statistical Manual of Mental Disorders V* (*DSM-5*), published by the American Psychiatric Association in 2013, is the official diagnostic manual for mental and emotional illnesses. This manual provides the classifications of mental illness used by the medical establishment for admission into hospitals and other medical facilities, and by medical practitioners for prescribing psychotropic medicines. Equally important is insurance companies' use of the *DSM* in deciding what treatments they will cover. The response to the text has been well summarized by Jay Lebow (2013), who stated, "Reaction has been intense as advocates claim advances in the scientific basis of classification, while critics castigate the extension of what they regard as an artifice that has little to do with the realities of experiencing and coping with human problems" (p.155).

During the 1970's and 1980's, it was not uncommon to hear marriage and family therapists state that they did not engage in diagnostic practices. In part, they took this position for philosophical reasons. These therapists would argue that diagnosis in the practice of marriage and family therapy is inappropriate because they worked with the family, not the individual. In fact, Denton (1990), in discussing the hesitancy of marriage and family therapists to use the *DSM*, argues, "the scientific paradigms underlying these two approaches [MFT and psychiatry] are fundamentally different and incompatible" (p. 113). However, as marriage and family therapists began to work more with individuals, they became more comfortable with the medical model. Likewise, when marriage and family therapists became more legitimized, clients started to seek reimbursement from their insurance companies for their treatment, and marriage and family therapists began to work with other mental health providers. This provided an increased interest in diagnosis. A study by Denton, Patterson, and Van Meir (1997) found that 91% of MFT training programs provide coursework that trains therapists how to use the *DSM*, and "Interdisciplinary communication improved chances of employment and cooperation with third-party payers were the main reasons for teaching in this area" (p. 85).

Denton and his colleagues further concluded that the use of the *DSM* is largely a pragmatic issue, rather than a reflection of a shift in the field's position on individual diagnosis. Thus, use of the *DSM* remains poorly integrated into the practice of marriage and family therapy, where the medical model coexists without overlapping. As Strong (1993) concludes, "family therapists are often expected to straddle both of those worlds, using *DSM* diagnosis for administrative purposes while offering descriptions of solvable problems to clients in lay terms" (p. 250). Systems theory, particularly postmodern theory, provides a potential bridge. From a postmodern perspective, all theory is fiction, and what becomes important to the therapist is which reality (fiction) is most helpful to the client (Keeney 1983). If we extend this idea, we see that diagnosis, like all theory, is an occasionally useful perspective. Furthermore, we can view a medical diagnosis as one reality that has certain benefits and costs to both the consumer and practitioner. In the current reality of professional standards, diagnosis is expected for treatment. From here, decisions can be made as to what degree the diagnosis drives treatment.

Relational Ethics

To promote ethical practice and high professional standards, organizations devoted to providing therapeutic and counseling services publish a code of ethics. To become a legitimate mental health profession, marriage and family therapists needed to develop and enforce their own code of ethical behaviors. Here again the AAMFT has taken a leadership role and published a code of ethics (see Appendix A). Other organizations also have statements about working with families in their code, which assists in representing the acceptance of family treatment as a mainstream approach to helping.

Members of AAMFT are ethically and in some states legally mandated to report peers who are in violation of the ethical standards. This provides for ongoing peer review of clinicians' practice. The best way to avoid unethical practices is to seek consultation as need. In fact this is so useful that the preamble of the ethics code encourages consultation. Many states have adopted AAMFT ethical standards as a legal standard for appropriate practice. Violations of ethical practice can be reported to both the state licensure board and AAMFT, or another professional association. The level of sanction for a violation is a function of the potential and actual harm done to a client. For minor violations, the situation might be remedied by supervision and education. However, for severe infractions, the sanction might be expulsion from a professional association or suspension of licensure. Because of the potential damage of unethical practice, most training programs offer an entire course on professional practice and ethics. In addition, AAMFT provides free phone consultation with ethics consultants for member clinicians.

The current AAMFT ethical standards were adopted in 2015 (see Appendix). The standards are divided into nine sections, which are (1) responsibility to clients, (2) confidentiality, (3) professional competence and integrity, (4) responsibility to students and supervisees, (5) research and publications, (6) technology-assisted professional services, (7) professional evaluations, (8) financial arrangements (9) advertising. While these ethics are similar to the ethical standards of other professions, unique issues are involved in the practice of family therapy. Noteworthy in the most recent standards are a section concerning the ethical uses of technology assisted professional services. As the use of technology and social media becomes more accessible to families, professionals will be drawn further into the digital world with their professional practices. It is becoming increasingly important for family therapists to understand the digital context that they are practicing in. Issues like jurisdiction are more complex in the digital world than in the physical world. For example with my North Carolina license am I able to work sitting at my computer with a client who is in California sitting at their computer and be with in the jusrtiction of that license. Am I practicing in California, North Carolina or would you see my practice as occurring in both locations simultaneously?

Since family therapy treats the family system as a whole, there can be instances where what is good for the family may not be good for the individual. In fact, Hare-Mustin (1980) wrote an article titled "Family Therapy May Be Dangerous to Your Health." One way out of this difficulty is to focus on negotiating with members of the family a clear therapeutic contract. A therapeutic contract is an agreement regarding what the focus and desired outcome of the therapy will be. In negotiation, therapists must be able to take a stance that is based on their personal and professional values. If the therapist does not clearly state these values and stand by them, the therapy will lack integrity. For example, a client was depressed over the stress of concealing his affair from his wife, whom he reported he still loved. The therapist informed the client that he did not think depression could be treated in someone having an affair. The therapist suggested they spend a number of sessions exploring whether he would end the affair or end his marriage. This was a contract both parties could agree to, and a treatment plan was developed to fulfill the contract.

A client's right to understand and choose not to participate in services has become a critical issue in all helping professions. Marriage and family therapy is no exception, and part of every therapy situation involves explaining to clients what they should expect from treatment. Part of the way this is accomplished is by presenting each client with a copy of an informed consent form (see Figure 15.1). The therapist and client discuss the informed consent during the first session, and after the client signs the forms, he or she is given a copy for future reference.

Confidentiality

In addition to following ethical guidelines, family therapists protect the public by maintaining confidentiality. Confidentiality serves to ensure the privacy of clients and to allow them to be comfortable in disclosing information that they would not disclose in other settings. However, to ensure the protection of the public at large, there are specific instances where a therapist would have to break confidence. These include (1) when the therapist is ordered to do so by a court, (2) when mandated by law in cases of child abuse or elder abuse (3), when clients present as a danger to themselves or others, and (4) when the client has provided written permission to make disclosures. Permission to make disclosures may be granted by the client for a variety of reasons, such as assigning insurance benefits and coordination of care with other professionals.

| FIGURE 15.1 | Sample Informed Consent Form |

Professional Disclosure Statement
Consent for treatment
Jon L. Winek, Ph.D.
895 State Farm Rd.
Suite 103
Boone NC 28607
(828) 260-1864

Qualifications:

Dr. Winek holds a master's degrees in both Sociology and Marriage and Family Therapy (1990), along with a doctorate in Sociology (1992), from the University of Southern California. He has been providing clinical services since 1986. A copy of his vita outlining his experiences is available upon request. Dr. Winek is currently licensed as a Marriage and Family Therapist (#605) and a Licensed Professional Counselor (#3515).

Consent to treat:

I freely give my consent to be treated by Dr. Winek. I understand these services may include and are not limited to: assessment, treatment planning, psychotherapy, referral, and release of information as designated by law or permission and follow up as needed.
I understand that I may deal with emotional issues, which may, at times, lead to unanticipated stress, as well as improvement. I understand that there are no warranties or guarantees of a particular outcome given or implied.

Dr. Winek treats families, couples, and individuals from a systemic perspective. His work is informed by both empirical studies and theoretical models. He assists clients with a variety of emotional, personal, and relations problems.

Dr. Winek does not discriminate or refuse professional services to anyone on the basis of race, gender, religion, national origin, sexual orientation or identity. If you need care at a greater level than can be provided in an outpatient practice, Dr. Winek will make a referral for appropriate care.
In case of an emergency please call 911 or go to an emergency room. If you need to talk with Dr. Winek between sessions call 828 260-1864. If he is not available, leave a message and he will return your call when he is available.

Confidentiality:

Relationships are built on respect, trust and honesty. Conversations with Dr. Winek will be confidential, except in two instances where there is a legal mandate to report. These situations are 1) If you express intent to harm yourself or someone else, and 2) If a child or elderly person has been abused or neglected. In addition, a court might order Dr. Winek to testify about your therapy. Dr. Winek will make every effort to inform you regarding any issue pertinent to the confidentiality of our relationship. Of course, Dr. Winek will release your information to which

| FIGURE 15.1 | **Sample Informed Consent Form** |

you consent by signing a "consent to release information" form.

As part of his work with you, Dr. Winek will enter into your records a diagnosis of your condition. Be aware that this will remain part of your record. If you choose to release your information to your insurance company it will likely become part of your medical record.

Dr. Winek has a personal Facebook page and a professional LinkedIn page. In order to protect your confidentially, he cannot respond to friend or contact requests over social media. Please do not contact him by email because that is not a confidential means of communication. If you contact him via email he will assume you are comfortable releasing the information you put in the email. Also, it should be noted that this is not an effective way to make or cancel appointments, because it is not checked as frequently as his voicemail.

Financial Arrangements:

Dr. Winek's fee is $____ for a 50 minute session. Payment with cash or check is expected at the time service is rendered unless prior arrangements have been made. He does not accept credit or debit cards. There is a $25 fee for returned checks. He does not bill insurance directly, but clients will be given a two-part receipt with diagnostic and procedure codes that they can submit to their insurance company. Dr. Winek reserves the right to bill for damages to office facilities caused by willful acts on the part of clients or their minor children.

Complaint Procedures:

If you are dissatisfied with any aspect of your treatment, please discuss it with Dr. Winek. If you cannot resolve the problem and would like to file a complaint against him, do so with the organization listed below. Also, should you feel he is in violation of any of the ethics listed in the code of ethics, take your concerns to the organization listed below. Dr. Winek abides by the ACA & AAMFT Codes of Ethics.

I have read, understand and received a copy of the above disclosed statement and consent to
     treat.

_____ _____   _____ _____
Client's Signature   Date   Parent/Guardian Signature   Date

_____ _____   _____ _____
  _____

Parent/Guardian Signature Date   Witness Signature   Date

_____ _____   _____ _____
  _____

In family therapy, issues of confidentiality are much more complex than they are in individual therapy or counseling. In many ways this situation is parallel to issues of confidentiality that arise in group therapy. Therapists can assure clients that they will not disclose what goes on in the session. However, family members are free to discuss what they want with whomever they want outside the therapy setting. Clients are not bound by the same ethical standards as family therapists. Therefore, it is best practice to discuss with the family what they are comfortable discussing with others outside the session and to help them reach a decision regarding what is reasonable.

A related issue, and potential pitfall, is the handling of secrets in family therapy. If a therapist sees only whole families, this is not an issue, but in reality, most practitioners see a variety of subsystems over the course of treatment. For example, if you meet with a teen and agree to keep what he says confidential and he discloses drug usage, it would be difficult not to disclose this information to his parents in a later session. In practice, even if therapists do not agree not to disclose information to other parts of the family system, clients still make significant disclosures. So, in the above example, the therapist would be in a position to help the teen talk with his parents about his drug usage in a productive way. This is also a significant issue in marital therapy where one member of the couple discloses a secret. It is important that family therapists have policies on disclosure that is consistent with the theoretical orientation of the treatment.

A Stance Against Violence and Abuse in Relationships

The treatment of violence and abuse that occurs in significant relationships is an issue that has not come to the forefront of marriage and family therapy until very recently. It was not until feminism was well enough established in the field that the focus could shift to issues as dark as violence and abuse in relationships.

Like the feminist movement, the antiviolence movement seemed to arrive suddenly. In 1991, Avis, Bograd & Kaufman presented a Plenary session titled "Abuse and Violence: The Dark Side of the Family," at the annual meeting of the American Family Therapy Association. It was later published in a special section of the *Journal of Marital and Family Therapy* (Avis, 1992; Bograd, 1992; Kaufman, 1992). This session propelled the profession to look at basic assumptions of therapy and to consider the role of therapy as a means of social control.

Sexual abuse is a common occurrence in North America. Between 18% and 44% of women report being sexually victimized during their lives (Casey & Nurivs, 2006; Russell & Bolen, 2000; Tjaden & Thoennes, 1998). Abuse of women also occurs with alarming frequency in former intimate relationships. Russell (1982) found that, in a nonclinical sample, 14% of women reported being raped by their ex-husbands.

It is clear that there is a strong association among violence, abuse, and gender. By far, the vast majority of violence is perpetrated by men. In North America, 95% of incest (Finkelhor, 1986; Rogers, 1990) and 95% of marital violence (Brown, 1987; Dobash & Dobash, 1979) is perpetrated by men. Every year in the United States, one out of six women is abused by a man she lives with (Avis, 1992). In their review of relationship violence, Simpson, Doss, Wheeler, and Christensen (2007) state that relationship aggression exists in 25% to 75% of distressed couples. Dutton (1988) found that violence occurs in 1 of 14 marriages, and on average, 35 incidents of violence occur before it is reported. Avis (1992) summarizes these and other statistics:

> These data lead us to the unavoidable conclusion that male violence and abuse directed against women and children in families is extremely common in Canadian and American families and that the consequences are highly destructive for individuals, families, and our collective well-being as societies. (p. 228)

Not only is violence an issue directly involving the victim of violence, but the whole family and the children's future family may be victims as well. A male child who watches a parent being abused is more strongly associated with being a future perpetrator of interpersonal violence than a victim is (Graham-Bermann, 1998). Girls who witness abuse have increased tolerance for being abused themselves in future relationships (Edleson, 1999). Likewise, mothers who are abused themselves are more likely to be abusive to their own children (Appel & Holden, 1998; Bancroft & Silverman, 2002). Thus we see that the total damage of violence in families is greater than the sum of its parts and the integrational transmission process can move it into multiple generations.

Treating Family Violence

Despite our desire for families to be safe havens for members the fact remains that families can be places where violence and abuse occur. The current trend is away from referring to violence in a relationship as domestic violence to calling it Intimate Partner Violence IPV. Family therapists who have taken an antiviolence position criticize the views of individual psychology, cycle-of-violence theories, and cybernetics systems thinking. In psychodynamic explanations, abuse is reduced to acts taken out of context and violence reinterpreted as "an ineffective attempt to meet ordinary human needs" (Herman, 1990, p.182). Writers from this perspective call attention to the abuser's psychological need for "recognition, acceptance, validation, affiliation, mastery, and control" (Groth, Hobson, & Gary, 1982, p. 137). This minimizes the impact on victims and increases the need to accept responsibility.

Cycle-of-violence theories view perpetrators as responding to violence acted upon them as a child. This theoretical model postulates an intergenerational effect of the violent lifestyle. However, the data do not bear out such a view. Of all the women who are victims, only a small minority are recruited into the cycle of violence. This theory cannot explain the "virtual male monopoly" on sexually violent behavior (Herman, 1990, p. 181). In addition, this perspective often calls for the relationship in which the violence occurs to be terminated. This happens when the victim is counseled in a shelter and the perpetrator is sent off to work on anger management issues. However, this approach often derails when, despite therapeutic recommendations, the couple continues the relationship.

Systems theories do not fare better in their treatment of violence. The act of abuse can be easily lost in the idea of recursion. The homeostatic view of equal responsibility can place blame on the victim by calling attention to the role of the victim in the violence. Perhaps Kaufman (1992) best summarizes this critique:

Constructivists and systems theorists who are enamored of speaking of the recursive sequences and the arbitrariness of punctuation in relationships, of cybernetic and Heisenbergian and other new-physics explanatory systems, should know this violence follows the old Newtonian physics of mass, velocity, momentum and inertia—as in a fist hitting a face breaking bones. (p. 236)

This critique is similar to that of feminist family therapists and is applied to systems theory in general.

As we take a deep look at domestic violence issues, we see that we must consider more complex conceptualizations of the issues. Greene and Bogo (2002) discuss the need for different approaches to treating intimate violence based on the style of violence. These types are (1) violence involving power and control by one (usually the male) partner, and (2) violence involving mutual conflict between partners. To make this clinical picture more complex, a study by Blasko, Winek, and Bieschke (2007) showed that marriage and family therapists' assessment of domestic violence situations varied as a function of the sexual orientation of the clients. In this research, therapists were asked to identify domestic violence in scenarios that were identical except for the sexual orientation of the couple. In the heterosexual scenario, therapists perceived the man as perpetrator, while in the same-sex scenarios, both partners were perceived to be both victim and perpetrator.

Safety is the key issue in treating family violence. The best approach is to assess violence perpetrated against children and in intimate relationships at intake. By asking about violence on intake forms, clients are alerted to your antiviolence stance. It may not present at first, but over time clients may feel comfortable discussing their concerns about violence. When faced with violence, it is important to emphasize both the safety of the victim and the responsibility of the perpetrator. Most states mandate child abuse reporting and provide penalties for professionals who fail to report, as well as protection under the law for those who make good-faith reports. When making a report, it is often useful to include the family in the process. If the therapist supports the perpetrator in self-reporting, making the report can become part of his or her healing process.

While we recognize the risks and controversies in treating domestic violence conjointly, we find that there is some benefit to this approach when it can be done safely. Rosen, Matheson, Stith, McCollum, and Locke (2003) discuss the positive aspects of working with both partners when using the common technique of time-outs for de-escalation. When both parties are present and when the time-out technique is taught, the couple will have a better chance of using the technique appropriately and effectively. In a recent follow up study Stith, McCollum, Amanor-Boadu & Smith (2012) find "available outcome research have demonstrated that for carefully screened couples who choose to stay together, systemic interventions decrease incidences of IPV and decreases the risk factors for IPV with no increases in risk" p.220.

Now that family therapists are aware of issues of abuse, there have been specific recommendations on how to address the issue. First, there is a need for recognition of the problem. Second, Avis (1992) reminds us:

We must recognize and address power dynamics in family relationships and avoid conceptualizations which view violence and abuse as systems dysfunctions rather than as abusive acts committed by one individual against another, or which in any way hold women and children responsible for the behavior of abusive men. (p. 230)

This relationship perspective allows for systemic treatment of domestic violence. Avis (1992) proposes three specific guidelines for the effective treatment of violence in families. First, abusive and controlling men must be seen as responsible for their violent, coercive, and abusive behavior and must be held accountable for it. The therapist must not minimize the acts of violence and should not apply a psychological or systemic theory that lets the perpetrator escape responsibility for his or her actions. Second, the primary focus of any therapeutic efforts must be on changing the violent behavior itself. Treatment should focus on details of the behavior's impact on others, and on the belief system that supports it. The focus when working with violence is always the removal of violence and the safety of the victims. The therapist must establish the goal of safety prior to addressing any personal or relational issues. Third, therapists should work in conjunction with the police and courts to use legal sanctions and mandated treatment. Because violence is such a difficult problem to overcome, the therapist must be willing to use as much leverage as possible to stop the violence. In some cases, the power of public institutions can be successfully used to force the termination of violence.

Stith, Rosen, and McCollum (2003) revived the literature on couple treatment of spousal abuse and drew some important conclusions. They concluded that there is some sparse empirical support for couple treatment for spousal abuse being at least as effective as traditional treatment, while posing no greater risk for injury to the woman. In addition, they find four key ingredients in effective treatment. These are as follows:

1. Clients are carefully screened into the program. Clients who have seriously injured their partner are excluded. Both clients (in separate interviews) must report that they want to participate in couple treatment and that they are not afraid to express their concerns to their partners.
2. The primary focus of treatment is on eliminating all forms of partner abuse (physical, emotional, verbal), not on saving marriages.
3. Most programs emphasize taking responsibility for one's own violence and include a skill building component including teaching such skills as recognizing when anger is escalating, de-escalating, and taking time outs.
4. Effectiveness in all the successful programs reviewed here is measured by reduction or elimination of violence. (p. 422)

Family violence remains a critical issue in working with family and for many family therapists working actively to address and prevent acts of violence is an important issue. Form many a pro safety stance is an ethical position. Collaboration with other systems such as protective services, attorneys, law enforcement, shelters, and other systems when appropriate and as need seems to be a wise course of action. Because of the risk and complexity of such case seeking consultation and supervision for other experienced therapist is a prudent course of action.

Training Processes

Training processes have to do with the development of skills necessary for practicing family therapy. First, we will discuss issues in accreditation of training programs in marriage and family therapy. Then, we will shift into how the supervision process impacts the training process in training the next generation of marriage and family therapists. Next, we discuss the development of core competencies that have been identified as being associated with competent practice. Finally, we look at issues of stress and management of stress in the training of marriage and family therapists.

The Commission on Accreditation for Marriage and Family Therapy Education

As discussed above, training in marriage and family therapy is accredited by the COAMFTE of AAMFT and is recognized by the Council for Higher Education. The commission issues standards of accreditation that guide accredited programs in providing quality education in marriage and family therapy. The standards are in their 12th edition and accredit program on the Masters, Doctorate and Post Degree Training level. To receive initial accreditation, programs undergo an extensive self-study and site visit by the commission. When the program demonstrates that it meets COAMFTE's standards, it is granted accreditation.

Of course, accredited marriage and family therapy programs are not the only places to get quality education in family therapy. Many other disciplines offer training and coursework in MFT. Most comprehensive training programs in marriage and family therapy are broken into two integrated steps. First, students are exposed to systems theory and theories of marriage and family therapy in the classroom setting. Second, interns engage in the supervised practice of marriage and family therapy.

Approved Supervision

The applied clinical portion of the training comes under the supervision of a master family therapist. Here AAMFT has taken a leadership role and established an advanced credential in supervision. The approved supervision designation is granted to therapists who have completed comprehensive training in supervision. This includes completion of a course in supervision, approval of a philosophy of training paper, and completion of a two-year clinical portion where the therapist's supervision is supervised by a supervisor mentor. Some states require that supervision of licensed marriage and family therapists be conducted by AAMFT-approved supervisors.

In supervision, case materials can be presented in a variety of ways. There are times when each modality of supervision is the preferred form of supervision. Let us look at each of these modalities and consider their strengths and weaknesses.

Co-therapy is the form of supervision often preferred by symbolic-experiential therapists. This allows the supervisor to remain in immediate proximity to both the supervisee and the client. The supervisor speaks with the supervisee about the case in front of the family. During these discussions, the supervisor and supervisee seek to become peers in a manner similar to that of good parents seeking to become peers with their children.

Another form of live supervision has the supervisor observing from behind a one-way mirror. Supervisors can provide feedback during the session using a variety of methods. They can talk to the therapist through an earphone, they can call in via telephone, and at designated times the supervisee can leave the treatment to conference with the supervisor. It is in this arrangement that supervisors often work with the treating therapist and client. This style of supervision was sometimes used during the development of the MRI, strategic, structural, Milan Systemic, and more recently, the brief family therapy theories, which changed the focus of therapy from content to process. This type of supervision, like co-therapy supervision, has the advantage of being conducted in real time.

Another mode of supervision involves the supervisor's playing back video or audio recordings of the client working. This modality allows the supervisor access to raw data on how the supervisee is working with clients. In addition, the supervisor can supervise via written or verbal reposts by the supervisee. In these modes of supervision, since the supervision is occurring after the fact, there is more time for the therapist to be invited to reflect on issues of theory and self of the therapist.

Since family therapy is a contextual approach, it is appropriate for supervision to take context into account. It is essential that supervisors help supervisees consider issues of where they practice. All too often novice therapists try to practice family therapy in a mental health system that does not accurately understand systems thinking and practice, and, as a result, the mental health system is not supportive of the MFT intern. In settings where supervision is provided on site, this issue is somewhat muted. However, often the supervision occurs off site and the context of supervision remains a salient issue. Consideration of context includes determining which mode of supervision might best promote professional development in the supervisee.

If we take a systems view of practice, we see that therapists need to be deliberate in their approach to gaining freedom to practice in a manner that seems to fit them best. For example, when working in an institution where there are unethical practices, therapists are responsible for their own ethical practices. How the institution is run is not an acceptable excuse for unethical practice. We can conclude that interventions are needed for the context of the therapist as well as for therapists' clients.

Core Competencies

In early 2003, AAMFT appointed a task force and charged them to develop a list of core competencies. Core competencies are a list of 128 basic skills a provider eligible for independent practice should possess (Nelson et al., 2007). After undergoing several revisions, with input from a wide variety of stakeholders, the version currently in effect is "D" (see Appendix B). This is part of a wider trend to assess the training and education of professionals. Miller, Todahl & Platt (2010) provide an analysis of the broader context in which marriage and family therapy is practiced, including both social forces and trends in related fields. Nelson and Graves (2011) conducted the single outcome of supervisors n = 135 assessing the training of their supervisees. For each of the competencies, they asked the supervisor these two questions: 1. "How important is it to your supervisory role that trainees master this competency before graduation?" and 2. "To what level has the average trainee mastered this competency upon graduation from her or his training program?" (Nelson & Graves, 2011, p. 432). They found that overall the mean of the supervisor scores for actual competency were below the mean of the desired scores. The authors concluded that the gap in what is expected and what graduates can do and what they should is a lag in training. Others including this author see this as the result of overly rigorous competencies where were not adequately empirically validated. In reading we see that the vast majority are general mental health skills with few addressing skills unique to working with couples and families. Perhaps the next version will have few competencies in general with more focusing on the additional skills family therapists bring to their work with couples and families.

MFT core competencies are divided into six domains, which are each further divided into five subdomains. The first four domains (admission to treatment, clinical assessment and diagnosis, treatment planning and case management, and therapeutic interventions) focus on the process of therapy itself, and the last two domains (legal issues, ethics, and standards and research and program evaluation) focus on the mental health care delivery processes. The five subdomains, listed below, focus on the family therapist's understanding and actions:

1. Conceptual skills focus on the family therapist's ability to understand systems thinking, family therapy models, and models of change.
2. Perceptual skills focus on the family therapist's ability to discern what is happening in the client system.
3. Executive skills focus on the family therapist's skill set in conducting the interview and delivering effective interventions.
4. Evaluative skills focus on interpreting feedback for the client system to assess therapeutic process.
5. Professional skills focus on the marriage and family therapist's development and professional identity. (Nelson et al., 2007)

Stress in Training

Lambert-Shute (2000) researched how stress affected graduate students who were training to become marriage and family therapists. She developed a normative model of the stress in two COAMFTE-accredited MFT master's programs. This model was developed by surveying all students in these training programs with both quantitative and qualitative questions.

The Lambert-Shute survey of 50 students produced some interesting results. According to Lambert-Shute (2000), "The majority (58%) fell into the 'Stress isn't a problem in your life' and 38% fell into the 'This is a moderate range of stress for a busy professional person'" (p. 64). Furthermore, Lambert-Shute identified several factors that were universally stressful: starting training, transitions, beginning internship, deadlines, classes, evaluation/feedback, trouble with professors, meeting new people, and personal issues. Additionally, she identified factors that increased and decreased stress. Factors that increased stress included the unknown, feelings of being overwhelmed, and fear of failure, while factors that reduced stress were such things as finishing assignments and transitions, breaks, and feelings of confidence. This study implies that it is important for supervisors and clinical faculty to monitor the level of stress in their supervisees and students. This will help to prevent burnout and increase students' ability to become competent marriage and family therapists.

Integrative Processes

The *integrative process* refers to the combining of two or more theories of family therapy, resulting in a new hybrid theory. As discussed in Chapter 2, this process has become common in family therapy. I will now discuss this process in more detail, and will provide some guidelines for integrating theories of family therapy. We will then discuss an integrative theory in detail and provide a case example of therapy conducted from an integrative theoretical orientation.

In Chapter 2, we briefly discussed the revolution that occurred in family therapy and led Lebow (1997) to declare that we have entered an 'era of integration in family therapy.' *Integration* refers to the process of blending a variety of theories together to develop a hybrid theory. It moves beyond mere eclectic practice. In eclectic practice, the practitioner freely borrows interventions from a variety of approaches without concern for theoretical issues. Furthermore, the concept of integration can be distinguished from blending techniques from different theories. As Lebow (1997) states, "bringing one distinctive intervention into an approach in which that concept is not employed (for example, genograms into strategic therapy) is more appropriately labeled 'assimilation'" (p. 4).

Integration is a much deeper process that involves a creation of a new theory. As Lebow (1997) states, "integration implies a melding not only at levels of strategy and intervention, but also some effort to construct a theory that transcends the approaches itself" (p. 4). If we look at the integration process from a second-order perspective, we see that in reality each working therapist has an integrative theory. The only therapists practicing from a completely homogenous approach are the originators of specific approaches. However, any unique, original theory is still evolving and subject to influence from other positions.

Not all voices are uniformly in favor of the call for integration. Simon (2003) makes an interesting case for theoretical purism in his text, *Beyond Technique in Family Therapy: Finding Your Therapeutic Voice*. In the preface, he argues that integrative and eclectic approaches threaten the diversity of theories in family therapy. In this book he provides a deep philosophical exploration of the bases and assumptions of theoretical approaches. I would agree that eclecticism poses a threat to the diversity of therapy and, without there being a theory and strategy of change associated with the interventions used in therapy, threatens to reduce therapy to pure technique. However, if integration is accomplished on a deep theoretical level, a level of analysis that Simon (2003) does so well, we can argue that a well-developed integration becomes a new theory in its own right and adds to the overall theoretical diversity.

We see that in choosing a theoretical orientation, we should not choose on the basis of a pure model versus an integrative model. Rather, the decision should be based on the model's fit with the self of the therapist. This means that the model selected, whether a pure model or an integrative approach, should fit the personality and thinking of the therapist. The assumptions that underlie the model should fit the therapist's assumptions of the world.

Criteria for Integration

If we adopt an integrative approach to therapy, we need to see that there is a good fit between the therapist's personal epistemology, or worldview, and the underlying assumptions of the integrative theory. It is also useful to develop some criteria for evaluating the integrative model. Having criteria will push integrative therapists to think deeply about their model and move past the level of superficial eclecticism.

In his analysis of what he calls the 'integrative revolution in couple and family therapy', Lebow (1997) describes three levels of content to consider when discussing an integrative model: theory, strategy, and intervention. While these levels overlap somewhat, seeing them as distinct is useful in facilitating the process of integration. Adopting these levels and using them as basic criteria gives us a method to evaluate the level of integration of a therapy. We can conclude that a theory is fully integrated if it blends two or more distinctive approaches on the levels of theory, strategy, and intervention. Let us consider these levels more closely.

Theoretical Integration

The deepest level of integration is at the theoretical level. At this level, a successful integration produces a new theory of family functioning and of how change occurs within the functioning of the family. If we consider a pure model at the theoretical level, we see that it is built on a set of assumptions that place the theory within a broader philosophical theoretical tradition. As Lebow (1997) states, "the theoretical foundation for an integration should include a description of each of the specific concepts involved and a consideration of how these ideas fit together" (p. 6). When integrating theories, the new theory must take the assumptions of the old theories and blend them together to produce a new synthesis.

In this task, we can see that the more closely related the underlying philosophical traditions of each theory integrated, the simpler the task. Some theories that are closely related, such as the Mental Research Institute model and strategic family therapy, have a similar set of assumptions and thus may be more easily integrated. However, some theories may have underlying assumptions that make integration of the theories difficult and in some instances even impossible. For example, Bowenian theory's emphasis on differentiation might appear to be incompatible with structural family therapy's emphasis on the function of structures in producing behaviors in family members. If they stand alone, they cannot be integrated. However, there is the possibility that with the development of new, mediating theoretical concepts, these theories can be integrated in the future.

We can also argue that at this level it is best to pay attention to issues of fit with the person of the therapist. If a therapist's personal worldview fits the theoretical model or integrated model, the therapist is able to be more fluid in his or her approach and interactions with clients. If there is not a good fit, the therapist is awkward and becomes less fluid in interacting. For example, if a therapist who believes that unconscious forces determine behavior adopts a structural or a solution-focused brief theoretical model for integration, the therapist will be in a bind. This integration makes it hard or even impossible for the therapist to be genuine with clients. The therapist will be trying to operate from a theoretical position outside his or her belief system. It is easier to adopt a new theory of change than it is to accept a new worldview.

Video Call Out 15.1: Strategic Medical Family Therapy

Before she was a Marriage and Family Therapist, Pamela Richey was a Registered Nurse. In her family therapy practice she works with families who have issues with fertility. Her work represents an integrative approach that is integrated deeply on all three levels. Her knowledge of medicine assists her in her work with these couples. At one point in the video she utilizes her medical knowledge to simply dismiss one of the couple's necrotic fears. Her confidence in assessing a zero risk situation for the couple is part of her strategy to help the couple have realistic expectations as they go through the infertility treatment process.

Strategic Integration

The next level to consider when integrating theories is the strategic level. Implicit in each theory is a concern for strategies for helping clients change their life situations. The integrative therapist must be careful to integrate only theories that are consistent in their strategies for producing change. Theories such as the structural and solution-focused brief models, which require the therapist to take a similar proactive stance, blend well. However, it would be difficult to integrate an approach such as Bowenian family therapy, with its emphasis on reducing anxiety during the interview, with the experiential approach, which depends on emotionally charged sessions.

At this level, we must also consider issues of the self of the therapist. Do the theories fit with the way the therapist tends to think? If not, the therapist might have to change his or her thinking. But this would require a second-order change, and, as we learned earlier, these are rather rare. It is also important that the therapist be comfortable working with the interview style implied in the strategy. If the blended strategy calls for the therapist to be directive, but the therapist has a passive, contemplative personality, this theory will be difficult to implement.

Intervention Integration

The final level of integration concerns the degree to which the interventions of the theories being integrated are compatible. Of the three levels, this is the most superficial, and thus most eclectic approaches are developed at this level. To be fully integrated, the theory must not only combine a series of interventions, but it also must include a strategy for change as well as a theoretical description of the relevant theoretical matter. It is important to link the choice of intervention to the hybrid strategy and theory.

The self of the therapist must again be considered at this level. The therapist must be comfortable engaging in the interventions included in the integration. If the therapist is unable to deliver an intervention, the approach will not have much utility no matter how well integrated the theory and strategy are. For, example a therapist might integrate a strategic behavioral approach that is robust on both the theoretical and strategic levels, and yet be unable to deliver a directive or behavioral prescription to the client family.

Video Call Out 15.2: Structural/Strategic Family Therapy

In the structural/strategic video we see that Dr. Edwards has also integrated these theorietical approach on the theoretical, strategic and intervention level. His work with substance abusing families is grounded in the strategic premise that the therapist is responsible for producing change which is integrated with the structural view that dysfunctional family structure maintains problems.

An Example: Structural, Strategic & Experiential Family Therapy Integration

To illustrate the process of integrating theories, I will now provide a description of the integration of three core theories of family therapy as developed by a practicing marriage and family therapist. This therapist has integrated structural family therapy (Chapter 9), strategic family therapy (Chapter 10), and symbolic-experiential family therapy (Chapter 7), in her theoretical model. The first two theories have a history of being integrated, going back to the founders of each approach. Minuchin and Haley worked together at the Philadelphia Child Guidance Center for nine years, where they influenced the development of each other's theories. Experiential theory is integrated into this hybrid model on multiple levels. Let us look at these three theories and attempt to integrate them on the theoretical, strategic, and intervention levels.

The first and deepest level of integration to consider is the theoretical level. Structural, strategic, and symbolic-experiential family therapies are cybernetics-based models. They look at how homeostasis is maintained in the system. Structural family therapy tends to look at how dysfunctional structure maintains the problem, and strategic family therapy tends to look how a client's paradoxical dilemma maintains a problem. Symbolic-experiential family therapy focuses on using spontaneity to disturb the homeostasis of the family system.

An important component of the experiential family therapy model that fits well with our therapist's personality is the concept of intensity. Experiential family therapy sees times of emotional crisis as opportunities for change. While the therapist making the integration in our example is calm and able to think clearly during times of emotional crisis in the family she is treating, she is not so comfortable with or good at building intensity. However, our therapist works with families of adolescents who have been referred by the courts and schools. Thus, she finds that intensity tends to build on its own in her practice. In addition, the therapist sees a common pattern where parents become overly responsible for their child's emotional well-being. This results in children who are emotionally unbalanced.

Other theoretical positions around which these theories can be integrated include the role of the therapist and the use of directives. In each of the three theories, the therapist takes the expert leadership position. This is done through the process of joining with the family. Joining, a term that originated in structural family therapy but has been assimilated into most family therapy approaches, describes how the therapist takes a position within the family. As a result, our hybrid model sees therapy as starting with the therapist's joining with the family and developing a therapy system, which is the family plus the therapist. Our therapist has also taken the notion of spontaneity from experiential family therapy. She believes that if she is joined with her clients on a deep level, her unconscious mind will think of creative ideas to suggest to them.

Structural family therapy pays particular attention to issues of boundaries and hierarchy, and strategic family therapy pays close attention to issues of the family life cycle. Our hybrid theory can integrate these two ideas by focusing on how families have difficulty with boundaries during the times of stress produced by transition into the next stage of development. In particular, our hybrid model focuses on how parents of teens respond to their teen's request for increased autonomy.

Our hybrid model is also integrated on the strategic level. At their core, both structural and strategic family therapy seek to interrupt dysfunctional patterns of interaction. Structural family therapy focuses on dysfunctional structures and makes deliberate moves to alter the dysfunctional structure. Strategic family therapy gives the therapist responsibility for altering patterns of problematic interaction. These two ideas can be combined to develop a hybrid theory that gives the therapist direct responsibility for changing the structures and patterns of interaction that are arresting the family's normal development.

Symbolic-experiential family therapy tends to use creativity to perturb the family's homeostasis. Our therapist has adopted the strategy of building a strong therapeutic relationship with the client until there is a crisis. When a crisis occurs, the therapist works with the parents on establishing appropriate boundaries and a more functional parental subsystem.

We are also able to integrate these theories in terms of the time period targeted by the theories' interventions. Structural and symbolic-experiential family therapy tend to target change in the here and now of the therapy room. They also place a secondary focus on the near future by giving the client things to try at home. Strategic family therapy focuses on the near future with ordeals and prescriptions and includes a secondary focus on change in the room. Our hybrid model combines these approaches, focusing on effecting change in the here and now of the therapy room, as well as in the near future through the use of directives and prescriptions.

On the level of intervention, there are a variety of techniques common to both the structural and strategic models. First, and most obvious, both approaches are directive. Therapists from these approaches feel free to make direct suggestions regarding actions family members should take. Second, the therapist takes an "I" position in giving directives. For example, the therapist might say, "Between sessions, I would like you to change..." Thus, the hybrid model involves giving direct instructions to the family.

In our hybrid model, interventions address boundary issues that are identified. Each specific intervention involves helping the family establish a functional hierarchy in the parental subsystem by assisting them in setting appropriate boundaries. This is accomplished by giving the parents directives. In addition, the parents are encouraged to set appropriate boundaries by selecting appropriate levels of autonomy for their teen.

Enactment, which originated in structural family therapy, allows the therapist to observe the client family's social interaction in the here and now and gives an opportunity to alter the structure directly. Our therapist has observed that enactments often create the intensity necessary to disturb the dysfunctional homeostasis. She is good at allowing her enactments to heat up enough emotionally to motivate clients to change.

Our therapist has adopted one final intervention from symbolic-experiential family therapy, which is a willingness to share with clients her unconscious process. When she has a thought or idea during the session, she shares it with the family to provoke change.

The Case of Runaway Nicole

To illustrate the process of practicing with an integrated model, let us look at a case treated by the therapist who developed the integrated theory described above. Since her theory has been integrated on all three levels and fits well with her personality, she is effective in her approach. She also is clear in her thinking about how to approach her clients and is able to respond to them in ways that they perceive as professional and caring. In describing this case, I have highlighted the interventions.

The identified client in this case is a 15-year-old girl, Nicole Hoffman, who has been referred by the courts. Nicole was arrested when she ran away from home after she and her mother, Mrs. Hoffmann, had gotten into an argument. As a result, she took her mother's car and drove to another state to visit a favorite cousin. When her aunt discovered Nicole and her daughter smoking pot, she called the authorities. Social services became involved and Nicole was charged. When the local district attorney found that Nicole had taken her mother's car out of state and that Mrs. Hoffmann did not report it, he threatened to charge her as well. At this point, Nicole was referred for treatment.

Nicole's biological father abandoned her when she was a baby, and neither she nor her mother has any idea where he is. She was adopted by her stepfather when she was five years old. Nicole has no siblings, and Mrs. Hoffmann reports that Nicole has had difficulty with anger since she was about 10. She also reports that Nicole has run away five times in the past four weeks. The therapist sets up a two-hour session the next day, and Mrs. Hoffmann agrees to attend with her husband and her daughter.

As the clients arrive, the therapist welcomes them and seeks to establish a positive therapeutic relationship. She does this by asking the parents what they are proud of in their lives and in their daughter's life. They tell how they were able to spend quality time together and travel a good bit when Nicole was younger. They talk about how Nicole is a good student and is involved in sports. After about 20 minutes of focusing on the family's strengths, the therapist turns to the parents and asks them, "What brings you to therapy today?" This questions set up an enactment where the therapist gets the parental subsystem to discuss their problem with Nicole.

Mrs. Hoffmann starts to tell about Nicole's recent running away and her arrest for smoking pot. Nicole becomes very quiet at this point and has a difficult time making eye contact. The therapist asks Mrs. Hoffmann how long Nicole has been smoking pot, and Mrs. Hoffmann states that, as far as she knows, that was the first time. Mr. Hoffmann disagrees with his wife and states that he has suspected it for some time now.

Nicole interrupts, stating that this is none of anyone's business and that she smoked pot only one time. Setting a boundary, the therapist asks Nicole to let her parents express their concerns without interruption. The therapist gently states, "Once I hear from your parents, I would like to hear your side of the story." Nicole's anger escalates as she tells her parents that she is not a drug addict. Gesturing toward the therapist, she states, "I knew she would blame this all on the drugs. It's their fault I ran away." The therapist calmly asks Nicole to lower her voice. After issuing a brief stream of profanity, Nicole storms out of the therapist's office.

After Nicole leaves, her parents start to get up, and the therapist gives a directive in the form of recommending that they finish the interview. Noticing how anxious the parents look, the therapist asks what they've done in the past when Nicole has acted like this. They explain that they go after her and try to calm her down so she doesn't run away. The therapist expresses concern that this makes them responsible for Nicole's feelings. She asks, "If you always rescue her, how will she learn to be responsible for her own feelings?" This provides information to the parents about emotional responsibility. The parents state that they've never thought about it that way. Mrs. Hoffmann is concerned that Nicole will run away again, and the therapist states that she shares that concern. However, the therapist points out, they can't stop her, especially if she is resourceful enough to get out of state. The therapist goes on to state that she is interested in helping Nicole find a way to stay and address her problems. She says that in her experience, when parents refrain from following teens who walk out of session, the teen returns.

To gain credibility with the parents, the therapist states that if Nicole returns, she will end the session for the day and have them come back in two days. During these two days, if Nicole runs away again, they will call the police and report her missing. Reluctantly the parents agree.

The therapist continues with the session, addressing with the parents issues in setting more appropriate boundaries. Shortly, Nicole returns, and she is in a much calmer mood. The therapist welcomes her back and compliments her on pulling herself together. The therapist models good boundaries and limits for the family. She states to Nicole that clients are allowed to leave the session if they are overwhelmed. She goes on to explain that while she was gone she and her parents worked on improving their parenting of her. The parents confirm that they worked on parenting issues while Nicole was gone. However, the therapist notes that the session is over and lets Nicole know that the family is returning in two days.

In this single session, we see how well integrated the theoretical model is. The therapist is able to go almost immediately into an enactment to address the family's core issue. We also see that she addresses emotional issues at the same time as she addresses structural and life stage issues. The ease with which the therapist uses these techniques in session speaks of her comfort with this integration on the theoretical, strategic, and intervention levels.

Summary

In this chapter we have explored how important having a grasp of family process is to practitioners of family therapy. Understanding the difference between process and content makes a family's pattern of interaction readily observable, allowing the therapist to know where to target his or her interventions. We explored the importance of observing how families maintain both physical and emotional relational space. The dynamic between bonding and buffering is an issue for all families, and it varies over the family's life course. We also explored what process families use to socialize each other. Recognizing strengths as well as challenges in a family's ability to socialize their children is an important skill for a family therapist to possess.

We next discussed the influence professional organizations have on the professional practice of marriage and family therapy. We looked at the relationship between the application of a medical model and the practice of systemic family therapy. While the history of the medical model has been somewhat distant from that of general systems theory, recently practitioners have developed a form of systemic thinking that incorporates the medical perspective. We also discussed concerns of relational ethics and confidentiality and their impact on the practice of family therapy.

Our discussion of training processes focused on the role of accreditation in ensuring quality of training in family therapy. Supervision is a key component in developing skills in the practice of family therapy. We explored the strengths and weaknesses of a variety of approaches to supervision. To address the question of what makes a family therapist competent, a list of core competencies has been developed. These competencies are categorized in terms of what they can contribute to the training of family therapists. We concluded our discussion of the training process by looking at the effect of stress on trainees. Research has demonstrated that while stress is a normative part of a marriage and family therapist's training, it typically increases during specific times. Given its predictability, therapists in training can take proactive steps to reduce the negative impact of that stress.

Last, we identified some key issues in the process of integrating theories of family therapy. We contrasted integration models with eclectic models of family therapy and developed criteria for the evaluation of a theoretical integration. Integration can occur on the levels of theory, strategy, and interventions. After developing the criteria, we looked at an example of how a therapist integrates structural, strategic, and symbolic-experiential family therapy.

Learning Exercises

1. Pair off with a peer and discuss what you think are the important elements in successful socialization of children. If you are comfortable, describe to what degree these ideas came from the practices you were socialized with.

2. Pair off with a colleague and take turns talking about your family of origin. What processes can you identify that have been important to your development? How have these process influenced—for better or worse—some of you personality traits?

3. Research the professional organization most closely related to your professional identity. What is required for student membership? What else is required for full membership?

4. Research the resources available in your community for addressing violence in families. Does your state mandate reporting the abuse of children? How is spousal abuse dealt with by the legal system? Is there a domestic violence shelter and prevention program? How do clients get access to these programs?

5. Devise a personal safety plan. Ask yourself the question, "If I had to get away from my partner to be safe, how could I do it?" What are the resources that would be available to you? Where could you stay that would be safe? Would you have money to support yourself, and if you could, how long could you support yourself? Discuss your plan with your peers. What did others include in their plans that could help you? As a group, try to develop elements that go into a good safety plan.

6. Become familiar with child abuse reporting laws in your state. Who takes child endangerment reports, and how are they processed?

Discussion Questions

1. How do different theories of family therapy address issues of bonding and buffering in marital relationships? In parent-child relationships?

2. What is the relationship between the need to protect the confidentiality and privacy of the client and the need to protect family members and the public at large? What role does licensure take in protecting the public?

3. From a broader systemic perspective, what do professional organizations do to support quality practice in marriage and family therapy?

4. What are the advantages and disadvantages of practicing from a purist theoretical model of family therapy? From an integrative model?

5. In what ways can systemic family therapy and a medical model of mental illness be integrated?

Web Resources

International Association of Marriage and Family Counselors IAMFC Webpage:

http://www.iamfconline.org/

Association for Family Therapy and Systemic Practice

http://www.aft.org.uk/view/index.html?tzcheck=1

Australian Association of Family Therapy AAMFT

http://www.aaft.asn.au/

Australian and New Zealand Journal of Family Therapy

http://onlinelibrary.wiley.com/journal/10.1002/(ISSN)1467–8438

Suggested Readings

Broderick, C. B. (1993). Understanding family process: Basics of family systems theory. Newbury Park, CA: Sage.

Kantor, D., & Lehr, W. (1975). Inside the family: Toward a theory of family process. San Francisco: Jossey-Bass.

Keeney, B. (1983). Aesthetics of Change. New York: Guilford Press.

Lebow, J. (1997). The integrative revolution in couple and family therapy. Family Process, 36, 1–24.

Stith, S, M., McCollum, E.E., Amanor-Boadu, Y., & Smith, D. (2012). Systemic perspectives of intimate partner violence treatment. Journal of Family Therapy 38(1)220–240.

CHAPTER

16

RESEARCH IN FAMILY THERAPY

Introduction

As we enter an age where accountability is becoming increasingly important, there is more pressure for marriage and family therapy (MFT) to show that it is an effective approach to helping people. While MFT's popularity has grown and has become legitimized as a profession, the time has come for it to prove its effectiveness. The field can no longer stand on the eloquence of its theoretical models and anecdotal reports of success. The time is now for the field to demonstrate its empirical validity. As we saw in Chapter 1, the field coevolved with research in schizophrenia and communication. However, over time the link between research and theory deteriorated, and as late as 1989 Werry criticized MFT by saying,

> Family therapy has many of the hallmarks of a religion with several competing sects led by feuding charismatic prophets each claiming to have a premium on the truth, but with few of the attributes of a profession rooted in ethics and skepticism. (p. 381)

More recently Crane, Wampler, Sprenkle, Sandberg, and Hovestadt (2002) have described family therapy this way:

Ours remains a field where it is still possible for a highly charismatic individual to create a model of family therapy, become successful in the workshop circuit, and get lucrative book contracts to promulgate the model without offering evidence for its efficacy beyond personal testimony. (p. 76)

It is empirical research on our practices that serves as a link between theory and practice in marriage and family therapy.

Following other professions some Marriage and Family Therapist are making calls for engaging in Evidence Based Practices. In their 2014 (Williams, Patterson & Edwards) text *Clinician's Guide to Research Methods in Family Therapy: Foundations of Evidence-Based Practice* the authors lay out the implications of trends towards evidence based practice in Family Therapy. They lay out 5 key advantages from an evidence based practice:

1. Research helps us understand our clients experience,

2. research helps us make better assessments and identify secondary factors associated with issues,

3. instrument developed for reseach can have clinical relevance,

4. research can guide us in selecting effective approach to issues,

5. research can identify what elements are important for success (Williams, Patterson & Edwards 2014).

To the authors ethical practice mandates being informed by current research knowledge.

Some marriage and family therapists complain that the research methods that have been developed out of a modern philosophical worldview do not apply to the postmodern theoretical view that has become central in the field. However, as with theory, it is a mistake to see research methodology as fixed. Research methods are dynamic and evolving processes, and changes occur in response to shifts in the theoretical environment. If we view empiricism as a tool of theory, we see that there will necessarily be a lag between theoretical development and the research methodology that is able to evaluate current theory accurately. Research can best be viewed as a tool that helps develop and further refine theoretical understanding.

It is in that spirit that this chapter explores the current state of research-informed theoretical understanding of family therapy theories. In each chapter of this book that has discussed a theoretical model (Chapters 4 through 14), a section highlighting empirical validations of that model has been included. This chapter goes beyond that empirical validation of specific models of family therapy and explores the state of the art in empirically validated models developed in the context of wider research projects as well as the research-determined efficacy of family therapy to address a variety of issues and diagnoses.

Empirically Validated Models

As marriage and family therapy enters an era of increased accountability, it is essential that models undergo further empirical validation. In prior chapters, as we examined each theoretical model, we looked at attempts to validate each model presented. For the most part, the major models of family therapy were developed as clinical innovations. However, some models of family therapy developed as part of larger research projects. In these instances, empirical validation and clinical development go hand in hand. In this chapter we will look at three such empirically validated models: functional family therapy, the circumplex model, and emotionally focused therapy.

Functional Family Therapy

FIGURE 16.1   **Functionfal Family Threrapy**

James F. Alexander and Thomas L. Sexton, "Functional Family Therapy Phases Of Change," Adapted from 'Functional Family Ttherapy: A Model for Treating High-Risk, Acting-Out Youth,' Comprehensive Handbook of Psychotherapy: Vol. 4, pp. 116. Copyright © 2002 by John Wiley & Sons, Inc.

Functional Family Therapy Clinical Model: Intervention Phases Across Time

	Engagement and Motivation	**Behavior Change**	**Generalization**
Phase goals	Develop alliances. Reduce negativity, resistance. Improve communication. Minimize hopelessness. Reduce dropout potential. Develop family focus. Increase motivation for change.	Develop and Implement Individualized change plans. Change presenting delinquency behavior. Build relational skills. (e.g., communication and parenting).	Maintain/generalize change. Prevent relapses. Provide community resources necessary to support change.
Risk and protective factors addressed	Negativity and blaming (risk). Hopelessness (risk). Lack of motivation (risk). Credibility (protective). Alliance (protective). Treatment availability (protective).	Poor parenting skills (risk). Negativity and blaming (risk). Poor communication (risk). Positive parenting skills (protective). Supportive communication (protective). Interpersonal needs (depends on context). Parental pathology (depends on context). Developmental level (depends on context).	Poor relationships with school/community (risk). Low level of social support (risk). Positive relationships with school/community (protective).
Assessment focus	Behavior (e.g., presenting problem and risk and protective factors). Relational problems sequence (e.g., needs/functions). Context (risk and protective factors).	Quality of relational skills (communication, parenting). Compliance with behavior change plan. Relational problem sequence.	Identification of community resources needed. Maintenance of change.
Therapist/ Interventionist skills	Interpersonal skills (validation, positive interpretation, reattribution, refraining. and sequencing). High availability to provide services.	Structure (session focusing). Change plan implementation. Modelling/focusing/ directing/training.	Family case manager Resource help. Relapse prevention interventions.

Functional family therapy (FFT) was first developed as an empirically validated model for working with at-risk youths as early as 1973 (Alexander, 1973; Alexander & Parsons, 1973; Parsons & Alexander, 1973). This approach has been used in a multitude of settings and is guided by a well-developed manual to direct clinical practice. In their recent review of functional family therapy, Alexander and Sexton (2002) assert, "As years of outcome data attest, FFT is an effective and efficacious change program for highly dysfunctional youth and their families" (p. 112).

Functional family therapy is a relatively short-term model lasting eight to 12 sessions for mild cases and up to 30 sessions for more difficult cases (Alexander & Sexton, 2002). Based on numerous outcome studies, FFT can reduce recidivism and/or the onset of offending from 25% to 60% when compared to other programs (Alexander & Sexton, 2002). In many texts FFT is classified as a behavioral model, and clearly behavioral therapy is at its core. It developed along with systems theory and is also a multisystemic theory. FFT makes extensive use of reframing, which was developed within the Mental Research Institute (MRI) model (see Chapter 7). It uses psychodynamic theory to understand relational motives in the complexities of family relationships (Alexander & Sexton, 2002).

At the core of its development, functional family therapy is an integrative theory. The integration takes place on the theoretical and practical levels, focusing on culturally sensitive issues. In addition, ongoing research findings and clinical wisdom were integrated into this model as it was developed. Recently the model has been influenced by cognitive theory and social psychology, which provide an understanding of the mechanism of attribution, as well as constructivist theory, which describes therapy as a social construction process (Alexander & Sexton, 2002).

Functional family therapy is based a multisystemic paradigm that recognizes that adolescents and their families exist in a variety of systems interconnected on a variety of levels. As Alexander and Sexton (2002) explain,

> within this framework, FFT focuses first and primarily on developing positive family functioning from within; we believe in helping the family move from hopelessness and frustration to an attitude of hope and self-efficacy, which is reflected in willingness to undertake positive change. (p. 115)

As change occurs, other systems that can support positive change are engaged to encourage additional positive functioning on the part of the family. This model is broken down into three phases that help to organize the approach for the clinician (see Figure 16.1). The three overlapping phases of the FFT model are (1) engagements and motivation, (2) behavioral change, and (3) generalization (Alexander & Sexton, 2002).

The engagement and motivation phases focus on developing in the family hope that they can overcome the pervasive negative and toxic interaction pattern that typically occurs in families with troubled adolescents. The therapist builds a positive therapeutic relationship based on respect for and understanding of each member, resulting in a balanced alliance with each member. It is important to engage and motivate the families before behavioral change is initiated (Alexander & Sexton, 2002).

The next phase is the behavioral change phase. According to Alexander and Sexton (2002), "during this phase, FFT clinicians develop intermediate and then long-term behavior change intervention plans that are culturally appropriate, contextually sensitive and individualized to the unique characteristics of each family member" (p. 117). While relationship skills on the part of the therapist remain important, the emphasis is on structuring the treatment. In this phase, a variety of interventions is introduced. These interventions include improving parenting skills, problem solving, communication skills, contracting, and conflict management. The goals of the interventions are based on the needs, values, and abilities of the family rather than the values of the therapist (Alexander & Sexton, 2002).

In the generalization phase, change is generalized into other areas of family life and to other situations. Change is retained through relapse prevention and is supported by linking the family to available community supports (Alexander & Sexton, 2002). It is this linkage to the community that makes FFT a multisystemic approach. Here social work skills are important in furthering the therapist's ability to facilitate the family's relationship with community support resources.

In the 35 plus years since functional family therapy was first introduced as a model for treating high-risk, acting-out youths, it has continued to evolve and be refined in an organized, deliberate manner. One of the strengths of FFT is how theory, practice, and research findings have been integrated to inform the model (Alexander & Sexton, 2002). Given the depth of the model and the degree to which it has been established, it will continue to be a model of choice for some time to come.

The Circumplex Model

The circumplex model of marital and family systems has generated a lot of interest and has remained influential in the field for 35 years (Olson, Sprenkle, & Russell 1979). This model and its related assessment instrument, the Family Adaptability and Cohesion Evaluation Scale, have been tested

PHOTO 16.1   David Olson

David Olson. Copyright © by David Olson. Reprinted with permission.

in over 500 studies (Kouneski, 2001). The circumplex model is based on two dimensions that have been central to many theories of family functioning: family cohesion and family adaptability. These variables were derived from reviewing the literature in various fields (Olson et al., 1979). Each of these dimensions is seen as having a curvilinear relationship to optimal functioning. That is, at low levels and high levels, these variables are less related to functioning than they are at the mid level. If we place the two dimensions on x and y axes of a graph, we have a circumplex where families in the center are seen as having better functioning than families on any edge.

Family cohesion is defined by Olson and colleagues (1979) as "the emotional bonding members have with one another and the degree of individual autonomy a person experiences in the family system" (p. 5). Since cohesion is conceptualized as a curvilinear variable, both the low end and high end of this dimension are seen as problematic for the family. Families that are disengaged have low levels of bonding and high levels of autonomy and fall on the low end of the cohesion dimension. Families that have too high a degree of cohesion can be enmeshed, with little or no autonomy for the members. In the model, cohesion serves as the x axis.

This is contrasted with the second dimension of this model, adaptability, or "the ability of a marital/family system to change its power structure, role relationships, and relationship rules in response to situational and developmental stress" (Olson et al., 1979, p. 12). Again, this is viewed as a curvilinear variable with the extreme ends marked by change (morphogenesis) and rigidity (morphostasis). Adaptability is the y axis in the circumplex model of family functioning.

As we can see in Figure 16.2, this creates a grid that describes 16 possible types of marital and family systems. At the center of the circumplex, families demonstrate a balance between cohesion and adaptability. As the family moves away from the intersection of cohesion and adaptability, each concentric circle represents an increase in level of dysfunction. One of the strengths of this model is its ability to describe clinical situations that therapists might treat in their practice. In addition, Olson and colleagues (1979) describe this model as being developmental in nature, with the assumption that families move about on the circumplex as they move through the family life cycle.

One of the most interesting elements of this model is its utility for guiding clinicians in their assessment of a family's level of cohesion and adaptability as well as its potential for guiding clinical treatment. This assessment function is furthered by the development of the Family Adaptability and Cohesion Evaluation Scale (FACES). This paper-and-pencil self-report instrument has undergone multiple revisions. Currently the FACES is in the IV verson Olson (2011) containing 6 scales. Cohesion is determined by the enmeshed, balanced cohesion, disengaged scales and Flexibility which is determined by chaotic, balanced flexibility and rigid scale.

Clinically, the circumplex model has utility in guiding family therapy in a variety of settings, and various clinical situations could benefit from focused treatment. Families assessed to be in an extreme range on either or both of the dimensions could benefit from treatment that brings the system to a more balanced position (Walsh & Olson, 1989). It is important to note that the goal of therapy under the circumplex model is not to change the style of functioning of the family, but to move the family to a more central and functional version of the same style of interacting. Let us look at a few examples of settings where this model has been applied.

The circumplex model has been applied to treat the severe family problems of sexual addiction (Carnes, 1989) and incest (Trepper & Sprenkle, 1989). In families that include adolescent members with sexual addiction, sex offenders when compared to other adolescents, report their families to be rigid and disengaged (Carnes, 1989). In this situation, treatment involves helping the families move to less extreme positions on the circumplex.

Trepper and Sprenkle (1989) found that families with incest commonly presented on the extreme enmeshed area of the model. In these families, "overinvolvement with each other's emotional life is typically present, with a desire for privacy equated with a lack of love" (Trepper & Sprenkle, 1989, p. 98). In part, treatment involves helping the family establish more healthy boundaries.

The circumplex model has been frequently used in research and treatment programs for nearly 30 years. The wealth of information it provides as well as the numbers of families it has helped make this a very well respected model. It will likely remain important as family therapy continues to evolve as a field.

FIGURE 16.2   **The Circumplex Model**

David Olson, Douglas Sprenkle, and Candyce Russell, "Circumplex Model Of Marital And Family Systems," adapted from "Circumplex Model of Marital and Family Systems: I. Cohesion and Adaptability Dimensions, Family Types, and Clinical Applications," Family Process, vol. 18, no. 1. Copyright © 1979 by John Wiley & Sons, Inc.

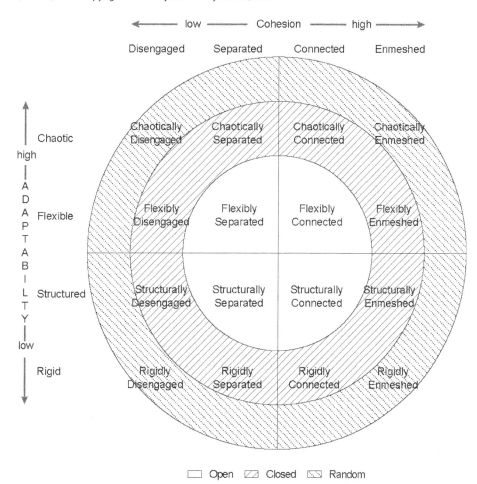

Emotionally Focused Therapy

The third empirically validated model we will explore is emotionally focused therapy for couples (Greenberg & Johnson, 1985, 1988). Treatment in emotionally focused therapy (EFT) is theoretically grounded in an integration of experiential theory, structural family therapy, and general systems theory. This model's understanding of love is based on attachment theory (Johnson & Greenman, 2006). In this approach, the negative interactional sequence is identified and underlying emotions are accessed (Greenberg & Johnson, 1988). Once the emotions are accessed, the goal of therapy is to restructure the couple's emotional bond. As Greenberg and Johnson (1988) state,

> in viewing the person as a self-organizing system in a continual process of becoming, in a field constituted both by internal intrapsychic influences and external interactional influences, change can be brought about both by changes in self and changes in context. (p. 53)

This model had continued to be further developed and validated and remains one of the most utilized approaches to working with couples.

The theory of relationships and the nature of love that informs EFT is based on the ideas of attachment theory (Bowlby, 1969 & 1973). In EFT, healthy relationships are marked by emotional engagement and mutual emotional responsiveness (Johnson & Greenman, 2006 Greenman & Johnson 2013 Johnson Wittenborn 2012). Couples who are in a critical angry pattern of nonresponsiveness to each other make emotional responsiveness and engagement difficult. From this perspective, interconnectedness based on "being there for each other" is the ideal in a relationship. This stands in contrast to Bowen's notion of differentiation. EFT has be applied to understanding forgiveness in couples therapy Woldarsky & Greenberg (2011) who describe forgiveness as moving from unfavorable emotional states to favorable in the couple. Johnson & Zuccarini (2010) place sexual functioning in the context of love and attachment helping to make EFT relevant for marital therapy.

Video Call Out 16.1: Emotionally Focused Therapy

In this session Chris Rodriguez, M.A. reflects with the couple regarding ways that partners come to interact and relate with one another, and how this typically becomes a pattern in the relationship. Chris reflects his understanding of the couple's pattern, pursue-withdrawal, to them and asks whether the couple believes this to be consistent with their relationship and typical interactions in conflict. He then suggests that the three continue to work with this pattern to break or mold it over time into something more conducive to the longevity of the relationship.

Video Call Out 16.2: Emotionally Focused Therapy

In addition, he asks the couple to consider their typical style and relate it to the incident brought up from there weekend. Chris provides each partner time to share their individual experience and continues to ask questions throughout to deepen both his understanding and the couple's pattern of interaction. Chris begins to refer to this pursue-withdrawal pattern as the 'dance' of the relationship, and asks the couple what it is like to hear this reflection. Later in the session Chris asks the couple what they want things in their relationship to be like now, upon having a stronger understanding of their relationship patterns and wants in the relationship. He then concludes the session by reflecting upon what the three of them have learned and covered in this session.

When couples are not able to meet each other's needs, anxiety arises in the relationship. Johnson and Greenman (2006) describe how partners respond: "People begin with protest, which usually takes the form of coercive anger, followed by clinging and seeking" (p. 599). In healthy relationships, partners respond to each other. In unhealthy relationships, the partners are either distracted from the relationship or become clingy. Frequently this can result in a pursuer-avoider pattern of relating.

This model is broken into nine steps, with progress through the steps being defined as circular. These steps have been developed to be completed in between 10 and 15 sessions (Johnson, 1996), making this approach attractive for its relatively short duration. According to Greenberg and Johnson (1988), the steps are as follows:

1. Delineate the issues presented by the couple and assess how these issues express core conflicts in areas of separateness-connectedness and dependence-independence.
2. Identify the negative interaction cycle.
3. Access unacknowledged feelings underlying interactional positions.
4. Redefine the problem(s) in terms of the underlying feelings.
5. Promote identification with disowned needs and aspects of self.
6. Promote acceptance by each partner of the other partner's experience.
7. Facilitate the expressions of needs and wants to restructure the interaction.
8. Establish the emergence of new solutions.
9. Consolidate new positions. (p. 66)

These steps have been further broken down into three stages of treatment. Stage 1 is cycle de-escalation (steps one through four), Stage 2 is restructuring interactional problems (steps five through seven), and Stage 3 is consolidation/integration (steps eight and nine; Johnson & Greenman, 2006).

In EFT, the therapist focuses her or his interventions on two main tasks. As Greenberg and Johnson (1988) state, these "tasks are accessing the emotional experience underlying interactional positions and using this emotional experience and expression to evoke new responses and change interactional positions" (p. 148). The focus on emotion explicit in this theory helps clients get past problematic patterns (structures) that inhibit their ability to experience healthy attachment.

In later works, Johnson, Makinen, and Millikin (2002) focus on treating couples who have experienced attachment injuries in the relationship. An attachment injury is an event such as an abandonment or betrayal that causes damage to the couple's ability to attach to each other. Johnson and colleagues (2002) note that "during the therapy process, . . . these events, which we have termed attachment injuries, often reemerge in an alive and intensely emotionally manner, much like a traumatic flashback, and overwhelm the injured partner" (p. 145). The injury can be something obvious, such as adultery, or something less obvious, such as not responding quickly enough to an intense call for support. For example, a wife experienced an attachment injury when her husband did not leave his work quickly to meet her at the hospital when she went into labor.

Attachment injuries are addressed early in the treatment, where the injured party articulates the impact of the injury to her or his partner. Supported by the therapist, one partner hears the other partner describe the injury. This partner then takes responsibility for the injury and seeks to comfort the other partner. This basic process has been preliminarily laid out in an eight-step model (Johnson et al., 2002) that is currently under empirical evaluation.

EFT has been successfully applied to a variety of situations. Walker, Johnson, Manion, and Cloutier (1996) found that EFT interventions led to clinical improvement in families with chronically ill children. In a two-year follow-up, Cloutier, Manion, Walker, and Johnson (2002) found that those families with chronically ill children were able to maintain the gains from treatment. Dankoski (2001) tells how EFT can be helpful to couples as they go through the family life cycle, describing how the model is developmentally appropriate for a wide variety of couples. Kowal, Johnson, and Lee (2003) describe the utility of EFT in helping couples dealing with chronic illness cope with the stress of the illness and Tie & Poulsen (2013) describe use of EFT with couple facing terminal illness. In a small well designed randomized study Denton Wittenborn & Golden (2012) EFT was utilized to augment antidepressant medication treatment of depressed women who also had relationship discord. The study found that the women reported improvement in the relationship compaired to those who did not receive EFT. This model promises to continue to be a treatment of choice for a good while. It has been well validated empirically and is theoretically rich, attracting a good deal of interest from the field.

Effectiveness Research

An important line of research in marriage and family therapy is effectiveness research, where researchers seek to empirically establish the types of problems that are effectively addressed by family therapy. As discussed previously, there has been a lag between the development of our theoretical understanding of family therapy and our empirical validation of the approach. In other words, our theories are running ahead of our research. However, despite the gap between research and practice, there has been recent headway in closing the gap. Sprenkle (2002a) argues that there is a fellowship between the thinking of good scientists and the thinking of clinicians. Given this, some theorists' rejection of scientific scrutiny seems ill founded. As Sprenkle (2002a) states, "Even if family therapy were to become much more informed by science, it will never become the equivalent of 'paint by numbers'" (p. 12). Three major works have gone a good distance toward closing this gap. The first is a special edition of the *Journal of Marital and Family Therapy* guest edited by Pinsof and Wynne (1995). Second is *Effectiveness Research in Marriage and Family Therapy*, edited by Sprenkle (2002b), which reviews the state of the art of the effectiveness research in the field. Most recently, Fred Piercy as editor the Journal of Marital and Family Therapy (2012 v1) move the tradition forward reviewing the state of the art in Effectiveness research in family therapy. Each article was written by leading researchers in their area of inquiry incorporating the research into practice. Let us look more closely at some of these areas.

Conduct Disorders and Delinquency

Family therapy has been demonstrated to be an effective approach to conduct disorders and delinquency in children. Henggeler and Sheidow (2002) have identified functional family therapy, multisystemic therapy, and The Oregon or Multidimentia treatment foster care as approaches that have been shown to be useful with this population. Functional family therapy (FFT) is an approach developed by Alexander and Parsons (1982) and further developed by Alexander and colleagues (1998) that focuses on developing parenting and communication skills. Multisystemic therapy (MST; Henggeler, Schoenwald, Borduin, Rowland, & Cunningham, 1998; Henggeler, Schoenwald, Rowland, & Cunningham, 2002) is a hybrid model designed to be a barrier-free, integrative approach based on strategic, structural, and parent training approaches. Oregon treatment foster care (OTFC; Chamberlain & Mihalic, 1998) is a manualized treatment approach rooted in social learning theory. This program closely monitors (with daily phone calls) delinquent youths who have been placed in foster care and tailors the treatment to the specific youth.

These approaches show promise in treating the difficult problem of conduct disorder by addressing several common factors identified by Henggeler and Sheidow (2002, 2012). First, all these models address the negative influence of antisocial peers. Second, they target family structure so the family can better monitor the youths' behavior. Finally, these approaches all use evidence-based techniques, specifically behavioral techniques. Henggeler and Sheidow (2002) conclude that the effectiveness of certain family-based treatments (e.g., FFT, MST, OTFC) in adolescents has "advanced to the point that major federal entities such as the Surgeon General have identified highly and promising or effective treatments, and stakeholders across the nation have requested that these treatments be transported to their communities" (p. 46).

Adolescent Substance Abuse and Delinquency

Family-based treatment for substance abuse and delinquency has recently received a good deal of research. Family life has an impact on the generation of substance abuse as well as being helpful in its treatment (Rowe & Liddle, 2002). Rowe and Liddle have identified three areas that have empirically demonstrated the effectiveness of family-based interventions: (1) engagement and retention in family-based treatment; (2) drug usage, school attendance, and performance; and (3) family functioning.

Teens who abuse substances and are delinquent are typically hard to engage and retain in therapy, but Rowe and Liddle (2002) have identified two approaches successful in engaging and retaining the families of these individuals. These are brief strategic family therapy (Szapocznik & Williams, 2000), a hybrid of structural and strategic family therapy, and multisystemic therapy (Henggeler & Borduin, 1990), which focuses on altering risk factors. Baldwin, Christian, Berkeljon, Shadish, Bean (2012) conducted an meta-analysis that identified brief strategic, functional family therapy, multidimensional family Therapy or multisystemic therapy that found the four to have a significant but modest effect as compared to treatment as usual and alternative therapies.

In treating substance abuse and delinquency in adolescents, the primary goal is to reduce and ultimately eliminate the client's use of drugs. Family therapy has been shown to be a highly effective treatment of choice. Not only does family therapy help adolescents stop their drug usage, but they also are able to maintain these changes for up to a year. As Rowe and Liddle (2002) conclude, "several studies ... suggest that certain family therapy approaches can more significantly impact drug usage than alternative state-of-the-art nonfamily treatment" (p. 59).

In other measures of success in treating adolescents who abuse substances and are delinquent, the results for family therapy as a treatment of choice have been equally impressive. Performance in school has been shown to improve with multidimensional family therapy (Liddle et al., 2001), multisystemic family therapy (Brown, Henggeler, Schoenwald, Brondino, & Pickrel, 1999), and behavioral family therapy (Azrin et al., 2001). Rowe and Liddle (2002) note, "There is growing evidence that family-based treatment improves family functioning" (p. 62). Family functioning is directly related to the ability of teens that abuse substances and are delinquent to be successful in treatment.

Childhood Mental Disorders

One area where a gap remains between theory and practice is family therapy that focuses on problems diagnosed in childhood. This is surprising, given that several models of family therapy were first developed by clinicians working with children. Northey, Wells, Silverman, and Bailey (2002) provide a comprehensive review of the research validating family therapy and family-based therapy in this area of application. Family-based treatments are treatments that focus on the identified patient (the child) but involve parents in some capacity. Usually the parents are involved in learning better parenting techniques and/or sitting in session and acting as a co-therapist. What this approach lacks is a focus on family processes other than parenting. However, in the most recent effectiveness review evidence based interventions were reviewed for a variety of disorder showing increased effectiveness Kaslow, Broth, Smith & Collins (2012).

In treating anxiety disorders in children, family- and group-based cognitive behavioral therapy have been shown to be effective approaches (Northey et al., 2002). Family Cognitive Behavioral Therapy, and several parenting program have been shown to be helpful with anxious children Kaslow, Broth, Smith & Collins (2012). Surprisingly, few studies have looked at depression in children. However, Northey and colleagues conclude, "The small number of studies provide preliminary support for family intervention" (p. 102). Since then little has changed and Kaslow, Broth, Smith & Collins (2012) comprehensive review only found "Stress-Busters" to be effective with school aged children.

In the treatment of oppositional–defiant disorder, parent training (see Chapter 4) has been well validated empirically and is the treatment of choice (Northey et al., 2002, Kaslow, Broth, Smith & Collins (2012)). The robustness of these findings makes sense in light of the fact that oppositional behavior by definition occurs in the context of a relationship, specifically the parent–child relationship. This is supported by observations that families with children with oppositional–defiant disorder have parents who are not very involved in their child's activities, provide poor supervision, and have harsh and inconsistent discipline practices (Loeber & Stouthamer-Loeber, 1986).

In treating attention-deficit hyperactivity disorders, the treatment of choice is stimulant medication. Klein and Abikoff (1997) have demonstrated that medication and psychosocial treatment produces better results than medication alone. Again, parent training has been shown to be effective in improving the results of a medication-only approach (Northey et al., 2002, Kaslow, Broth, Smith & Collins 2012). Given this, it seems useful that family therapy can help the family organize better to optimize the child's adaptation. This becomes obvious when we consider that children with attention issues most likely have parents who have had the same struggles.

Alcohol Abuse

Since alcohol abuse has such a profound impact on the entire family system, there has long been an association between family therapy and attempts to assist families with members who are addicted to alcohol. In their review of the literature on substance abuse, O'Farrell and Fals-Stewart (2002) looked at family therapy's effectiveness in treating alcoholism on two levels. First, they explored helping family members when the individual with alcoholism is unwilling to seek help, and second, they looked at how to help individuals address their alcoholism once they seek treatment. O'Farrell & Clements (2012) build on this work and finds the when the alcoholic is unwilling to enter treatment family therapy helps the family cope better and when the alcoholic enters therapy behavioral couples therapy is clearly more effective than individual treatment.

Families of people with alcoholism face several stressors, and Zetterlind, Hanson, Aberg-Orbeck, and Berglund (1998) have found that families can be helped even when the individual with alcoholism does not receive treatment. Al-Anon, a 12-step program supporting families dealing with the stressors of substance abuse, has been found to be an effective treatment in terms of helping family members cope with the drinking (Barber & Gilbertson, 1998; Rychtarik & McGillicuddy, 1998, 2002). Al-Anon facilitation therapy, a manualized guide for therapists working with clients involved with Al-Anon, has also been shown to be effective (Miller, Meyers, & Tonigan, 1999; Rychtarik & McGillicuddy, 1998).

O'Farrell and Fals-Stewart (2002) also evaluated approaches for engaging people with alcoholism in treatment. First, community reinforcement and family training is a manualized approach to improving the functioning of nonalcoholic family members and coaching them in encouraging the member with alcoholism to seek professional help (Meyers, Smith, & Miller, 1998). Community reinforcement was found to be effective in engaging people with alcoholism in treatment (Miller et al., 1999; Sisson & Azrin, 1986). The pressure-to-change approach (Barber & Crisp, 1995), designed for partners of people with alcoholism, has been shown in three studies to produce movement toward change (Barber & Crisp, 1995; Barber & Gilbertson, 1996, 1998). Finally, the popular Johnson Institute approach (Johnson, 1986), which has been referred to as an "intervention," did not receive empirical validation, and O'Farrell and Fals-Stewart (2002) recommend that programs discontinue using this approach.

Family therapy has also been empirically shown to be an effective approach to working with people with alcohol issues once the client has sought help. O'Farrell and Fals-Stewart (2002) reviewed 28 studies of behavioral couple therapy (BCT). This approach is based on building a better relationship between the person with alcoholism and her or his spouse or partner. It is in this intimate relationship that abstinence from alcohol is rewarded. According to O'Farrell and Fals-Stewart (2002), "in 12 of the 15 studies that compared BCT with a standard of individual-based treatment, positive results favored BCT" (p. 147). Family systems therapy (Steinglass, Bennett, Wolin, & Reiss, 1987), which blends general systems theory into a model of the "alcoholic" family, has also received empirical validation. O'Farrell and Fals-Stewart (2002) conclude,

> Family systems therapy (a) had less drinking than individual treatment of a waitlist control in 2 studies, (b) retained couples with more troubled relationships in treatment better than BCT, and (c) had the first studies to treat the entire family and examine children's ratings of outcome. (p. 154)

Marital Therapy

Susan Johnson (2002) provided a rigorous review of the literature on marital therapy. She concluded that only behavioral marital therapy and emotionally focused therapy have been empirically supported. The behavioral approach (Dunn & Schwebel, 1995; Jacobson & Addis, 1993) is based on a social exchange view of marital interaction. It focuses on negotiation skills, problem solving, and communication skill development. Emotionally focused therapy (Johnson, 1996) is grounded in attachment theory and involves assisting clients in repairing injury to the marital relationship through the restructuring of key emotional responses (see the previous section on EFT). Since then the updated effectiveness review Lebow, Chambers, Christensen, Johnson (2012) finds that 70% of couples are positively impacted by therapy. This is similar to individual therapies and superior to wait list control compairsons.

While there was limited support for marital therapy as an approach to repairing troubled relationships, Johnson (2002) explores couple therapy as a treatment of individual disorders. Since individual problems and marital problems often co-occur in a reciprocal manner, we would expect couple therapy to be effective for some individual disorders. Barlow, O'Brien, and Last (1984) found that the inclusion of a spouse in treatment significantly improved the treatment for agoraphobia. Several studies have supported the use of marital therapy for the treatment of depression using a behavioral approach (Beach, Whisman, & O'Leary, 1994; Jacobson, Dobson, Fruzzetti, Schmaling, & Salusky, 1991) and a couples version of interpersonal psychotherapy (Foley, Rounsaville, Weissman, Sholomaskas, & Cheveron, 1989). These studies have shown that marital therapy is as effective as individual therapy when marital distress is present and has the additional benefit of improving the marital relationship.

Since then Lebow, Chambers, Christensen, Johnson (2012) have reviewed significant improvement in the treatment of couples. Behavioral Family Therapy has been shown for provide for improvement in even seriously distressed couple and the change has been shown to last as long as

5 years (Lebow, Chambers, Christensen, Johnson 2012). Likewise EFT has been shown to produce significant change in couples relationship. Lebow, Chambers, Christensen, Johnson (2012) found that "Process studies that the active ingredient of EFT are depth of emotional expression in key the shaping of interactions where partners are able to clearly express attachment fears and needs and be emotionally responsive to each other's needs." p.152.

Intimate Partner Violence

Intimate partner violence causes direct damage to the victim and other members of the family and has an indirect impact on society as a whole. This issue has increasingly become a public concern, and law enforcement and the court system are paying it more attention. Stith, Rosen, and McCollum (2002) argue that current thinking focuses on providing protection for the victim while holding the aggressor accountable. This view came from a working with working with women (victims) at shelter and in the criminal justice system. However, we see a broader picture when we look a national survey data asking persons about the violent behavior we see that both genders can be violent in families. Stith, McClollum, Amanor-Boadu, Smith (2012) find increased understating in the nature of violence and that it is in part a result of family dysfunction including substance abuse.

To protect the victim, most treatment approaches run two separate and parallel groups for perpetrators and victims. Stith and colleagues (2002) found that these programs are the only ones to have been fully evaluated and that between 50% and 80% of batterers are nonviolent at time of evaluation. These are impressive statistics on the surface, but when one considers that from about one third to two thirds of participants do not complete the program, the success rate is less impressive.

A more controversial approach is treating domestic violence in conjoint sessions including both victim and perpetrator. Advocates of this approach see that there are different types of batterers. They suggest that batterers who hit only family members and who apparently have no additional psychopathology are most likely to benefit from conjoint treatment (Stuart & Holtzworth-Munroe, 1995). Additionally, Stith and colleagues (2002) argue that the high occurrence of violence in couples, the frequency with which couples seek to stay together after violence, and the degree to which relationship distress is associated with violence are reasons to approach domestic violence conjointly. After a comprehensive review of the literature, Stith and colleagues (2002) conclude, "Domestic violence–focused conjoint approaches with carefully screened couples appear to be at least as effective as gender specific treatment approaches" (p. 243). In addition, they conclude that conjoint therapy provides no documented increase in risk to the victim.

Since abuse is such a common occurrence, couple counselors are likely already treating couples who are abusive. This makes screening for violence in all couples important. When violence is discovered, it is important for the focus of therapy to shift to promoting the safety of all parties. Stith and colleagues (2002) have identified four common conditions in the empirically validated approaches:

1. Clients are carefully screened into the program.
   - Clients who have seriously injured their partner are excluded.
   - Both clients (in separate interviews) must report that they want to participate in couples treatment and that they are not afraid to express their concerns to their partner.

2. The primary focus of treatment is on eliminating all forms of partner abuse (physical, emotional, and verbal), not on saving the marriages.

3. Most programs emphasize taking responsibility for one's violence and include a skill-building component including teaching such skills as recognizing when anger is escalating, de-escalating, and taking time outs.

4. Effectiveness in all the successful programs reviewed here is measured by reduction or elimination of violence. (p. 249)

While the area of domestic violence still needs a good deal of research, we know that couple therapy can be effective. Stith, McClollum, Amanor-Boadu, Smith (2012) conclude "It is clear from these studies that it is possible to treat IPV in heterosexual couples using systemic intervention"p.234. These authors are also cautious giving the dangers in working with such populations and the complexity of this issues. What is lacking is an approach to working with whole families, given what we know about the impact of violence on the entire family system. However, they also note that there is increased concern from the legal system and they are hope that there will be increased funding for future research.

Severe Mental Illness

Family therapy and helping families with severe mental illnesses have a long history of co-evolution. Initially, family therapy assumed that family dysfunction generated psychopathology in the first place. However, there was a shift away from this perspective in the 1970s. McFarlane, Dixon, Lukens, and Lucksted (2002) describe the reasons for the shift:

> Perhaps the leading influence was the growing realization that conventional family therapy, in which family dysfunction is assumed and becomes the target of intervention for the alleviation of symptoms, proved to be at least ineffective and perhaps damaging to patient and family well-being. (p. 255)

Over time, families became seen as essential providers of support, such as case management and helping clients deal with pragmatic issues such as housing. This has evolved to a family psychoeducational paradigm, where the family provides a variety of supportive functions to assist the client who has the severe mental illness.

From this perspective, the goal is to reduce relapse and rehospitalization. Controlled studies of the family psychoeducational approach have demonstrated that this approach is empirically validated (McFarlane et al., 2002). Family therapists can provide an important service to the community by having an understanding of issues associated with severe mental illness and an ability to help families coordinate services for a member with a severe mental illness. McFarlane and colleagues suggest that, for this to be successful, "family therapists primarily need to see the family as a resource for, not the source of, the disorder, as being equally the victim of a neurological disorder in a loved one as is the patient" (p. 280).

Affective Disorders

In his review of the research on effectiveness of family therapy for clients with affective disorders, Beach (2002) points out that depressive disorders are prevalent among persons with marital discord or family difficulties. There is currently enough empirical evidence for Beach (2002) to conclude, "It is now possible to suggest that marital therapy and perhaps parent training are necessary and medically prudent in many cases of adult unipolar depression, and that these interventions should be more widely available than they are currently" (p. 290).

There is a well-documented relationship between marital distress and depression. Whisman (2001) found that marital relationships are more likely to be distressed when one partner is depressed. Zlotnick, Kohn, Keitner, and Della Grotta (2000) found that partners with depression reported that their partners did not meet their needs and had difficulty discussing problems with their partners. Cano and O'Leary (2000) found that humiliating events such as threatened divorce and infidelity significantly increase the risk of depression. In his review, Beach (2002) found behavioral marital therapy, emotionally focused therapy, insight-oriented marital therapy, and strategic marital therapy to be efficacious or possibly efficacious for persons with depression who also have marital distress. Beach & Whisman (2012) found Coping Oriented Couple Therapy and Brief Couple Therapy to be effective in well-designed manualized treatment protocals.

There is also a long-documented relationship between depression and problems in parenting (Weissman & Paykel, 1974). More recently Lovejoy, Gracyk, O'Hare, and Newman (2000) found that mothers with depression exhibit more withdrawal behaviors toward their children. Depression limits the parent's ability to be responsive to the needs of her children. Beach (2002) & Beach & Whisman (2012) notes that parent management training is an effective approach and suggests its use for reducing stress in parents with depression.

Beach (2002) makes some recommendations regarding which clients with depression are best suited for marital versus parenting interventions. When individuals with depression report little problem in their marriage or parenting, family therapy can be useful. When such clients report marital and parenting difficulties that developed before the depression, Beach (2002) suggests that "an initial approach that focuses on systemic problems (e.g., marital therapy or enhanced parent training) may produce positive outcomes and provide benefits that are greater than those obtained from an individual focus" (p. 301).

Common Factor Research

An important line of scientific inquiry is the effectiveness of psychotherapy in general. This research supports the effectiveness of family therapy in general. Rather than comparing theoretical models against one another, this line of inquiry seeks to answer the question, why does psychotherapy work? Sparks, Duncan, and Miller (2008) conclude that, on average, 80% of treated clients are better off after treatment than individuals who are not treated. This finding is consistent across all models of psychotherapy.

As early as 1973, Frank concluded that the various forms of psychotherapy could best be thought of as "a single entity." Since factors that can be attributed to the therapeutic model account for only

1% of change in psychotherapy (Wampold, 2001), some claim that there is little to be gained from research that compares and contrasts psychotherapy models. Looking at what common factors make psychotherapy work for the client at this time offers a real promise to shape the practice of psychotherapy in the future.

Much of psychotherapy is based on models of personality that view the client as having a deficit. If family therapists were to follow the medical model proposed by the *Diagnostic and Statistical Manual of Mental Disorders* V(American Psychiatric Association, 2013), they would assume that over time this deficit would lead to a mental disorder or illness. However, many people face and overcome severe issues and traumas in their lives and recover, often without ever seeking professional assistance. Asay and Lambert (1999) found that, in people facing such problems, 40% of improvement is attributable to client factors. An alternative perspective has been offered by Duncan, Miller, and Sparks (2004) in their book *The Heroic Client*. With the client's being responsible for explaining the majority of change in therapy, we find that change in therapy is largely attributable to the quality and depth of the therapeutic relationship.

An emphasis on the therapeutic relationship can be traced to Rogers (1957), who sought to identify necessary and sufficient conditions in helping clients change. According to Sparks and colleagues (2008), Roger's focus has evolved into the notion of therapeutic alliance and is one of the most researched variables. Bordin (1979) defines a therapeutic alliance as being composed of (1) the client's level of connection with the therapist, (2) agreement on goals, and (3) agreement on tasks necessary for achieving the goals. In their review of the research, Sparks and colleagues (2008) found that "the amount of change attributable to the alliance is about seven times that of a specific model or technique" (p. 462). These findings allow us to conclude that, regardless of the therapeutic model, each therapist must pay attention to factors in the therapeutic alliance.

Two important variables that have been shown to be associated with client improvement are the therapist–client relationship and timing. Therapists who emphasize their relationship with their clients tend to be more effective than therapists who do not stress the relationship (Vocisano et al., 2004). We also see that in therapy, change happens early, most notably before the first session and within the first seven sessions (Sparks et al., 2008). This tells us that therapy that is quick to develop a cooperative relationship, that works quickly, and that is driven by the client's needs is most likely to be successful.

Since we know that psychotherapy works, we need to more know about how it works. One way this can be accomplished is by paying attention to how clients and therapists build and maintain a therapeutic relationship. This explains why we find more variance in effectiveness between a beginning and expert therapist with the same theoretical orientation than between two experts from different schools of family therapy. This insight has implications for the beginning family therapist. In selecting a theory of family therapy in which to gain expertise, it is important to consider your level of comfort with the type of relationship inherent in the approach. Rather than selecting the best model, look for a good fit between the model and how you would like to practice.

Summary

In this chapter we explored how family therapy is meeting the demands of an era of empirically validated practice in the mental health field. We see that several successful models of families have been developed as part of an empirical research program. These models set the benchmark for strong empirical validation of the practices of family therapy. We explored three of the models that have a long history of influence in the field and are likely to be influential as theory and practice continue to develop. The first model, functional family therapy, is a model of family therapy. The second, the circumplex model, is a model of family functioning. Finally, emotionally focused therapy is an example of an empirically validated model of couple therapy.

Next we focused on a comprehensive review of family therapy outcome research. We explored conduct disorders and delinquency, adolescent substance abuse, childhood mental disorders, alcohol abuse, marital therapy, domestic violence, severe mental illness, and affective disorders. Each of these issues has provided varying but significant degrees of support for the conclusion that family therapy is an effective approach to treatment.

We concluded this chapter by looking beyond outcome studies and explored common factors associated with successful psychotherapy in general. We looked at how issues that are not specific to the therapist's approach impact treatment. Finally, we discovered that the therapeutic relationship and timing are the two most important factors in predicting success.

Given the lines of inquiry into the scientific validation of family therapy, we can conclude that family therapy is an effective approach to treating a variety of problems. It has proven to be the treatment of choice for many of them. The amount and quality of research in family therapy has increased, and family therapy clearly remains a leader in conducting research that has direct implications for treatment.

Learning Exercises

1. Interview a professional healer, such as a marriage and family therapist, counselor, social worker, massage therapist, or medical professional, about the aspects of her relationship with her clients that she thinks are most helpful. Share your findings in class and discuss common themes in the healers' views of what is important in relationships with clients.

2. Read a research-oriented journal article and share with your peers how that research may impact clinical practice.

Discussion Questions

1. There has been ongoing debate as to whether family therapy is more of an art or a scientifically validated, technical enterprise. How can family therapy be seen as an art that can be scientifically practiced?

2. Why is it necessary for a family therapist to remain current of the research in the field?

3. In what way does research on common factors influence each of the approaches to family therapy?

Web Resources

Functional family therapy

http://www.fftllc.com/sites/

The International Centre for Excellence in Emotionally Focused Therapy

eft. ca

Emotionally Focused Therapy Wikipedia page

https://en.wikipedia.org/wiki/Emotionally_focused_therapy

Multisystemic therapy

http://mstservices.com/

Suggested Reading

Baldwin, S. A., Christian, S., Berkeljon, A., & Shadish, W. R. (2012). The effects of family therapies for adolescent delinquency and substance abuse: A meta-analysis. Journal of Marital and Family Therapy, 38(1), 281–304.

Beach, S. R., & Whisman, M. A. (2012). Affective disorders. Journal of Marital and Family Therapy, 38(1), 201–219.

Henggeler, S. W., & Sheidow, A. J. (2012). Empirically supported family-based treatments for conduct disorder and delinquency in adolescents.Journal of Marital and Family Therapy, 38(1), 30–58.

Kaslow, N. J., Broth, M. R., Smith, C. O., & Collins, M. H. (2012). Family-based interventions for child and adolescent disorders. Journal of Marital and Family Therapy, 38(1), 82–100.

Lebow, J. L., Chambers, A. L., Christensen, A., & Johnson, S. M. (2012). Research on the treatment of couple distress. Journal of Marital and Family therapy, 38(1), 145–168.

O'Farrell, T. J., & Clements, K. (2012). Review of outcome research on marital and family therapy in treatment for alcoholism. Journal of Marital and Family Therapy, 38(1), 122–144.

Stith, S. M., McCollum, E. E., Amanor-Boadu, Y., & Smith, D. (2012). Systemic perspectives on intimate partner violence treatment. Journal of Marital and Family Therapy, 38(1), 220–240.

Williams, L., Patterson, J., & Edwards, T. M. (2014). Clinician's guide to research methods in family therapy: Foundations of evidence-based practice. New York, NY: Guilford Publications.

APPENDIX

CODE OF ETHICS

PREAMBLE

The Board of Directors of the American Association for Marriage and Family Therapy (AAMFT) hereby promulgates, pursuant to Article 2, Section 2.01.3 of the Association's Bylaws, the Revised AAMFT Code of Ethics, effective January 1, 2015.

Honoring Public Trust

The AAMFT strives to honor the public trust in marriage and family therapists by setting standards for ethical practice as described in this Code. The ethical standards define professional expectations and are enforced by the AAMFT Ethics Committee.

Commitment to Service, Advocacy and Public Participation

Marriage and family therapists are defined by an enduring dedication to professional and ethical excellence, as well as the commitment to service, advocacy, and public participation. The areas of service, advocacy, and public participation are recognized as responsibilities to the profession equal in importance to all other aspects. Marriage and family therapists embody these aspirations by participating in activities that contribute to a better community and society, including devoting a portion of their professional activity to services for which there is little or no financial return. Additionally, marriage and family therapists are concerned with developing laws and regulations pertaining to marriage and family therapy that serve the public interest, and with altering such laws and regulations that are not in the public interest. Marriage and family therapists also encourage public participation in the design and delivery of professional services and in the regulation of practitioners. Professional competence in these areas is essential to the character of the field, and to the well-being of clients and their communities.

Seeking Consultation

The absence of an explicit reference to a specific behavior or situation in the Code does not mean that the behavior is ethical or unethical. The standards are not exhaustive. Marriage and family therapists who are uncertain about the ethics of a particular course of action are encouraged to seek counsel from consultants, attorneys, supervisors, colleagues, or other appropriate authorities.

Ethical Decision-Making

Both law and ethics govern the practice of marriage and family therapy. When making decisions regarding professional behavior, marriage and family therapists must consider the AAMFT Code of Ethics and applicable laws and regulations. If the AAMFT Code of Ethics prescribes a standard higher than that required by law, marriage and family therapists must meet the higher standard of the AAMFT Code of Ethics. Marriage and family therapists comply with the mandates of law, but make known their commitment to the AAMFT Code of Ethics and take steps to resolve the conflict in a responsible manner. The AAMFT supports legal mandates for reporting of alleged unethical conduct.

Marriage and family therapists remain accountable to the AAMFT Code of Ethics when acting as members or employees of organizations. If the mandates of an organization with which a marriage and family therapist is affiliated, through employment, contract or otherwise, conflict with the AAMFT Code of Ethics, marriage and family therapists make known to the organization their commitment to the AAMFT Code of Ethics and take reasonable steps to resolve the conflict in a way that allows the fullest adherence to the Code of Ethics.

Binding Expectations

The AAMFT Code of Ethics is binding on members of AAMFT in all membership categories, all AAMFT Approved Supervisors and all applicants for membership or the Approved Supervisor designation. AAMFT members have an obligation to be familiar with the AAMFT Code of Ethics and its application to their professional services. Lack of awareness or misunderstanding of an ethical standard is not a defense to a charge of unethical conduct.

Resolving Complaints

The process for filing, investigating, and resolving complaints of unethical conduct is described in the current AAMFT Procedures for Handling Ethical Matters. Persons accused are considered innocent by the Ethics Committee until proven guilty, except as otherwise provided, and are entitled to due process. If an AAMFT member resigns in anticipation of, or during the course of, an ethics investigation, the Ethics Committee will complete its investigation. Any publication of action taken by the Association will include the fact that the member attempted to resign during the investigation.

Aspirational Core Values

The following core values speak generally to the membership of AAMFT as a professional association, yet they also inform all the varieties of practice and service in which marriage and family therapists engage. These core values are aspirational in nature, and are distinct from ethical standards. These values are intended to provide an aspirational framework within which marriage and family therapists may pursue the highest goals of practice.

The core values of AAMFT embody:

1. Acceptance, appreciation, and inclusion of a diverse membership.
2. Distinctiveness and excellence in training of marriage and family therapists and those desiring to advance their skills, knowledge and expertise in systemic and relational therapies.
3. Responsiveness and excellence in service to members.
4. Diversity, equity and excellence in clinical practice, research, education and administration.
5. Integrity evidenced by a high threshold of ethical and honest behavior within Association governance and by members.
6. Innovation and the advancement of knowledge of systemic and relational therapies.

Ethical Standards

Ethical standards, by contrast, are rules of practice upon which the marriage and family therapist is obliged and judged. The introductory paragraph to each standard in the AAMFT Code of Ethics is an aspirational/explanatory orientation to the enforceable standards that follow.

STANDARD I

RESPONSIBILITY TO CLIENTS

Marriage and family therapists advance the welfare of families and individuals and make reasonable efforts to find the appropriate balance between conflicting goals within the family system.

1.1 Non-Discrimination. Marriage and family therapists provide professional assistance to persons without discrimination on the basis of race, age, ethnicity, socioeconomic status, disability, gender, health status, religion, national origin, sexual orientation, gender identity or relationship status.

1.2 Informed Consent. Marriage and family therapists obtain appropriate informed consent to therapy or related procedures and use language that is reasonably understandable to clients. When persons, due to age or mental status, are legally incapable of giving informed consent, marriage and family therapists obtain informed permission from a legally authorized person, if such substitute consent is legally permissible. The content of informed consent may vary depending upon the client and treatment plan; however, informed consent generally necessitates that the client: (a) has the capacity to consent; (b) has been adequately informed of significant information concerning treatment processes and procedures; (c) has been adequately informed of potential risks and benefits of treatments for which generally recognized standards do not yet exist; (d) has freely and without undue influence expressed consent; and (e) has provided consent that is appropriately documented.

1.3 Multiple Relationships. Marriage and family therapists are aware of their influential positions with respect to clients, and they avoid exploiting the trust and dependency of such persons. Therapists, therefore, make every effort to avoid conditions and multiple relationships with clients that could impair professional judgment or increase the risk of exploitation. Such relationships include, but are not limited to, business or close personal relationships with a client or the client's immediate family. When the risk of impairment or exploitation exists due to conditions or multiple roles, therapists document the appropriate precautions taken.

1.4 Sexual Intimacy with Current Clients and Others. Sexual intimacy with current clients or with known members of the client's family system is prohibited.

1.5 Sexual Intimacy with Former Clients and Others. Sexual intimacy with former clients or with known members of the client's family system is prohibited.

1.6 Reports of Unethical Conduct. Marriage and family therapists comply with applicable laws regarding the reporting of alleged unethical conduct.

1.7 Abuse of the Therapeutic Relationship. Marriage and family therapists do not abuse their power in therapeutic relationships.

1.8 Client Autonomy in Decision Making. Marriage and family therapists respect the rights of clients to make decisions and help them to understand the consequences of these decisions. Therapists clearly advise clients that clients have the responsibility to make decisions regarding relationships such as cohabitation, marriage, divorce, separation, reconciliation, custody, and visitation.

1.9 Relationship Beneficial to Client. Marriage and family therapists continue therapeutic relationships only so long as it is reasonably clear that clients are benefiting from the relationship.

1.10 Referrals. Marriage and family therapists respectfully assist persons in obtaining appropriate therapeutic services if the therapist is unable or unwilling to provide professional help.

1.11 Non-Abandonment. Marriage and family therapists do not abandon or neglect clients in treatment without making reasonable arrangements for the continuation of treatment.

1.12 Written Consent to Record. Marriage and family therapists obtain written informed consent from clients before recording any images or audio or permitting third-party observation.

1.13 Relationships with Third Parties. Marriage and family therapists, upon agreeing to provide services to a person or entity at the request of a third party, clarify, to the extent feasible and at the outset of the service, the nature of the relationship with each party and the limits of confidentiality.

STANDARD II

CONFIDENTIALITY

Marriage and family therapists have unique confidentiality concerns because the client in a therapeutic relationship may be more than one person. Therapists respect and guard the confidences of each individual client.

2.1 Disclosing Limits of Confidentiality. Marriage and family therapists disclose to clients and other interested parties at the outset of services the nature of confidentiality and possible limitations of the clients' right to confidentiality. Therapists review with clients the circumstances where confidential information may be requested and where disclosure of confidential information may be legally required. Circumstances may necessitate repeated disclosures.

2.2 Written Authorization to Release Client Information. Marriage and family therapists do not disclose client confidences except by written authorization or waiver, or where mandated or permitted by law. Verbal authorization will not be sufficient except in emergency situations, unless prohibited by law. When providing couple, family or group treatment, the therapist does not disclose information outside the treatment context without a written authorization from each individual competent to execute a waiver. In the context of couple, family or group treatment, the therapist may not reveal any individual's confidences to others in the client unit without the prior written permission of that individual.

2.3 Client Access to Records. Marriage and family therapists provide clients with reasonable access to records concerning the clients. When providing couple, family, or group treatment, the therapist does not provide access to records without a written authorization from each individual competent to execute a waiver. Marriage and family therapists limit client's access to their records only in exceptional circumstances when they are concerned, based on compelling evidence, that such access could cause serious harm to the client. The client's request and the rationale for withholding some or all of the record should be documented in the client's file. Marriage and family therapists take steps to protect the confidentiality of other individuals identified in client records.

2.4 Confidentiality in Non-Clinical Activities. Marriage and family therapists use client and/or clinical materials in teaching, writing, consulting, research, and public presentations only if a written waiver has been obtained in accordance with Standard 2.2, or when appropriate steps have been taken to protect client identity and confidentiality.

2.5 Protection of Records. Marriage and family therapists store, safeguard, and dispose of client records in ways that maintain confidentiality and in accord with applicable laws and professional standards.

2.6 Preparation for Practice Changes. In preparation for moving a practice, closing a practice, or death, marriage and family therapists arrange for the storage, transfer, or disposal of client records in conformance with applicable laws and in ways that maintain confidentiality and safeguard the welfare of clients.

2.7 Confidentiality in Consultations. Marriage and family therapists, when consulting with colleagues or referral sources, do not share confidential information that could reasonably lead to the identification of a client, research participant, supervisee, or other person with whom they have a confidential relationship unless they have obtained the prior written consent of the client, research participant, supervisee, or other person with whom they have a confidential relationship. Information may be shared only to the extent necessary to achieve the purposes of the consultation.

STANDARD III

PROFESSIONAL COMPETENCE AND INTEGRITY

Marriage and family therapists maintain high standards of professional competence and integrity.

3.1 Maintenance of Competency. Marriage and family therapists pursue knowledge of new developments and maintain their competence in marriage and family therapy through education, training, and/or supervised experience.

3.2 Knowledge of Regulatory Standards. Marriage and family therapists pursue appropriate consultation and training to ensure adequate knowledge of and adherence to applicable laws, ethics, and professional standards.

3.3 Seek Assistance. Marriage and family therapists seek appropriate professional assistance for issues that may impair work performance or clinical judgment.

3.4 Conflicts of Interest. Marriage and family therapists do not provide services that create a conflict of interest that may impair work performance or clinical judgment.

3.5 Maintenance of Records. Marriage and family therapists maintain accurate and adequate clinical and financial records in accordance with applicable law.

3.6 Development of New Skills. While developing new skills in specialty areas, marriage and family therapists take steps to ensure the competence of their work and to protect clients from possible harm. Marriage and family therapists practice in specialty areas new to them only after appropriate education, training, and/or supervised experience.

3.7 Harassment. Marriage and family therapists do not engage in sexual or other forms of harassment of clients, students, trainees, supervisees, employees, colleagues, or research subjects.

3.8 Exploitation. Marriage and family therapists do not engage in the exploitation of clients, students, trainees, supervisees, employees, colleagues, or research subjects.

3.9 Gifts. Marriage and family therapists attend to cultural norms when considering whether to accept gifts from or give gifts to clients. Marriage and family therapists consider the potential effects that receiving or giving gifts may have on clients and on the integrity and efficacy of the therapeutic relationship.

3.10 Scope of Competence. Marriage and family therapists do not diagnose, treat, or advise on problems outside the recognized boundaries of their competencies.

3.11 Public Statements. Marriage and family therapists, because of their ability to influence and alter the lives of others, exercise special care when making public their professional recommendations and opinions through testimony or other public statements.

3.12 Professional Misconduct. Marriage and family therapists may be in violation of this Code and subject to termination of membership or other appropriate action if they: (a) are convicted of any felony; (b) are convicted of a misdemeanor related to their qualifications or functions; (c) engage in conduct which could lead to conviction of a felony, or a misdemeanor related to their qualifications or functions; (d) are expelled from or disciplined by other professional organizations; (e) have their licenses or certificates suspended or revoked or are otherwise disciplined by regulatory bodies; (f) continue to practice marriage and family therapy while no longer competent to do so because they are impaired by physical or mental causes or the abuse of alcohol or other substances; or (g) fail to cooperate with the Association at any point from the inception of an ethical complaint through the completion of all proceedings regarding that complaint.

STANDARD IV

RESPONSIBILITY TO STUDENTS AND SUPERVISEES

Marriage and family therapists do not exploit the trust and dependency of students and supervisees.

4.1 Exploitation. Marriage and family therapists who are in a supervisory role are aware of their influential positions with respect to students and supervisees, and they avoid exploiting the trust and dependency of such persons. Therapists, therefore, make every effort to avoid conditions and multiple relationships that could impair professional objectivity or increase the risk of exploitation. When the risk of impairment or exploitation exists due to conditions or multiple roles, therapists take appropriate precautions.

4.2 Therapy with Students or Supervisees. Marriage and family therapists do not provide therapy to current students or supervisees.

4.3 Sexual Intimacy with Students or Supervisees. Marriage and family therapists do not engage in sexual intimacy with students or supervisees during the evaluative or training relationship between the therapist and student or supervisee.

4.4 Oversight of Supervisee Competence. Marriage and family therapists do not permit students or supervisees to perform or to hold themselves out as competent to perform professional services beyond their training, level of experience, and competence.

4.5 Oversight of Supervisee Professionalism. Marriage and family therapists take reasonable measures to ensure that services provided by supervisees are professional.

4.6 Existing Relationship with Students or Supervisees. Marriage and family therapists are aware of their influential positions with respect to supervisees, and they avoid exploiting the trust and dependency of such persons. Supervisors, therefore, make every effort to avoid conditions and multiple relationships with supervisees that could impair professional judgment or increase the risk of exploitation. Examples of such relationships include, but are not limited to, business or close personal relationships with supervisees or the supervisee's immediate family. When the risk of impairment or exploitation exists due to conditions or multiple roles, supervisors document the appropriate precautions taken.

4.7 Confidentiality with Supervisees. Marriage and family therapists do not disclose supervisee confidences except by written authorization or waiver, or when mandated or permitted by law. In educational or training settings where there are multiple supervisors, disclosures are permitted only to other professional colleagues, administrators, or employers who share responsibility for training of the supervisee. Verbal authorization will not be sufficient except in emergency situations, unless prohibited by law.

4.8 Payment for Supervision. Marriage and family therapists providing clinical supervision shall not enter into financial arrangements with supervisees through deceptive or exploitative practices, nor shall marriage and family therapists providing clinical supervision exert undue influence over supervisees when establishing supervision fees. Marriage and family therapists shall also not engage in other exploitative practices of supervisees.

STANDARD V

RESEARCH AND PUBLICATION

Marriage and family therapists respect the dignity and protect the welfare of research participants, and are aware of applicable laws, regulations, and professional standards governing the conduct of research.

5.1 Institutional Approval. When institutional approval is required, marriage and family therapists submit accurate information about their research proposals and obtain appropriate approval prior to conducting the research.

5. 2 Protection of Research Participants. Marriage and family therapists are responsible for making careful examinations of ethical acceptability in planning research. To the extent that services to research participants may be compromised by participation in research, marriage and family therapists seek the ethical advice of qualified professionals not directly involved in the investigation and observe safeguards to protect the rights of research participants.

5. 3 Informed Consent to Research. Marriage and family therapists inform participants about the purpose of the research, expected length, and research procedures. They also inform participants of the aspects of the research that might reasonably be expected to influence willingness to participate such as potential risks, discomforts, or adverse effects. Marriage and family therapists are especially sensitive to the possibility of diminished consent when participants are also receiving clinical services, or have impairments which limit understanding and/or communication, or when participants are children. Marriage and family therapists inform participants about any potential research benefits, the limits of confidentiality, and whom to contact concerning questions about the research and their rights as research participants.

5.4 Right to Decline or Withdraw Participation. Marriage and family therapists respect each participant's freedom to decline participation in or to withdraw from a research study at any time. This obligation requires special thought and consideration when investigators or other members of the research team are in positions of authority or influence over participants. Marriage and family therapists, therefore, make every effort to avoid multiple relationships with research participants that could impair professional judgment or increase the risk of exploitation. When offering inducements for research participation, marriage and family therapists make reasonable efforts to avoid offering inappropriate or excessive inducements when such inducements are likely to coerce participation.

5.5 Confidentiality of Research Data. Information obtained about a research participant during the course of an investigation is confidential unless there is a waiver previously obtained in writing. When the possibility exists that others, including family members, may obtain access to such information, this possibility, together with the plan for protecting confidentiality, is explained as part of the procedure for obtaining informed consent.

5.6 Publication. Marriage and family therapists do not fabricate research results. Marriage and family therapists disclose potential conflicts of interest and take authorship credit only for work they have performed or to which they have contributed. Publication credits accurately reflect the relative contributions of the individual involved.

5.7 Authorship of Student Work. Marriage and family therapists do not accept or require authorship credit for a publication based from student's research, unless the marriage and family therapist made a substantial contribution beyond being a faculty advisor or research committee member. Co-authorship on student research should be determined in accordance with principles of fairness and justice.

5.8 Plagiarism. Marriage and family therapists who are the authors of books or other materials that are published or distributed do not plagiarize or fail to cite persons to whom credit for original ideas or work is due.

5.9 Accuracy in Publication. Marriage and family therapists who are authors of books or other materials published or distributed by an organization take reasonable precautions to ensure that the published materials are accurate and factual.

STANDARD VI

TECHNOLOGY-ASSISTED PROFESSIONAL SERVICES

Therapy, supervision, and other professional services engaged in by marriage and family therapists take place over an increasing number of technological platforms. There are great benefits and responsibilities inherent in both the traditional therapeutic and supervision contexts, as well as in the utilization of technologically-assisted professional services. This standard addresses basic ethical requirements of offering therapy, supervision, and related professional services using electronic means.

6.1 Technology Assisted Services. Prior to commencing therapy or supervision services through electronic means (including but not limited to phone and Internet), marriage and family therapists ensure that they are compliant with all relevant laws for the delivery of such services. Additionally, marriage and family therapists must: (a) determine that technologically-assisted services or supervision are appropriate for clients or supervisees, considering professional, intellectual, emotional, and physical needs; (b) inform clients or supervisees of the potential risks and benefits associated with technologically-assisted services; (c) ensure the security of their communication medium; and (d) only commence electronic therapy or supervision after appropriate education, training, or supervised experience using the relevant technology.

6.2 Consent to Treat or Supervise. Clients and supervisees, whether contracting for services as individuals, dyads, families, or groups, must be made aware of the risks and responsibilities associated with technology-assisted services. Therapists are to advise clients and supervisees in writing of these risks, and of both the therapist's and clients'/supervisees' responsibilities for minimizing such risks.

6.3 Confidentiality and Professional Responsibilities. It is the therapist's or supervisor's responsibility to choose technological platforms that adhere to standards of best practices related to confidentiality and quality of services, and that meet applicable laws. Clients and supervisees are to be made aware in writing of the limitations and protections offered by the therapist's or supervisor's technology.

6.4 Technology and Documentation. Therapists and supervisors are to ensure that all documentation containing identifying or otherwise sensitive information which is electronically stored and/or transferred is done using technology that adhere to standards of best practices related to confidentiality and quality of services, and that meet applicable laws. Clients and supervisees are to be made aware in writing of the limitations and protections offered by the therapist's or supervisor's technology.

6.5 Location of Services and Practice. Therapists and supervisors follow all applicable laws regarding location of practice and services, and do not use technologically-assisted means for practicing outside of their allowed jurisdictions.

6.6 Training and Use of Current Technology. Marriage and family therapists ensure that they are well trained and competent in the use of all chosen technology-assisted professional services. Careful choices of audio, video, and other options are made in order to optimize quality and security of services, and to adhere to standards of best practices for technology-assisted services. Furthermore, such choices of technology are to be suitably advanced and current so as to best serve the professional needs of clients and supervisees.

STANDARD VII

PROFESSIONAL EVALUATIONS

Marriage and family therapists aspire to the highest of standards in providing testimony in various contexts within the legal system.

7.1 Performance of Forensic Services. Marriage and family therapists may perform forensic services which may include interviews, consultations, evaluations, reports, and assessments both formal and informal, in keeping with applicable laws and competencies.

7.2 Testimony in Legal Proceedings Marriage and family therapists who provide expert or fact witness testimony in legal proceedings avoid misleading judgments, base conclusions and opinions on appropriate data, and avoid inaccuracies insofar as possible. When offering testimony, as marriage and family therapy experts, they shall strive to be accurate, objective, fair, and independent.

7.3 Competence. Marriage and family therapists demonstrate competence via education and experience in providing testimony in legal systems.

7.4 Informed Consent. Marriage and family therapists provide written notice and make reasonable efforts to obtain written consents of persons who are the subject(s) of evaluations and inform clients about the evaluation process, use of information and recommendations, financial arrangements, and the role of the therapist within the legal system.

7.5 Avoiding Conflicts. Clear distinctions are made between therapy and evaluations. Marriage and family therapists avoid conflict in roles in legal proceedings wherever possible and disclose potential conflicts. As therapy begins, marriage and family therapists clarify roles and the extent of confidentiality when legal systems are involved.

7.6 Avoiding Dual Roles. Marriage and family therapists avoid providing therapy to clients for whom the therapist has provided a forensic evaluation and avoid providing evaluations for those who are clients, unless otherwise mandated by legal systems.

7.7 Separation of Custody Evaluation from Therapy. Marriage and family therapists avoid conflicts of interest in treating minors or adults involved in custody or visitation actions by not performing evaluations for custody, residence, or visitation of the minor. Marriage and family therapists who treat minors may provide the court or mental health professional performing the evaluation with information about the minor from the marriage and family therapist's perspective as a treating marriage and family therapist, so long as the marriage and family therapist obtains appropriate consents to release information.

7.8 Professional Opinions. Marriage and family therapists who provide forensic evaluations avoid offering professional opinions about persons they have not directly interviewed. Marriage and family therapists declare the limits of their competencies and information.

7.9 Changes in Service. Clients are informed if changes in the role of provision of services of marriage and family therapy occur and/or are mandated by a legal system.

7.10 Familiarity with Rules. Marriage and family therapists who provide forensic evaluations are familiar with judicial and/or administrative rules prescribing their roles.

STANDARD VIII

FINANCIAL ARRANGEMENTS

Marriage and family therapists make financial arrangements with clients, third-party payors, and supervisees that are reasonably understandable and conform to accepted professional practices.

8.1 Financial Integrity. Marriage and family therapists do not offer or accept kickbacks, rebates, bonuses, or other remuneration for referrals. Fee-for-service arrangements are not prohibited.

8.2 Disclosure of Financial Policies. Prior to entering into the therapeutic or supervisory relationship, marriage and family therapists clearly disclose and explain to clients and supervisees: (a) all financial arrangements and fees related to professional services, including charges for canceled or missed appointments; (b) the use of collection agencies or legal measures for nonpayment; and (c) the procedure for obtaining payment from the client, to the extent allowed by law, if payment is denied by the third-party payor. Once services have begun, therapists provide reasonable notice of any changes in fees or other charges.

8.3 Notice of Payment Recovery Procedures. Marriage and family therapists give reasonable notice to clients with unpaid balances of their intent to seek collection by agency or legal recourse. When such action is taken, therapists will not disclose clinical information.

8.4 Truthful Representation of Services. Marriage and family therapists represent facts truthfully to clients, third-party payors, and supervisees regarding services rendered.

8.5 Bartering. Marriage and family therapists ordinarily refrain from accepting goods and services from clients in return for services rendered. Bartering for professional services may be conducted only if: (a) the supervisee or client requests it; (b) the relationship is not exploitative; (c) the professional relationship is not distorted; and (d) a clear written contract is established.

8.6 Withholding Records for Non-Payment. Marriage and family therapists may not withhold records under their immediate control that are requested and needed for a client's treatment solely because payment has not been received for past services, except as otherwise provided by law.

STANDARD IX

ADVERTISING

Marriage and family therapists engage in appropriate informational activities, including those that enable the public, referral sources, or others to choose professional services on an informed basis.

9.1 Accurate Professional Representation. Marriage and family therapists accurately represent their competencies, education, training, and experience relevant to their practice of marriage and family therapy in accordance with applicable law.

9.2 Promotional Materials. Marriage and family therapists ensure that advertisements and publications in any media are true, accurate, and in accordance with applicable law.

9.3 Professional Affiliations. Marriage and family therapists do not hold themselves out as being partners or associates of a firm if they are not.

9.4 Professional Identification. Marriage and family therapists do not use any professional identification (such as a business card, office sign, letterhead, Internet, or telephone or association directory listing) if it includes a statement or claim that is false, fraudulent, misleading, or deceptive.

9.5 Educational Credentials. Marriage and family therapists claim degrees for their clinical services only if those degrees demonstrate training and education in marriage and family therapy or related fields.

9.6 Employee or Supervisee Qualifications. Marriage and family therapists make certain that the qualifications of their employees and supervisees are represented in a manner that is true, accurate, and in accordance with applicable law.

9.7 Specialization. Marriage and family therapists represent themselves as providing specialized services only after taking reasonable steps to ensure the competence of their work and to protect clients, supervisees, and others from harm.

9.8 Correction of Misinformation. Marriage and family therapists correct, wherever possible, false, misleading, or inaccurate information and representations made by others concerning the therapist's qualifications, services, or products.

APPENDIX

MARRIAGE AND FAMILY THERAPY
CORE COMPETENCIES©

DECEMBER, 2004

The marriage and family therapy (MFT) core competencies were developed through a collaborative effort of the American Association for Marriage and Family Therapy (AAMFT) and interested stakeholders. In addition to defining the domains of knowledge and requisite skills in each domain that comprise the practice of marriage and family therapy, the ultimate goal of the core competencies is to improve the quality of services delivered by marriage and family therapists (MFTs). Consequently, the competencies described herein represent the minimum that MFTs licensed to practice independently must possess.

Creating competencies for MFTs and improving the quality of mental health services was considered in the context of the broader behavioral health system. The AAMFT relied on three important reports to provide the framework within which the competencies would be developed: *Mental Health: A Report of the Surgeon General*; the President's New Freedom Commission on Mental Health's *Achieving the Promise: Transforming Mental Health Care in America*; and the Institute of Medicine's *Crossing the Quality Chasm*. The AAMFT mapped the competencies to critical elements of these reports, including IOM's 6 Core Values that are seen as the foundation for a better health care system: 1) Safe, 2) Person-Centered, 3) Efficient, 4) Effective, 5) Timely, and 6) Equitable. The committee also considered how social, political, historical, and economic forces affect individual and relational problems and decisions about seeking and obtaining treatment.

The core competencies were developed for educators, trainers, regulators, researchers, policy-makers, and the public. The current version has 128 competencies; however, these are likely to be modified as the field of family therapy develops and as the needs of clients change. The competencies will be reviewed and modified at regular intervals to ensure the competencies are reflective of the current and best practice of MFT.

The core competencies are organized around 6 primary domains and 5 secondary domains. The primary domains are:

1. **Admission to Treatment**—All interactions between clients and therapist up to the point when a therapeutic contract is established.
2. **Clinical Assessment and Diagnosis**—Activities focused on the identification of the issues to be addressed in therapy.
3. **Treatment Planning and Case Management**—All activities focused on directing the course of therapy and extra-therapeutic activities.
4. **Therapeutic Interventions**—All activities designed to ameliorate the clinical issues identified.
5. **Legal Issues, Ethics, and Standards**—All aspects of therapy that involve statutes, regulations, principles, values, and mores of MFTs.
6. **Research and Program Evaluation**—All aspects of therapy that involve the systematic analysis of therapy and how it is conducted effectively.

The subsidiary domains are focused on the types of skills or knowledge that MFTs must develop. These are: a) Conceptual, b) Perceptual, c) Executive, d) Evaluative, and e) Professional.

Although not expressly written for each competency, the stem "Marriage and family therapists..." should begin each. Additionally, the term "client" is used broadly and refers to the therapeutic system of the client/s served, which includes, but is not limited to individuals, couples, families, and others with a vested interest in helping clients change. Similarly, the term "family" is used generically to refer to all people identified by clients as part of their "family system," this would include fictive kin and relationships of choice. Finally, the core competencies encompass behaviors, skills, attitudes, and policies that promote awareness, acceptance, and respect for differences, enhance services that meet the needs of diverse populations, and promote resiliency and recovery.

Domain 1: Admission to Treatment

Number	Subdomain	Competence
1.1.1	Conceptual	Understand systems concepts, theories, and techniques that are foundational to the practice of marriage and family therapy
1.1.2	Conceptual	Understand theories and techniques of individual, marital, couple, family, and group psychotherapy
1.1.3	Conceptual	Understand the behavioral health care delivery system, its impact on the services provided, and the barriers and disparities in the system.
1.1.4	Conceptual	Understand the risks and benefits of individual, marital, couple, family, and group psychotherapy.

Number	Subdomain	Competence
1.2.1	Perceptual	Recognize contextual and systemic dynamics (e.g., gender, age, socioeconomic status, culture/race/ethnicity, sexual orientation, spirituality, religion, larger systems, social context).
1.2.2	Perceptual	Consider health status, mental status, other therapy, and other systems involved in the clients' lives (e.g., courts, social services).
1.2.3	Perceptual	Recognize issues that might suggest referral for specialized evaluation, assessment, or care.
1.3.1	Executive	Gather and review intake information, giving balanced attention to individual, family, community, cultural, and contextual factors.
1.3.2	Executive	Determine who should attend therapy and in what configuration (e.g., individual, couple, family, extrafamilial resources).
1.3.3	Executive	Facilitate therapeutic involvement of all necessary participants in treatment.
1.3.4	Executive	Explain practice setting rules, fees, rights, and responsibilities of each party, including privacy, confidentiality policies, and duty to care to client or legal guardian.
1.3.5	Executive	Obtain consent to treatment from all responsible persons.
1.3.6	Executive	Establish and maintain appropriate and productive therapeutic alliances with the clients.
1.3.7	Executive	Solicit and use client feedback throughout the therapeutic process.
1.3.8	Executive	Develop and maintain collaborative working relationships with referral resources, other practitioners involved in the clients' care, and payers.
1.3.9	Executive	Manage session interactions with individuals, couples, families, and groups.
1.4.1	Evaluative	Evaluate case for appropriateness for treatment within professional scope of practice and competence.
1.5.1	Professional	Understand the legal requirements and limitations for working with vulnerable populations (e.g., minors).
1.5.2	Professional	Complete case documentation in a timely manner and in accordance with relevant laws and policies.
1.5.3	Professional	Develop, establish, and maintain policies for fees, payment, record keeping, and confidentiality.

Domain 2: Clinical Assessment and Diagnosis

Number	Subdomain	Competence
2.1.1	Conceptual	Understand principles of human development; human sexuality; gender development; psychopathology; psychopharmacology; couple processes; and family development and processes (e.g., family, relational, and system dynamics).
2.1.2	Conceptual	Understand the major behavioral health disorders, including the epidemiology, etiology, phenomenology, effective treatments, course, and prognosis.
2.1.3	Conceptual	Understand the clinical needs and implications of persons with comorbid disorders (e.g., substance abuse and mental health; heart disease and depression).
2.1.4	Conceptual	Comprehend individual, marital, couple and family assessment instruments appropriate to presenting problem, practice setting, and cultural context.
2.1.5	Conceptual	Understand the current models for assessment and diagnosis of mental health disorders, substance use disorders, and relational functioning.
2.1.6	Conceptual	Understand the strengths and limitations of the models of assessment and diagnosis, especially as they relate to different cultural, economic, and ethnic groups.
2.1.7	Conceptual	Understand the concepts of reliability and validity, their relationship to assessment instruments, and how they influence therapeutic decision making.
2.2.1	Perceptual	Assess each clients' engagement in the change process.
2.2.2	Perceptual	Systematically integrate client reports, observations of client behaviors, client relationship patterns, reports from other professionals, results from testing procedures, and interactions with client to guide the assessment process.
2.2.3	Perceptual	Develop hypotheses regarding relationship patterns, their bearing on the presenting problem, and the influence of extra-therapeutic factors on client systems.
2.2.4	Perceptual	Consider the influence of treatment on extra-therapeutic relationships.
2.2.5	Perceptual	Consider physical/organic problems that can cause or exacerbate emotional/interpersonal symptoms.
2.3.1	Executive	Diagnose and assess client behavioral and relational health problems systemically and contextually.
2.3.2	Executive	Provide assessments and deliver developmentally appropriate services to clients, such as children, adolescents, elders, and persons with special needs.
2.3.3	Executive	Apply effective and systemic interviewing techniques and strategies.
2.3.4	Executive	Administer and interpret results of assessment instruments.

Number	Subdomain	Competence
2.3.5	Executive	Screen and develop adequate safety plans for substance abuse, child and elder maltreatment, domestic violence, physical violence, suicide potential, and dangerousness to self and others.
2.3.6	Executive	Assess family history and dynamics using a genogram or other assessment instruments.
2.3.7	Executive	Elicit a relevant and accurate biopsychosocial history to understand the context of the clients' problems.
2.3.8	Executive	Identify clients' strengths, resilience, and resources.
2.3.9	Executive	Elucidate presenting problem from the perspective of each member of the therapeutic system.
2.4.1	Evaluative	Evaluate assessment methods for relevance to clients' needs.
2.4.2	Evaluative	Assess ability to view issues and therapeutic processes systemically.
2.4.3	Evaluative	Evaluate the accuracy and cultural relevance of behavioral health and relational diagnoses.
2.4.4	Evaluative	Assess the therapist-client agreement of therapeutic goals and diagnosis.
2.5.1	Professional	Utilize consultation and supervision effectively.

Domain 3: Treatment Planning and Case Management

Number	Subdomain	Competence
3.1.1	Conceptual	Know which models, modalities, and/or techniques are most effective for presenting problems.
3.1.2	Conceptual	Understand the liabilities incurred when billing third parties, the codes necessary for reimbursement, and how to use them correctly.
3.1.3	Conceptual	Understand the effects that psychotropic and other medications have on clients and the treatment process.
3.1.4	Conceptual	Understand recovery-oriented behavioral health services (e.g., self-help groups, 12-step programs, peer-to-peer services, supported employment).
3.2.1	Perceptual	Integrate client feedback, assessment, contextual information, and diagnosis with treatment goals and plan.
3.3.1	Executive	Develop, with client input, measurable outcomes, treatment goals, treatment plans, and after-care plans with clients utilizing a systemic perspective.
3.3.2	Executive	Prioritize treatment goals.
3.3.3	Executive	Develop a clear plan of how sessions will be conducted.
3.3.4	Executive	Structure treatment to meet clients' needs and to facilitate systemic change.
3.3.5	Executive	Manage progression of therapy toward treatment goals.

Continued.

Number	Subdomain	Competence
3.3.6	Executive	Manage risks, crises, and emergencies.
3.3.7	Executive	Work collaboratively with other stakeholders, including family members, other significant persons, and professionals not present.
3.3.8	Executive	Assist clients in obtaining needed care while navigating complex systems of care.
3.3.9	Executive	Develop termination and aftercare plans.
3.4.1	Evaluative	Evaluate progress of sessions toward treatment goals.
3.4.2	Evaluative	Recognize when treatment goals and plan require modification.
3.4.3	Evaluative	Evaluate level of risks, management of risks, crises, and emergencies.
3.4.4	Evaluative	Assess session process for compliance with policies and procedures of practice setting.
3.4.5	Professional	Monitor personal reactions to clients and treatment process, especially in terms of therapeutic behavior, relationship with clients, process for explaining procedures, and outcomes.
3.5.1	Professional	Advocate with clients in obtaining quality care, appropriate resources, and services in their community.
3.5.2	Professional	Participate in case-related forensic and legal processes.
3.5.3	Professional	Write plans and complete other case documentation in accordance with practice setting policies, professional standards, and state/provincial laws.
3.5.4	Professional	Utilize time management skills in therapy sessions and other professional meetings.

Domain 4: Therapeutic Interventions

Number	Subdomain	Competence
4.1.1	Conceptual	Comprehend a variety of individual and systemic therapeutic models and their application, including evidence-based therapies and culturally sensitive approaches.
4.1.2	Conceptual	Recognize strengths, limitations, and contraindications of specific therapy models, including the risk of harm associated with models that incorporate assumptions of family dysfunction, pathogenesis, or cultural deficit.
4.2.1	Perceptual	Recognize how different techniques may impact the treatment process.
4.2.2	Perceptual	Distinguish differences between content and process issues, their role in therapy, and their potential impact on therapeutic outcomes.
4.3.1	Executive	Match treatment modalities and techniques to clients' needs, goals, and values.

Number	Subdomain	Competence
4.3.2	Executive	Deliver interventions in a way that is sensitive to special needs of clients (e.g., gender, age, socioeconomic status, culture/race/ethnicity, sexual orientation, disability, personal history, larger systems issues of the client).
4.3.3	Executive	Reframe problems and recursive interaction patterns.
4.3.4	Executive	Generate relational questions and reflexive comments in the therapy room.
4.3.5	Executive	Engage each family member in the treatment process as appropriate.
4.3.6	Executive	Facilitate clients developing and integrating solutions to problems.
4.3.7	Executive	Defuse intense and chaotic situations to enhance the safety of all participants.
4.3.8	Executive	Empower clients and their relational systems to establish effective relationships with each other and larger systems.
4.3.9	Executive	Provide psychoeducation to families whose members have serious mental illness or other disorders.
4.3.10	Executive	Modify interventions that are not working to better fit treatment goals.
4.3.11	Executive	Move to constructive termination when treatment goals have been accomplished.
4.3.12	Executive	Integrate supervisor/team communications into treatment.
4.4.1	Evaluative	Evaluate interventions for consistency, congruency with model of therapy and theory of change, cultural and contextual relevance, and goals of the treatment plan.
4.4.2	Evaluative	Evaluate ability to deliver interventions effectively.
4.4.3	Evaluative	Evaluate treatment outcomes as treatment progresses.
4.4.4	Evaluative	Evaluate clients' reactions or responses to interventions.
4.4.5	Evaluative	Evaluate clients' outcomes for the need to continue, refer, or terminate therapy.
4.4.6	Evaluative	Evaluate reactions to the treatment process (e.g., transference, family of origin, current stress level, current life situation, cultural context) and their impact on effective intervention and clinical outcomes.
4.5.1	Professional	Respect multiple perspectives (e.g., clients, team, supervisor, practitioners from other disciplines who are involved in the case).
4.5.2	Professional	Set appropriate boundaries, manage issues of triangulation, and develop collaborative working relationships.
4.5.3	Professional	Articulate rationales for interventions related to treatment goals and plan, assessment information, and systemic understanding of clients' context and dynamics.

Domain 5: Legal Issues, Ethics, and Standards

Number	Subdomain	Competence
5.1.1	Conceptual	Know state, federal, and provincial laws and regulations that apply to the practice of marriage and family therapy.
5.1.2	Conceptual	Know professional ethics and standards of practice that apply to the practice of marriage and family therapy.
5.1.3	Conceptual	Know policies and procedures of the practice setting.
5.1.4	Conceptual	Understand the process of making an ethical decision.
5.2.1	Perceptual	Recognize situations in which ethics, laws, professional liability, and standards of practice apply.
5.2.2	Perceptual	Recognize ethical dilemmas in practice setting.
5.2.3	Perceptual	Recognize when a legal consultation is necessary.
5.2.4	Perceptual	Recognize when clinical supervision or consultation is necessary.
5.3.1	Executive	Monitor issues related to ethics, laws, regulations, and professional standards.
5.3.2	Executive	Develop and assess policies, procedures, and forms for consistency with standards of practice to protect client confidentiality and to comply with relevant laws and regulations.
5.3.3	Executive	Inform clients and legal guardian of limitations to confidentiality and parameters of mandatory reporting.
5.3.4	Executive	Develop safety plans for clients who present with potential self-harm, suicide, abuse, or violence.
5.3.5	Executive	Take appropriate action when ethical and legal dilemmas emerge.
5.3.6	Executive	Report information to appropriate authorities as required by law.
5.3.7	Executive	Practice within defined scope of practice and competence.
5.3.8	Executive	Obtain knowledge of advances and theory regarding effective clinical practice.
5.3.9	Executive	Obtain license(s) and specialty credentials.
5.3.10	Executive	Implement a personal program to maintain professional competence.
5.4.1	Evaluative	Evaluate activities related to ethics, legal issues, and practice standards.
5.4.2	Evaluative	Monitor attitudes, personal well-being, personal issues, and personal problems to insure they do not impact the therapy process adversely or create vulnerability for misconduct.
5.5.1	Professional	Maintain client records with timely and accurate notes.
5.5.2	Professional	Consult with peers and/or supervisors if personal issues, attitudes, or beliefs threaten to adversely impact clinical work.

Number	Subdomain	Competence
5.5.3	Professional	Pursue professional development through self-supervision, collegial consultation, professional reading, and continuing educational activities.
5.5.4	Professional	Bill clients and third-party payers in accordance with professional ethics, relevant laws and polices, and seek reimbursement only for covered services.

Domain 6: Research and Program Evaluation

Number	Subdomain	Competence
6.1.1	Conceptual	Know the extant MFT literature, research, and evidence-based practice.
6.1.2	Conceptual	Understand research and program evaluation methodologies, both quantitative and qualitative, relevant to MFT and mental health services.
6.1.3	Conceptual	Understand the legal, ethical, and contextual issues involved in the conduct of clinical research and program evaluation.
6.2.1	Perceptual	Recognize opportunities for therapists and clients to participate in clinical research.
6.3.1	Executive	Read current MFT and other professional literature.
6.3.2	Executive	Use current MFT and other research to inform clinical practice.
6.3.3	Executive	Critique professional research and assess the quality of research studies and program evaluation in the literature.
6.3.4	Executive	Determine the effectiveness of clinical practice and techniques.
6.4.1	Evaluative	Evaluate knowledge of current clinical literature and its application.
6.5.1	Professional	Contribute to the development of new knowledge.

References

Ackerman, N. (1970). Child participation in family therapy. *Family Process, 9*(4), 403–410.

Ainsworth, M. D. S., Blehar, M. C., Waters, E., & Wall, S. (1978). *Patterns of attachment: A psychological study of the strange situation.* Hillsdale, NJ: Erlbaum.

Alexander, J. F. (1973). Defensive and supportive communications in family systems. *Journal of Marriage and the Family, 35,* 613–617.

Alexander, J. F., Barton, C., Gordon, D., Grotpeter, J., Hansson, K., Harrison, R., et al. (1998). *Functional family therapy* (Blueprints for Violence Prevention, Vol. 3). Boulder, CO: Center for the Study and Prevention of Violence.

Alexander, J. F., & Parsons, B. V. (1973). Short-term behavior interventions with delinquent families: Impact on family process and recidivism. *Journal of Abnormal Psychology, 81,* 219–225.

Alexander, J. F., & Parsons, B. V. (1982). *Functional family therapy: Principles and procedures.* Carmel, CA: Brooks/Cole.

Alexander, J. F., & Sexton, T. L. (2002). Functional family therapy: A model for treating high-risk, acting-out youth. In F. W. Kaslow & J. Lebow (Eds.), *Comprehensive handbook of psychotherapy: Vol. 4. Integrative/eclectic* (pp. 111–132). New York: Wiley.

Allen, A. J., Davey, M. P., Davey, A. (2009). Being examples to the flock: The role of church leaders and African American families seeking mental health services. *Contemporary Family Therapy. 32*(1), 117–134.

American Association for Marriage and Family Therapy. (n.d.). *Directory of MFT licensure and certification boards.* Retrieved April 7, 2009, from http://www.aamft.org/resources/Online_Directories/boardcontacts.asp

American Association for Marriage and Family Therapy. (2001, July). *AAMFT code of ethics.* Retrieved September 28, 2008, from http://www.aamft.org/resources/lrm_plan/Ethics/ethicscode2001.asp

American Association for Marriage and Family Therapy. (2004, December). *Marriage and family therapy core competencies.* Retrieved September 28, 2008, from http://www.aamft.org/institutes/2008si/refresher/mft%20core%20 compentenciesdecember%202004.pdf

American Psychiatric Association. (1973). *Diagnostic and statistical manual of mental disorders* (2nd ed.). Washington, DC: Author.

American Psychiatric Association. (1994). *Diagnostic and statistical manual of mental disorders* (4th ed.). Washington, DC: Author.

American Psychiatric Association. (2000). *Diagnostic and statistical manual of mental disorders* (4th ed., text revision). Washington, DC: Author.

American Psychiatric Association. (2013). Diagnostic and Statistical Manual of Mental Disorders (5th ed.). Washington, DC: Author.

Andersen, T. (1991). The reflecting team: Dialogues and dialogues about the dialogues. New York: Norton.

Anderson, H. (1993). On a roller coaster: A collaborative language systems approach to therapy. In S. Friedman (Ed.), *The new language of change.* New York: Guilford Press.

Anderson, H. (1994). Rethinking family therapy: A delicate balance. *Journal of Marital and Family Therapy, 20,* 145–149.

Anderson, H. D. (1995). Collaborative language systems: Toward a postmodern therapy. In R. H. Mikesell, D. Lusterman, & S. H. McDaniel (Eds.), *Integrating family therapy: Handbook of family psychology and systems theory* (pp. 27–44). Washington, DC: American Psychological Association.

Anderson, H. (1997). Conversation, language, and possibilities: A postmodern approach to therapy. New York: Basic Books.

Anonymous. (1972). Differentiation of self in one's family. In J. Framo (Ed.), *Family interaction* (pp. 111–173). New York: Springer.

Aponte, H. J. (1992). Training the person of the therapist in structural family therapy. *Journal of Marital and Family Therapy, 18,* 269–281.

Aponte, H. J., & VanDeusen, J. H. (1981). Structural family therapy. In A. S. Gurman & D. P. Kniskern (Eds.), *Handbook of family therapy* (Vol. 1, pp. 310–360). New York: Brunner/Mazel.

Appel, A., & Holden, G. (1998). The co-occurrence of spouse and physical child abuse: A review and appraisal. *Journal of Family Psychology, 12*, 578–599.

Asay, T. P., & Lambert, M. J. (1999). The therapeutic relationship. In M. A. Hubble, B. L. Duncan, & S. D. Miller (Eds.), *The heart and soul of change: What works in therapy* (pp. 133–178). Washington, DC: American Psychological Association.

Avis, J. M. (1992). Where are all the family therapists? Abuse and violence within families and family therapy's response. *Journal of Marital and Family Therapy, 18*, 225–232.

Azar, S. T., Nix, R. L., Makin-Byrd, K. (2005). Parenting schemas and the process of change. *Journal of Marital and Family Therapy, 3*(11), 45–58.

Azrin, N. H., Donohue, B., Teichner, G. A., Crum, T., Howell, J., & DeCato, L. A. (2001). A controlled evaluation and description of individual-cognitive problem solving and family-behavior therapies in dually-diagnosed conduct-disordered and substance-dependent youth. *Journal of Child and Adolescent Substance Abuse, 11*(1), 1–43.

Baldwin, S. A., Christian, S., Berkeljon, A., & Shadish, W. R. (2012). The effects of family therapies for adolescent delinquency and substance abuse: A meta-analysis. *Journal of Marital and Family Therapy, 38*(1), 281–304.

Bancroft, L., & Silverman, J. (2002). The batterer as parent: The impact of domestic violence on family dynamics. Thousand Oaks, CA: Sage.

Banmen, J. (2002). The Satir model: Yesterday and today. *Contemporary Family Therapy, 24*(1), 7–22. doi:10.1023/A:1014365304082

Barber, J. G., & Crisp, B. R. (1995). The "pressure to change" approach to working with the partners of heavy drinkers. *Addiction, 90*, 269–276.

Barber, J. G., & Gilbertson, R. (1996). An experimental study of brief unilateral intervention for the partners of heavy drinkers. *Research on Social Work Practice, 6*, 325–336.

Barber, J. G., & Gilbertson, R. (1998). Evaluation of a self-help manual for the female partners of heavy drinkers. *Research on Social Work Practice, 8,* 141–151.

Barlow, D. H., O'Brien, G. T., & Last, C. G. (1984). Couples treatment of agoraphobia. *Behavior Therapy, 15,* 41–58.

Barnes, J. S., & Bennett, C. E. (2002, February). *The Asian population: 2000* (Census 2000 Brief No. C2KBR/01-16). Retrieved March 16, 2009, from http://www.census.gov/prod/2002pubs/c2kbr01-16.pdf

Barry, D. (1997). Telling changes: From narrative family therapy to organizational change and development. *Journal of Organizational Change Management, 10*(1), 30–46.

Bateson, G. (1972). *The cybernetics of "self": A theory of alcoholism.* In G. Bateson (ed.), *Steps to an ecology of mind* (pp. 309–337). Chicago, IL: University of Chicago Press.

Bateson, G., Jackson, D., Haley, J., & Weakland, J. (1956). Toward a theory of schizophrenia. *Behavioral Science, 1*(4), 251–264.

Bateson, G., Jackson, D. D., Haley, J., & Weakland, J. H. (1972). Toward a theory of schizophrenia. In G. Bateson, *Steps to an ecology of mind* (pp. 201–227). Northvale, NJ: Jason Aronson.

Baucom, D. H., & Hoffman, J. A. (1986). The effectiveness of marital therapy: Current status and applications to the clinical setting. In N. S. Jacobson & A. S. Gurman (Eds.), *Clinical handbook of marital therapy* (pp. 576–620). New York: Guilford Press.

Beach, S. (2002). Affective disorders. In D. H. Sprenkle (Ed.), *Effectiveness research in marriage and family therapy* (pp. 289–309). Alexandria, VA: American Association for Marriage and Family Therapy.

Beach, S. R. H., & Whisman, M. A. (2012). Affective disorders. *Journal of Marital and Family Therapy, 38*(1), 201–219.

Beach, S. R. H., Whisman, M., & O'Leary, K. D. (1994). Marital therapy for depression: Theoretical foundations, current status and future directions. *Behavior Therapy, 25,* 345–371.

Beck, A.T. (1976). *Cognitive therapy and the emotional disorder*. New York, NY: International Universal Press.

Becvar, D. S. (1997). *Soul healing*. New York: Basic Books.

Becvar, D. S., & Becvar, R. J. (1988). *Family therapy: A systemic integration* (1st ed.). Boston: Allyn & Bacon.

Becvar, D. S., & Becvar, R. J. (1993). *Family therapy: A systemic integration* (2nd ed.). Boston: Allyn & Bacon.

Becvar, D. S., Caldwell, K. L., & Winek, J. L. (2006). The relationship between marriage and family therapists and complementary and alternative medicine approaches: A qualitative study. *Journal of Marital and Family Therapy, 32,* 115–126.

Benson, M. J., Schnindler-Zimmerman, T., & Martin, D. (1991) Accessing children's perception of their family: Circular questioning revisited. *Journal of Marital and Family Therapy*, 17(4), 363–372.

Bentovim, A., & Kinston, W. (1991). Focal family therapy: Joining systems theory with psychodynamic understanding. In Gurman, A. S., & Kniskern, D. P. (Eds.), *Handbook of family therapy* (Vol. 2). New York, NY: Brunner/Mazel.

Bepko, C., & Johnson, T. (2000). Gay and lesbian couples in therapy: Perspectives for the contemporary family therapist. *Journal of Marital and Family Therapy, 26,* 409–419.

Berg, I. K., & Gallagher, D. (1991). Solution focused brief treatment with adolescent substance abusers. In T. Todd & M. D. Selekman (Eds.), *Family therapy approaches with adolescent substance abusers* (pp. 93–111). Boston: Allyn & Bacon.

Berg, I. K., & Miller, S. (1992). Working with the problem drinker: A solution-focused approach. New York: Norton.

Berg, I. K., & Reuss, N. (1997). Solutions step-by-step: A substance abuse treatment manual. New York: Norton.

Berger, P., & Luckman, T. (1966). The social construction of reality: A treatise in the sociology of knowledge. New York: Anchor Press.

Bergin, A. E., & Garfield, S. L. (1994). Overview, trends, and future issues. In A. E. Bergin & S. L. Garfield (Eds.), *Handbook of psychotherapy and behavior change*. New York: Norton.

Bermudez, J. M., & Bermudez, S. (2002). Altar-making with Latino families: A narrative therapy perspective. *Journal of Family Psychotherapy, 13*(3/4), 329–347.

Besa, D. (1994). Evaluating narrative family therapy using single-system research designs. *Research on Social Work Practice, 4,* 309–325.

Bigner, J. J., & Gottlieb, A. R. (Eds.) (2006). Intervention with families of gay, lesbian, bisexual, and transgender people: From the inside out. New York: Harrington Press.

Black, L., & Jackson, V. (2005). Families of African origin: An overview. In M. McGoldrick, J. Giordano, & N. Garcia-Preto (Eds.), *Ethnicity and family therapy* (3rd ed). (pp. 77–86). New York, NY: Guilford Press.

Blanton, P. G. (2013). *Mind over marriage: Transforming your relationship using centering prayer and neuroscience.* New York, NY: Lantern Books.

Blasko, K., Winek, J., & Bieschke, K. (2007). Therapists' prototypical assessment of domestic violence situations. *Journal of Marital and Family Therapy, 33,* 258–269.

Bograd, M. (1992). Values in conflict: Challenges to family therapists' thinking. *Journal of Marital and Family Therapy, 18,* 245–257.

Bond, C., Woods, K., Humphrey, N., Symes, W., & Green, L. (2013). Practitioner review: The effectiveness of solution focused brief therapy with children and families: A systematic and critical evaluation of the literature from 1990–2010. *The Journal of Child Psychology and Psychiatry, 54*(7), 707–723.

Bordin, E. S. (1979). The generalizability of the psychoanalytic concept of the working alliance. *Psychotherapy, 16,* 252–260.

Bowen, M. (1974). Alcoholism as viewed through family systems theory and family psychotherapy. *Annals of the New York Academy of Sciences, 233,* 125–132.

Bowen, M. (1978). On the differentiation of a self. In M. Bowen, *Family therapy in clinical practice* (pp. 467–528). Northvale, NJ: Jason Aronson.

Bowen, M. (1988). *Family therapy in clinical practice.* Northvale, NJ: Jason Aronson.

Bowers, M. (2007). The making of the MFT profession: Standards, regulation, and the AAMFT. *Family Therapy Magazine, 6*(4), 12–18.

Bowlby, J. (1969 & 1973). *Attachment and loss* (12 vols.). New York: Basic Books.

Bowlby, J. (1979). *The making and breaking of affectional bonds.* London: Tavistock Publications.

Bowlby, J. (1988). *A secure base: Clinical applications of attachment theory.* London: Routledge.

Boszormenyi-Nagy, I. (1972). Loyality implications of the transference model in psychotherapy. *AMA Achieves of General Psychiatry, 27,* 374–380.

Boszormenyi-Nagy, I., & Krasner, B. R. (1986). *Between give and take.* New York, NY: Brunner/Mazel.

Boyd-Franklin, N. (1989). *Black families in therapy: A multisystems approach.* New York: Guilford Press.

Braveman, L. (Ed.). (1988). *Women, feminism, and family therapy.* New York: Haworth Press.

Broderick, C. B. (1993). Understanding family process: Basics of family systems theory. Newbury Park, CA: Sage.

Broderick, C. B., & Schrader, S. S. (1991). The history of professional marriage and family therapy. In A. S. Gurman & D. P. Kniskern (Eds.), *Handbook of family therapy* (Vol. 2, pp. 3–40). New York: Brunner/Mazel.

Brott, P. E. (2004). Constructivist assessment in career counseling. Journal *of Career Development, 30*(3), 189–200.

Brown, A. (1987). *When battered women kill.* New York: Free Press.

Brown, T. L., Henggeler, S. W., Schoenwald, S. K., Brondino, M. J., & Pickrel, S. G. (1999). Multisystemic treatment of substance abusing and dependent juvenile offenders: Effects on school attendance at posttreatment and 6-month follow-up. *Children's Services: Social Policy, Research and Practice, 2,* 81–93.

Bureau of Labor Statistics, U.S. Department of Labor. (January 8, 2014). *Mental Health Counselors and Marriage and Family Therapists.* Retrieved from: http://www.bls.gov/ooh/community-and-social-service/mental-health-counselors-and-marriage-and-family-therapists.htm

Butler, W. R., & Powers, K. V. (1996). Solution-focused grief therapy. In S. D. Miller, M. A. Hubble, & B. L. Duncan (Eds.), *Handbook of solution-focused brief therapy* (pp. 228–247). San Francisco: Jossey-Bass.

Caldwell, K. L., Winek, J. L., & Becvar, D. S. (2006). The relationship between marriage and family therapists and complementary and alternative medicine: A national survey. *Journal of Marital and Family Therapy, 32,* 101–114.

Calvert, S., & Calvert, P. (1993). *Latin America in the twentieth century.* New York: St. Martin's Press.

Campbell, D., Draper, R., & Cruthley, E. (1991). The Milan systemic approach to family therapy. In A. S. Gurman & D. P. Kniskern (Eds.), *Handbook of Family Therapy* (Vol. II). New York, NY: Brunner/Mazel.

Campbell, T. L., & Patterson, J. M. (1995). The effectiveness of family interventions in the treatment of physical illness. *Journal of Marital and Family Therapy, 21,* 545–583.

Cano, A., & O'Leary, K. D. (2000). Infidelity and separations precipitate major depressive episodes and symptoms of nonspecific depression and anxiety. *Journal of Counseling and Clinical Psychology, 68,* 774–781.

Caplan, P. J., & Hall-McCorquodale, I. (1985). Mother-blaming in major clinical journals. *American Journal of Orthopsychiatry, 55,* 345–353.

Carlson, T. D. (1997). Using art in narrative therapy: Enhancing therapeutic possibilities. *American Journal of Family Therapy, 25,* 271–283.

Carlson, T. D., Kirkpatrick, D., Hecker, L., & Killmer, M. (2002). Religion, spirituality, and marriage and family therapy: A study of family therapists' beliefs about the appropriateness of addressing religious and spiritual issues in therapy. *American Journal of Family Therapy, 30,* 157–171.

Carneiro, R. (2013) The impact of Christianity on therapy with Latino families) *Contemporary Family Therapy.* 35(1)137–146.

Carnes, P. J. (1989). Sexually addicted families: Clinical use of the circumplex model. In D. H. Olson, C. S. Russell, & D. H. Sprenkle (Eds.), *Circumplex model: Systemic assessment and treatment of families* (pp. 113–140). New York: Haworth Press.

Carson, T. S., McGeorge, C. R., & Anderson, A. (2011). The importance of spirituality in couple and family therapy: A comparative study of therapists' and educators' beliefs. *Contemporary Family Therapy, 33,* 3–16.

Casey, E. A., & Nurivs, P. S. (2006). Trends in the prevalence and characteristics of sexual violence: A cohort analysis. *Violence and Victims, 22,* 629–644.

Casey, J. A., & Buchan, L. G. (1997). Family approaches to school psychology: Brief strategic intervention. In W. M. Walsh & G. R. Williams (Eds.), *Schools and family therapy: Using systems theory and family therapy in the resolution of school problems* (pp. 69–73). Springfield, IL: Charles C Thomas.

Chamberlain, P., & Mihalic, S. (1998). *Multidimensional treatment foster care* (Blueprints for Violence Prevention, Vol. 8). Boulder, CO: Center for the Study and Prevention of Violence.

Chamberlain, P., & Rosicky, J. (1995). The effectiveness of family therapy in the treatment of adolescents with conduct disorders and delinquency. *Journal of Marital and Family Therapy, 21,* 441–459.

Chen, R., (2012) Narrative therapy for Chinese adults raised as an only child. *Contemporary Family Therapy 34* (1) 104–111.

Cloutier, P. F., Manion, I. G., Walker, J. G., & Johnson, S. M. (2002). Emotionally focused interventions for couples with chronically ill children: A 2-year follow-up. *Journal of Marital and Family Therapy, 28,* 391–398.

Coenen, M. (1998). Helping families with homosexual children: A model for counseling. *Journal of Homosexuality, 36*(2), 73–85.

Colapinto, J. (1991). Structural family therapy. In A. S. Gurman & D. P. Kniskern (Eds.), *Handbook of family therapy* (Vol. 2, pp. 417–443). New York: Brunner/Mazel.

Constantine, L. (1986). Family paradigms: The practice of theory in family therapy. New York: Guilford Press.

Cowdery, R. S., Scarborough, N., Kudson-Martin, C., Seshadri, G., Lewis, M., Mahoney, A. R. (2009). Gendered power in cultural contexts: Part II middle class African American heterosexual couples with children. *Family Process, 48*(1), 24–39.

Cordova, J. V., & Jacobson, N. S. (1993). Couple distress. In D. H. Barlow (Ed.), *Clinical handbook of psychological disorders: A step-by-step treatment manual* (2nd ed., pp. 481–512). New York: Guilford Press.

Cotton, S., Larkin, E., Hoopes, A., Cromer, B. A., & Rosenthal, S. L. (2005). The impact of adolescent spirituality on depressive symptoms and health risk behaviors. *Journal of Adolescent Health, 36,* 529.

Crane, D. R., Wampler, K. S., Sprenkle, D. H., Sandberg, J. G., & Hovestadt, A. J. (2002). The scientist- practitioner model in marriage and family therapy doctoral programs. *Journal of Marital and Family Therapy, 28,* 75–83.

Crane, D. R., & Christenson, J. (2014). A summary report of cost effectiveness: Recognizing the value of family therapy in health care. In J. Hodgson, A. Lamson, T. Mendenhall, & R. Crane (Eds.), *Medical family therapy: Advanced applications.* New York, NY: Springer.

Dankoski, M. E. (2001). Pulling on the heart strings: An emotionally focused approach to family life cycle transitions. *Journal of Marital and Family Therapy, 27,* 177–187.

Dattilio, F. M. (2001). Cognitive-behavioral family therapy: Contemporary myths and misconceptions. *Contemporary Family Therapy, 23*(1), 3–18.

Dattilio, F. M. (2005). The restructuring of family schemas: A cognitive-behavioral perspective. *Journal of Marital and Family Therapy, 31*(1), 15–30.

Davey, J. (1999). Constructionist approaches to bereavement and therapy: Part 2. *Counseling Psychology Review, 14,* 3–11.

de Castro, S., & Guterman, J. T. (2008). Solution-focused therapy for families coping with suicide. *Journal of Marital and Family Therapy, 34,* 93–106.

De Jong, P., & Hopwood, L. E. (1996). Outcome research on treatment conducted at the Brief Family Therapy Center 1992–1993. In S. D. Miller, M. A. Hubble, & B. L. Duncan (Eds.), *Handbook of solution-focused brief therapy* (pp. 272–298). San Francisco: Jossey-Bass.

Denton, W. H. (1990). A family systems analysis of *DSM-III-R*. *Journal of Marital and Family Therapy, 16,* 113–125.

Denton, W. H., Patterson, J. E., & Van Meir, E. S. (1997). Use of the *DSM* in marriage and family therapy programs: Current practices and attitudes. *Journal of Marital and Family Therapy, 23,* 81–86.

Denton, W. H., Wittenborn, A. K., & Golden, R. N. (2012). Augmenting antidepressant medication treatment of depressed women with emotionally focused therapy for couples: A randomized pilot study. *Journal of Marital and Family Therapy, 38*(s1), 23–38.

de Shazer, S. (1978). Brief therapy with couples. *International Journal of Family Counseling, 6,* 17–30.

de Shazer, S. (1979). Brief therapy with families. *American Journal of Family Therapy, 7,* 83–95.

de Shazer, S. (1982). Pattern of brief family therapy: An ecosystemic approach. New York: Guilford Press.

de Shazer, S. (1984). The death of resistance. *Family Process, 23,* 11–17.

de Shazer, S. (1985). *Keys to solutions in brief therapy.* New York: Norton.

de Shazer, S. (1987). Minimal elegance. *Family Therapy Networker, 11*(5), 57–60.

de Shazer, S. (1988). Clues: Investigating solutions in brief therapy. New York: Norton.

de Shazer, S. (1994). *Words were originally magic.* New York: Norton.

de Shazer, S., & Berg, I. K. (1985). A part is not apart: Working with only one of the partners present. In A. Gurman (Ed.), *Casebook of marital therapy* (pp. 97–110). New York: Guilford Press.

de Shazer, S. & Dolan, Y. (2007). *More than miracles: The state of the art of solution-focused therapy.* London & New York: Routledge.

Deutsch, M., & Brown, B. (1964). Social influence in Negro-white intellectual differences. *Journal of Social Issues, 20,* 27–36.

Dickerson, V. C., & Zimmerman, J. (1992). Families with adolescents: Escaping problem lifestyles. *Family Process, 31,* 341–353.

Dickerson, V. C. (2010). Positioning oneself within an epistemology: Refining our thinking about integrative approaches. *Family Process, 49(3),* 349–368.

Dobash, R. E., & Dobash, R. P. (1979). *Violence against wives: A case against the patriarchy.* New York: Free Press.

Doherty, W. J., McDaniel, S. H., & Hepworth, J. (2014). Contributions of medical family therapy to the changing health care system. *Family Process, 53(3),* 529–543.

Dolan, Y. M. (1991). Resolving sexual abuse: Solution-focused therapy and Ericksonian hypnosis for adult survivors. New York: Norton.

Duncan, B., Miller, S. D., & Sparks, J. A. (2004). The heroic client: A revolutionary way to improve effectiveness through client-directed, outcome-informed therapy. San Francisco: Jossey-Bass.

Dunn, R., & Schwebel, A. (1995). Meta-analytic review of marital therapy outcome research. *Journal of Family Psychology, 9,* 58–68.

Dutton, D. G. (1988). The domestic assault of women: Psychological and criminal justice perspectives. Toronto, Ontario, Canada: Allyn & Bacon.

Edleson, J. (1999). Children's witnessing of adult domestic violence. *Journal of Interpersonal Violence, 14,* 839–870.

Efron, D., & Veenendaal, K. (1993). Suppose a miracle doesn't happen: The non miracle option. *Journal of Systemic Therapies, 12,* 11–18.

Ellis, A. (1962). *Reason and emotion in psychotherapy.* New York, NY: Lyle Sturt.

Ellis, A. (1978). Family therapy: A phenomenological and action directive approach. *Journal of Marriage and Family Counseling, 4(2),* 43–50.

Ellis, A., & Harper, R. A. (1961). *A guide to rational living.* Englewood Cliffs, NJ: Prentice Hall.

Engel, G. L. (1977). The need for a new medical model: A challenge for biomedicine. *Science, 196,* 129–136.

Engel, G. L. (1980). The chemical application of the biopsychosocial model. *American Journal of Psychiatry, 137*, 535–544.

Ennis, S. R., Rios-Vargas, M., & Albert, N. G. (2011). The Hispanic population: 2010 Census briefs. Retrieved from http://www.census.gov/prod/cen2010/briefs/c2010br-04.pdf

Eppler, C., & Carolan, M. T. (2005). Biblionarrative: A narrative technique uniting oral and written life-stories. *Journal of Family Psychotherapy, 16*(4), 31–43.

Epston, D. (1994). Extending the conversation. *Family Therapy Networker, 18*(6), 31–37, 62–63.

Falicov, C. (1982). Mexican families. In M. McGoldrick, J. K. Pearce, & J. Giordano (Eds.), *Ethnicity and family therapy* (1st ed., pp. 134–163). New York: Guilford Press.

Falicov, C. (1996). Mexican families. In M. McGoldrick, J.Giordano, & J. K. Pearce (Eds.), *Ethnicity and family therapy* (2nd ed., pp. 169–182). New York: Guilford Press.

Falloon, I. R. H. (1991). Behavioral family therapy. In A. S. Gurman & D. P. Kniskern (Eds.), *Handbook of family therapy* (Vol. 2, pp. 65–95). New York: Brunner/Mazel.

Fernandes, E. M. (2007). When what I wish makes me worse... to make coherence flexible. *Psychology and Psychotherapy: Theory, Research and Practice, 80*, 165–180.

Finkelhor, D. (1986). Abusers: Special topics. In D. Finkelhor and Associates (Eds.), *A sourcebook on child sexual abuse* (pp. 119–142). Beverly Hills, CA: Sage.

Fish, S. L., & Harvey, R. G. (2005). *Nurturing queer youth: Family therapy transformed*. New York, NY: W. W. Norton.

Fishman, H. C. (2006). Juvenile anorexia nervosa: Family therapy's natural niche. *Journal of Marital and Family Therapy, 32*, 505–514.

Flemons, D., Liscio, M., Gordon, A. B., Hibel, J., Gutierrez-Hersh, A., & Rebholz, C. L. (2010). Fostering solutions: Bringing brief-therapy principles and practices to the child welfare system. *Journal of Marital and Family Therapy, 36*(1), 80–95.

Focht, L., & Beardslee, W. R. (1996). "Speech after long silence": The use of narrative therapy in a preventive intervention for children of parents with affective disorder. *Family Process, 35,* 407–422.

Foley, S. H., Rounsaville, B. J., Weissman, M. M., Sholomaskas, D., & Cheveron, E. (1989). Individual versus conjoint interpersonal therapy for depressed patients with marital disputes. *International Journal of Family Psychiatry, 10,* 29–42.

Frank, J. D. (1973). *Persuasion and healing* (2nd ed.). Baltimore: Johns Hopkins University Press.

Fraenkel, P., Hameline, T. & Shannon, M. (2009) Narrative and Collaborative practices in work with families that are homeless. *Journal of Marital and Family Therapy 35*(3) 325–342.

Franklin, A. J. (1993). The invisibility syndrome. *Family Therapy Networker, 17*(4), 33–39.

Frazier, E. F. (1966). *The Negro family in the United States.* Chicago: University of Chicago Press.

Freedman, J., & Combs, G. (1996). *Narrative therapy: The social construction of preferred realities.* New York, NY: Norton.

Freedman, J. & Combs, G. (2009) Narrative ideas for consulting with communities and organuzations: *Ripples from the gathering. Family Process 48*(3) 347–362.

Friedman, E. H. (1991). Bowen theory and therapy. In A. S. Gurman & D. P. Kniskern (Eds.), *Handbook of family therapy* (Vol. 2, pp. 134–170). New York: Brunner/Mazel.

Fromm-Reichmann, F. (1948). Notes on the development of treatment of schizophrenics by psychoanalytic psychotherapy. *Psychiatry, 11,* 263–274.

Gallup Poll Inc. (2008). *Religion.* Retrieved from *http://www.gallup/poll/1690/Religion.aspx*

Gallup Poll Inc. (2011). *More Than 9 in 10 Americans continue to believe in God*. Retrieved from http://www.gallup.com/poll/147887/ Americans-Continue-Believe-God.aspx?utm_source=Believe%20in%20 god&utm_medium=search&utm_campaign=tiles

Garcia-Preto, N. (1996). Latino families. In M. McGoldrick, J. Giordano, & J. K. Pearce (Eds.), *Ethnicity and family therapy* (2nd ed., pp. 141–154). New York, NY: Guilford Press.

Garcia-Preto, N. (2005). Latino families: An overview. In M. McGoldrick, J. Giordano, & N. Garcia-Preto (Eds.), *Ethnicity and family therapy* (3rd ed., pp. 141–154). New York, NY: Guilford Press.

Gergen, K. J. (2009). An invitation to social construction (2nd ed.). Thousand Oaks, CA: Sage.

Gerson, R., McGoldrick, M., & Petry, S. (2008). Genograms: Assessment and intervention (3rd ed.). New York, NY: Norton.

Gibson, D., M. (2013) Ambiguous roles in a stepfamily: Using maps of narrative practice to develop a new family story with adolescents and Parents. *Contemporary Family Therapy* 35(4) 793–805.

Gibson, J. M. (1993). Use of Bowen theory. *Journal of Addictions and Offender Counseling, 14*(1), 25–36.

Gingerich, W. J., & Eisengart, S. (2000). Solution-focused brief therapy: A review of the outcome research. *Family Process, 39,* 477–498.

Golann, S. (1988). On second order family therapy. *Family Process, 27,* 51–65.

Goldner, V. (1985). Feminism and family therapy. *Family Process, 24,* 31–47.

Goldner, V. (1988). Generation and gender: Normative and covert hierarchies. *Family Process, 27,* 17–33.

Goldner, V. (1993). Power and hierarchy: Let's talk about it! *Family Process, 32,* 157–162.

Gordon, S. B., & Davidson, N. (1981). Behavioral parent training. In A. S. Gurman & D. P. Kniskern (Eds.), *Handbook of family therapy* (Vol. 1, pp. 517–555). New York: Brunner/Mazel.

Graham-Bermann, S. (1998). The impact of woman abuse on children's social development: Research and theoretical perspectives. In G. Holden, R. Geffner, & E. Jouriles (Eds.), *Children exposed to marital violence: Theory, research, and applied issues* (pp. 21–54). Washington, DC: American Psychological Association.

Greenberg, L. S., & Johnson, S. (1985). Emotionally focused couples therapy: An effective systemic approach. In N. S. Jacobson & A. S. Gurman (Eds.), *Handbook of clinical and marital therapy* (pp. 253–278). New York: Guilford Press.

Greenberg, L. S., & Johnson, S. M. (1988). *Emotionally focused therapy for couples*. New York: Guilford Press.

Greene, K., & Bogo, M. (2002). The different faces of intimate violence: Implications for assessment and treatment. *Journal of Marital and Family Therapy, 28,* 455–466.

Greenman, P. S., & Johnson, S. M. (2013). Process research on emotionally focused therapy (EFT) for couples: Linking theory to practice. *Family Process, 52*(1), 46–61.

Greenson, R. R. (1965). The working alliance and the transference neurosis. *Psychoanalytic Quarterly, 34*(1) 155–181.

Groth, A. H., Hobson, W. F., & Gary, T. S. (1982). The child molester: Clinical observations. In J. Conte & D. Shor (Eds.), *Social work and child sexual abuse* (pp. 129–142). New York: Haworth Press.

Guerin, P. J., & Pendagast, E. G. (1976). Evaluation of family system and genogram. In P. J. Guerin (Ed.), *Family therapy* (pp. 450–464). New York: Gardner Press.

Gurman, A. S., & Kniskern D. P. (1978). Behavioral marriage therapy: II. Empirical perspective. *Family Process, 17,* 139–148.

Gurman, A. S., & Kniskern, D. P. (1981). Family therapy outcome research: Knowns and unknowns. In A. S. Gurman & D. P. Kniskern (Eds.), *Handbook of family therapy* (Vol. 1, pp. 742–775). New York: Brunner/Mazel.

Gurman, A. S., & Knudson, R. M. (1978). Behavioral marriage therapy: I. A psychodynamic-systems analysis and critique. *Family Process, 17,* 121–138.

Guttman, H. (1991). Systems theory, cybernetics, and epistemology. In A. S. Gurman & D. P. Kniskern (Eds.), *Handbook of family therapy* (Vol. 2, pp. 41–61). New York: Brunner/Mazel.

Guzmán, B. (2001, May.) *The Hispanic population: 2000* (Census 2000 Brief No. C2KBR/01-3). Retrieved March 16, 2009, from http://www.census.gov/prod/2001pubs/c2kbr01-3.pdf

Haley, J. (1973). Uncommon therapy: The psychiatric techniques of Milton H. Erickson, M.D. New York: Norton.

Haley, J. (1980). Leaving home: The therapy of disturbed young people. New York: McGraw-Hill.

Haley, J. (1984). Ordeal therapy: Unusual ways to change behavior. San Francisco: Jossey-Bass.

Haley, J. (1987). *Problem solving therapy.* San Francisco: Jossey-Bass.

Hanson, B. G. (1995). *General systems theory: Beginning with wholes.* Washington, DC: Taylor and Francis.

Hanson, R. F., & Spratt, E. G. (2000). Reactive attachment disorders: What we know about the disorder and the implications for treatment. *Child Maltreatment: Journal of the American Professional Society on the Abuse of Children, 5*(2), 132–154.

Hardy, K. (1994). Marginalization or development? A response to Shields, Wynne, McDaniel, and Gawinski. *Journal of Marital and Family Therapy, 20,* 139–143.

Hardy, K. V. (1989). The theoretical myth of sameness: A critical issue in family therapy training and treatment. *Journal of Psychotherapy & the Family,* 6(1–2), 17–33.

Hare-Mustin, R. T. (1978). A feminist approach to family therapy. *Family Process, 17,* 181–194.

Hare-Mustin, R. T. (1980). Family therapy may be dangerous to your health. *Professional Psychology, 11,* 935–938.

Harvey, A. and Feagin, J. R. (2013). *Yes we can?*: White racial framing and the Obama presidency. (2nd ed.). New York, NY. Routledge.

Hayland, P. S. (1990). Family therapy in the hospital treatment of children and adolescents. *Bulletin of the Menninger Clinic, 54*(1), 48–64.

Heider, F. (1946). Attitudes and cognitive organization. *Journal of Psychology, 21,* 107–112.

Helmeke K. B., & Bischof, G. H. (2002). Recognizing and raising spiritual and religious issues in therapy: Guidance for the timid. *Journal of Family Psychotherapy, 13,* 195–214.

Hendricks, B., Bradley, L. J., Southern, S., Oliver, M., & Birdsall, B. (2011). Ethical code of the international association of marriage and family counselors. *The Family Journal: Counseling and Therapy for Couples and Families, 19*(2), 217–224.

Henggeler, S. W., & Borduin, C. M. (1990). Family therapy and beyond: A multisystemic approach to treating the behavior problems of children and adolescents. Pacific Grove, CA: Brooks/Cole.

Henggeler, S. W., Schoenwald, S. K., Borduin, C. M., Rowland, M. D., & Cunningham, P. B. (1998). *Multisystemic treatment of antisocial behavior in children and adolescents.* New York: Guilford Press.

Henggeler, S. W., Schoenwald, S. K., Rowland, M. D., & Cunningham, P. B. (2002). *Serious emotional disturbance in children and adolescents: Multisystemic therapy.* New York: Guilford Press.

Henggeler, S. W., & Sheidow, A. J. (2002). Conduct disorder and delinquency. In D. H. Sprenkle (Ed.), *Effectiveness research in marriage and family therapy* (pp. 27–51). Alexandria, VA: American Association for Marriage and Family Therapy.

Henggeler, S. W., & Sheidow, A. J. (2012). Empirically supported family-based treatments for conduct disorder and delinquency in adolescents. *Journal of Marital and Family Therapy, 38*(1), 30–58.

Herman, J. L. (1990). Sex offenders: A feminist perspective. In W. L. Marshall, D. R. Laws, & H. E. Barbarea (Eds.), *Handbook of sexual assault: Issues, theories, and treatment of the offender* (pp. 177–193). New York: Plenum Press.

Hertlein, K. M., & Killmer, J. M. (2004). Towards differentiated decision-making: Family systems theory with the homeless clinical population. *American Journal of Family Therapy, 32,* 255–270.

Hines, P. M., & Boyd-Franklin, N. (1982). Black families. In M. McGoldrick, J. K. Pearce, & J. Giordano (Eds.), *Ethnicity and family therapy* (1st ed., pp. 84–107). New York: Guilford Press.

Hines, P. M., & Boyd-Franklin, N. (1996). African American families. In M. McGoldrick, J. Giordano, & J. K. Pearce (Eds.), *Ethnicity and family therapy* (2nd ed., pp. 66–96). New York: Guilford Press.

Ho, M. K. (1987). *Family therapy with ethnic minorities.* Newbury Park, CA: Sage.

Hodgson, J., Lamson, A., Mendenhall, T., & Crane, R. (2012). Medical family therapy: Opportunity for workforce development in healthcare. *Contemporary Family Therapy, 34*(2), 143–146.

Hodgson, J., Lamson, A., Mendenhall, T., & Crane, R. (2014). *Medical family therapy: Advanced applications.* New York, NY: Springer.

Hoeffel, E. M., Rastogi, S., Kim M. O., & Shahid, H (2012). The Asian population: 2010 Census briefs. Retrieved from https://www.census.gov/prod/cen2010/briefs/c2010br-11.pdf

Hooks, B. (2000a). *Feminist Theory: From margin to center.* (2nd ed.). Cambridge, MA: South End Press.

Hooks, B. (2000b). *Where we stand: Class matters.* New York, NY: Routledge.

Hooks, B. (2001). Feminism is for everybody: Passionate politics. Pluto Press.

Hosking, D. M., & Bass, A. (2001). Constructing changes in relational processes: Introducing a social constructivist approach to change work. *Career Development International, 6,* 348–360.

Huber, C. V. H., & Baruth, L. G. (1989). Rational-emotive family therapy: A systems perspective. New York, NY: Springer.

Inclan, J., & Hernandez, M. (1992). Cross-cultural perspectives and codependence: The case of poor Hispanics. *American Journal of Orthopsychiatry, 16,* 244–255.

Jackson, D. D. (1965). The study of the family. *Family Process, 4,* 1–20.

Jacobson, N. S. (1978). Specific and non-specific factors in the effectiveness of behavioral approaches to the treatment of marital discord. *Journal of Consulting and Clinical Psychology, 46,* 442–452.

Jacobson, N. S. (1991). To be or not to be behavioral when working with couples. *Journal of Family Psychology, 4,* 436–445.

Jacobson, N. S. (1992). Behavioral couple therapy: A new beginning. *Behavior Therapy, 23,* 493–506.

Jacobson, N. S., & Addis, M. E. (1993). Research on couples and couple therapy: What do we know? Where are we going? *Journal of Consulting and Clinical Psychology, 61,* 85–93.

Jacobson, N. S., Dobson, K., Fruzzetti, A. E., Schmaling, D. B., & Salusky, S (1991). Marital therapy as treatment for depression. *Journal of Consulting and Clinical Psychology, 59,* 547–557.

Jacobson, N. S., & Margolin, G. (1979). Marital therapy: Strategies based on social learning and behavioral exchange principles. New York, NY: Brunner/Mazel.

Jacobson, N. S., Schmaling, K. B., & Holtzworth-Munroe, M. (1987). Component analysis of behavioral marital therapy: Two year follow-up and prediction of relapse. Journal *of Marital and Family Therapy, 13,* 187–195.

Jacobson, N. S., & Weiss, R. L. (1978). Behavioral marriage therapy: III. The contents of Gurman et al. may be hazardous to our health. *Family Process, 17,* 149–163.

James, K., & MacKinnon, L. (1990). The incestuous family revisited: A critical analysis of family therapy myths. *Journal of Marital and Family Therapy, 16,* 71–88.

Johnson, S. (2001). Family therapy saves the planet: Messianic tendencies in the family systems literature. *Journal of Marital and Family Therapy, 27*(1), 3–11.

Johnson, S. M. (1996). Creating connection: The practice of emotionally focused marital therapy. New York: Brunner/Mazel.

Johnson, S. M. (2002). Emotionally focused couple therapy with trauma survivors: Strengthening attachment bonds. New York: Guilford Press.

Johnson, S. M., & Greenman, P. S. (2006). The path to a secure bond: Emotionally focused couple therapy. *Journal of Clinical Psychology: In Session, 62*, 597–609.

Johnson, S. M., Makinen, J. A., & Millikin, J. W. (2002). Attachment injuries in couple relationships: A new perspective on impasses in couples therapy. *Journal of Marital and Family Therapy, 27*, 145–155.

Johnson, S. M., & Wittenborn, A. K. (2012). New research findings on emotionally focused therapy: Introduction to special section. *Journal of Marital and Family Therapy, 38*(s1), 18–22.

Johnson, S. M., & Zuccarini, D. (2010). Integrating sex and attachment in emotionally focused couple therapy. *Journal of Marital and Family Therapy, 36*(4), 431–445.

Johnson, V. E. (1986). *Intervention: How to help someone who doesn't want help*. Minneapolis, MN: Johnson Institute Books.

Jones, K. E., Lettenberger, C. L., and Wickel, K. (2011) A Structural/Strategic Lens in the Treatment of Children with Obesity. *The Family Journal: Counseling and Therapy for couples and Families, 19(3)*, 340–346.

Jones, A., & Seagull, A. (1977). Dimensions of the relationship between the black client and the white therapist. *American Psychologist, 32*, 851.

Juhnke, G. A., & Coker, J. K. (1997). A solution-focused intervention with recovering, alcoholic-dependent, single parent mothers and their children. *Journal of Addictions and Offender Counseling, 17*(2), 77–88.

Jung, M. (1984). Structural family therapy: Its implications to Chinese families. *Family Process, 23*, 365–374.

Kantor, D., & Lehr, W. (1975). *Inside the family: Toward a theory of family process*. San Francisco: Jossey-Bass.

Kaplan, H. S. (1974). *The sex therapy*. New York, NY: Quadrangle Books.

Kaslow, N. J., Broth, M. R., Smith, C. O., & Collins, M. H. (2012). Family-based interventions for child and adolescent disorders. *Journal of Marital and Family Therapy, 38*(1), 82–100.

Kaufman, G. (1992). The mysterious disappearance of battered women in family therapists' offices: Male privilege colluding with male violence. *Journal of Marital and Family Therapy, 18,* 233–245.

Keeney, B. (1983). *Aesthetics of Change.* New York, NY: Guilford Press.

Kelcher-Oliver, M., & Smith, C. O. (2015). Using an evidence-based parenting intervention with African American parents, *23*(1), 26–32.

Kerr, M., & Bowen, M. (1988). Family evaluation: An approach based on Bowen theory. New York: Norton.

Kim, J. M. (2003). Structural family therapy and its implications for the Asian American family. *Family Journal: Counseling and Therapy for Couples and Families, 11,* 388–392.

Kim, S. (1985). Family therapy of Asian Americans: A strategic-structural framework. *Psychotherapy, 22,* 342–348.

Kindsvatter, A., Duba, J. D., Dean, E. P. (2008). Structural techniques for engaging reluctant parents in counseling. *The Family Journal: Counseling and Therapy for Couples and Families, 16(3),* 204–211.

King, J. (1991). Dysconcious racism: Ideology, Identity, and the miseducation of teachers. *The Journal of Negro Education, 60*(2), 133–146.

Kiser, D. J., Piercy, F. P., & Lipchik, E. (1993). The integration of emotion in solution-focused therapy. *Journal of Marital and Family Therapy, 19,* 233–242.

Klein, M. (1956). On identification. In M. Klien, D. Heimann, & R. E. Money-Kryle (Eds.), *New Directions in Psychoanalysis.* New York, NY: Basic Books.

Klein, R. G., & Abikoff, H. (1997). Behavior therapy and methylphenidate in the treatment of children with ADHD. *Journal of Attention Disorders, 2,* 89–114.

Kohut, H. (1984). *How does analysis cure?* Chicago, IL: University of Chicago Press.

Korin, E. C. (1994). Social inequalities and therapeutic relationship: Applying Freire's ideas in clinical practice. In R. Almedia (Ed.), *Expansions of feminist family therapy through diversity* (pp. 75–88). New York: Haworth Press

Korin, E. C. (1996). Brazilian families. In M. McGoldrick, J. Giordano, & J. K. Pearce (Eds.), *Ethnicity and family therapy* (2nd ed., pp. 200–213). New York: Guilford Press.

Kouneski, E. (2001). *Circumplex model and FACES: Review of literature.* Retrieved March 15, 2009, from http://www.pe-resources.com/public/Studies_using_FACES.pdf

Kowal, J., Johnson, S. M., & Lee, A. (2003). Chronic illness in couples: A case for emotionally focused therapy. *Journal of Marital and Family Therapy, 29,* 299–310.

Krupnick, J. L. (2002). Brief psychodynamic treatment of PTSD. *Psychotherapy in Practice, 58(8),* 919–932.

Kuhn, T. (1962). *The structure of scientific revolutions.* Chicago: University of Chicago Press.

Lambert-Shute, J. J. (2000). *Stressors in marriage and family therapy training: An exploratory study.* Unpublished master's thesis, Appalachian State University, Boone, NC.

Larner, G. (1996). Narrative child family therapy. *Family Process, 35,* 423–440.

Lambie, G., W., & Milsom, A. (2010) A narrative approach to supporting students with learning disabilities. *Journal of Counseling and Development 88(2)* 196–203.

LaSala, M. C. (2002). Walls and bridges: How coupled gay men and lesbians manage their intergenerational relationships. *Journal of Marital and Family Therapy, 28,* 327–339.

Launer, J. (2002). *Narrative-based primary care: A practical guide.* Abingdon, TN: Radcliffe Medical Press.

Laura, T., & Kindsvatter, A. (2014). A structural approach to assisting families recovering from job loss. *The Family Journal: Counseling and Therapy for Couples and Families, 18(4),* 344–348.

Lebow, J. (1997). The integrative revolution in couple and family therapy. *Family Process, 36,* 1–24.

Lebow, J. (2013). Editorial: DSM-V and family therapy. *Family Process, 52*(2), 155–160.

Lebow, J. L., Chambers, A. L., Christensen, A., & Johnson, S. M. (2012). Research on the treatment of couple distress. *Journal of Marital and Family therapy, 38*(1), 145–168.

Lee, B. K. (2002). Development of a congruence scale based on the Satir model. *Contemporary Family Therapy, 24*(1), 217–239. Retrieved from: http://doi.org/10.1023/A:1014390009534

Lee, B. K. (2008). Congruence in Satir's model: Its spiritual and religious significance. In J. Banmen's (ed.) *Satir transformational systemic therapy*. Mountain View, CA: Science and Behavior Books.

Lee, E. (1996). Asian American families: An overview. In M. McGoldrick, J. Giordano, & J. K. Pearce (Eds.), *Ethnicity and family therapy* (2nd ed., pp. 227–267). New York: Guilford Press.

Lever, K., & Wilson, J. (2005). Encore parenting: When grandparents fill the role of primary caregiver. *Family Journal: Counseling and Therapy for Couples and Families, 13,* 167–171.

Liberman, R. P. (1970). Behavioral approaches to family and couple therapy. *American Journal of Orthopsychiatry, 40,* 106–118.

Liberman, R. P., Wheeler, E., deVisser, L. A., Kuehnel, J., & Kuehnel, T. (1980). *Handbook of marital therapy: A positive approach to helping troubled relationships*. New York: Plenum Press.

Liddle, H. A., & Dakof, G. A. (1995). Family-based treatment for adolescent drug use: State of the science. In E. Rahdert (Ed.), *Adolescent drug abuse: Clinical assessment and therapeutic interventions* (NIDA Research Monograph No. 156, NIH Publication No. 95-3908, pp. 218–254). Rockville, MD: National Institute on Drug Abuse.

Liddle, H. A., Dakof, G. A., Parker, K., Diamond, G. S., Barrett, K., & Tejeda, M. (2001). Multidimensional family therapy for adolescent drug abuse: Results of a randomized clinical trial. *American Journal of Drug and Alcohol Abuse, 27,* 651–688.

Lim, S. & Nakamoto, T. (2008). Genograms: Use in therapy with Asian families with diverse cultural heritages. *Contemporary Family Therapy, 30*(1), 199–219.

Lipchik, E. (1992). A reflecting interview. *Journal of Strategic and Systemic Therapies, 11*(4), 55–74.

Lipchik, E. (1993). "Both/and" solutions. In S. Friedman (Ed.), *The new language of change* (pp. 25–49). New York: Guilford Press.

Lipchik, E. (2002). Beyond technique in solution-focused therapy: Working with emotions and the therapeutic relationship. New York: Guilford Press.

Loeber, R., & Stouthamer-Loeber, M. (1986). Family factors as correlates and predictors of juvenile conduct problems and delinquency. In N. Morris & M. Tonry (Eds.), *Crime and justice* (Vol. 7, pp. 29–149). Chicago: University of Chicago Press.

Long, J., Bonomo, J., Andrews, B., & Brown, B. (2006). Systemic therapeutic approaches with sexual minorities and their families. In J. J. Bigner & A. R. Gottlieb (Eds.), *Interventions with families of gay, lesbian, bisexual, and transgender people: From the inside out.* New York: Harrington Press.

Lopez, F. G. (1993). Attachment theory as an integrative framework for family counseling. *The Family Journal: Counseling and Therapy for Couples and Families, 3*(1), 11–17.

Lovejoy, M. C., Gracyk, P. A., O'Hare, E., & Newman, G. (2000). Maternal depression and parenting behavior: A meta-analytic review. *Clinical Psychology Review, 20,* 561–592.

Luepnitz, D. (1988). The family interpreted: Feminist theory in clinical practice. New York: Basic Books.

Madanes, C. (1990). *Sex, love, and violence.* New York: Norton.

Madanes, C. (1991). Structural family therapy. In A. S. Gurman & D. P. Kniskern (Eds.), *Handbook of family therapy* (Vol. 2, 396–417). New York: Brunner/Mazel.

Mallouk, T. (1982). The interpersonal context of object relations: Implications for family therapy. *Journal of Marital and Family Therapy, 8*(4), 429–441.

Marek, L. I., Sandifer, D. M., Beach, A., Coward, R. L., & Protinsky, H. O. (1994). Supervision without the problem: A model of solution-focused supervision. *Journal of Family Psychotherapy, 5*(2), 57–64.

Mason, W. H., Chandler, M. C., & Grasso, B. C. (1995). Solution-based techniques applied to addictions: A clinic's experience in shifting paradigms. *Alcoholism Treatment Quarterly, 13,* 39–49.

Masters, W. H., & Johnson, V. E. (1966). *Human sexual response.* Boston: Little, Brown.

Masters, W. H., & Johnson, V. E. (1970). *Human sexual inadequacy.* Boston: Little, Brown.

Maxwell, M. (2007). Career counseling is personal counseling: A constructivist approach to nurturing the development of gifted female adolescents. *Career Development Quarterly, 55,* 206–224.

McAdoo, H. P. (Ed.). (1981). *Black families.* Beverly Hills, CA: Sage.

McCollum, E. E., & Trepper, T. S. (2001). Family solutions for substance abuse clinical and counseling approaches. Binghamton, NY: Haworth Press.

McDaniel, S., Hepworth, J., & Doherty, W. (1992). Medical family therapy: A biopsychosocial approach to families with health problems. New York: Basic Books.

McFarlane, W. R., Dixon, L., Lukens, E., & Lucksted, A. (2002). Severe mental illness. In D. H. Sprenkle (Ed.), *Effectiveness research in marriage and family therapy* (pp. 255–288). Alexandria, VA: American Association for Marriage and Family Therapy.

McGoldrick, M. (1982). Ethnicity and family therapy: An overview. In M. McGoldrick, J. K. Pearce, & J. Giordano (Eds.), *Ethnicity and family therapy* (1st ed., pp. 3–29). New York: Guilford Press.

McGoldrick, M., & Carter, B. (2001). Advances in coaching: Family therapy with one person. *Journal of Marital and Family Therapy, 27,* 281–300.

McGoldrick, M., & Gerson, R. (1985). *Genograms in family assessment.* New York: Basic Books.

McGoldrick, M., Giordano, J., & Pearce, J. K. (Eds.). (1996). *Ethnicity and family therapy* (2nd ed.). New York: Guilford Press.

McGoldrick, M. & Hardy, K. (2008). *Re-visioning family therapy: Race, culture, and gender in clinical practice*. New York, NY: Guilford.

McGoldrick, M., Pearce, J. K., & Giordano, J. (Eds.). (1982). *Ethnicity and family therapy* (1st ed.). New York: Guilford Press.

McGoldrick, M., Giordano, J., & Garcia-Preto, N. (Eds.). (2005). *Ethnicity and family therapy* (3rd ed.). New York, NY: Guilford Press.

McLuckie, A. (2005). Narrative family therapy for paediatric obsessive compulsive disorder. *Journal of Family Psychotherapy, 16*(4), 83–106.

Meneses, C. W., & Greenberg, L. S. (2011). The construction of a model of the process of couples' forgiveness in emotion-focused therapy for couples. Journal of Marital and Family Therapy, 37(4), 491–502.

Messina, K., Kolbert, J. B., Hyatt-Burkhart, D., & Crothers, L. M. (2015). The role of mental health counselors in promoting school-family collaborative with the tiered school–wide positive behavioral intervention and support (SWPBIS) model. *The Family Journal: Counseling and Therapy for Couples and Families, 19(1)*, 1–9.

Metcalf, L. (1995). Counseling towards solutions: A practical solution-focused program for working with students, teachers, and parents. Englewood Cliffs, NJ: Simon & Schuster.

Meyers, R. J., Smith, J. E., & Miller, E. J. (1998). Working with the concerned significant other: Community reinforcement and family training. In W. R. Miller & N. Heather (Eds.), *Treating addictive behaviors: Processes of change* (2nd ed., pp. 149–162). New York: Plenum Press.

Milan, S., & Keiley, M. K. (2000). Biracial youth and families in therapy: Issues and interventions. *Journal of Marital and Family Therapy, 26*, 305–315.

Miller, A., Vernon, T., Wu, V., & Russo, K. (2014). Social skill group interventions for adolescents with autism spectrum disorders: A systematic review. *Journal of Autism and Developmental Disorders, 1*(4), 254–265.

Miller, G. (2003). *Incorporating spirituality in counseling and psychotherapy: Theory and technique*. Hoboken, NJ: John Wiley and Sons.

Miller, J. K., Todahl, J. L., & Platt, J. J. (2010). The core competency movement in marriage and family therapy: Key considerations for other disciplines. *Journal of Marital and Family Therapy, 36*(1), 59–70.

Miller, R., Anderson, S., & Keala, D. (2004). Is Bowen theory valid? A review of basic research. *Journal of Marital and Family Therapy, 30,* 453–466.

Miller, S. D., & Berg, I. K. (1995). The miracle method: A radical new approach to problem drinking. New York: Norton.

Miller, W. R., Meyers, R. J., & Tonigan, J. S. (1999). Engaging the unmotivated in treatment for alcohol problems: A comparison of three strategies for intervention through family members. *Journal of Consulting Clinical Psychology, 67,* 688–697.

Minuchin, S. (1974). *Families and family therapy.* Cambridge, MA: Harvard University Press.

Minuchin, S. (1998). Where is the family in narrative family therapy? *Journal of Marital and Family Therapy, 24,* 397–404.

Minuchin, S., Baker, L., Rosman, B., Liebman, R., Milman, L., & Todd, T. C. (1975). A conceptual model of psychosomatic illness in children. *Archives of General Psychiatry, 32,* 1031–1038.

Minuchin, S., & Fishman, H. C. (1981). *Family therapy techniques.* Cambridge, MA: Harvard University Press.

Minuchin, S., Montalvo, B., Guerney, B. G., Rosman, B., & Schumer, F. (1967). *Families of the slums: An exploration of their structure and treatment.* New York: Basic Books.

Minuchin, S., Rosman, B. L., & Baker, L. (1978). *Psychosomatic families: Anorexia nervosa in context.* Cambridge, MA: Harvard University Press.

Mitten, T. J., & Connell, G. M. (2004). The core variable of symbolic-experiential therapy: A qualitative study. *Journal of Marriage and Family Therapy, 30,* 467–478.

Montag, K. R., & Wilson, G. L. (1992). An empirical evaluation of behavioral and cognitive-behavioral group marital treatment with discordant couples. *Journal of Sex and Marital Therapy, 18,* 255–272.

Moynihan, D. D. (1950). *The Negro family: The case for national action.* Washington, DC: U.S. Department of Labor.

Murphy, J. J. (1996). Solution-focused brief therapy in the school. In S. D. Miller, M. A. Hubble, & B. L. Duncan (Eds.), *Handbook of solution-focused brief therapy* (pp. 184–204). San Francisco: Jossey-Bass.

Murray, S. B. (2014). A Case of Strategic Couples Therapy in Adult Anorexia Nervosa: The Importance of Symptoms in Context. *Contemporary Family Therapy, 39,* 392–397.

Napoliello, A. L., & Sweet, B. S. (1992). Salvador Minuchin's structural family therapy and its application to Native Americans. *Family Therapy, 19,* 155–165.

Nardone, G. (1995). Brief strategic therapy of phobic disorders: A model of therapy and evaluation research. In J. H. Weakland & W. A. Ray (Eds.), *Propagations: Thirty years of influence from the Mental Research Institute* (pp. 91–105). New York: Haworth Press.

Nelson, T. S., Chenail, R. J., Alexander, J. F., Crane, D. R., Johnson, S. M., & Schwallie, L. (2007). The development of core competencies for the practice of marriage and family therapy. *Journal of Marital and Family Therapy, 33,* 417–438.

Nelson, T. S., & Graves, T. (2011). Core competencies in advanced training: What supervisors say about graduate training. *Journal of Marital and Family Therapy, 37*(4), 429–451.

Newmark, M., & Beels, C. (1994). The misuse and use of science in family therapy. *Family Process, 33,* 3–17.

Ng, K., & Smith, S. D. (2006). The relationship between attachment theory and intergenerational family systems theory. *The Family Journal: Counseling and Therapy for Couples and Families, 14*(4), 430–440.

Nichols, M. P. (1984). *Family therapy: Concepts and methods.* New York: Gardner Press.

Nichols, M. P., & Fellenberg, S. (2000). The effective use of enactments in family therapy: A discovery-oriented process study. *Journal of Marital and Family Therapy, 26,* 143–152.

Nims, D. R., & Duba, J. D. (2011). Using play therapy techniques in a Bowenian theoretical context. *The Family Journal, 19*(1), 83–89.

Nobles, W. (1980). African philosophy: Foundations for black psychology. In R. Jones (Ed.), *Black psychology* (2nd ed., pp. 18–32). New York: Harper & Row.

Northey, W. F., Wells, K. C., Silverman, W. K., & Bailey, C. E. (2002). Childhood behavioral and emotional disorders. In D. H. Sprenkle (Ed.), *Effectiveness research in marriage and family therapy* (pp. 89–122). Alexandria, VA: American Association for Marriage and Family Therapy.

Novas, H. (1994). *Everything you need to know about Latino history.* New York: Plume/Penguin Books.

Nwoye, A., (2007) Memory and narrative heling process in HIV counseling: A view from Africa. *Contemporary Family Therapy 30*(1)15–

O'Farrell, T. J., & Clements, K. (2012). Review of outcome research on marital and family therapy in treatment for alcoholism. *Journal of Marital and Family Therapy, 38*(1), 122–144.

O'Farrell, T. J., & Fals-Stewart, W. (2002). Alcohol abuse. In D. H. Sprenkle (Ed.), *Effectiveness research in marriage and family therapy* (pp. 123–162). Alexandria, VA: American Association for Marriage and Family Therapy.

Olson, D. (2011). FACES IV and the circumplex model: Validation study. *Journal of Marital and Family Therapy, 37*(1), 64–80.

Olson, D. H., Sprenkle, D. H., & Russell, C. S. (1979). Circumplex model of marital and family systems: I. Cohesion and adaptability dimensions, family types and clinical application. *Family Process, 18,* 3–28.

Osmond, M. W., & Thorne, B. (1993). Feminist theories: The social construction of gender in families and society. In P. G. Boss, W. J. Doherty, R. LaRossa, W. R. Schuman, & S. K. Steinmetz (Eds.), *Sourcebook of family theories and methods: A contextual approach* (pp. 591–625). New York: Plenum Press.

Palazzoli, M. S. (1978). Self-starvation: From individual to family therapy in the treatment of anorexia nervosa (A. Pomerans, Trans.). New York, NY: Jason Aronson. (Original work published 1977).

Palazzoli, M. S. (1984). Behind the scenes of the organization: Some guidelines for the expert in human relations. *Journal of Marital and Family Therapy*, 6(2), 299–307.

Palazzoli, M. S., (1984). The emergence of a comprehensive systems approach: Supervision and team problems in a district psychiatric center. *Journal of Marital and Family Therapy*, 7(1), 135–146.

Palazzoli, M. S., Boscolo, L., Cecchin, G., & Prata, G. (1974). The treatment of children through brief therapy of their parents. *Family Process*, 13(4), 429–442.

Palazzoli, M. S., Boscolo, L., Cecchin, G. & Prata, G. (1977). Family ritual a powerful tool in family therapy. Family Therapy, 16(4), 445–453.

Palazzoli, M. S., Boscolo, L., Cecchin, G., & Prata, G. (1978). *Paradox and Counterparadox*. New York, NY: Jason Aronson Incorporated.

Palazzoli, M. S., Boscolo, L., Cecchin, G. & Prata, G. (1980). Hypothesizing-circularity-neutrality: Three guidelines for the conductor of the session. *Family Process, 19*, 3-12.

Palazzoli, M. S., Boscolo, L., Cecchin, G., & Prata, G. (1980). The problem of the referring person. *Journal of Marital and Family Therapy*, 6, 3-9.

Palma, T. V., & Stanley, J. L. (2002). Effective counseling with lesbian, gay, and bisexual clients. *Journal of College Counseling, 5*(1), 74–90.

Paniagua, F. A. (1994). Assessing and treating culturally diverse clients. Thousand Oaks, CA: Sage.

Parsons, B. V., & Alexander, J. F. (1973). Short-term family intervention: A therapy outcome study. *Journal of Consulting and Clinical Psychology, 41*, 195–201.

Parsons, T., & Bales, R. F. (1955). *Family, socialization, and interaction process.* Glencoe, IL: Free Press.

Patalano, F. (1997). Developing the working alliance in marital therapy: A psychodynamic perspective. *Contemporary Family Therapy, 19*(4), 497–505.

Patterson, G. R. (1971). Families: Applications of social learning theory to family life. Champaign, IL: Research Press.

Patterson, G. R., & Brodsky, A. (1966). A behavioral modification program for a child with multiple behavioral problems. *Journal of Child Psychology and Psychiatry, 7,* 277–295.

Patterson, G. R., Jones, R., Whittier, J., & Wright, M. (1965). A behavioral modification technique for a hyperactive child. *Behavioral Research and Therapy, 2,* 217–226.

Patterson, G. R., McNeal, S., Hawkins, S., & Phelps, R. (1967). Reprogramming the social environment. *Journal of Child Psychology and Psychiatry, 8,* 181–195.

Pavlov, I. P. (1934). An attempt at a psychological interpretation of obsessional neurosis and paranoia. *Journal of Mental Science, 80,* 187–197.

Piercy, F. P., Lipchik, E., & Kiser, D. (2000). Miller and de Shazer's article on "Emotions in solution-focused therapy." *Family Process, 39,* 25–28.

Piercy, F. P., & Sprenkle, D. H. (1990). Marriage and family therapy: A decade review. *Journal of Marriage and Family Therapy, 16,* 1116–1126.

Pinsof, W. M., & Catherall, D. R (1986). The integration psychotherapy alliance: Family, couple, and individual therapy scales. *Journal of Marital and Family Therapy, 12*(1), 137–151.

Pinsof, W. M., & Wynne, L. C. (Eds.). (1995). *Family therapy effectiveness: Current research and theory.* Washington, DC: American Association for Marriage and Family Therapy.

Rastogi, S., Johnson, T. D., Hoeffel, E. M., & Drewery, M. P., Jr. (2011). The Black population: 2010 Census briefs. Retrieved from https://www.census.gov/prod/cen2010/briefs/c2010br-06.pdf

Raymond, L., Freelander, M. L., Heatherington, L., Ellis, M. V., & Sargent, J. (1993). Communication processes in structural family therapy: Case study of an anorexic family. *Journal of Family Psychology, 6,* 308–326.

Richeport-Haley, M. (1998). Approaches to madness shared by cross-cultural healing systems and strategic family therapy. *Journal of Family Psychotherapy, 9*(4), 61–75.

Rippentrop, E., Altmaier, E. M., Chen, J. J., Found, E. M., & Keffala, V. J. (2005). The relationship between religion/spirituality and physical health, mental health, and pain in a chronic pain population. *Pain, 116,* 311–321.

Roberto, L. G. (1991). Symbolic-experiential family therapy. In A. S. Gurman & D. P. Kniskern (Eds.), *Handbook of family therapy* (Vol. 2, pp. 444–476). New York: Brunner/Mazel.

Rogers, C. (1957). The necessary and sufficient conditions of therapeutic personality change. *Journal of Counseling Psychology, 21,* 95–103.

Ramey, H., L., Tarulli, D., Frijters, J.,C. & Fisher, L. (2009) A sequential analysis of externalizing in narrative therapy with children. *Contemporary Family Therapy 31*(2) 262–279.

Rogers, R. (1990). Reaching for solutions: The summary report of the Special Advisor to the Minister of National Health and Welfare on child sexual abuse in Canada. Ottawa, Ontario, Canada: National Clearinghouse on Family Violence, Health and Welfare.

Rosen, K. H., Matheson, J. L., Stith, S. M., McCollum, E. E., & Locke, L. D. (2003). Negotiated time-out: A de-escalation tool for couples. *Journal of Marital and Family Therapy, 29,* 291–298.

Rosman, B. L., Minuchin, S., & Liebman, R. (1975). Family lunch session: An introduction to family therapy in anorexia nervosa. *American Journal of Orthopsychiatry, 45,* 846–853.

Rowe, C. L., & Liddle, H. A. (2002). Substance abuse. In D. H. Sprenkle (Ed.), *Effectiveness research in marriage and family therapy* (pp. 53–87). Alexandria, VA: American Association for Marriage and Family Therapy.

Ruble, N. (1999). The voices of therapists and children regarding the inclusion of children in family therapy: A systemic research synthesis. *Contemporary Family Therapy, 21*(4), 485–503.

Russell, D. E. H. (1982). *Rape in marriage.* New York: Collier Books.

Russell, D. E. H., & Bolen, R. M. (2000). *The epidemic of rape and child sexual abuse in the United States.* Thousand Oaks, CA: Sage.

Rychtarik, R. G., & McGillicuddy, N. B. (1998). *Effects of skill training and twelve-step facilitation on posttreatment coping skills in women with alcoholic partners.* Poster presented at the International Conference on the Treatment of Addictive Behaviors, Santa Fe, NM.

Rychtarik, R. G., & McGillicuddy, N. B. (2002). *Reducing violence against women with alcoholic partners*. Poster presented at the Research Society on Alcoholism meeting, San Francisco, CA.

Safran, J. D. (1993). Breaches in the therapeutic alliance: An arena for negotiating authentic relatedness. *Psychotherapy, 30*(1), 11–24.

Sarwer, D. B., & Durlak, J. A. (1997). A field trial of effectiveness of behavioral treatment for sexual dysfunctions. *Journal of Sex and Marital Therapy, 23*, 87–97.

Satir, V. (1988). *The new peoplemaking*. Mountain View, CA: Science and Behavior Books.

Sauerheber, J. D., Nims, D., & Carter, D. J. (2014). Counseling Muslim couples from a Bowen family systems perspective. *The Family Journal, 22*(2), 231–239.

Savin-Williams, R. C. (1994). Verbal and physical abuse as stressors in the lives of lesbians, gay males, and bisexual youths: Associations with school problems, running away, substance abuse, prostitution, and suicide. *Journal of Consulting and Clinical Psychology, 62*, 261–269.

Savin-Williams, R. C., & Cohen, K. M. (1996). Psychological outcomes of verbal and physical abuse among lesbian, gay, and bisexual youths. In R. C. Savin-Williams & K. M. Cohen (Eds.), *The lives of lesbians, gays, and bisexuals: Children to adults* (pp. 180–191). New York: Jason Aronson.

Schnarch, D. M. (1991). Constructing the sexual crucible: An integration of sexual and marital therapy. New York: Norton.

Schnarch, D. M. (1997). Passionate marriage: Keeping love and intimacy alive in a committed relationship. New York: Norton.

Scopetta, M. A., Szapocznik, J., King, O. E., Ladner, R., Alegre, C., & Tillman, W. S. (1977). *The Spanish Drug Rehabilitation Research Project: Final report* (NIDA Grant No. H81 DA 01696-03). Miami, FL: University of Miami, Spanish Family Guidance Center.

Scott, W. (1994). Group therapy for male sex offenders: Strategic interventions. *Journal of Family Psychotherapy, 5*(2), 1–20.

Selvini Palazzoli, M. (1984) Behind the scenes of the organization: Some guidelines for the expert in human relations. *Journal of Marital and Family Therapy*, 6(2), 299–307.

Selvini Palazzoli, M. (1984) The emergence of a comprehensive systems approach: Supervision and team problems in a district psychiatric center. *Journal of Marital and Family Therapy*, 7(1), 135–146.

Selvini Palazzoli, M., Boscolo, L., Cecchin, G., & Prata, G. (1978) *Paradox and Counterparadox*. New York: Jason Aaronson.

Selvini Palazzoli, M., Boscolo, L., Cecchin, G., & Prata, G. (1974) The treatment of children through brief therapy of their parents. *Family Process, 13*(4), *429–442.*

Selvini Palazzoli, M., Boscolo, L., Cecchin, G., & Prata, G. (1977) Family ritual: A powerful tool in family therapy. *Family Therapy, 16*(4), 445–453.

Selvini-Palazzoli (1978). Self-starvation. From individual to family therapy in the treatment of anorexia nervosa (translator, A. Pomerans). New York Jason Aronson, Selvini Palazzoli, M., Boscolo, L., Cecchin, G., & Prata, G. (1980). Hypothesizing-circularity-neutrality: Three guidelines for the conductor of the session. *Family Process, 19*, 3–12.

Selvini Palazzoli, M., Boscolo, L., Cecchin, G., & Prata, G. (1980). The problem of the referring person. *Journal of Marital and Family Therapy, 6*, 3–9.

Siegel, L. (1991). Brief therapy: The MRI approach. In A. S. Gurman & D. P. Kniskern (Eds.), *Handbook of family therapy* (Vol. 2, pp. 171–200). New York: Brunner/Mazel.

Siegel, L. I. (1991). Projective identification: Pros and cons. An Essay review of Samuel Slipp: The technique and practice of object relations family therapy. *Contemporary Family Therapy, 13*(3), 275–296.

Shapiro, L. E., & Henderson, J. G. (1992). Brief therapy for encopresis: A case study. *Journal of Family Psychotherapy, 3*(3), 1–12.

Shields, C., Wynne, L., McDaniel, S., & Gawinski, B. (1994). The marginalization of family therapy: A historical and continuing problem. *Journal of Marital and Family Therapy, 20*, 117–138.

Shon, S., & Ja, D. (1982). Asian families. In M. McGoldrick, J. K. Pearce, & J. Giordano (Eds.), *Ethnicity and family therapy* (1st ed., pp. 208–228). New York: Guilford Press.

Shorris, E. (1992). *Latinos: A biography of the people.* New York: Norton.

Simon, G. M. (1992). Having a second order mind while doing first order therapy. *Journal of Marital and Family Therapy, 18,* 377–389.

Simon, G. M. (2003). Beyond technique in family therapy: Finding your therapeutic voice. Boston: Allyn & Bacon.

Simpson, L. E., Doss, B. D., Wheeler, J., & Christensen, A. (2007). Relationship violence among couples seeking therapy: Common couple violence or battering? *Journal of Marital and Family Therapy, 33,* 270–283.

Sirles, E. A., Lipchik, E., & Kowalski, K. (1993). A consumer's perspective on domestic violence interventions. *Journal of Family Violence, 8*(3), 267–276.

Sisson, R. W., & Azrin, H. H. (1986). Family-member involvement to initiate and promote treatment of problem drinkers. *Journal of Behavior Therapy and Experimental Psychiatry, 17,* 15–21.

Slipp, S. (1988). *The technique and practice of object relations family therapy.* North Vale, NJ: Jason Aronson.

Sluzki, C. E., & Ransom, D. C. (1976). Preface. In C. E. Sluzki & D. C. Ransom (Eds.), *Double bind: The foundation of the communicational approach to the family.* New York: Grune & Stratton.

Smock, S. A., Trepper, T. S., Wetchler, J. L., McCollum, E. E., Ray, R., & Pierce, K. (2008). Solution-focused group therapy for Level 1 substance users. *Journal of Marital and Family Therapy, 34,* 107–120.

Soo-Hoo, T. (1995). Implementing brief strategic therapy within a psychiatric residential/daytreatment center. In J. H. Weakland & W. A. Ray (Eds.), *Propagations: Thirty years of influence from the Mental Research Institute* (pp. 107–128). New York: Haworth Press.

Soroka, Y. (1995). Unfaithfulness in the marital system: Paradoxical therapy using the idea of revenge. In J. H. Weakland & W. A. Ray (Eds.), *Propagations: Thirty years of influence from the Mental Research Institute* (pp. 73–84). New York: Haworth Press.

Sparks, J. A., Duncan, B. L., & Miller, S. D. (2008). Common factors in psychotherapy. In J. L. Lebow (Ed.), *Twenty-first century psychotherapies: Contemporary approaches to theory and practice* (pp. 453–497). Hoboken, NJ: Wiley.

Sprenkle, D. H. (2002a). Editor's introduction. In D. H. Sprenkle (Ed.), *Effectiveness research in marriage and family therapy* (pp. 9–25). Alexandria, VA: American Association for Marriage and Family Therapy.

Sprenkle, D. H. (Ed.). (2002b). *Effectiveness research in marriage and family therapy*. Alexandria, VA: American Association for Marriage and Family Therapy.

Stack, C. (1970). All our kin: Strategies for survival in a black community. New York: Harper & Row.

Stander, V., Piercy, F. P., MacKinnon, D., & Helmeke, K. (1994). Spirituality, religion and family therapy: Competing or complementary worlds? American *Journal of Family Therapy, 22*(1), 27–41.

Stanton, M. D., & Todd, T. C. (1979). Structural therapy with drug addicts. In E. Kaufman & P. Kaufman (Eds.), *Family therapy of drug and alcohol abuse* (pp. 55–59). New York: Guilford Press.

Staples, R. (1994). *Black family: Essays and studies* (5th ed.). New York: Van Nostrand Reinhold.

Stein, S. J., Mozdzierz, A. B., & Mozdzierz, G. J. (1998). The kinship of Adlerian family counseling and Minuchin's structural family therapy. *Journal of Individual Psychology, 54*(1), 90–107.

Steinglass, P., Bennett, L., Wolin, S., & Reiss, D. (1987). *The alcoholic family*. New York: Basic Books.

Stith, S. M., McCollum, E. E., Amanor-Boadu, Y., & Smith, D. (2012). Systemic perspectives of intimate partner violence treatment. *Journal of Family Therapy, 38*(1), 220–240.

Stith, S. M., Rosen, K. H., & McCollum, E. E. (2002). Domestic violence. In D. H. Sprenkle (Ed.), *Effectiveness research in marriage and family therapy* (pp. 223–254). Alexandria, VA: American Association for Marriage and Family Therapy.

Stith, S. M., Rosen, K. H., & McCollum, E. E. (2003). Effectiveness of couples treatment for spouse abuse. *Journal of Marital and Family Therapy, 29,* 407–426.

Storm, C. (1991). The remaining thread: Matching change and stability signals. *Journal of Strategic and Systemic Therapies, 10,* 114–117.

Strong, T. (1993). *DSM-IV* and describing problems in family therapy. *Family Process, 32,* 249–253.

Stuart, G. L., & Holtzworth-Munroe, A (1995). Identifying subtypes of martially violent men: Descriptive dimensions, correlates and causes of violence, and treatment implications. In S. M. Stith & M. A. Straus (Eds.), *Understanding partner violence: Prevalence, causes, consequences and solutions* (pp. 162–172). Minneapolis, MN: National Council on Family Relations.

Stuart, R. B. (1969). Operant-interpersonal treatment of marital discord. *Journal of Consulting and Clinical Psychology, 33,* 675–682.

Stuart, R. B. (1980). Helping couples change: A social learning approach to marital therapy. New York: Guilford Press.

Sue, S., & McKinney, H. (1975). Asian Americans in the community health care system. *American Journal of Orthopsychiatry, 45,* 111–118.

Sue, S., & Zane, N. (1987). The role of cultural techniques in psychotherapy: A critique and reformulation. *American Psychologist, 42,* 37–45.

Szapocznik, J., & Kurtines, W. M. (1989). Breakthroughs in family therapy with drug abusing problem youth. New York: Springer.

Szapocznik, J., Rio, A., Murray, E., Cohen, E., Scopetta, M., Rivas-Vazquez, A., et al. (1989). Structural family versus psychodynamic child therapy for problematic Hispanic boys. *Journal of Counseling and Clinical Psychology, 57,* 571–578.

Szapocznik, J., & Williams, R. A. (2000). Brief strategic family therapy: Twenty-five years of interplay among theory, research and practice in adolescent behavior problems and drug abuse. *Clinical Child and Family Psychological Review, 3*(2), 117–134.

Szykula, S. A., Morris, S. B., Sayger, T. V., & Sudweeks, C. (1987). Child-focused behavior and strategic therapies: Outcome comparisons. *Psychotherapy, 24*(3S), 546–551.

Tambling, R. B. (2012). Solution-oriented therapy for survivors of sexual assault and their partners. *Contemporary Family Therapy, 34*(3), 391–401.

Thibaut, J., & Kelley, H. H. (1959). *The social psychology of groups.* New York, NY: Macmillan.

Tie, S., & Poulsen, S. (2013). Emotionally focused couple therapy with couples facing terminal illness. *Contemporary Family Therapy, 35*(3), 557–567.

Tjaden, P., & Thoennes, N. (1998). Prevalence, incidence and consequences of violence against women: Findings from the national violence against women survey. Washington, DC: National Institute of Justice.

Toman, W. (1961). *Family constellations.* New York: Springer.

Tomm, K. (1984a). One perspective on the Milan systemic approach: Part I. Overview of development, theory and practice. *Journal of Marital and Family Therapy, 10*(2), 113–125.

Tomm, K. (1984b). One perspective on the Milan systemic approach: Part II. Description of session format, interviewing style and interventions. *Journal of Marital and Family Therapy, 10*(3), 253–271.

Trepper, T. S., & Sprenkle, D. H. (1989). The clinical use of the circumplex model in the assessment and treatment of intrafamily child sexual abuse. In D. H. Olson, C. S. Russell, & D. H. Sprenkle (Eds.), *Circumplex model: Systemic assessment and treatment of families* (pp. 93–111). New York: Haworth Press.

Uba, L. (1994). Asian Americans: Personality patterns, identity, and mental health. New York: Guilford Press.

U.S. Census Bureau. (n.d.). *Profile of general demographic characteristics: 2000: California.* Retrieved March 16, 2009, from http://factfinder.census.gov/servlet/QTTable?_bm=y&-geo_id=04000US06&-qr_name=DEC_2000_SF1_U_DP1&-ds_name=DEC_2000_SF1_U

U.S. Census Bureau. (2014). *Quickfacts.* Retrieved February 22, 2016, from http://www.census.gov/quickfacts/table/RHI225214/00

Vaughn, K., Young, B. C., Webster, D. C., & Thomas, M. R. (1996). Solution focused work in the hospital: A continuum-of-care model for inpatient treatment. In S. D. Miller, M. A. Hubble, & B. L. Duncan (Eds.), *Handbook of solution-focused brief therapy* (pp. 99–127). San Francisco: Jossey-Bass.

Vetere, A. (2001). Structural family therapy. *Child Psychology and Psychiatry Review, 6*(3), 133–139.

Vetere, A., & Dowling, E. (2005). Narrative therapies with children and their families: A practitioners' guide to concepts and approaches. New York: Routledge.

Vocisano, C., Klein, D. F., Arnow, B., Rivera, C., Blalock, J., Rothbaum, B., et al. (2004). Therapist variables that predict symptom change in psychotherapy with chronically depressed outpatients. *Psychotherapy: Theory, Research, Practice, Training, 41,* 255–265.

von Bertalanffy, L. (1968). *General systems theory.* New York: George Braziler.

Waldner, L., & Magruder, B. (1999). Coming out to parents: Perceptions of family relations, perceived resources, and identity expressions as predictors of identity disclosures for gay and lesbian adolescents. *Journal of Homosexulaity, 37*(2), 83–100.

Walker, J. G., Johnson, S., Manion, I., & Cloutier, P. (1996). Emotionally focused marital intervention for couples with chronically ill children. *Journal of Consulting and Clinical Psychology, 64,* 1029–1036.

Walsh, F. (1993). *Normal family processes.* New York: Guilford Press.

Walsh, F. (1999). *Spiritual resources in family therapy.* New York: Guilford Press.

Walsh, F., & Olson, D. H. (1989). Utility of the circumplex model with severely dysfunctional family systems. In D. H. Olson, C. S. Russell, & D. H. Sprenkle (Eds.), *Circumplex model: Systemic assessment and treatment of families* (pp. 51–78). New York: Haworth Press.

Wampold, B. E. (2001). The great psychotherapy debate: Models, methods, and findings. Hillsdale, NJ: Lawrence Erlbaum.

Watson, J. B., & Raynor, R. (1920). Conditioned emotional reactions. *Journal of Experimental Psychology, 3*(1), 14.

Watson, W. L., Bell, J. M., & Wright, L. M. (1992). The medical map is not the territory: Or, "Medical Family Therapy?"—Watch your language. *Family Systems Medicine, 10(1)*, 35–39.

Watzlawick, P. (1966). A structured family interview. *Family Process, 2*, 256–271.

Watzlawick, P., Bavelas, J. B., & Jackson, D. D. (1967). *Pragmatics of human communication: A study of interactional patterns, pathologies, and paradoxes.* New York, NY: Norton.

Watzlawick, P., Weakland, J., & Fisch, R. (1974). *Change: Principles of problem formation and problem resolution.* New York, NY: Norton.

Weakland, J. H., Fisch, R., Waltzlawick, P., & Boden, A. M. (1974). Brief therapy: Focused problem resolution. *Family Process, 13*, 141–168.

Weakland, J. H., & Ray, W. A. (Eds.). (1995). Propagations: Thirty years of influence from the Mental Research Institute. New York: Hayworth Press.

Weakland, J. H., Watzlawick, P., & Riskin, J. (1995). Introduction: MRI—A little background music. In J. H. Weakland & W. A. Ray (Eds.), *Propagations: Thirty years of influence from the Mental Research Institute* (pp. 1–15). New York: Haworth Press.

Webster, D. C. (1990). Solution-focused approaches in psychiatric/mental health nursing. *Perspectives in Psychiatric Care, 26*, 17–21.

Webster, D. C., Vaughn, K., & Martinez, R. (1994). Introducing solution-focused approaches to staff in inpatient psychiatric settings. *Archives of Psychiatric Nursing, 8(4)*, 254–261.

Weinberg, G. (1972). *Society and the healthy homosexual.* Garden City, NY: Anchor Press.

Weingarten, K. (1998). The small and the ordinary: The daily practice of a postmodern narrative therapy. *Family Process, 37*, 3–15.

Weissman, M. M., & Paykel, E. S. (1974). *The depressed woman: A study of social relationships.* Chicago: University of Chicago Press.

Werner-Wilson, R. J., & Davenport, B. R. (2003). Distinguishing between conceptualizations of attachment: Clinical implications in marriage and family therapy. Contemporary Family *Therapy, 25*(2), 179–193.

Werry, J. S. (1989). Family therapy: Professional endeavor or successful religion? *Journal of Family Therapy, 11,* 377–382.

Wetchler, J. L. (1990). Solution-focused supervision. *Family Therapy, 17,* 129–138.

Whisman, M. A. (2001). The association between depression and marital dissatisfaction. In S. R. H. Beach (Ed.), *Marital and family processes in depression: A scientific foundation for clinical practice* (pp. 2–24). Washington, DC: American Psychological Association.

Whitaker, C. A. (1975). Psychotherapy of the absurd: With a special emphasis on the psychotherapy of aggression. *Family Process 17,* 1–15.

Whitaker, C. A. (1976). The hindrance of theory in clinical work. In P. J. Guerin (Ed.), *Family therapy: Theory and practice* (pp. 154–164). New York: Gardner Press.

Whitaker, C. A. (1977). Process techniques of family therapy. *Interaction, 1*(1), 4–19.

Whitaker, C. A. (1989). *Midnight musings of a family therapist.* New York: Norton.

Whitaker, C. A., & Bumberry, W. M. (1988). *Dancing with the family: A symbolic-experiential approach.* New York: Brunner/Mazel.

Whitaker, C. A., & Malone, T. P. (1953). *The roots of psychotherapy.* New York: Blakiston.

White, M. (1989). *Selected papers.* Adelaide, Australia: Dulwich Center Publications.

White, M. (1993). Deconstruction and therapy. In S. Gilligan & R. Price (Eds.), *Therapeutic conversations* (pp. 22–61). New York: Norton.

White, M. (2007). *Maps of narrative practice.* New York: Norton.

White, M., & Epston, D. (1990). *Narrative means to therapeutic ends.* New York: Norton.

Wiener, N. (1948). Cybernetics. *Scientific American, 179*(5), 14–18.

Wilber, K. (2000). *A brief history of everything.* Boston, MA: Shambhala Publications.

Williams, L., Patterson, J., & Edwards, T. M. (2014). *Clinician's Guide to Research Methods in Family Therapy: Foundations of Evidence-based Practice.* New York, NY: Guilford Publications.

Willie, C. (1981). Dominance in the family: The black and white experience. *Journal of Black Psychology, 7*(2), 91–97.

Willie, C., & Greenblatt, S. (1978). Four "classic" studies of power relationships in black families: A review and look to the future. *Journal of Marriage and the Family, 40,* 691–694.

Winek, J. L. (1998). A qualitative study of the co-construction of therapeutic reality: A process and outcome model. Lewiston, NY: Edwin Mellen Press.

Winek, J. L., & Carlin-Finch, S. C. (1997). Constructions of therapy, race, ethnicity and gender: An anthropological metaphor. *Contemporary Family Therapy, 19,* 523–535.

Wiselberg, H. (1992). Family therapy and ultra-orthodox Jewish families: A structural approach. *Journal of Family Therapy, 14,* 305–329.

Wolpe, J. (1948). *An approach to the problem of neurosis based on the conditioned response.* Unpublished M.D. thesis, University of Witwaterstand, Johannesberg, South Africa.

Wright, L. M., Watson, W. L., & Bell, J. M. (1996). *Beliefs: The heart of healing in families and illness.* New York, NY: Basic Books.

Yaccarino, M. E. (1993). Using Minuchin's structural family therapy techniques with Italian-American families. *Contemporary Family Therapy, 15,* 459–466.

Young, T. L., Negash, S. M., & Long, R. M. (2009). Enhancing sexual desire and intimacy via the metaphor of a problem child: Utilizing structural–strategic family therapy. *Journal of Sex and Marital Therapy, 35,* 402–417.

Zeig, J. K., Ritterman, M., & Welter-Enderman, R. (n.d.). *In memoriam Jay Haley, 1923–2007.* Retrieved April 24, 2008, from http://www.familyprocess.org/featured_articles_display.asp?id=69

Zetterlind, U., Hanson, H., Aberg-Orbeck, K., & Berglund, M. (1998). *Coping skill therapy, group support and information for spouses of alcoholics: A controlled randomized study.* Poster presented at the International Conference on the Treatment of Addictive Behaviors, Santa Fe, NM.

Zlotnick, C., Kohn, R., Keitner, G., & Della Grotta, S. A. (2000). The relationship between quality of interpersonal relationships and major depressive disorder: Findings from the National Comorbidity Survey. *Journal of Affective Disorders, 59,* 205–215.

CPSIA information can be obtained
at www.ICGtesting.com
Printed in the USA
FSOW03n1808171016
26254FS